820.9382   Garcia, Humberto,
GAR   1978-

245865

Islam and the English
enlightenment, 1670-
1840.

D1572680

Islam and the English Enlightenment,
1670–1840

Islam and the English Enlightenment, 1670–1840

HUMBERTO GARCIA

The Johns Hopkins University Press

Baltimore

© 2012 The Johns Hopkins University Press
All rights reserved. Published 2012
Printed in the United States of America on acid-free paper

2 4 6 8 9 7 5 3 1

The Johns Hopkins University Press
2715 North Charles Street
Baltimore, Maryland 21218-4363
www.press.jhu.edu

Library of Congress Cataloging-in-Publication Data

Garcia, Humberto, 1978–
Islam and the English enlightenment, 1670–1840 / Humberto Garcia.
     p.   cm.
Includes bibliographical references and index.
ISBN-13: 978-1-4214-0353-3 (hardcover : alk. paper)
ISBN-10: 1-4214-0353-6 (hardcover : alk. paper)
1. Islam in literature. 2. English literature—18th century—History and criticism.
3. English literature—19th century—History and criticism. 4. Enlightenment—
Great Britain. 5. Great Britain—Relations—Islamic countries. 6. Islamic countries—
Relations—Great Britain. I. Title.
PR149.I8G37 2011
820.9'38297—dc22   2011011299

A catalog record for this book is available from the British Library.

*Special discounts are available for bulk purchases of this book. For more information,
please contact Special Sales at 410-516-6936 or specialsales@press.jhu.edu.*

The Johns Hopkins University Press uses environmentally friendly book materials,
including recycled text paper that is composed of at least 30 percent
post-consumer waste, whenever possible.

For Shimy

MAHOMET

Utter the Song, O my Soul! the flight and return of Mohammed,
Prophet and Priest, who scatter'd abroad both Evil and Blessings,
Huge wasteful Empires founded and hallow'd slow Persecution,
Soul-withering, but crush'd the blasphemous Rites of the Pagan
And idolatrous Christians.—For veiling the Gospel of Jesus,
They, the best corrupting, had made it worse than the vilest.
Wherefore Heaven decreed th' enthusiast Warrior of Mecca,
Choosing Good from Iniquity rather than Evil from Goodness.

Loud the Tumult in Mecca surrounded the Fane of the Idol;—
Naked and Prostrate the Priesthood were laid—the People with mad shouts
Thundering now, and now with saddest Ululation
Flew, as over the channel of rock-stone the ruinous River
Shatters its waters abreast, and in mazy uproar bewilder'd,
Rushes dividuous all—all rushing impetuous onward.

SAMUEL TAYLOR COLERIDGE, "Mahomet" (composed 1799)

CONTENTS

This volume examines how sympathetic literary and cultural representations of the Islamic republic contributed significantly to Protestant Britain's evolving self-definition between 1670 and 1840. Radical Protestant accounts about the Islamic republic—in which the Prophet Muhammad, the wise legislator, restored constitutional rule—captured the political imagination of many eighteenth-century and Romantic-era writers who rejected, or were troubled by, the democratic principles that were implemented in Georgian Britain, its overseas empire, and revolutionary France. Although writers such as Edmund Burke, Samuel Taylor Coleridge, and Percy Bysshe Shelley eventually abandoned their commitments to Islam, their short-term infatuation with this faith reminds twenty-first-century readers that our secular predecessors often hailed the Prophet an Enlightened Promethean hero.

In making the case for radical Protestant interpretations of Mahometanism (a Christian nomenclature for Islam), this study offers a corrective addendum to the late Edward Said's groundbreaking study *Orientalism* (1978), which argues for a hegemonic imperialist discourse that sought to construct and dominate the Orient by the late eighteenth century. Avoiding Said's anachronistic application of the East-West binary in the early modern period, I offer an alternative story about the emergence of Islamic-inspired secularization in eighteenth-century Britain. This story should not be read as a subaltern approach to "histories from below" or as a victimization narrative about an overpowering West and a correspondingly subjugated East. Rather, I foreground Islam's contribution to the English Enlightenment in the interest of "provincializing Europe," the analytic term coined by Dispesh Chakrabarty to dislodge Europe as the center of world history and the culmination of secular modernity.[1] I challenge an exclusionist Judeo-Christian Enlightenment by engaging with precolonial perceptions of Islam. As such, this book is not only for eighteenth-century and Romantic literature specialists, but also for scholars of history, philosophy, postcolonialism, religion, and Islam and the Middle East. In general, this book is for those who are weary of a post-9/11 world in which conflicts between East and West have ushered in a new phase in the consolidation of US global hegemony.

Doing historical work that links Islam to developments in the English Enlightenment is a daunting task following 9/11 and the US invasion of Afghanistan and Iraq. These major events are usually read as guideposts for what Bernard Lewis and Samuel Huntington dub "the clash of civilizations." Lewis, an academic historian of Islam and the Middle East, refers to Muslims and Western Christians as opposed blocs that have been in conflict for over a millennium and that are destined for even greater hostilities after the 9/11 terrorists attacks on the World Trade Center. In a 2004 book chapter titled "The Roots of Muslim Rage" (first published in 1990), he describes the strained relationship between the United States and the Muslim world as an "irrational but surely historical reaction of an ancient rival against our Judeo-Christian heritage, our *secular present*, and the worldwide expansion of both."[2] The "clash of civilizations" phrase popularized in his essay but previously coined by him, began to circulate widely among academics when it was later borrowed by Samuel Huntington. His much-disputed *Foreign Affairs* article and book cast Islam as the West's new rival after the fall of Soviet Communism in 1989.[3] After 9/11, the "clash" rhetoric became the Bush administration's foreign policy mantra, a justification for the illegal occupation of Afghanistan and Iraq in the name of fighting the "War on Terror." In fact, Lewis has acquired a reputable name among White House officials; *What Went Wrong* and *The Crisis of Islam*, his two best-selling books in the United States, have provided an intellectual rationale for the neoconservative interpretation of the Muslim world. Lewis has not only defended US military aggression in Afghanistan, Iraq's connection to the 9/11 plot, and the need for toppling Saddam Hussein, but he has also addressed the White House and advised Dick Cheney and Richard Perle on foreign policy.[4] As the *Wall Street Journal* aptly puts it, "The Lewis doctrine, in effect, had become US policy."[5] Said was right when he described Lewis's "liberal objective scholarship" as "propaganda *against* his subject material."[6]

Unfortunately, Lewis's "propaganda" has dominated public debate in the United States, Britain, and Europe. On September 3, 2005, the Danish newspaper *Jyllands-Posten* published twelve editorial cartoons of the Prophet Muhammad, deliberately provocative and degrading, which ignited a fierce international controversy. Even though the newspaper editors disregarded the Muslim (especially Sunni) prohibition against visually portraying the Prophet, they claimed that their publication was part of a goodwill effort to encourage a cross-cultural dialogue, as well as to expand censorship limits and reaffirm democratic values.[7] And yet these offensive images—reprinted throughout the Netherlands, Germany, Scandinavia, Belgium, and France between October 2005 and January 2006—revived the anti-Islamic sentiments of the 1990s Rushdie affair. In 2008, *Jyllands-Posten* and many other Danish newspapers reprinted the images in retaliation against renewed Muslim threats.[8] Even an April 2006 *South Park* episode aired a spoof of this scandal, exposing the secular hypocrisy entailed in "freedom of speech": Islamic jihadists produce a show featuring George Bush and Jesus defecating on each other and the American flag in response to an airing of an uncensored Muhammad image on an American TV show (Comedy Central, *South Park*'s network, only censored the latter image).[9] Two 2010 South Park episodes satirized these double standards when Comedy Central removed all images and references to the Prophet while retaining offensive caricatures of Buddha snorting cocaine and Jesus watching Internet porn.[10] The mass publicity surrounding the Danish cartoon scandal has reconfirmed the clash of civilizations thesis: Islam represents a decadent civilization fundamentally at odds with Western modernity, and, as such, it *must* eventually embrace the West's secular values. Otherwise, this false theology is destined to collide with the Enlightenment.[11]

Ironically, this scandal reached its apocalyptic climax in US state universities, the revered strongholds of a tolerant liberal education. Free speech advocates from Michigan State University, the University of California Irvine, the Ayn Rand Institute at New York University, the University of Chicago, Harvard University, and the University of Illinois Urbana-Champaign vehemently defended the Enlightenment legacy by reprinting the cartoons. They appealed to a secularist rhetoric that evoked the "latent Orientalism" that Edward Said scrutinized in 1978.[12] For many progressive liberals, Muslim values are fundamentally opposed to, and even threaten, the Enlightenment project. To combat Muslim bigotry, some critics have hailed the restaging of Voltaire's 1741 play *Mahomet the Impostor* as an exemplary response to Muslims who cannot respect the secular values enshrined in Western toleration.[13]

Many liberal intellectuals, including Ayaan Hirsi Ali and Salman Rushdie, published a pro-Enlightenment "Manifesto" in *Jyllands-Posten* as an act of solidarity with the newspaper's decision to print the offensive images. By conflating twentieth-century fascism with the seventeenth-century religious wars, this polemic condemns the political-theological "obscurantism" concealing the "new totalitarianism"—the Islamic faith itself—and recasts Lewis's and Huntington's rhetoric in *philosophe* terms: "It is not the clash of civilizations nor an antagonism of West and East that we are witnessing, but a global struggle that confronts democrats and theocrats" (22:30).[14] Unfortunately, the Huntington-Lewis-Bush doctrine has assumed the aura of an unquestionable dogma among many liberals who, unwittingly, have aligned their politics with neoconservative "democrats" in an effort to rescue Judeo-Christian modernity from Muslim "theocrats."[15] This doctrine persists unabated in popular and academic discourses, across the political spectrum, despite President Barack Obama's engagement with the Muslim world in the language of mutual respect rather than religious clashes.

Moving beyond theses skewed debates, this work offers a counternarrative to the "clash of civilizations" story. It challenges long-standing biases in cultural and literary criticism that cast Islam as the wayward and bastard child of the Enlightenment. Long overdue, this revisionist gesture should not be read as an attempt to dispense with secular values or as an apology for twenty-first-century Islam, but as an invitation—now more than ever—to rewrite the received narratives of the Enlightenment and explore different genealogies of secular modernity. My research shows that "our Judeo-Christian heritage" and "our *secular present*" is not the exclusive property of Western Europe but a shared yet too-often forgotten heritage in which cross-cultural exchange between the early modern Christian West and the Muslim world was not unfathomable or even predominantly hostile.

In trying to foreground these moments of cross-cultural exchange, I focus only on writers and works that most critics have frequently neglected or not completely understood: Henry Stubbe, John Toland, and Walter Savage Landor; Samuel Taylor Coleridge's "Mahomet," Percy Shelley's *The Assassins: A Fragment of a Romance*, and Mary Shelley's *The Last Man*. William Beckford, Lord Byron, Thomas Moore, and Thomas De Quincey lie beyond the scope of this study.[16] Likewise, I do not give any sustained attention to the 1706 *Arabian Nights* English translation. Even as these Oriental tales have had an undeniable influence on European representations of Islam and the literary works I will be examining, *Arabian Nights* scholarship has marginalized other media for conveying heretical ideas about Mahometanism, ignoring widespread images of Islam that were circulating among radical circles before 1706.[17] This book includes only those works that self-consciously illustrate the long historical continuity between radical heterodox writings on Mahometanism and national discourses on civic republicanism. Because of this meticulous focus on England and English writers (apart from Edmund Burke), this study is also narrow in its regional coverage. Although I refer to "Britain" and "England" interchangeably when discussing imperial nationhood, I am not making any claims about the Scottish and Irish

Enlightenments, nor do I consider provincial towns and cities beyond London. These limitations in literary and regional coverage will, I hope, inspire research on topics that could not be properly addressed in a book that covers an expansive chronological scale. Notwithstanding these limitations, I will have performed a valuable service to my readers if my work helps dismantle "the West and the Rest" paradigm that has framed post-9/11 discussions of Islam.

A book of this massive scale and chronology will inevitably be disputed among scholars for years to come, but the many debts I have acquired while writing it, from a dissertation to a final manuscript, are beyond dispute. My primary debt is to Robert Markley. As a dedicated advisor and meticulous reader, he spent innumerable hours reading and rereading multiple drafts of this book during different stages. His constructive feedback and encouragement have helped me rewrite and reorganize this book and figure out what I actually wanted to say. I also have benefited from the strong encouragement and engaging criticism of Bernadette Andrea, Ted Underwood, and Leon Chai. I also thank Vanderbilt University for a one-year research leave that enabled me to complete revisions for this book, as well as Vanderbilt colleagues who have offered their advice and support. In particular, I want to recognize Jonathan Lamb, Bridget Orr, and James Epstein for providing invaluable suggestions—and even challenges to—different chapters and parts of this book. The Johns Hopkins reader Rajani Sudan undoubtedly helped to make this book more coherent, effective, and readable. Matthew McAdam has proved to be a very attentive editor who was willing to take on, without reservations, the ambitious and lengthy project of a first-time author. I thank David Coen for a fine copyediting job and the hardworking staff at the Johns Hopkins University Press for overseeing the publication of this book.

The theoretical inspiration for this work was kindled, in part, during my participation in a two-week seminar sponsored by the University of California Humanities Research Institute Seminar in Experimental Critical Theory and titled "Cartographies of the Theological-Political," convened at UC Irvine by Saba Mahmood and Charles Hirschkind in the summer of 2007. Composed of speakers, faculty, and graduate students representing many disciplines and fields, this seminar reflected on interrelated questions about Islam, secularization, and religious belief that have changed the way I look at the eighteenth century. I acknowledge the members of the Southern California Eighteenth-Century Studies Group, particularly Felicity Nussbaum, for providing last-minute feedback on a precirculated version of chapter 2, "Letters from a Female Deist: Lady Mary Wortley Montagu, Muslim Women, and Freethinking Feminism." I thank the Huntington and Clark Memorial Libraries for allowing me to use their collections, without which this book's research would have remained incomplete. Funding for this library research was generously provided by the Vanderbilt Summer Scholars Program in 2008. I also made extensive use of the library of the University of Illinois at Urbana-Champaign. I am especially grateful to Jack Stillinger for nurturing my interest in Romantic Orientalism; he was the first scholar to listen attentively to a young graduate student raving about visionary poets and Islamic republics.

I thank the University of Pennsylvania Press for permission to use material in chapter 1 that appeared in an earlier version in "A Hungarian Revolution in Restoration England: Henry Stubbe, Radical Islam, and the Rye House Plot," *The Eighteenth Century: Theory and Interpretation* 51.1–2 (2010): 1–25; and the Trustees of Boston University for permission to use material in chapter 4 that appeared in an earlier version in "The Hermetic Tradition of Arabic Islam and the Colonial Politics of Landor's *Gebir*," *Studies in Romanticism* 46.4 (2007): 433–59.

Finally, I wish to thank my parents and my wife, Shimy, who has firmly stood by my scholarly endeavors through good and bad times.

Islam and the English Enlightenment,
1670–1840

Introduction

Rethinking Islam in the Eighteenth Century

Our common "culture"... is more manifestly Christian, barely even
Judaeo-Christian. No Muslim is among us, alas ...just at the
moment when it is towards Islam, perhaps, that we ought to begin
by turning our attention. No representative of other cults either.
Not a single woman! We ought to take this into account: speaking
on behalf of these mute witnesses without speaking for them, in
place of them, and drawing from this all sorts of consequences.

Jacques Derrida, *Faith and Knowledge: The Two Sources of "Religion"*
at the Limits of Reason Alone

Islamic republicanism is a term that describes how radical Protestants in eighteenth-century England self-consciously recast Islam in constitutional-nationalist
terms, and in this book I argue for this action's crucial significance. My theoretical premise is that "Mahometanism" (a commonplace Christian nomenclature
for Islam) marks the occasion for what Jacques Derrida designates as the return
to Abraham's revelation. He describes the Abrahamic as that which preexists and
follows, conditions and disrupts, creates and destroys the self-enclosed civilizations of Judaism, Christianity, and Islam. This disruptive revelation renders the
concept of religion an obscure and unreadable signifier that explodes the ideological hyphen that forcefully joins "Judeo" and "Christianity" in Western secular
thought. By unsettling Europe's identity as essentially Greco-Roman, Christian,
and secular, the Abrahamic resists the West's cultural, political, and linguistic
monopoly over prophetic history. According to Gil Anidjar's historical reassess-
ment of the Abrahamic, Islam—along with Judaism and other forgotten heresies
as well as women's repressed contribution to this vision—"demands that history
... be rethought, a history that is all too sedimented in the manifest progression of the Abrahamic as the history of 'western' religions ... from Judaism to
Christianity, from Christianity to Islam."[1] The present work "desediments" this

Eurocentric progression by treating radical Protestant interpretations of Mahometanism as central to the English Enlightenment rather than as a marginal anomaly to be ignored.

Largely forgotten by literary critics today, Samuel Taylor Coleridge's "Mahomet," which was composed in 1799 and serves as this book's epigraph, answers Derrida's plea about the need to desediment the West's secular history. Opening with a "Song" celebrating "the flight and return of Mohammed," this intriguing fourteen-line poem casts the Prophet as a Protestant revolutionary: he is "th' enthusiast Warrior of Mecca" who "crushed the blasphemous Rites of the Pagan / And idolatrous Christians.—For veiling the Gospel of Jesus" (lines 7, 4–5). For Coleridge, Islamic republicanism anoints the Abrahamic by asking a pressing question—can there be another revelation after Christ?—that threatens to disrupt Europe's identity as Christian and secular. Although deism, Arianism, and Unitarianism have disparate historical chronologies and do not even share the same beliefs and practices, they invoke Islamic monotheism in trying to answer this pressing question, albeit in a heretical way. These heresies realign an iconoclastic Protestant Reformation with a rival prophetic faith that spurns what they identify as an "idolatrous" Christian orthodoxy: the Trinity, the atonement, and the clergy. As such, the smashing of orthodoxy's false idols is tantamount to replacing the established church and state with an Islamic constitutional republic modeled after the original primitive Christianity. As I demonstrate in chapter 5, Coleridge's "enthusiast Warrior" reveals a just social equality during a period when English dissenters became disillusioned with the French Revolution, especially after Napoleon's imperialist ambitions became obvious during his 1798–99 Egyptian occupation. In Coleridge's imagination, Mahomet replaces Napoleon as the new republican prophet who leads "the People with mad / shouts" to the "ruinous River"—a revolutionary energy "all rushing impetuous onward"— recalling "Kubla Khan"'s sublime scenery (lines 10–11, 15). The revolutionary Prophet ambivalently points forward to Christ's egalitarian vision—the Second Coming—while also returning to the sublime tyranny and Oriental despotism of earlier centuries.

Insofar as Mahometanism functions as an unstable supplement, this Abrahamic faith is not, as Derrida sees it, a fixed irreducible alterity whose only role is to deconstruct (rather than construct) European-Christian identity. Islamic republicanism reaffirms a republican philosophy and ethos latent in biblical monotheism while also suggesting a deficiency in Christian modernity (the Passion, Trinity, the church, etc.) that needs to be replaced by Islamic iconoclasm, albeit in a tentative and incomplete manner. Many Britons viewed North African Muslim societies in Morocco, Algiers, Tripoli, and Tunisia (the last three regions being military provinces in the Ottoman empire) as the seat of tyranny, barbarism, and white slavery. By contrast, English freethinkers such as the young Coleridge cast the Ottoman empire in Hungary, Turkey, and Egypt and the Mughal empire in India as the custodians of England's ancient republican constitution.[2] In their imagination, these Islamic republics confirm, yet promise to resolve, the short-comings plaguing the Christian prophetic monarchy in England: the downfall of Cromwell's government followed by the restoration of the Stuart regime and the high Anglican church; disenfranchised nonconformists barred from hold-ing public office, including property rights, and preferment due to the Test and Corporation Acts; women's inability to own wealth and property under English common law; and the gradual disillusionment with the French Revolution com-bined with a conservative backlash and governmental suppression of radicals in England. For these freethinkers, Islam was not yet subsumed within what Derrida calls late-nineteenth-century "globalatinization," which reduced the Prophet's universal message to an alien geopolitical religion existing outside Latin Chris-tendom. Instead, Islamic republicanism promised to recuperate pre-Latinate-Roman virtue once Christ's teachings were accepted as the living legacy of a rival and successful prophetic faith in the East. But as my reading of Coleridge's poem suggests, this supplementation is postponed for a Second Coming that never oc-curs, so the Islamic republic evokes the political disillusionment that originally characterized the negative freethinking response to Latinate-Roman Christianity. This political disillusionment, I argue, does not reflect Briton's inherent preju-dice against Islam itself but the shifting social, economic, and political alliances among Protestant England, Catholic Europe, and the Muslim world.

This book thus challenges anachronistic postcolonial readings that project a dichotomy between a superior Christian Occident and an inferior Islamic Ori-ent onto the early modern period. In refusing to posit a hegemonic British em-pire in the eighteenth century, this study is not proposing the equally fallacious move of arguing for philo-Islamism: English literature's culturally unmediated sympathy for Islam—or as Maxime Robinson puts it, the "mystique of Islam" as seen "through fraternal and understanding eyes."[3] Instead, this book argues that positive (and negative) perceptions of Islam were conditioned by Anglo-Islamic encounters in India, Ottoman Europe, and elsewhere in the Muslim world. As a result, the radical Enlightenment was in constant dialectical engagement with Islam.[4] Britain was economically and politically subordinate to powerful Islamic empires that, from their relatively hegemonic position, exercised control over the East-West dissemination of goods, peoples, ideas, religions, literature, and revolutions. Although the topic lies beyond the present study, this dialectical engagement does not foreclose other conditions that informed Anglo-Islamic relations, such as the eighteenth-century British fascination with Judaism, Confucianism, Zoroastrianism, Hinduism, and Buddhism.

Building on the pioneering scholarship of early modern scholars,[5] I argue for the need to foreground Mahometanism's centrality in the works of Lady Mary Wortley Montagu, Edmund Burke, Walter Savage Landor, Samuel Taylor Coleridge, Robert Southey, and Percy and Mary Shelley. In doing so, I revise a progressivist Whig paradigm that renders religion reactionary. My argument decolonizes the historical imagination by approaching early modern Afro-Eurasia as an integrated whole, complicating nationalist and imperialist histories of eighteenth-century Britain.

I resist a diffusionist model in which the West is the prime mover and the East its passive beneficiary, for diffusionism occludes the various connections that defined a polycentric world before 1800, when Western superiority and Eastern subjugation were not yet rigidly defined.[6] Hailing Derrida's plea and Coleridge's "Song," I treat eighteenth-century Muslim Afro-Eurasia as a formidable economic, political, and cultural force, in turn remapping the interrelationship among radicalism, Orientalism, and secularization in this transitional period. In the following sections I will redefine these three complex terms from the vantage of Islamic republicanism.

Radicalism between the Revolutions

In "Radical Criticisms of the Whig Order in the Age between Revolutions," J. G. A. Pocock frames radicalism's historical continuity in the long eighteenth century as a pressing problem: "To begin our study in 1688 involves us in some problems of continuity . . . the problem of relating radical criticism of the Whig order to the great explosion of plebeian and sectarian speech and action which had marked the years of the Civil War and Interregnum."[7] To talk about the continuities among the 1688, 1776, and 1789 revolutions raises the bloody specter of the 1640s and 1650s. In other words, Pocock asks us to consider how mid-seventeenth-century radical Protestant dissent—plebeian and sectarian movements that spurned the Church of England's authority—informed country and commonwealthean opposition to Britain's Whig-Walpolean oligarchy in the 1730s and '40s, the American democratic upheavals, and French Jacobin politics despite its defeat in 1660. If 1789 or 1688 repeats history, then how does one account for the transmission of radical ideas in this period? This section argues that Islamic republicanism is enabled by a heterodox biblical hermeneutics associated with (but not confined to) the English deist movement. To think about what lies *between* the revolutions involves long and complicated national debates about Mahometanism, a supplementary prophetic faith that helped transmit and renew radical ideas in England.

In terms of literary chronology, Islamic republicanism begins with Henry Stubbe's *The Rise and Progress of Mahometanism* (c. 1671), a subversive work that portrays Mahomet as a wise legislator who reinstituted primitive Christianity's republican order. Accordingly, Christianity began as egalitarian Jewish sect with Ebonite and Arian leanings that refused the corrupt doctrine of Trinity as decreed by the Nicene Council in AD 325. As I argue in chapter 1, Stubbe's antitrinitarian manuscript circulated privately among radical clandestine circles from the late seventeenth to the late eighteenth century. James R. Jacob cleared him from the charge that he abandoned his prior commitments to Sir Henry Vane and the Interregnum government. He also argues that his manuscript is a missing historical link between the Restoration's dissenting Protestantism and the early Enlightenment's Whig deism.[8] Owing to Jacob's revisionist work, I show that Voltaire's *Mahomet the Impostor* (1741), staged and reprinted several times in England,[9] is atypical of the eighteenth-century stance on Mahometanism. His despotic Prophet does not represent the multifaceted—and even sympathetic—accounts of Islam that were widely circulating during that period.

According to Jacob, "Stubbe must . . . be reckoned as one of the founders of English deism, though his creed wore the guise of 'Mahometan Christianity.'"[10] Mahometanism not only conveniently masked Stubbe's deist critique. By the eighteenth century, many deists preferred Mahometanism over the dogmatic Christianity codified in the Anglican church and state. Thomas Morgan, Matthew Tindal, and Peter Annet variously employed Islamic *tawhid,* or unity of God, to discredit the scriptural basis of revelation, liturgical practices, apostolic succession, the Trinity, the incarnation, miracles, and original sin. In particular, they used Islamic toleration as a beating stick against English toleration—the entitlement to freedom of conscience that, in practice, excluded many nonconformists from citizenship.[11] Because of the Corporation (1662) and Test (1673) Acts—which remained in effect after the 1689 Toleration Act—the Anglican state barred Unitarians, Quakers, Catholics, and antitrinitarians from holding public office, obtaining legal preferment, and earning degrees from Oxford and Cambridge.

For this reason, deism not only implies a preference for natural religion over scriptural authority and revealed truth but also an open-ended investigation in which various primitive monotheisms—Arian, Ebonite, Jewish, or Islamic—can be used to explore republican-democratic models that promote civic equality despite confessional affiliation and socioeconomic differences.[12] By reading the scriptures beside profane histories, deists helped shape the *Historica monotheistica*, a comparativist study that challenges Christocentric history and politics. Radical dissenters used this study to question the theological authority of an exclusionist Anglican establishment.[13] From Stubbe onward, deism implied a temper or attitude toward England's toleration policy and religious plurality rather than a systematic creed.[14]

In other words, deists studying the *Historica monotheistica* deemphasized the need to establish a unified theological-philosophical doctrine and instead adopted a historicist approach to the problem of particularity: how can human salvation hinge on a particular moment in human history as affirmed by orthodox Christianity, if Christ taught a universal message? Why would a rational and benevolent God allow a particular event and place—Moses' liberation of the Jews in the Holy Land and Christ's resurrection in Jerusalem—to shape world history, reducing various religions, histories, and cultures to insignificance, or worst yet, to eternal damnation? The deists solved this problem by insisting that a universal and reasonable religion, in its "natural" and simple form, would avoid ascribing a partial will to an arbitrary God. This tidy solution would require not only an unbiased comparative investigation of Judaism, paganism, and Islam, but also the categorical denial of the belief that Jesus was the Son of God. Deists could not accept that this divine mediator determined human history, and that his sacrifice has atoned for humanity's original sin through God's forgiveness. The deist solution to the problem of particularity requires the wholesale rejection of original sin, the Trinity, the incarnation, divine revelation, and the atonement. In their imagination, these erroneous "pagan" doctrines were concocted by priests, popes, and kings to dupe their subjects into voluntary submission.[15]

The problem of particularity has its deep-seated roots in Western Europe's religious fragmentation following the Protestant Reformation and sectarian disputes over the meaning of "religion(s)." Protestant reformers raised unsettling questions about the relationship between natural pagan beliefs and practices and Christian doctrine. They were also concerned about the role of rival monotheistic faiths—Judaism and Islam—in Christendom's parochial conflicts.[16] After the Protestant Reformation, the need to account for providential history before and after Luther's break with the church led to an extensive search for commonalities among the three Abrahamic faiths. Unlike Judaism, however, Islam posed the longest and greatest threat, theologically and politically, to the Christian narrative of redemption: the socioeconomic and military superiority of the Ottoman, Safavid, and Mughal empires threatened to supplement and thus displace Christocentric views of history and politics. For instance, E. Baker's map, *Eslam or the Countries Which Have Professed the Faith of Mahomet* (1804, 1817), would have taught English Protestants about the rapid expansion of "Mahometan Sovereignties" in Afro-Eurasia and India—the various caliphates and sultanates that geographically dwarfed Western European countries from the late seventh to the early nineteenth century. Implicitly, this map records the successful propagation of a rival prophetic faith that eclipsed Christianity's centrality in world affairs (fig. 1). Mahometanism's worldwide triumph poses a perplexing problem for an orthodox Christianity that sees itself as the final political theology that supersedes all previous revelations.

For deists, on the other hand, Christendom's fragmentation from within and without its porous borders is not a problem, because Mahometanism and the Protestant Reformation symbolize the providential unfolding of the *Historica monotheistica*. Mahomet, as well as Christ, is one among many prophets belonging to Abraham's natural religion. In other words, if Christian Europe is to overcome religious pluralism as the subject of political and theological contention, it must abandon its obsession with a particular time and event: a diachronic history that is grounded on Christ's incarnation in first-century Jerusalem. Instead, deists concluded that, ideally, religious plurality is the universal essence of history: a synchronic monotheism that interprets Islam's worldwide triumph as anticipating the Protestant Reformation. In their imagination, Muhammad is an earlier and more radical reformer than Luther.

Hence, Stubbe has no qualms about justifying Islam's rise to geopolitical domination, because the true opponents to the Christian faith are the Trinitarians, the "enemies to all human Learning": St. Athanasius, for his false teachings about the "son of God," and Emperor Constantine, for rigging the Nicene Council elections in favor of the Trinitarian heresy.[17] Stubbe argues that Islam was spread not through the sword but by the word. Mahomet's mission was not to establish a military empire but to restore the

> old Religion, not to introduce a new one. He taught his followers to abolish idolatry everywhere, and that all the World was obliged to the profession of these truths, that there was one God, that he had no Associates, that there was a Providence, & a Retribution hereafter proportionate to the good or ill Actions of Men, just as the Jews thought themselves obliged to bring all Mankind . . . under the observation of the Law of Nature

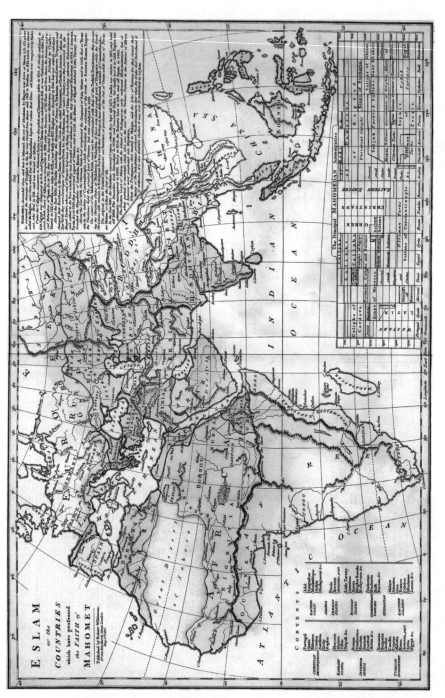

Figure 1. E. Baker, *Eslam, or the Countries Which Have Professed the Faith of Mahomet,* 1817. Special Collections and University Archives, The Gelman Library, The George Washington University.

contained in the seven precepts of Noah. But that all Mankind were to be forced to the profession of his Religion . . . is a falsehood. (180)

Mahometanism is modeled after the egalitarian teachings of the "Judaizing Christians," the first practitioners of Christ's simple faith (145). As such, Mahomet granted liberty of religion to Jews and Christians living in his empire after paying a small tribute (184). He began the Reformation eight hundred years before Luther. Appearing in Coleridge's "Mahomet" over a century later, Stubbe's Protestant Prophet resurrected civic republicanism. In solving the problem of particularity, Islam offers an attractive counterpoint to the restrictive policy of Anglican toleration.

As evident in Coleridge's poem, Islamic republicanism makes a dramatic comeback in 1790s London. In 1800, William Hamilton Reid, a dissenting republican who (like Stubbe) became a "turncoat" to avoid government persecution, published *The Rise and Dissolution of the Infidel Societies in this Metropolis*, an anti–French revolutionary exposé in imitation of Abbe Barruel's highly acclaimed *Memoirs* (1798). Claiming to have uncovered a "secret" Jacobin conspiracy in England, he argues that French revolutionary principles originated in Europe's freemason and Rosicrucian secret societies, which, for him, naturally stem from London's deist infidelity. This republican discourse has posed a threat to church and state since the English Civil War.[18] Among the heretical ideas circulating in the London's infidel circles, he references the deist defense of Islam: English deists, in their support of French Jacobinism, believe that the "Mahometans" are closer to "the standard of reason" than the Christians, suggesting that the heretical maxims of the Islamic prophecy are compatible with modern infidelity (65, 68). In this case, he may be alluding to deists such as Thomas Chubb, who upheld Mahometanism as tolerant in contrast to historical Christianity's persecuting spirit.[19] Arguing against those who claim that Islam was not propagated by the sword, Reid favors Christian morality over "the Mahometan or Infidel system" (79). He insists that Mahometanism's rise to geopolitical domination does not supplement Christocentric history and politics (70).

Reid's antideist contention remains ambivalent, however. The deist argument favoring powerful Islamic states' triumph over Christendom "makes nothing against the universality of the Christian Religion," because, as he explains, pagan and Muslim believers could embody Christ's universal message: "among Pagans and Mahometans, there are . . . many who, living above the dictates of those false systems, are, in the best sense, true Christians." Ironically, his antideist argument subscribes to a deist outlook: pagan and Mahometan belief in Christ's teachings, however corrupted, shows that "Christianity . . . is more of a *principle* than a *profession*" (71; emphasis original). Christianity is about practicing universal morality rather than adhering to a doctrinal system. To support this broad interpretation, he quotes two passages from the New Testament: 10 Acts, 5:34, 35, which state that "God is no respecter of persons, but in every nation he who feareth him and worketh righteousness is accepted with him"; and 3 Romans 5:1, in which passage Paul preaches that the Jews could more easily attain righteousness than the gentiles (71). Freethinkers used these passages, among many others from Paul's epistles, to defend the Ancient Theology, the tradition of *the prisca theologia*: an apologetic theology showing that vestiges of the true universal religion were taught among the Greeks, the Jews, and others, originating with Noah and his sons (or the antediluvians) and passed down to Confucius, Zoroaster, Hermes, Brahmins, Druids, Orpheus, Pythagoras, Plato, and the Sibyls. The Ancient Theology, or the *Historica monotheistica*, was used by orthodox churchmen to justify the need to covert pagans and Jews. As deployed by Reid and deist infidels, this study promotes a radical scriptural hermeneutics. "The Laws of nature" and the virtuous teachings of paganism, Judaism, and Mahometanism are faithful to Christ's "universal principles."[20] Even though he insists that his account is not subversive, his emphatic attack on Mahometan infidelity ironically renders Christianity a dispensable revelation (57). As Iain McCalman has shown, Reid wrote an anti-Jacobin exposé as a ruse for evading William Pitt's antiradical persecution campaign. After publishing *The Rise and Dissolution*, he became an ardent spokesman for the republican cause.[21]

Reid's clever use of subversive rhetoric is an example of what Jon Mee describes as 1790s bricolage discourse: the linguistic term borrowed from Levi-Strauss refers to the eclectic mixture of various political, theological, and intellectual repertoires used by radicals to refashion elements from a previous discourse into a new linguistic medium for conveying ideas that are too dangerous to discuss otherwise.[22] However, this discursive eclecticism is not unique to the 1790s. From Stubbe to Reid, Mahometanism was a useful bricolage medium for a diverse group of writers from various political and religious backgrounds. John Toland, Lady Mary Wortley Montagu, Edmund Burke, Samuel Taylor Coleridge, and Percy Shelley variously understood Mahometanism to provide both a model and an idiom for the definition of political liberty. In this context, English radicalism is defined not as a linear history of ideas but as a series of subversive practices and eclectic discursive techniques that are culturally situated.[23] James R. Jacob has shown that these culturally situated practices inform the writings of Henry Stubbe, who, in various works, deploys irony, understatement, innuendo, and paradox to outfox government censorship. Jacob's analysis reveals that ironic self-distancing and rhetorical indirection defined the radical Enlightenment. In order to evade severe censorship laws, many deists relied on the "rhetoric of subterfuge" and "the Art of Theological Lying."[24] These subversive rhetorical techniques are common in English deist discourse, especially in heterodox writings on Mahometanism.

Despite its deist roots, Islamic republicanism does not reflect any fixed set of ideological assumptions, nor does it belong to any particular coterie of writers and thinkers or to any intellectual tradition. Rather, it mediates the various contradictions that permeate England's constitutional idiom—the vexed language describing the balance among the king, the Parliament, and the people—blurring the boundaries that distinguish the interregnum commonwealth of the 1640s and '50s from the parliamentary limited monarchy of 1688. Stories about Mahomet's egalitarian republic complicate any coherent reading of British political history, especially after 1789. By continually supplementing England's Judeo-Christian "ancient constitution,"[25] Islamic republicanism is a highly malleable discourse that encompasses republican leveling, Tory opposition, Whig reform, and, during and after the 1790s, Jacobin revolution. As a bricolage imprint of England's heterogeneous past, the rise and progress of Mahometanism equally lends itself to the "conservative" Edmund Burke and the "radical" Percy Shelley, both of whom use Islam to reinvent British constitutional history for their self-serving political agenda (to be discussed in chapters 3 and 6).

In short, Islamic republicanism is part of what Charles Taylor calls the modern "social imaginary": the "images, stories, and legends" through which people in England could imagine their everyday existence, "the deeper normative notions and images that underlie [social] expectations" about their constitutional past and present.[26] In English political life, Islam is one of the principal mediums for imagining cultural transmission and transformation. Converting to a Mahometan is therefore a process of radical self-fashioning for those who believe that England's constitutional model has excluded them from participating in the symbolic rites of Anglican citizenship. For many English nonconformists, Islam offers a renovated constitutional idiom for reclaiming political subjectivity and national identity, reworking the universal ideals of liberty, equality, and fraternity into a new vocabulary for redefining the power struggle among state sovereignty, church authority, and the people. Employed in this manner, Islamic republicanism augments English nonauthoritarian liberty while dispensing with exclusionist and oppressive Christian policies.

Taking my cue from Derrida, this book examines how Islamic republicanism reinvents English revolutionary history, providing sociopolitical empowerment for marginalized "mute witnesses": deists, Unitarians, Gnostics, and Arians, among other forgotten heretics, and heterodox women who championed female-friendly versions of the prophetic past. Islamic republicanism's political reinvention—enabled through reprinted republican tracts and recirculated subversive manuscripts—creates a historical continuity among the 1640s, 1688, 1776, and 1789.[27] This imaginative process ties together the various events that took place between the eighteenth-century revolutions. Mythical accounts about Mahometanism's worldwide triumph constitute a lived cultural heritage that underwrites the English social imaginary. Hence, this book covers literary history up to 1840, the year in which Thomas Carlyle remade Mahomet into a national icon worthy of hero worship. Joining Luther, Cromwell, and Napoleon, he becomes modern Britain's pioneer republican in Carlyle's work. From the late seventeenth to the mid-nineteenth century, Islamic republicanism captivated the radical Anglo-Protestant imagination and redefined reformed orthodoxy in England, North America, and the transatlantic world, only to be silenced by the anti-Islamic sentiments that gripped Victorian culture after the 1857 Indian Mutiny.[28]

Beyond Orientalism

In the past two decades, anthropologists and religious studies critics have pointed out that the application of religion-as-belief to a non-Western context is specific to the West's cultural, theological, and colonial history.[29] Yet literary critics continue to treat "religion" as if it were self-evident and universal. Even though Edward Said condemned the "clash of civilizations" model for its essentialism, he nonetheless posits a *religious* difference between the Christian West and the Islamic East: "[T]he European encounter with the Orient . . . turned Islam into the very epitome of an outsider against which the whole of European civilization . . . was founded."[30] This influential statement might explain why Islamic republicanism has never received any sustained academic attention. Of course, postcolonial critics have examined the complex links among Orientalism, Romanticism, and imperial culture, questioning the idea that the Romantic fascination with the East produces a hegemonic self-consistent knowledge that helps consolidate colonial domination.[31] Equally significant are recent strands of criticism overturning scholarly stereotypes that presume a lack of intercultural contact between England and the Muslim world.[32] Nonetheless, these studies cannot explain how radicals appropriated Islamic ideas to interrogate, transform, and expand eighteenth-century England's constitutionalist framework. Moving beyond Orientalism requires, as I will argue, that critics cease to treat Islam as a "religion" distinct from Judaism and Christianity, because this scholarly interpretation reproduces an imperialist taxonomy in which Europe is the privileged center of world history.

Contrary to Said's assumptions, Islam was not always "diametrically inferior" to Europe (72). During the early modern period, Mahometanism metaphorically encoded the "non-Christian" as an alterity that threatens the Occident from within—what Michel de Certeau identifies as the "bipolar structure" of the Christian infidel. By projecting this "bipolar structure" onto the Mahometan Christian bogyman, post-Reformation Europe's religious differences can be explained.[33] Various sects exploited Islamophobia to posit a unified Christendom that stands in an imaginary opposition to an internal and external enemy. Indeed, comparisons with Mahometanism were central to Luther's understanding of the true believer and debates about church reform.[34] This process of metaphorical displacement confirms Said's thesis that the East "was always *like* some aspect of the West," except that this simile does not presume a preexisting difference between the Occident and the Orient (67, emphasis original). Orthodox Anglicans invoke the Mahometan Christian bogyman to rationalize the exclusion of dissenters from the rites of citizenship. Radical dissenters, on the other hand, used this figure to question Anglican national hegemony, which, by the 1790s, suppressed revolutionary fervor at home and bolstered missionary and imperialist zeal abroad.[35]

Said's model cannot explain Islamic republicanism because of what Herbert Butterfield diagnoses as "the Whig interpretation of history": a teleological model that celebrates past Protestant actors for anticipating the progressive Whig reformers who championed nineteenth- and twentieth-century secular liberalism, made possible by the post-enlightenment decline of religious belief. Said's work is predicated on this "Whig fallacy."[36] He traces modern Orientalism to a secularized Protestant outlook that, in dissolving the biblical interpretive framework in the late eighteenth century, released the Islamic East from the Christian West's "narrowly religious scrutiny." He argues that this de-Christianizing process, rooted in the Reformation's challenge to institutional authority, transposed theology onto aesthetics. In turn, this process enabled the imperialist appropriation and restructuring of the Orient (120–21). By displacing religion as a social category, Orientalism recast Eastern religions as alien and reactionary in contradistinction to the "Enlightened" and "progressive" West.

Following Said's *Orientalism*, most postcolonial critics have assumed that eighteenth-century England, under the sway of Enlightenment skepticism, witnessed the birth of an Orientalist discourse that abandons theological polemic for an aesthetics that essentialized the East-West binary. According to Norman Daniel, the image of Islam as alterity, which, for him, first appeared in Antoine Galland's translation of *A Thousand and One Nights*, led to an eighteenth-century aesthetics whose aim was to "reduce polemic, and to replace it by exotic entertainment." For Kenneth Parker, Orientalism is a logical extension of the Enlightenment attitude toward the rarefied "Other." Following Nigel Leask's assessment of Romantic Orientalism, Ros Ballaster maintains that, unlike the religious-moral discourses earlier in the century, late-eighteenth-century Orientalism produced alterity and difference, so reading the Oriental tale in the Romantic era signifies "an aesthetic outlook of the world, rather than the acquisition of political or moral truth(s)."[37] In these Whiggish accounts, "religion" becomes a transparent auxiliary for aesthetic enjoyment. Since Said, postcolonial criticism assumes an unproblematic divide between politics and aesthetics in which the transformation and privatization of religion, made possible only through the triumph of Protestantism in the West, is the wedge separating artistic representation from politics. This cultural division is treated as the ideological precondition that made possible the imperialist restructuring of the East circa 1800. That few postcolonial critics have questioned the historical basis of this division as it operates in late-eighteenth-century Orientalist discourse is a testament to the enduring paralysis of the Whig fallacy.[38]

Within a Saidean framework, literary representations of the Islamic republic can be interpreted only as a rare historical abnormality rather than, as it should be, a productive engagement with British culture and politics. This interpretive bias is not surprising given that the late eighteenth century has always served as the launching pad for secular modernity's grand narratives. Despite the many challenges leveled against Whig historiography, some scholars continue to treat the eighteenth century as a period that witnessed widespread religious decline and a concomitant secular liberalism.[39] Because of this progressivist bias, Islamic republicanism appears as an odd conundrum when yoked to the radical Enlightenment. The inability to recognize radical Protestant interpretations of Islam says more about Whig historiography's unconscious appeal than it does about the eighteenth century. I argue that the Whig fallacy has not only infiltrated the discipline of literary studies but has also become the unquestionable dogma of a postcolonial mode of criticism that always casts Islam as the European Self's exotic alter ego—a foreign eastern religion that, most critics presume, has made no significant contributions to the secular West.

This Whig fallacy is a product of what Edward Said, following M. H. Abrams, calls the natural supernaturalism model, the cultural narrative that explains the secularization process in the late eighteenth century. According to Said, Orientalism was enabled by a displaced Protestant theology in the secular guise of Romantic philosophy and literature: a natural supernaturalism that, for Abrams, inaugurated modernity as the aesthetization of the Christian and esoteric tradition. In this regard, Romanticism entails "the secularization of inherited ideas and ways of thinking," whereby revolutionary politics is transposed onto the aesthetic imagination, a "non-political" realm.[40] Said incorporates Abrams's definition: Romantic Orientalism "retained, as an undislodged current in its discourse, a reconstructed religious impulse, a naturalized supernaturalism" (121). The secularization process shaped "[m]odern Orientalist theory and praxis. . . . a set of structures inherited from the past, secularized, redisposed, and re-formed by such disciplines as philology, which in turn were naturalized, modernized, and laicized substitutes for (or versions of) Christian supernaturalism" (122). Said reads modern Orientalism as a politically suspicious Romanticism that, in displacing Protestant theology, produced an ideological split between politics and aesthetics. Religion's exclusion from public discourse justified, in turn, the imperialist distinction between a "backward" East that mixes theology with politics and a "progressive" West that adheres to the separation of church and state.

Primarily in the last decade, many literary critics have contested Abrams's natural supernaturalism.[41] Most notably, Colin Jager has redefined romantic secularization as institutional "differentiation," in which the religious sphere competes among other forms of sociopolitical organization—such as science and the nation-state—for the authority once vested exclusively in religious institutions. He borrowed this term from José Casanova's *Public Religions in the Modern World*. This work describes differentiation as the "emancipation of the secular spheres—primarily the state, the economy, and science—from the religious sphere and the concomitant differentiation and specialization of religion within its own newly found religious sphere."[42] Jager relies on this definition to argue against two dominant theories about secular modernity: "the decline-of-religion thesis," which posits religion's gradual disappearance from world affairs, and "the privatization thesis," which sees religion's marginalization as resulting from its repositioning in the private sphere.[43] In debunking these two theories, Jager rereads Romantic secularization not as a transpositioning—*x* is a secularized version of *y*—but as an institutional reconfiguration in which literature takes up some questions that were formerly under purview of religious institutions, which are forced to undergo further specialization as a result. He avoids the ideologically suspect move made by Abrams and Said: that secularization inaugurates the teleological unfolding of a single (Western) modernity in which literature and aesthetics are supplements to religion. As in Hans Blumenberg's critique of Carl Schmitt, Jager refuses to interpret the analogy between religion and aesthetics as the Romantic transformation of theological concepts into the secular idiom of a self-legitimated modernity.[44]

Jager's criticism questions the Saidean assumption that Islam can only signify the otherworldly in contrast to the worldly West. For instance, Bonaparte's 1798–99 Egyptian invasion, which Said treats as an inaugural event in Orientalist praxis, does not adhere to the story of natural supernaturalism (80–89). Bonaparte not only sought to restructure Egypt—an imperialist will to power—but also to re-interpret European republican culture in an enlightened Islamic context. Indeed, after invading Cairo, he assumed the authority of the Ottoman sultanate and redefined deist doctrine as Islamic law in order to consolidate French colonial power among the Egyptian ulema, the Muslim clerical class.[45] Almost two de-cades after the unsuccessful Egyptian expedition, Bonaparte continued to praise Islam as a rational faith that, compared with a heathenish Trinitarian Christian-ity, "is the finest of all."[46] However, Said interprets Bonaparte's praise as a pro-paganda campaign "to wage a uniquely benign and selective war against Islam" (82). This hasty dismissal is revealing. Politically suspect as his foreign policies may be, Bonaparte's long-lasting fascination with Islam defies the binary logic of Orientalism: far from exemplifying natural supernaturalism, Islam is implicated in a process of institutional differentiation in which French republican rule and Egyptian-Ottoman authority are negotiated and reorganized. Juan Cole describes this process as "Euro-Muslim creolization," in which the mixed cultural and in-stitutional forms of authority practiced by colonizer and colonized are mutu-ally transformed. On this account, institutional differentiation-as-creolization consolidated French republican savants and Egyptian Muslim clerics into a joint ruling class who, despite strong religious differences, shared a rationalist disdain for the otherworldly superstition of the illiterate lower classes, East and West.[47]

Natural supernaturalism's inability to make sense of French Egypt and de-ist Islam points to a secularist obsession with treating "religion" as a sui generis concept existing outside history and politics. Talal Asad has shown that this con-cept emerged from the Western tendency to separate private belief from practice, distinguishing, in effect, the modern (Christian) age from everything that came before and rendering the Muslim world unmodern as a result.[48] For Richard King and Tomoko Masuzawa, this concept not only erases the heterogeneity of hu-man experience across various traditions but also is operative in an academic discourse that is complicit with an imperialist tendency to "other" the East as the exemplary site of religion. Rendering the European West secular and the rest spiritual, the late-nineteenth-century drive to classify all faith-based teachings became "a vital operating system within the colonial discourse of Orientalism."[49] By treating Islam as distinct from other monotheisms, the growing academic taxonomy of religions redefined European (Christian) identity as essentially secular. Despite its universalist-pluralist ethos, designating Islam a "world religion" indirectly rendered Muslims (and Jews) degenerate "Semites" who, historically speaking, have no legitimate claim to the Judeo-Christian Enlightenment.

Most post-Saidean criticism continues to rely on a sui generis concept of religion that identifies civilizations through their common doctrinal beliefs. Amartya Sen has noted that this imperialist tendency has been mostly taken for granted among historians who deploy it as an organizing trope that, in practice, impedes "our understanding of other aspects of the global history of ideas."[50] The attempt to categorize world religions through their universal essence feeds into a Eurocentric taxonomy of the world. Notwithstanding the contemporary relevance of Said's critical legacy, the study of Islamic republicanism requires a paradigm shift that moves beyond the Islamic Orient as a byproduct of supernatural religion.

The Prophetic Tradition

Norman O. Brown's 1982 essay "The Prophetic Tradition" was the first to suggest the paradigm shift in the study of Islamic republicanism, even as most scholars were (and still are) unwilling to heed its message. Inspired by the "Copernican Revolution" launched in Marshall Hodgson's *The Venture of Islam* (1974), a three-volume revisionist work that challenges Eurocentric historiography by including Irano-Semitic civilization, Brown argues that William Blake needs to be resituated within a larger prophetic tradition in which Islam is integral to Judeo-Christian history rather than a backward and derivative religion. For Brown, the Prophet's seventh-century mission represents the first "Protestant Reformation" to recuperate a Mosaic prophetic revelation: "Islam represents a return to the original Mosaic theocratic or theopolitical idea."[51] Muhammad's teachings overhaul the corrupt "Roman Law" that gave birth to orthodox Trinitarian Christianity. Islam supplements Trinitarianism in a Derridean sense: as an egalitarian monotheism, Christianity—despite its pagan degeneration in the Roman-Latinate world—is worthy of an enhanced Muslim recuperation (a process, I would argue, that finds its historical-literary analogue in eighteenth-century Islamic republicanism). In this context, Blake's anti-imperialist prophecies are indebted to an unacknowledged rival prophetic tradition. Although the aim of Brown's essay is to reframe Blakean prophecy within an esoteric Judeo-Christian-Islamic worldview, his definition of the prophetic tradition offers a useful alternative to natural super-natural Orientalism.

According to Brown, if the full story behind "Blake and Tradition" is to be told entirely, then scholars need to treat the prophetic tradition as continuous with Judaism, Christianity, and Islam. This egalitarian tradition renders Islam a legitimate response to the apocalyptic failure of Western Trinitarianism, the orthodox Christocentric worldview. Like (Stubbe's) Muhammad, Blake resists a corrupt Roman Christianity; he is a radical poet who wants to restore primitive monotheism to its egalitarian-prophetic roots in the ancient Near East. As a lit-eral affirmation of this poet-prophet identity, he renames himself "Mahomet" in a self-portrait sketch (fig. 2). Mahomet's image is included among the Visionary Heads of Edward I, King John, and David, the first two names as emblematic of long-standing debates about Anglo-Saxon liberty and the 1216 Magna Charter. Mahomet's physical appearance resembles the younger poet if compared with Thomas Phillips's 1807 oil portrait (fig. 3). George Bentley notes the parallel fea-tures found in these two images, drawing attention to the striking similarities in the calm facial expression, tight lips, curly hair, and penetrating gaze.[52] These par-allels are not evident in the other sketches of the Visionary Heads. The sketches were probably executed about 1819–25, with the following words written at the bottom of the pages: "All Genius Varies Thus."[53] Blake's Mahomet not only mani-fests the "Poetic Genius" dormant in all religions but also finds his reincarnation in the "White" English poet. Mahomet's whitewashing is an example of what Srinivas Aravamudan describes as the "tropological" revision of imperial and racial ideologies: rather than assimilating Mahomet's head to an abstract Anglo or Caucasian-European model (an imperialist gesture), the viewer is compelled to imagine the Islamicizing of a "White" English individual (a disruption of the English national imaginary).[54] Blake refuses to orientalize Islam: Mahomet does not resemble the dark-skinned, turban-wearing despot traditionally depicted in Western writings. Instead, Mahomet, the Blakean poet against empire, signifies, congruently, the virtuous restoration of King David's worldly theocratic king-dom and the prophetic anticipation of Edward I's and King John's rule by con-stitutional law.

Blake's tropological revision has profound implications for what Brown, in one of his footnotes, calls "the politics of Orientalism." To understand that Blake can "speak again" only through the Qur'an is to acknowledge that "it is time to discard the time-honored prejudice that treats Koranic theology as a confused echo of half-understood Jewish or Christian traditions, selected and polemi-cally distorted to concoct a newfangled monotheism to supply 'backward' Arabs

Figure 2. William Blake, *Mahomet*, 1819–1825. Santa Barbara Museum of Art, Gift of F. B. Vanderhoef, Jr.

with a 'cultural identity.'"[55] In other words, Hodgson's anti-Eurocentric model of history entails a thorough repudiation of defining civilizations through their religious beliefs, thereby denying a diffusionist logic that ascribes Islam only to the Arabs, a "religious" people. Following Hodgson's lead, Brown argues that Islam also belongs to the prophetic history of Western Europe. By offering a radical reorientation of the historical and geographical assumptions behind Islam's place in the world, Brown undermines any Eurocentric prejudices that posit a fundamental difference between East and West. He reads Blakean poetics as a challenge to Said's essentialist historicism: namely, that revolution first belonged to Western Europe and then to the Muslim world.[56]

For Brown, Hodgson's historiography redefines prophecy as the social and

Figure 3. William Blake by Thomas Phillips, oil on canvas, 1807. © National Portrait Gallery, London.

political vehicle of secularization, which spans thousands of years and traverses cultural and historical frontiers. That is to say, his holistic approach to the prophetic tradition accounts for the social, commercial, and technological transformations that characterize the "Urban Revolution," or the movement from the agrarian village to the urban city, that spread from the "Nile to Oxus" about 3000 BC. In this regard, the prophetic voice channels the perception of social change within the potentialities inherent in the sociopolitical order's massive transformations, which results from commercial and technological developments. Thus, the prophetic tradition redirects the "Urban Revolution," and ends "the injustice, inequality, anomie, the state of war . . . that has been its history from start to finish."[57] According to Brown, Hodgson's historiographical model is unique not in the sense that prophecy is the site of political protest, a thesis that has been advanced by many historians;[58] rather, his model is illuminating because it encodes republicanism in a biblical-Qur'anic idiom that condemns the state, church, and commerce for defacing civic virtue. As such, this model severs the one-to-one link between secularization and Western modernity as repeatedly asserted in traditional European historiography. Relying on Hodgson's research, Brown redefines secularization as modern urbanization in the Afro-Eurasian world. This socioeconomic process questions traditional state and church authority, redefining the vexed relationship among political sovereignty, class interests, and theological dogma thousands of years before the rise of the secular West. For Hodgson, secular modernity's challenge to religious and political traditions is not exceptional to "Western Europe," because "All traditions are open and in motion" and *"every generation makes its own decisions"* (emphasis original).[59] In Hodgson's account of Irano-Semitic culture—"Islamicate civilization" as world history—Brown discovers the social and historical mechanism by which religious traditions have been continually reorganized under various sociopolitical institutions for several millennia. For him, the worldwide manifestation of this secularization process first occurred in the Arab-Islamic age of the seventh century rather than in the Western European world of the late eighteenth century.

Following Hodgson's lead, Brown's model of the prophetic tradition overcomes two of the limitations facing Whiggish historiography: first, that prophetic discourse underwent a sharp decline during Blake's era, and thus religion was excluded from the revolutionary sphere; and second, that with the privatization of religious belief, Islam's prophetic teachings became diametrically opposed to the West's Christian and secular values. By overcoming these limitations, the prophetic tradition could be taken as an inclusive explanatory model that does not render Islamic republicanism a historical abnormality. On the contrary, Brown's model casts Islam as part of a historical pattern existing across all civilizations. Islam is therefore not a "religion" distinct from Judaism and Christianity, nor is this prophetic faith reducible to a fixed set of propositional beliefs or to any specific geographical locale. In adopting this holistic approach, I will treat Romanticism as the messianic return of the Islamic republic on a global scale, rather than as the privileged site for natural supernaturalism. As Blake's self-portrait sketch suggests, the Romantic poet finds his lyric voice in the Prophet's revolutionary persona.

The decision to avoid using the term *Orientalism* to describe Islamic republicanism requires some qualifications. First, my post-Orientalist historiography does not imply a political transcendence free from ideological complicity with the agents of empire. No discourse on the East can claim this kind of neutrality. By heuristically adopting terms such as *Mahometan Christianity, deist Islam, Arab-Islamic hermeticism,* and *Muslim Unitarianism* to describe radical Protestant interpretations of Islam, I want to defamiliarize the political effects of our own secularist obsessions in categorizing the Islamic East as a distinct "religious" civilization. The terms I prefer to use are Christocentric misnomers that nonetheless cast a wider interpretive net than is possible under postcolonial criticism's limited and anachronistic vocabulary. My goal is not to belittle postcolonial studies of Orientalism as it applies to other fields and disciplines but to place Blake and other such radicals within the Islamic prophetic tradition. In doing so, I hope to avoid the diffusionist historicism that, since Said, has infiltrated postcolonial accounts of the early modern period. This book calls for an inclusive, nonessentialist paradigm that treats Mahomet in the same light that Coleridge and Blake saw him: as a Promethean protagonist in the global narrative of secular and republican modernity.

Eurasian Secularization

Many critics have insisted that the modern secular age was inherited from the Judeo-Christian West, ignoring developments in the non-European world.[60] By locating secularization as an event internal to early modern Europe, these insular narratives pretend that there were no outsiders to Latin Christendom. Critics who trace constitutional republicanism exclusively to developments in Europe inadvertently cast the Islamic world as nonprogressive. To avoid this Eurocentric bias, critics need to see the eighteenth-century Enlightenment as part of a wider process of Eurasian secularization. As I argue in this section, references to the ancient Islamic republic cannot be explained away by appealing to any clear-cut distinction between the histories of the secular West and the Islamic East.

The mythical search for a virtuous "righteous republic" has a wider intellectual and political history outside the West. For J. G. A. Pocock, civic republicanism is rooted in classical antiquity and Renaissance Italy, incorporated into English constitutional concepts and values during the English Civil War and the subsequent formation of Anglo-Atlantic republicanism in the eighteenth century.[61] In *Birth of the Modern World, 1780–1914,* C. A. Bayly expands this familiar historical narrative. He argues that the "righteous republic" can be found throughout the Afro-Eurasian world, where, couched in a reformist Islamic idiom that sought to limit the power of kings, civic humanism shaped what Bayly calls the "converging Revolutions" before 1776 and 1789.[62] Given Islam's theological-political language of reformation in many parts of the globe, radical Protestant admiration for Islamic republics could be interpreted, in part, as a diffuse expression of civic republicanism. Brown's understanding of prophetic history suggests that this Afro-Eurasian (mainly Muslim) republicanism is present in the works of Dante, Blake, and other Western writers. The prophetic tradition is another way of referring to what Bayly calls "archaic globalization": an interdependent and interconnected early modern world in which the initial breakdown of the old regimes occurred not in Europe but in the Ottoman, Safavid, and Mughal empires. By the late eighteenth century, the rise of industrialization, advances in science and technology, the growth of world trade, transformations in the political order, and the emergence of a republican ethos and philosophy cannot be read as Western European miracles.

"Archaic globalization" challenges the natural supernatural narrative that I have been criticizing thus far. Indeed, Colin Jager's account of secularization-as-differentiation tries "to expand the time line and lift a teleological and narrative burden from the concept of modernity."[63] Using Casanova's theory as a corrective to Abram's model, he argues that "romantic secularization [is] that which reorders the relationship of this world to the next world by transforming divine into human content," making this "form of differentiation a reordering of categories *within* this world" (emphasis original).[64] Accordingly, a secularized religious outlook negotiates the relationship between political power and socioeconomic transformations *within* the existing civic order rather than *between* the natural realm and an asocial afterlife. Institutional specialization resists the political ossification of religious dogma and ecclesiastical hierarchy under earlier autocratic governments. According to this definition, secularism-as-differentiation does not belong exclusively to the industrial modernity of the Romantic period, because this process can be traced to the earlier part of the eighteenth century, before the rise of industry and revolution. Once transformation from the religious past to the modern future ceases to be the dominant trope, Romantic secularization can be seen as a key site for exploring how the autonomous domain of aesthetics and literature makes available alternative modes of secularity that are not confined to an essentialist interpretation of world religions.[65]

One could argue that these alternative modes are operative within the prophetic tradition. This argument, however, would require a slight readjustment of Jager's definition of romantic secularization. Faithful to José Casanova's traditional historiography, Jager assumes that secularization-as-differentiation is a social process incited by the Protestant Reformation. For them, secularization culminated in the West's three modern achievements: state formation, capitalist growth, and the scientific revolution. Casanova and Jager choose to ignore the "developmental processes of secularization from a universal-historical perspective."[66] This theoretical maneuver ignores the global realities of early modern Eurasia. It does not account for the process by which religious differentiation—the reordering of social, economic, and political institutions—defines most of Afro-Eurasian civilization. This process reached its zenith in the Prophet Muhammad's mission: to overthrow idolatrous beliefs and practices that form the backbone of autocratic church-state governments and to protect the "religions of the Book" (and not just Judaism and Christianity) under a reconstructed civil order centered on prophecy's egalitarian truths. Radical freethinkers such as Stubbe, Blake, and Coleridge recognized this prophetic model when they rewrote the history of Moses' and Christ's virtuous republic from the perspective of Muhammad's challenge to and reorganization of religious, social, and political institutions.

By reconfiguring romantic secularization-as-differentiation as a later yet distinct phase of the prophetic tradition, I treat Islamic republicanism as a useful dialogical model for understanding Eurasian modernity in the global eighteenth century. This approach is not that unusual when considering that the span between 1670 and 1800 coincides with a turbulent age of reformation and revolution throughout the Muslim world. Contrary to scholarly stereotypes that label the eighteenth century an era of religious stagnation, this period witnessed many Islamic revivals and rebellions against unstable old regimes: the Ottoman empire's loss of significant territory to European powers in 1699; the collapse of the century-old Iranian Safavid state in 1722; the split of the Mataram sultanate in present-day Indonesia in 1755; and the gradual fragmentation of the Mughal empire in South Asia between 1739 and 1759. Independent from any direct Western influence, eighteenth-century Muslim revivalism represents a radical reworking of an old prophetic-millenarian vocabulary. Far from being reactionary, this revivalism emerged from an interconnected global network that opposed the militarized autocratic state, an intrusive taxation system, and official clerical dogma: to name a few notable examples, the late-seventeenth-century Naqshbondiyyah Sufi order challenged the Ottomans and, after moving from Central Asia to Western China, openly rebelled against Qing imperial rule in 1781; the many West African jihads that led to fledgling Caliphate states during the early eighteenth century; the Usuli Shi'ite school's victory in post-Safavid Iran under Nadir Shah's revolutionary regime, resulting in a reformed Shi'ite jurisprudence; and the Sufi-led reformation of the Mughal Shar'ia (Islamic law), which helped extend toleration to non-Muslims.[67] These movements suggest that Islamic republicanism diffused outward from Eastern Europe, the Levant, Africa, Central Asia, and South and Southeast Asia. Indeed, the "Age of Revolutions," from 1760 to 1840, can be understood only in an Afro-Eurasian (predominantly Muslim) context.[68]

Thus, this book analyzes English republican writings as coeval with developments in the eighteenth-century Muslim world—specifically in Ottoman Europe, the Maghreb, India, and Egypt—although it does not offer a comparative account that considers Muslim and English works side by side. Comparative accounts are very valuable, and yet they often reproduce essentialist distinctions among different parts of the globe. My work, on the other hand, relies on a broad definition of prophetic history that treats early Eurasian modernity as an intricate whole. In doing so, this book emphasizes what Sanjay Subrahmanyam calls "connected histories" as opposed to "comparative histories." I adopt this global approach to historical analogy because, as I have argued, the attempt to compare separate geo-national units under distinct "religions" fails to account for the connected flow of ideas across civilizations. For Subrahmanyam, early Eurasia was united ideologically through a prophetic language that evokes "a shared sense of millenarian expectation in the century after Columbus."[69] These pancultural millenarian myths encompassed the Ottoman empire, Safavid Iran, Mughal India and the Deccan as well as west of Eurasia in Portugal, the Christian Mediterranean, and the Americas. The language of prophetic renewal accounts for "the circulation of powerful myths and ideological constructs ... in early modern Eurasia."[70] Islamic republicanism is one of those myths that, as Bayly points out, converge with French revolutionary millenarianism as part of a transnational Eurasian-prophetic idiom.[71]

Nonetheless, I do not want to suggest that Muslim Afro-Eurasia issued its own Enlightenment that English radicals simply imitated. The "Islamic Enlightenment" is a highly problematic term. Not only does it erase the distinctive contributions of the English radical Enlightenment but also risks imposing Western ideas of anthropocentric reason on the Muslim world.[72] Likewise, I am not espousing a "nativist" history by adopting Brown's model of the prophetic tradition. Countering Eurocentrism with Islamocentrism reinscribes essentialist presuppositions that carve out the world into centers and peripheries, neglecting the fluidity and heterogeneity existing among the Abrahamic faiths. Attentive to different modes of secularization specific to particular times and places, I employ the umbrella term Eurasian secularization, heuristically and cautiously, to underscore a common iconoclastic monotheism that lends itself to multiple appropriations. This value-laden monotheism entails social justice regardless of religious affiliation.[73] For many eighteenth-century Jews, Christians, and Muslims, overturning theological and political "idols" involves a mode of humanistic secularity that, as William Blake writes, seeks to embrace difference in the "human form,/In heathen, turk or jew."[74] From the seventh century onward, Islam helped disperse monotheism's iconoclastic virtues throughout Afro-Eurasia, inciting reforms and revolutions made possible through elaborate intellectual exchanges among Abraham's prophetic followers. By the late eighteenth century, a cosmopolitan "Islamic public sphere" emerged in Arabia, the Ottoman regions, North and West Africa, India, Malaysia, and South Asia that paralleled, if not surpassed, the Anglo-Atlantic republic of letters.[75] This global public sphere is wide enough to encompass Britain's Islamic republicanism, from Stubbe's *The Rise and Progress of Mahometanism* to Carlyle's lecture on Mahomet the "hero-prophet."

Overview of the Book

In charting Britain's evolving intercultural ties to Muslim Afro-Eurasia, the following chapters are roughly organized in geographical and chronological order. They center on key authors/texts that lend coherence to this order, often at the expense of other important but tangential histories, ideas, and texts. Each chapter contextualizes English literary engagements with Islamic republicanism within various critical junctures in the long history of British constitutional thought.

In chapter 1, I analyze Stubbe's *The Rise and Progress of Mahometanism* as a positive response to Imre Thököly, a leading Hungarian rebel who defended Protestant toleration under the Ottoman empire's protection only to experience defeat when his Catholic foes halted the Turkish siege of Vienna in 1683. The negative reception surrounding the "Count Teckeley" conspiracy in Restoration England provides the political backdrop for understanding how Islam sparked heated constitutionalist debates in England and shaped Whig radicalism, an underground movement that fueled the anti-Stuart politics of the Popish and Rye House Plots. A key member of this movement, Stubbe wrote a defense of Islam that prompted an onslaught of anti-Islamic, antirepublican Tory satires, which inadvertently advertised his ideas. Post-1688, the deist John Toland further advertised his ideas as an attack on Anglican toleration. I argue that the Hungarian Revolution shaped subsequent responses to Islamic republicanism, a model of civic virtue that served as a counterweight to Catholic Europe.

In chapter 2, I trace Stubbe's post-1688 republican legacy to Lady Mary Wortley Montagu and her appropriation of radical Tory feminism. I demonstrate that Montagu's *The Turkish Embassy Letters* (1763) adopts a subversive deist voice that defends Turkish women's socioeconomic freedom under Islamic law. Montagu finds this law, as practiced in the Ottoman empire, preferable to Englishwomen's lack of property rights under the English common law of coverture. I argue that Montagu, along with Mary Astell and Delarivier Manley, reject a male-only contractual rights discourse for an Ottoman-Islamic language that valorizes women's sexual autonomy. This feminist interpretation was enabled by a Tory oppositional politics that has traditionally approached Whig civic republicanism with suspicion, especially for these writers in relation to gender inequality.

In chapter 3, I examine a critical stage in the formation of British rule in Mughal India, between the Battle of Plassey in 1757 and Edmund Burke's defense of Mahometan-republican virtue during the 1788 impeachment trial of Warren Hastings—the governor-general of the East India Company in Bengal charged with violating India's ancient constitution. Opposed to Hastings's defense (that all Muslim societies are based on arbitrary laws), Burke deploys a Mughal imperial idiom that, originating in Indo-Persian myths, exalts Timur's prophetic recovery of Islamic republicanism in India. I hold that Burke's anticolonial discourse relies on older radical ideals that, given the constitutional turmoil of the 1780s, he and other oppositional Whigs used to criticize the king's encroaching power over Parliament.

In chapter 4, I read Walter Savage Landor's *Gebir* (1798) as a radical extension of Burke's anticolonial discourse. I align this Egyptian-themed Oriental tale, which celebrates Bonaparte's messianic arrival, with radical Restoration works on hermeticism, most of which (like *Gebir*) derive from Arabic-Islamic sources. The Islamic hermeticism of *Gebir*, I argue, reflects (by the 1803 edition of the poem) a desperate attempt to salvage an anticolonial politics despite Landor's disillusionment with revolutionary France and Bonaparte's unsuccessful attempt to institute an Islamic republic in Egypt during 1798–99. In chapter 5, I continue to explore this theme of disillusionment in Coleridge's "Mahomet" and "Kubla Khan" and in Robert Southey's *Thalaba the Destroyer* (1801), poems that sought to replace the tragic narrative of the French Revolution with a radical Unitarian account on the triumphant rise of Islamic republicanism in the Near East. After abandoning their collaborative literary project, a proposed epic on "the flight and return of Mohammed," Coleridge and Southey continued to cautiously incorporate Qur'anic motifs in their poems, even though they eventually abandoned Islam after becoming conservative defenders of the Anglican church and state.

In chapter 6, I propose that colonialist-patriarchal representations of harem slavery should not be read as the master trope of Romantic feminism. I argue that Mary Shelley's *The Last Man* (1826), a novel that registers the Ottoman empire's rapid decline in the early nineteenth century, mobilizes the domestic harem as the site from which to satirize Mary Wollstonecraft's Eurocentric feminism. Recalling Lady Mary Wortley Montagu's freethinking feminism, Shelley inverts the terms of her mother's anti-Islamic rhetoric by relying on images of "freeborn" harem women and "enslaved" Englishwomen. This inversion is contextualized in relationship to Percy Shelley's *The Assassins: A Fragment of a Romance* (1814–15), a Gnostic account about the early history of the unified Abrahamic faiths that Mary helped edit and transcribed. By considering this incomplete fragment, I reframe the bizarre eschatology narrated in *The Last Man*: the defeat of the Turks does not usher a golden age of democratic reform but the emergence of an Eastern-originating "feminine" infection that undercuts nineteenth-century Britain's hypermasculine and imperialist ideologies.

Although in chapter 6 I consider one of the last major instances of Islamic republicanism, the epilogue briefly considers its twentieth-century reincarnation. I focus on the original publication of Stubbe's *The Rise and Progress of Mahometanism* in 1911 by the Indo-Muslim Urdu linguist and philologist Hafiz Mahmud Khan Shairani (1881–1946). In his introduction to this publication, Shairani praises Stubbe for having refuted Orientalism. I argue that Shairani's timely publication sought to overcome Victorian stereotypes about backward Muslims by recovering romantic views of the Islamic republic to further the Indian anti-imperial struggle and the pan-Islamic cause. Using Shairani's publication as an example of Islamic republicanism's resilient constitutional idiom, in the epilogue I counteract the post-9/11 tendency to cast Islam as a retrograde ideology.

This book is undeniably inspired by Derrida's plea to have a constructive dialogue between Islam and the West, post-9/11, without any preconditions or unwarranted assumptions about the clash between secular democracy and Islamic fundamentalism. Offered as one of his last reflections before his untimely death, Derrida argues that to defend the Enlightenment legacy of secularization requires progressive interpretations of the Islamic prophetic tradition: "The task consists in doing everything to help, first in the Islamic world, by allying ourselves with forces that struggle not only for the secularization of the political . . . but also for an interpretation of the Koranic heritage that emphasizes from deep within potentialities, which are no doubt no more visible to the naked eye and by that name than they were in the Old and the New Testaments."[76] Derrida further notes that Islam is "the only religious culture that up to now would have resisted a European (Greco-Christian and globalization) process of secularization." In the spirit of Derrida's Abrahamic faith, this book makes visible the "potentialities" of a progressive "Koranic heritage" as evident in radical eighteenth-century writings on Mahometanism. Islam, rather than resisting "a

European process of secularization," facilitated this process as early as the late seventeenth century.

In advancing these claims, I need to distinguish my methodology from Derrida's approach. I do not call for a dialogue, however embracing, in which Islam is addressed only as "the other recognized as other, recognized in his alterity."[77] I call instead for a cross-cultural dialogue that emphasizes the strong connections and continuities bridging the West to the Muslim world. Islam should not be filtered through a "world religion(s)" discourse which renders it the West's "religious" alter ego/other, a rival monotheistic specter coming back to haunt European (Judeo-Christian) modernity. In the chapters that follow I tell the story of how Islamic republicanism temporarily eclipsed Christocentric history and politics in the West (even as Mahometanism reconstituted a Christian worldview), casting a long shadow over our eighteenth-century predecessors who, like Coleridge, eagerly awaited "th' enthusiast Warrior of Mecca" in England.

CHAPTER ONE

A True Protestant Mahometan

Henry Stubbe, Ottoman Hungary, and the Siege of Vienna

> *Teck[ely]*: I swear by *Mahomet*, that your *true Protestants* are rare
> fellows, to make a Conventicle a kind of Baudy House. What do
> their adversaries talk of them for taking part, (as they say) with
> Infidels?
>
> *Eng[lish] True P[rotestant]*: Why they represent them a parcel of
> Factious, Self Interested, Rebellious, Irreligious, Atheistical
> sort of People. And indeed they don't contradict the charge, by
> their Practice. Their Lives are so Lewd, their Conversation is so
> Treacherous; that they won't admit them fit for humane Society.
> Every step they make is towards, or in favour of a Rebellion.
> Their Principles are so visible [. . .] that their Malignants boldly
> affirm, that as long as there's a Conventicle in the Kingdom, we
> shall never be without a Republican Atheist, or a *true Protestant
> Mahometan*. Farewel[l] Brother, and next Meeting expect a new
> *Teckelitish* Letany.
>
> *Great news from Count Teckely, or, An Account of Some Passages 'twixt
> a True Protestant English Volunteer, and a Teckelytish MAHOMETAN
> in the Turkish Camp sent over by the Counts secretary to a brother in
> London* (London, 1684)

Radical Protestantism achieved historical, philosophical, and ideological coherence in part through its sympathetic identification with Islamic republicanism, a flexible trope that casts Mahomet's Christian prophetic monarchy as a supplement to English constitutional virtue. As Matthew Birchwood and Nabil Matar have consistently shown, images of Islam and the dreaded Ottoman Turk contributed to imagining national identity and religious difference since the Restoration, if not before.[1] During the Exclusion Crisis (1679–81), Catholic France was not England's only worry; a growing Ottoman military presence in Hungary and

Eastern Europe took center stage in national debates about monarchical succession and religious authority, even as these remote regions might initially appear alien to late Stuart culture and politics.

Polemical allusions to Hungary's Turkish sympathies suggest that European-Ottoman affairs were not far removed from England's national concerns. The epigraph records a transcultural dialogue between Imre Thököly (known in England as "Count Teckely"), the Hungarian rebel who sided with the Ottoman empire in retaliation against the oppressive rule of Catholic Austria, and his faithful recruit, a "True Protestant English Volunteer." Set in a "Turkish Camp," this anonymous Tory burlesque ties together two different but related events: the spread of conventicles—nonconformist congregations illegally existing outside the Anglican church—and the Austrian-Polish defeat of the Ottoman Turks and their Hungarian allies at Vienna in 1683. The burlesque posits religious, political, and familial commonalities between Hungarian rebels ("the Counts secretary") and English dissenters ("a brother in London"). In order to discredit the nonconformist defense of religious toleration, *Great news* casts dissenting conventicles as a pretense for concealing an international conspiracy between radical Protestants and Muslims. Allegedly, these infidels plan to overthrow Christendom, renew the English Civil War, and welcome an Ottoman invasion. As hysterical as these accusations may seem, they reflect late-seventeenth-century attitudes toward Eastern Europe's ongoing religious wars. To understand how Restoration writers read their national crisis analogically in relation to Ottoman-Hungarian affairs, I argue that Tory satires mocking "Teckelites," or domestic radicals, were inadvertently advertising Henry Stubbe's well-known defense of Islamic toleration—*The Rise and Progress of Mahometanism* (circa 1671; published in 1911).[2]

Anti-Teckelite satires may have been responding to the vibrant radical Protestantism that permeates Stubbe's manuscript. In *Henry Stubbe, Radical Protestantism and the Early Enlightenment*, James R. Jacob has reconstructed the freethinking political context that imbued Mahometanism with an anti-Stuart, anticonformist message. Jacob argues against previous historians who have inaccurately portrayed Stubbe as a turncoat who, after 1660, betrayed "the good old cause" and became an ideologue for the established church, the monarchy, and scholastic learning. A loyal member of the Stuart court, he nonetheless remained secretly committed to Sir Henry Vane's republicanism until his death in 1676. He saw in Mahometanism the blueprints for a dissenter-inclusive toleration policy, as championed by Anthony Ashley Cooper, First Earl of Shaftesbury. Jacob's historical reconstruction centers on Stubbe's Mahomet, a wise legislator who founded a tolerant republican monarchy modeled after that of the primitive Christians. Circulating privately for over a century, *The Rise and Progress of Mahometanism* bridges mid-seventeenth-century civic republicanism to early-eighteenth-century radical Whiggism, confirming what some historians describe as a continuous commonwealthean tradition that survived its political defeat in 1660.[3] Accordingly, Islam is the ally of the radical Enlightenment, an underground international movement that defined its theological and political heterodoxy through borrowed legends, stories, and motifs associated with various prophetic strains of near eastern monotheism.[4] As the "English True Protestant" solemnly admits, republicans' secret Mahometan "Principles" have become "visible" to those who fear that the tolerationist cause will trigger another civil war in late Stuart England.

This chapter departs from Jacob's pioneering scholarship by treating Stubbe's Mahometanism as a by-product of Eurasian (Muslim) secularization (see the Introduction) and not as an insular phenomenon exclusive to England's national borders. I argue that Tory burlesques, like most Restoration satires, exploit secrecy about real and imagined conspiracies to generate publicity. By reading Hungary's Islamic revolution as an analogy for England's Exclusion Crisis, Tory burlesques rendered "secrets" about *The Rise and Progress of Mahometanism* accessible to a wider English audience than did heretical manuscripts confined to private circulation.[5] Targeting those who used Islam as a beating stick against revelation, the clergy, and the existing political order, paranoid Tories relied on incoming reports about the siege of Vienna to satirize their Exclusionist opponents as seditious "Protestant Mahometans." They were reacting to what they perceived as Shaftesbury's appropriation of Stubbe's ideas. Thus, Tory satires sought to raise public awareness about the "Turkish" constitutional ideals shared by English Whigs and Hungarian rebels. Post-1688, Islamic republicanism reappears in a new guise. In his deist mock-theology *Nazarenus: or, Jewish, Gentile, and Mahometan Christianity* (1718), John Toland uses Mahometanism to launch a Whig assault against the Toleration Act's antinonconformist strictures. I argue that royalists and radicals, Tories and Whigs, conformist and dissenters appropriated Islamic republicanism for their self-serving agenda. As such, I treat the buildup to the 1688 "Whig triumph" as a diffuse response to the Ottoman-Hungarian alliance, a counterweight to Catholic Europe that promises to check an encroaching counterreformation.

The Count Teckely Conspiracy

When Charles II's brother, James Duke of York, married the Catholic Mary of Modena, general suspicions about a Catholic succession and arbitrary government ignited the Exclusion Crisis. The attempt to exclude James from the succession revived heated controversies about constitutional authority that had plunged England into a national crisis almost forty years earlier.[6] In July 1683, Vizer Kara Mustafa Pasha launched a joint Ottoman-Hungarian campaign against Catholic Vienna, while England experienced political gridlock following Charles II's decision to dissolve Parliament before it had a chance to review the Exclusion Bill preventing a Catholic succession. Although Austria halted the siege of Vienna, the battle's outcome was not decisive. Given the continuing threat of an Ottoman invasion, few Britons read this event as the "final clash" between a defeated East and a victorious West.[7] The 1699 Treaty of Carlowitz—arranged, in part, by English ambassador Lord Paget—was the first event to signal a shift in power. This treaty rendered the Ottoman empire a weaker military and political presence. In the context of these events, Stubbe's call for Islamic toleration would have aggravated the civil war crisis that the Restoration settlement had yet to resolve. Tory burlesques sought to contain this crisis by casting Count Teckely's political and military failure as a sign of divine retribution against the infidels, Muslims and Protestants alike.

Burlesques such as *Great news* allegorized Teckely's defeat as another instance of the old English commonwealth's inherent failure. They reassured the reader that the tolerationist cause was doomed by God to follow the same tragic steps as Teckely's Protestant Mahometans, who, differing "only in name," share with their English counterparts a commitment to the "good old cause" (1). Indeed, the broadside's conversational dialogue reveals that these "Conventiclers" live in the same anti-Christian culture that "Teckelyte Mahometans" inhabit. This satiric critique functions primarily as anti-conventicle propaganda. After the 1664 Conventicle Act (rigorously reinforced in 1670), religious worship and assembly outside the church was penalized as seditious activity, preventing nonconformist clergy from forming dissenting congregations. In 1672, King Charles II's Declaration of Indulgence, which temporarily repealed all penal laws against nonconformists and Catholics and led to the licensing of many conventicles, incited paranoid Tory speculations about a secret nonconformist conspiracy to thwart church and state. While it was not the first time that Protestant reformers were stigmatized as disguised Muslims,[8] satires such as *Great news* are unique in treating this conspiracy as existing under the auspices of Count Teckely.

By the 1680s, Count Teckely had become a menacing figure for orthodox Christians who associated his tolerationist politics with the attempt to supplement Christendom with Islamic rule. To combat the counterreformation, Teckely accepted Ottoman-Islamic law in order to protect Protestant Hungary's constitutional right to free worship, clerical independence, and national sovereignty. Because Hungary's ancient rights to determine monarchical succession and military appointments were annulled under the Hapsburg's Catholic domination, Teckely fought to turn his country into a semiautonomous tributary state under the Ottomans. His reformist politics countered a unified Christian ideology as dictated under the 1648 Treaty of Westphalia. Bringing Catholic-Protestant conflicts during Germany's Thirty Years' War (1618–48) to a peaceful resolution, this treaty postulated the urgent need for a combined Christian alliance to drive the sultan out of occupied eastern European territories. With the rise of Hapsburg-Catholic power in the 1660s, Protestant Hungary became a contested site for the political and theological viability of a unified Christian ideology.

The 1669 Hungarian-Ottoman alliance tested this ideology. In desperation, Hungarian noblemen asked the Ottoman court in Istanbul for protection against German-Austrian attempts to restore Catholic hegemony, eliminate the free election of their leaders, and place their military under strict Viennese supervision. These "conspirators," as they were called, sought the religious toleration that the Ottoman Porte granted to all Protestants, including Unitarians, living in the tributary state of Transylvania. The conspirators' plan eventually failed, and the Hungarian constitution was suspended under direct Austrian rule. By 1674, this imperial initiative led to the persecution and death of hundreds of Protestant clergymen and noblemen for their alleged "Turkish" sympathies. By 1680, the Hungarian nobleman Imre Thököly wanted to redress his country's oppression by becoming the commander in chief of the *Kurvc* movement (the name deriving from the word *crusader*). His army of "malcontents" sought to reclaim their Protestant country from Austrian authoritarianism. Having achieved several military victories in upper Hungary, Teckely refused peace negotiations with the Hapsburg court in 1681 and instead looked toward the Turks as allies. A poignant threat to Christian unification, Teckely accepted the Ottoman Porte's appointment as the crowned prince of upper Hungary in 1682.

The Westphalia treaty was put to its greatest test in 1683, when Teckely convinced the grand vizier, Kara Mustafa, to attack Vienna and overthrow the Hapsburg empire. Turks, Tartars, Transylvanian troops (mostly Unitarians), and Teckely's rebels composed the huge Ottoman army. Hapsburg emperor Leopold I halted the siege, thanks, in major part, to Pope Innocent XI's Holy League alliance, which involved military aid from Charles of Lorraine, with troops and support from thirty German princes, the prince of Venice, and the King of Poland. The Ottomans were routed, sustaining heavy military casualties and a substantial loss of territory. Teckely experienced defeat and humiliation after having escaped Austrian captivity, effectively ending his political career. The Holy League continued in its military campaign against the Turks, and, with Prince Eugene of Savoy's aid, western and central Hungary, including Buda, was freed from Ottoman control by 1686. These rapid victories reinforced the need for a unified Christian front as set forth in the Treaty of Westphalia almost forty years earlier. In this regard, the Ottoman defeat at Vienna and its aftermath mark the restoration of European absolutism and papal authority in central Europe, Hungary, and, by 1690, Transylvania. Having failed to defend Transylvania's independence from the Hapsburgs, Count Teckely retired from politics, only to die in 1705 as an exile in Turkey. With the signing of the 1699 Treaty of Carlowitz, which forced Sultan Mustafa II to make large-scale territorial concessions to the Holy League, Teckely's radical Protestantism was frequently branded as godless, disloyal, and shameful by those who celebrated God's restoration of a unified Christendom in central and Eastern Europe.[9]

Despite its defeat, "Teckelite" politics continued to pose a serious threat to Christian peace. John Shirley's *The History of the State of the Present War in Hungary, Austria, Croatia, Moravia, and Silesia* (London, 1683) documents, in detail, Count Teckely's alliance with the Turks. This work's epistle to the reader describes the "oppression of the Turkish sword" as having almost destroyed the Hapsburg empire by exploiting sectarian divisions between Catholics and Protestants. Shirley casts Count Teckely as the chief culprit who has aided the Turks by exasperating these sectarian divisions and, in turn, undermining the power of Christian-Roman unity. To underscore this point, the opening illustration to the first section of Shirley's history includes a brief inscription: "Behold the Wounded Empire, Bleeding Lyes./By Rebells Rage and Turkish Cruelties/(But what's the cause) it springs from Christian was/The Turkes still Triumphs when the Christians jar" (fig. 4). The Roman Hapsburg empire's "wounded" state "springs" from European infidelity and not Ottoman might, because "Turkish Cruelties" can only triumph in central Europe when Christians "jar" or rebel. In other words, Count Teckely is to blame for disturbing Christendom's *Pax Romana*, symbolized in the laurel wreath worn by the victorious "Emperour of Germany." In Shirley's account, the siege of Vienna contains a divine warning: the Catholic Hapsburg empire's integrity is in the best interest of Christendom, so any Ottoman encroachments into central Europe requires a unified Christian coalition if Prot-

Figure 4. John Shirley, *The History of the State of the Present War in Hungary, Austria, Croatia, Moravia, and Silesia* (London, 1683). © The British Library Board. 9135.a.13.

estant England is to survive as God's favored nation. In this case, Teckelite-style politics indirectly poses as an ideological danger to England's national security, though the English reading public clearly knew that the Holy League had effectively subdued Count Teckely after 1683.

And yet central Europe's Christian integrity was not always in England's best security interests. Nor can Anglo-Ottoman relations be described as predominately hostile. On the contrary, late Stuart England continued to maintain friendly commercial relations with the Ottoman Porte since the late sixteenth century and, even after the Treaty of Westphalia, occasionally promoted the sultan's interest even if it ran counter to the lofty ideal of a unified Christian coalition.[10] After the Treaty of Dover (1670), the Stuart kings, Charles II and James II, expressed outright disdain for the Hapsburg emperor Leopold I and secretly supported the French King Louis XIV, who gained political prominence in Europe between 1661 and 1715 by forming an alliance with the Ottomans to weaken the Hapsburg eastern front and forestall Leopold's claims to the Spanish throne. Some English critics saw this Franco-Ottoman alliance as an anti-Christian conspiracy spearheaded by Count Teckely, Louis XIV, and, implicitly, the Stuarts to eliminate Austria as the only buffer zone protecting Western Europe from an Ottoman invasion.[11] Although England assumed a neutral position on Austrian-Ottoman conflicts, the Stuarts' unwavering dependence on French military aid—while ignoring Louis's opportunistic alliance with the sultan—could be interpreted as pro-Ottoman. In this case, anti-Stuart opponents used Mahometanism metaphorically to condemn the "Turkish" tyranny promoted by English royalists, who prevented any possibility for forming a combined Christian bloc against the infidels.

Even as England's foreign policy shifted from pro-French to pro-Hapsburg with William III's ascension to the throne, Islamic republicanism should not be read as a literal alternative to the Stuart-Anglican order. As deployed by Tories, this satiric trope should instead be read as an allegorical reference to domestic policies on the legal status of subjects existing *within* that order: namely, English Teckelites, or radical dissenters who grounded a reformist agenda on constitutional principles that required a heretical rereading of the Islamic prophetic tradition. Stubbe promoted such an agenda during the same period that the Hungarian "malcontents" were forming an alliance with the Ottoman Porte. *The Rise and Progress of Mahometanism* makes three controversial claims: first, that Islam revived Arian Christianity, an anticlerical messianic Judaism that upheld Christ as a prophet and, as a result, was marginalized by the persecution of corrupt Trinitarian churches. Second, that Christianity's decline and Islam's rise is a legitimate response to the combined influence of Trinitarianism and the clergy, political theologies that promote despotic monarchies. And third, that Mahomet, a wise legislator, replaced Christian dogmas with popular myths on the restoration of constitutional law. According to Stubbe, Mahometanism is a natural faith worthy of admiration. The Prophet's civic laws have accomplished in less than a century what Trinitarian Christians could not in over a millennium: his laws have anchored a state-sponsored (rather than ecclesiastical) toleration policy for all religious minorities on a solid constitutional foundation that originated with Noah's covenant as prophetically renewed by Abraham, Moses, and Christ. Like Teckely, Stubbe treats Islamic toleration as the antidote to the religious and political contentions that have plagued Europe and England since the Protestant Reformation.

Not surprisingly, High Anglican polemicists stigmatized Teckelite politics as Protestant conversion to Mahometanism under the pretense of promoting toleration. Indeed, Stubbe's account lacks the proselytizing rhetoric that typically accompanies Anglican polemics on Islam. He elevates Mahomet's prophetic status to that of civic legislator, but without ever suggesting that Muslims need to be converted to the true Protestant faith. On the contrary, Stubbe foregrounds the need for Christians to abandon their superstitious ignorance and come closer to Islam's tolerationist principles. Relying on Edward Pococke's *Specimen historiae Arabum* (1650),[12] he deplores the negative myths found in Christian polemics against Islam and the Prophet: Mahomet's revelation as a symptom of the "falling sickness" (epileptic seizures), the pigeon who eats from his ear, his suspended coffin between two lodestones, and the Nestorian monk (Sergius) and Jew (Abdalla) who allegedly wrote the Qur'an, among many others. Stubbe dedicates an entire chapter, with an appendix, to condemning medieval accounts of the Prophet's life as "a great deal of fabulous, ridiculous trash" (141–55, 193–238, 142). Pocock's work on Arabic Islam is invested in a similar critique but, unlike Stubbe, only to help convert Muslims to a "rational" Anglican faith as opposed to an irrational and ineffective Catholicism. In fact, Pocock, an orthodox scholar of Oriental languages and religion, produced an Arabic translation of Grotius's *De Veritate Religionis Christianae, Liber VI*—which refutes Mahometanism as a false religion propagated by the sword—in 1660 to help convert Jews and Muslims in the Levant.[13] Stubbe deploys his orthodox scholarship to subvert the dominant proselytizing rhetoric that, by the 1670s, heavily relied on Grotius's anti-Islamic polemic. Not only does Stubbe argue that Islam was propagated by the word rather than the sword, but he also writes in a Muslim vein by always calling Jesus *Isa* (the Qur'anic name for Christ). His account suggests that Christians have more to learn from Mahomet's tolerationist outlook than Muslims do from the clergy's false teachings. As a result, Stubbe's Mahometanism can be interpreted literally as his de facto conversion to Islam.

Count Teckely's acceptance of Ottoman protection was interpreted as such. Published anonymously in London in 1683, *The Sum of Nine Articles lately ratified and mutually countercharged, between the Ottoman Emperour and Count Emeric Techli* confirmed orthodox Anglicans' worst suspicion: Teckely had abandoned the Christian faith for a legal system under which non-Muslims accept the Qur'an's binding authority as absolute. According to the articles' terms, Teckely was willing to turn Hungary into a tributary state if the sultan was willing to grant religious toleration, guarantee democratic elections for future Hungarian kings, not retain any property rights in Hungary, and offer protection from enemies abroad (1–6). These conditions were not impossible to fulfill during the *Pax Ottomanica* of the sixteenth and seventeenth centuries.[14] Under the millet system, Ottoman subjects were forced to accept the sultan's authority despite their religious affiliation yet retain their independence if they paid the required poll tax (*jizya*) and did not threaten the empire's political and economic interests. Jewish, Protestant, Catholic, and Greek Orthodox communities exercised relative autonomy over civil matters such as marriage, inheritance, property rights, clerical leadership, and education. As Ezel Kural Shaw has argued, the Ottoman world offered European Protestants fleeing religious persecution a political asylum.[15] For Teckely, the price for this asylum was worth paying: complete submission to the Shari'a (Islamic Law) in exchange for protecting constitutional principles, property rights, liberty of conscience, free elections, and independent congregations. From his enemies' perspective, his submission is comparable to a long and shameful tradition of Christian captives who voluntarily "turned Turk" for economic and political gain.[16]

In Restoration England, orthodox Christians consider Teckely a "radical" only in that his actions counter the terms of the Test and Corporation Acts, which prohibit those who refrain from taking the Anglican sacrament or deny some or all the Thirty-nine Articles from holding local, civil, military, or national offices and obtaining degrees from Oxford and Cambridge. Even after the 1689 Toleration Act, nonconformists could not acquire English citizenship because, under these Acts, they did not have the same constitutional guarantees, property rights, and religious protection that were granted to conforming members of the Church of England. In this context, Stubbe's writing has radical implications in that Islamic toleration signals "the Progress of that Stupendous Revolution" (2). He argues that the Judaizing Christians lived in an autonomous republic under the Roman empire, and, based on the laws of Noah and Moses, they practiced toleration and elected their leaders. These first Christians were early Nazarenes and Ebionites (Jewish heretics) whose only belief was that Christ, the temporal Messiah, was destined to restore the kingdom of Israel. They did not believe in God's incarnation, the Trinity, and a separate clergy (5–6, 11–20). The sacrament, baptism, and Lord's Supper were pagan inventions foisted on Christianity by the gentiles, who abandoned the Mosaic law for superstitious dogmas: the Trinity, cosubstantiation, and eternal generation (29). These corrupt Trinitarians, the "enemies of all human learning," spread their fabrications under St. Paul, the apostle who first codified the gentiles' "mysteries." Imperial Rome institutionalized this pagan religion under Emperor Constantine, who, after assembling the rigged Nicene council in AD 325, reduced Christianity to "one uniform doctrine" (43, 56, 30–35).

Christianity was thereby transformed into a "court religion" (44). From Stubbe's radical perspective, England's Test and Corporation Acts are rooted in the corrupt "pagan" doctrines espoused by the Roman empire.

Likewise, Mahomet's Nazarene republicanism finds its latest manifestation in the Ottoman sultanate, a preferable republican monarchy than England's proto-Catholic government. According to Stubbe, primitive Christianity sank into oblivion owing to severe Trinitarian persecution until it was resuscitated by Mahomet centuries later. During his extensive travels, Mahomet learned about the sad plight of the original Christians, the Nestorians, Jacobites, and Arians; based on their principles, he erected a civic religion that eliminated Arab-pagan idolatry, condemned the Trinity as idolatrous, and sanctified Judaizing Christianity (70, 75, 78, 82, 128). Stubbe writes that Mahomet "was a convert to the Judaizing Christians and formed his Religion as far as possible in resemblance of theirs" (145). He was a virtuous republican who promoted the seven Noahetic precepts, the Mosaic law, and Christ's word. Stubbe's account offers a reassuring message for English nonconformists: in an age dominated by Trinitarian persecution, only Islam's tolerant principles can guarantee a constitutional republicanism that would allow them to become citizens equally entitled to rights, property, and privilege. These ideas are revolutionary because they implicitly suggest that Islamic law should replace and supplement ineffective Christian regimes. The Teckely character in *Great news* invokes this supplementation when posing a mock-rhetorical question to his English coreligionist: "Here's Paradice before thee Lad, and a good *Old Cause*; and who would not be a Friend to the Grand *Signeour* upon such Honorable Propositions ['liberty of Conscience']" (1). For a "true Protestant Mahometan" to fulfill the "good old cause" requires that they refashion the Anglican nation in accordance with the Ottoman sultanate, an updated version of the Nazarene prophetic republic.

That many English dissenters continued to form illegal conventicles therefore implies the same seditious activity that resulted in the divine punishment of Turks and Hungarian rebels. For instance, the English translation of Jean Le Clerc's *Memoirs of Emeric Count Teckely* in 1693 includes a preface that ties the radical Protestant cause in England to Teckely's alleged anti-Christian crusade. Accordingly, English nonconformists calling for toleration put "themselves and the nation into such a condition as must inevitably end in the Destruction of the late king, the whole Royal Family, or the Ruine of the Protestant Religion, and the Civil Liberties of England."[17] This paranoid commentator assumes that expanding toleration is regicidal because it implies a Hungarian-inspired rebellion against the divinely ordained monarchy and established religion. For those reading his published memoirs in England, Teckely recalls sectarian and political conflicts, past and present, that threatened to fragment English national unity from within.

Thus, *The Rise and Progress of Mahometanism* could never have been published in the late seventeenth century. Even though Stubbe may have been more invested in reforming than abolishing the Stuart-Anglican regime, the publication of his manuscript would have resulted only in greater harm to the reformist cause at home and abroad; it would have confirmed Tory fears about a Muslim-Protestant conspiracy to launch a revolution in Restoration England. Defending the Mahometan "good old cause" following the failed Ottoman-Hungarian alliance could only have exacerbated England's political and religious scars. According to my historical reconstruction of post-Reformation and Ottoman Europe, Stubbe's manuscript serves as the backdrop against which to set Tory burlesques that used Teckely as an ideological grid for indirectly addressing a sensitive domestic problem: English reformers who may have looked toward Hungary's Islamic revolution as a source of inspiration.

The Turkish Plot

In a satire titled *The rebels association in Hungary for reformation of religion and advancement of Empire* (London, 1682), the anonymous writer references Teckely's politics to smear Whig Exclusionists as allies of the Turkish cause: "The Teckelites are in Discipline and Principles much the same with those they call Whigs in England, Religion being the ground of their Exorbirances. Under pretense of Religion (which is indeed but Rebellion,) they will Levy Arms against the Emperour, and for Defence of the Gospel, join with the Turk against their Christian Sovereign"(1).

Teckelites and Whigs are alike in that both have joined the Turks to protect a limited Protestant monarchy, bring "a Bill of Exclusion to cast off the Succession," and "revenge [the King's] Death on the Papists" (2). This analogy renders dissenting "Religion," "Rebellion," and anti-Catholicism the common tie between English Exclusionists and Hungarian rebels. Indeed, two years after Stubbe's death in 1676, English reformers used his writings on toleration, property rights, and a Protestant succession for the Exclusionist cause, anticipated, in part, when Stubbe's allegiances shifted with the First Earl of Shaftesbury's from "Court" to "Country" politics in late 1673.[18] Stubbe's reformist appeal leads Jacob to conclude that his manuscript signaled "a continuity of actual political organization emanating from and revolving around the First Earl himself."[19] Unlike Jacob,

I locate this sociopolitical continuity in a wider transnational context, in what remains unspoken yet central to the anxiety-ridden rhetoric of Tory burlesques: the Whigs are involved in a Turkish plot to replace the Anglican state with an Islamic republic.

Tory burlesques mock Teckelite politics to ease worries about England's "Turkish" reformers. *The rebels association* offers a rhetorical strategy for containing the possibility for a domestic revolution. According to this rhetorical strategy, English reformers and Hungarian rebels share a freethinking biblical hermeneutics, a republican reading of the Psalms:

> [The Teckelites] . . . Love the *Psalms* above any part of Canonical Scripture, because it mentions, the Binding of Kings in Chains, and their Nobles in Fetters. Fear God and Honour the King, is their *Apocripha*. The Beast with many Horns, their *Revelations*. The Seditious City, who in Defence of their Liberties, dare lose their Charter, and forfeit their Indentures, to become Free-men. They are for a King too, provided it be a Rebel, and of their own Choosing, and being Chosen, to Change him as oft as they shall think fit. Yet never did Rebels carry it on with greater pretence of Loyalty, then these Teckelites; when at the very same time, they were Enter'd into an Association to Levy War, to Rout out Religion and Monarchy, and undermine the very Foundation of the Empire. . . . (1)

This burlesque suggests that Teckelites prefer Old Testament prophecies to New Testament salvation. As such, their innovative interpretations turn the sociopolitical order upside down: a revolutionized limited monarchy—"the Binding of Kings in Chains, and their Nobles in Fetters"—is rendered orthodox and a royalist absolute monarchy—"Fear of God and Honour of King"—"Apocripha." What is most striking about this transvaluation is how Tory burlesques remain cautiously silent about the 1640s and '50s. They displace earlier fears about England's Interregnum and Cromwellian regimes on the Hungarian uprising. In other words, *The rebels association* performs an act of historical and political self-effacement in refusing to name an internal enemy: English Protestants who privately share Stubbe's "Mahometan" hermeneutics.[20] Tory satires choose to remain secretive about this internal enemy by projecting national fears about Islamic republicanism in England onto bizarre conspiracy theories centered on Teckely's affairs in Europe. They treat Whig Teckelites as an allegory for radical Protestants sympathetic to the Mahometan cause. For paranoid Tory satirists wary of popularizing subversive ideas, the allegory is too dangerous to be addressed directly and literally in print.

John Dryden mobilizes the allegory in the epilogue he wrote for Nathaniel Lee's *Constantine the Great* (1684). As in *The rebels association,* he aligns the

Whig ("Wights") opposition to a Stuart-Catholic succession with Teckely's anti-Catholic campaign, "a Foreign Rebel's Cause":

Besides all these, there were a sort of Wights,

(I think my Author calls them *Teckelites;*)

Such hearty Rogues, against the King and Laws,

They favour'd even a Foreign Rebel's Cause.

When their own damn'd Design was quash'd and aw'd,

At least they gave it their good Word abroad.

As many a Man, who, for a quiet Life,

Breeds out his Bastard, not to nose his Wife;

Thus o're their Darling Plot, these *Trimmers* cry;

And tho' they cannot keep it in their Eye,

They bind it Prentice to Count *Teckely.*

They believe not the last Plot, may I be curst,

If I believe they e're believ'd the first;

No wonder their own Plot, no Plot they think;

The Man that makes it, never smells the Stink.

And, now it comes into my Head, I'le tell

Why these damn'd *Trimmers* lov'd the *Turks* so well.

The Original *Trimmer,* tho' a Friend to no man,

Yet in his heart ador'd a pretty Woman:

He knew that *Mahomet* laid up for ever,

Kind black-eyed Rogues, for every true Believer:

And, which was more than mortal Man e're tasted,

One Pleasure that for threescore Twelve-months lasted:

To turn for this, may surely be forgiven:

Who'd not be circumcis'd for such a Heav'n![21]

Dryden accuses Whig "Teckelites," "Trimmers" (insincere Tories), and Mahometans of having formed a new conspiracy against the king. The Turkish plot has been carried out under the smokescreen of the Popish Plot, a paranoid conspiracy theory concocted by Teckelites to distract Parliament with fabricated evidence about Papist plans to hijack the government while they secretly formed an anti-Stuart alliance with Hungarian rebels. The epilogue incriminates the "damn'd Designs" of these Whig "Rogues ... against the King and Laws," since their Popish Plot in "Prentice to Count *Teckely*" has been "quash'd and aw'd." In Dryden's eyes, the Whigs stand condemned as regicidal Muslim converts; by befriending Count Teckely, they have been "circumcis'd" for the sake of Mahomet's lust-filled paradise, a false republican utopia. In an age in which secret histories about court intrigues, hidden alliances, and paranoid plots shaped the public sphere in England, Dryden's epilogue—along with other such satires—publicly circulated and inadvertently advertised clandestine information about the radical Whig fascination with Mahometanism.

Dryden published the epilogue separately and in the printed edition of Nathaniel Lee's play *Constantine the Great*, an allegory on the Earl of Shaftesbury's fall from court favor after the foiled Rye House Plot to assassinate the king.[22] This controversy weakened efforts to exclude Charles II's bid to appoint his Catholic brother, James Duke of York as his successor. Consequently, Shaftesbury fled the country and Tory royalism reasserted itself in the fall of 1683. Given these decisive events, Dryden, a staunch Tory, uses the Turkish plot trope to tie the Rye House Plot to an international conspiracy inspired by the Hungarian uprising. For him, the Whigs can never smell the "Stink" of their own Islamic-inspired designs owing to their unrealistic obsession with "Papist" plots to thwart church and state. By comically mimicking the anti-Catholic rhetoric of Islamic republicanism in a low burlesque mode, Dryden's epilogue mocks radical Whigs who sympathize with the Mahometan cause at home and abroad.

For Dryden, the Rye House Plot and siege of Vienna are interrelated events. While Ottoman-Hungarian forces were preparing to overthrow the Catholic-Hapsburg monarchy, radical Whigs were plotting to assassinate the king and the Duke of York near a property named the Rye House. They were ready to launch a revolution that would have led either to the establishment of a republican commonwealth under parliamentary control or a weakened monarchy under the Duke of Monmouth, the illegitimate Protestant son of Charles II. The discovery of this foiled conspiracy resulted in the execution of two Whig Lords, William Russell and Algernon Sydney, for their supposed share in the plot; the suicide of Arthur Capel, Earl of Essex; and the exile of Monmouth. The Rye House Plot confirmed the Tory view that the Whigs were not just regicides but—in their support for the failed siege of Vienna—accomplices to Teckely's plot to place Christendom under the sultan's rule. In his effort to make this Turkish plot known to the public, Dryden casts suspicion on Whig "Teckelites" and "Trimmers," who "turn'd Addressing *Tory*" to conceal their sympathy for the plot. He wrote an epilogue to a play that could be alluding to the plight of antitrinitarian radicals: the plotters who, secretly headed by the false councilor Arius (Shaftesbury), tragically failed to overthrow Trinitarian Christianity during the fourth-century reign of Emperor Constantine, heroically represented as Charles II in Lee's play and treated as a "Bastard" in Stubbe's manuscript (35). In this case, Dryden approaches Ottoman-Hungarian relations just as he uses the contemporary Indian history of Aurangzeb: to discuss religious and political concerns about monarchal succession that otherwise might have been censored into silence.

Dryden is not the only Tory polemicist to blast Whig Exclusionists' anti-Catholic politics. *A Letter from Count Teckely to the Salamanca doctor: giving an account of the siege of Vienna, and the state of the Ottoman Empire* (1683), almost identical to the burlesque mode used in *Great news,* treats the Popish Plot as an extension of Teckely's rebellion. This fictional letter from Teckely expresses an interest in forming an Anglo-Hungarian alliance with the "Grand Seignior." According to this satire, Titus Oates, the "Salamanca doctor" who in 1678 disclosed false evidence about a supposed Catholic plan to assassinate the king, has furthered the cause of "true Protestant Rebels." By generating mass paranoia about a "Papist" conspiracy in his narrative account,[23] he has kept Parliament in the dark about Hungarian-Ottoman plans to invade England. As such, the Teckely character wishes to strike a bargain with Oates: in exchange for militarily aiding the "Mahometan good old cause" in England and abroad, he promises to secure "liberty of Conscience" in England and, for Oates, a lucrative position as "Mufti, or Chief Priest of *Mahomet*" in the sultan's court (2). As in Dryden's epilogue, this satire describes the Popish Plot as a cover-up for a sinister plan to launch an Islamic-style revolution in a country on the brink of another civil war.

Oates writes a friendly reply to Teckely's offer in another fictional letter, *Dr. Oates Answers to Count Teckleys Letter Intercepted at Dover* (1683). Signing his letter under the self-title "Mufti to the Grand Turk," Oates is portrayed comically: he is an accomplice to Teckely's rebellion and afraid that he and his radical Whig conspirators might find themselves in a misfortune situation once the Popish Plot is exposed as a sham for concealing their secret plans (2). This "intercepted" letter concludes with a postscript reaffirming Oates's support despite the setbacks of the siege of Vienna; he promises to provide Teckely with "a detachment of fifty thousand French Protestant Mahometans, which *Shaftesbury* sent . . . over to be ready upon such occasions" (2). This Oates-Teckely partnership should not be read only as a polemical blow aimed at Shaftesbury's prodissenting and anti-Hapsburg French policies but also as an implicit acknowledgment that Shaftesbury is secretly invested in Stubbean politics. Written in a low burlesque mode, these Tory broadsides deprecate Whig loyalty to the crown by reducing their efforts to pass the Exclusion Bill to a vulgar fascination with Titus Oates's false testimony, satirically cast as a facade concealing Whig support for the Mahometan cause at home and abroad.

By 1681, Oates becomes a symbolic figure for Whig betrayal. His elaborate evidence for a Papist uprising, which led to the imprisonment of up to two thousand innocent Catholics, began to collapse on closer inspection. Moreover, his scandalous involvement in lies, treachery, perjury, and sodomy did not help the Whig opposition when, taking advantage of the anti-Catholic sentiments generated by the Popish Plot, Shaftesbury and his allies brought the Exclusion Bill before the House of Commons. To make matters worse, the Rye House Plot raised Tory fears that Oates's scare tactics were part of a republican conspiracy to exploit popular sentiments in order to prepare for an anti-Stuart revolution. Referring to the June 23, 1683, proclamation for the apprehension of John Rumsey, Nathaniel Wade, and other Whig conspirators, *The Salamanca Doctors Comment Upon the Proclamation* (1683) portrays Oates as a villain who conducted the Popish Plot for powerful Whig lords ready to perpetuate a second regicide under the excuse of preventing a Papist takeover. According to this anti-Whig satire, his plan was to aid the Whigs in assassinating the king by placing the blame on the Catholics. However, his plan failed when Shaftesbury fled the country to escape treason charges. Oates is a betraying "Judas" who, having been exposed for his involvement in the plot, can save his life only by comically reproducing the false allegations that he had used to fabricate the now discredited Popish Plot (2). Likewise, *Dr. Oates answer to Count Teckly's Letter giving him a true account of the present horrible plot* (1683) states that his false testimony "was to the Earl of Shaftesbury's contrivance," creating "the sham *Popish plot*" to advance the "Mahometan cause" in London and Vienna (1). For Tories distressed over these "Whig" plots, Oates evokes the shadowy presence of Stubbean radicals running amok in England.

At the height of the Exclusion Crisis, Oates's notorious reputation was bound with the distrustful Turk who failed to occupy Vienna. Even after the Popish Plot was exposed as a hoax, the Titus-Turk figure featured in many anti-Whig satires remained "both the real enemy within and the projected enemy without."[24] This dual symbolic association becomes polemically charged when Tory satires imagine Oates as a willing accomplice in Count Teckely's anti-Christian conspiracy. Given the strong parallel between the Whigs' anti-Catholic agenda and Teckely's anti-Austrian policy, he is a key figure for rendering religious connections between radical Whigs and Hungarian rebels publicly visible, and for plotting these two events as part of a shared narrative about the comic plight of Mahometan republicans on the retreat. Indeed, *Dr. Oates answer to Count Teckleys letter Intercepted* suggests that the discovery of the Rye House Plot leaves Oates with no choice but to join Teckely in a "Sarraglio," along with his Whig gang of "Bums," "Whores," and "Bauds." By seeking "refuge" in the sultan's harem, he "intend[s] to out-do *Solloman* in *Letchery*, *Mahomet* in *Blasphemy*, and *Judas* in *Perjury* and *treachery*" (2). As confirmed by Tory satires, English reformers and Hungarian rebels share the same destiny: these infidels abandoned Christian dogma for the libertine pleasures of the Islamic East.

Oates's sexual misconduct exemplifies "rebellion as seduction."[25] This figurative mode of writing secret histories associates prominent individuals with notorious groups, historical and imaginary, in order to frame public events, including rebellions, through recourse to "private" affairs. Scandals about Oates's homosexuality, blasphemy, perjury, and lies were frequently projected on his secret identity as a disguised renegade. His detractors believed that during his visit to Algiers—where he claims to have first heard rumors about the Popish Plot[26]—he converted to Islam to live a life of debauchery. Tory satires referenced his Mahometan lifestyle not only to debase the Whigs' moral character but also to represent rebellion as stemming from sexual self-interest alone.[27] In his epilogue, Dryden relies on this figurative mode when he traces the Turkish plot to an "Original Trimmer," Oates, who sanctified his forbidden pleasures by converting to Mahomet's law.

In reducing rebellion to a story about sexual seduction in the Islamic East, Oates's scandalous affairs prefigure Shaftesbury's Mahometan politics. In John Norris's *A Murnival of knaves, or Whiggism plainly displa'd, and (if not grown shameless) burlesqu't out of countenance* (1683), Shaftesbury is comically portrayed as following Oates's immorality. In this regard, Shaftesbury's inclusive toleration policy could appeal only to a "wicked crew" of Whigs who secretly support the "good old cause" (23, 5). According to John Northleigh, his "argument for befriending *Turks* and *Mahometans*" in a tolerant state dispenses with all moral, religious, and political laws.[28] In the Tory-burlesque mode, representing rebellion as sexual seduction has the effect of rendering Stubbe's defense of Islam publicly recognizable as well as nonthreatening. Tory burlesques contain the threat of revolution by rewriting the events of the Exclusion Crisis and propagandizing a self-congratulatory narrative about Islamic republicanism's worldwide defeat after 1683.

For this narrative logic to make sense, Tory satires need to connect Stubbe's Mahometanism to Shaftesbury's republicanism. Jacob draws attention to this connection by exploring the parallels between their careers: both supported the Declaration for Indulgence for repealing penal laws against dissenters (legalizing conventicles), made an economic argument for expanding toleration (lifting the Test and Cooperation Acts is beneficial for trade), and shifted their political allegiances to "Country" opposition in late 1673.[29] Moreover, Jacob insists that Stubbe, not Shaftesbury, was the first to readapt the older republican language of Harringtonianism into a "Country" program opposed to absolutist monarchies, commercial corruption, ministerial influence, and standing armies. To account for monarchical restoration after 1660, Stubbe modified Harringtonian-commonwealthean language by transforming the republican balance between the Few (the oligarchy) and the Many (the people) into a constitutional balance among the monarch, the House of Lords, and the House of Commons. In recasting the monarchy in sympathetic terms, "neo-Harringtonianism" allowed radical Protestants to no longer anchor constitutional principles in a remote Christian-Roman past.[30] Thus, Stubbe realigns the Harringtonian ancient virtue with Mahomet's "Prophetic monarchy" (128). Jacob argues that this "Mahometan" Harringtonianism "was likely to be more palatable to a 'Country' Whig than to a Courtier during the 1680s."[31] Indeed, many Tory satirists saw this new ideology as a "Country" and radical Whig invention.

In effect, neo-Harringtonianism recasts England's constitutional idiom in Islamic terms. J. G. A. Pocock has shown that appeals to the "ancient Constitution" shaped English legal thought and political argumentation in the early modern period.[32] Stubbe was no exception. In his manuscript, ancient constitutionalism, revived in the Judaizing Christians' "Mosaical Constitutions," seeks legitimacy in the Islamic past, which he treats as an authoritative source of public virtue, common law, and ancient custom (171). Mahomet, a prophet-legislator, founded a republic based on Niccolò Machiavelli's idea of virtue: "The dexterity of the Prophet shew'd that the prudent may be absolute without Tyranny or without regretting their subjects or enfeebling their spirits, that the Arts of Government consist not in the show but use of Authority, the true use whereof is to insinuate itself into men's affections or convince their Reason, not to impose upon their understanding or force their will" (93–94).

Like Machiavelli's prince, Mahomet is not a tyrant; he creates complacent and nonrebellious subjects through the "arts of Government" and not through violent authoritarian rule. Stubbe adopts a Machiavellian trope central to English constitutional rhetoric yet treats Mahomet like another version of Moses: an armed prophet who, as a political innovator bound to the temporal world, requires the sword to govern his "Military Empire" (169).[33] As Pocock accurately points out, "the Machiavellian and prophetic perspectives lay not far apart" in seventeenth-century constitutional thought.[34] Stubbe's prophet-legislator embodies this dual perspective, rendering Islam an idealized model for imagining England's republican past.

Accordingly, Islamic republicanism espouses the same constitutional principles that Shaftesbury and his "Country" supporters defended, as they refashioned

Machiavellian republicanism into a neo-Harringtonian political program.[35] Stubbe's prophet-legislator subscribes to the same principles that defined "Country" opposition to the Stuart crown. Mahomet avoided civil strife by granting toleration to Christians and Jews who preferred to pay a small tribute and retain their property rights under Muslim protection than to live under Catholic and Greek orthodox persecution (180–81, 110). To prevent his subjects from growing "effeminate through Luxury or mutinous by means of their Riches," he established charitable alms-giving ("Zacot"), a kind of "Grecian levelling Law" meant to limit an affluent upper class and reduce poverty (170). Likewise, he outlawed usury and gambling to reduce "Discord & Poverty" and prevent commercial corruption under his egalitarian governance (175–78). The mandatory practice of the five *salats* (prayers), fasting, and pilgrimage helps create productive subjects who, as citizen-soldiers of the republic, relieve the government from having to use public funds to support an expensive professional army (169). By eliminating the powerful "hereditary nobility," Mahomet's "prophetic monarchy" is immune to aristocratic and ministerial corruption (128). For Stubbe, Mahomet's Machiavellian republic can help guide a Country politics determined to protect England's virtuous commonwealth from corrupt ministers, despotic kings, intolerant Anglicans, parasitic aristocrats, monied interest, and standing armies.

Given the tragic failure of the Ottoman-Hungarian cause, Tory satirists feared that the defense of Islamic republicanism was part of a radical Whig attempt to foment a second revolution in England. In Stubbe's case, they may have been correct. He employs Islam as a constitutional model that is perhaps more radical than Shaftesbury and the Whigs ever advocated: extending toleration to anti-trinitarians and abolishing ecclesiastical institutions altogether. For Stubbe, Mahometanism established an Erastian regime that unites the civil and ecclesiastical branches under one absolute (Machiavellian) sovereign. In this respect, his absolute sovereign can be traced to Thomas Hobbes's radical writings. In his strong distaste for clerical pretensions, Hobbes, who Stubbe knew well, locates the civil commonwealth in Mosaic law and Abraham's covenant, a social contract that excludes the establishment of a separate priesthood.[36] Hobbes claims that Christ's mission was to restore the Hebrew Covenant with the civil sovereign (the Old Testament prophets), dispensing with corrupt clerical power and bringing about "the Independency of the primitive Christians."[37] Stubbe's account adheres to this Erastian model by rejoicing in Mahomet's "uniting the Civil and Ecclesiastical Powers in one Soveraign!" (178). In effect, he reduces a "Country" program to an Erastian politics that, by 1683, had its analogue in Ottoman-Hungarian efforts to abolish (Catholic) ecclesiastical authority.

The link between the reformist cause and Erastian-style politics is publicly exposed through Tory burlesques that mock Islamic republicanism. Allegedly written as Titus Oates's confidential letter to the Duke of Monmouth, *Oates new shams discovered: and how they carried it on from time to time sent in a letter to his Grace James Duke of Monmouth from Doctor Titus Oates* (London, 1688?) satirizes the various "shams" perpetuated by Whig rebels who have fathered the Popish Plot, personified as a bastard child reared in the secret womb of the English body politic. Shaftesbury, Lord Russell, Lord Essex, Lord Gray, and other Rye House conspirators were each, in turn, its "midwives," but only "Perking Teckely," prior to Monmouth, fell "to work . . . upon the Brat." Teckely wants to claim "an un-doubted Right to the Imperial Crown of *England*" (1). This satire casts him as the principal instigator in the larger drama of Whig betrayal, suggesting that English Exclusionists will repeat Teckely's tragic failure by helping beget a sham Popish Plot for the Mahometan cause:

> a great many more made the like attempt, with such or worse success—and some hang'd, some in hold, some turn'd Trimmers, and the rest run away: for just in the interim when the *K.* was to have been Murthered comes me in—one *Howard, Rumsey, West,* and *Keeling*—and undertook to deliver this great Belly—and upon the word of a *Priest,* they handled it with such Dexterity, that in a fort-nights time, they brought out this great Monster—and what do you think it was that made all this nois-e'en honest *Presbyter John*—a Delicate Babe, but so stuft with' *Soiciations,* Noble *Feer's Speech; Holy Leagues,* and *Covenants,* & c. that it was Farting full again: And being *Incubus* it spoke as soon as it was Born, and names above six-Hundred Fathers that were at the getting on't *Shaftsbury, Tongue,* and my self, three of the Chief-then dr[a]wing its Mouth on one side; cry'd, You must all turn *Turks* or be damn'd-and ever since I have had a great Ambition to leave off my Hypocritical Jump, and turn *Muffty.* But how do you think this *Brat* served us at last; for all we have lick't it into five hundred shapes and colours nothing serves its turn but speaking truth with a Pox to the *Rascal:* and has spoiled all our future proceedings; and we have lost the Charter into the bargain. (2)

By casting Whig rebellion as a perverted and shameful act of sexual impregna-tion, this burlesque discloses a "secret" about the conspiratorial Popish and Rye House Plots: the monstrous deformity in the "great Belly" of the body politic is a demonic "Incubus" who demands that all English citizens "turn Turk" by tak-ing recourse in the language of constitutional republicanism—the "Soiciations," "Holy Leagues," and "Covenants." By casting Shaftesbury, Israel Tonge, and Oates as the "chief" Turkish conspirators, Whig reformers are satirized as Teckelite de-mons who have raped the English nation, gendered as a sleeping female victim who gave illegitimate birth to the Popish Plot hoax. This elaborate conceit implies that Oates's addressee, Monmouth, will fail in his attempt to protect English constitutional virtue by trying to launch a "Turkish" rebellion against King James II in 1685. As the Oates figure sadly admits, Teckelite politics has "spoiled all our future proceedings; and we have lost the Charter into the bargain" (2). Ultimately, this Tory burlesque plots Islamic republicanism as a failed yet decisive episode in a mock-heroic epic about Whig-Erastian politics that would reach its climactic resolution in the events of 1688–91.

Steeped in hysterical paranoia, Tory burlesques seek to discredit Exclusionist politics by insisting that radical Whigs are accomplices in a Hungarian conspiracy against church and state, exposing the constitutional principle of a limited Protestant monarchy as founded on Islamic innovation rather than Christian tradition. For Tory satirists, Islam needs to be ridiculed because it poses a serious threat to England's political existence from within and without its porous borders. Humphrey Prideaux, an Anglican bishop, expresses this paranoia in the subtitle to his anti-Islamic polemic: *The True Nature of Imposture Fully display'd in the Life of Mahomet. With a discourse Annex'd for the Vindication of Christianity from this Charge. Offered to the Consideration of the Deists of the Present Age* (London, 1697), a popular work that ran through nine editions and is a coded response to rumors and satiric attacks on exaggerated caricatures of Stubbe's ideas.[38] Indeed, Charles Blount, a deist, plagiarized passages from Stubbe's manuscript in his letters to Thomas Hobbes and John Wilmot, the Earl of Rochester, a notorious freethinker. These two letters were prefixed to Blount's deist publication, *The Oracles of Reason* (London, 1693).[39] Hence, Prideaux's fear that the deists will "raise up some *Mahomet* against us" and incite a second civil war represents a Tory reaction to existing radical threats.[40] Such polemics imply that many High Anglicans would have known about Stubbe's work by the 1690s.

Respublica Islamica, Post-1688

As the fierce controversies of the Exclusion Crisis continued to find new outlets of expression in the 1680s, Islamic republicanism became an exploitable trope that lent itself to variety of satiric uses and could be potentially mobilized for almost any political cause. For Stubbe and radical Whigs, this trope was used to criticize the Stuart-Anglican regime's antidissenting policies; for Shaftesbury and his Exclusionist allies, to combat "Popery and arbitrary government" and justify the need to reform England's corrupted constitution; and in the hands of paranoid Tories, to launch a smear campaign against radical Protestants to secure their political interests in the Stuart court and display their unwavering loyalty to the restored Anglican monarchy. After the 1683 siege of Vienna, Islamic republicanism emerged as a culturally diffuse discourse that a new generation of radical Whigs, from the reign of Queen Anne (1702–14) to the early Georgian period, self-consciously appropriated and reinvented. I argue that John Toland's *Nazarenus: or, Jewish, Gentile, and Mahometan Christianity* (1718), a deist mock-theology, supplements Anglo-Protestant toleration with ideas inherited from the Islamic prophetic tradition. For Toland, Mahometanism's *Respublica Mosaica*, Moses' virtuous republic, enshrines the revolutionary (Whig) principles of 1688.

Stubbe's manuscript acquired a central polemical status in the deist controversy, especially after Toland published his views on "Mahometan Christianity."[41] Toland's work argues for the primordial identity among Judaism, Christianity, and Islam based on evidence from the lost Gospel of Barnabas, or the true "Mahometan Gospel," which synchronizes the continuity of the prophets, from Adam, Noah, Abraham, Moses, Jesus, to Mahomet. For him, this synchronized monotheism reflects "the Original Plan of Christianity," or the Nazarenes' primitive teachings. Accordingly, the Mahometans, whose Qur'an derives from the apocryphal Gospel of Barnabas ("the earliest documents of the Christian religion"), are "a sort of Christians, and not the worst sort neither" (166, 116).[42] They are closer to the original Nazarene system than the historical Christians, whose doctrines were perverted through faulty biblical texts (165–66). He shares three principal themes with Stubbe: first, primitive (Arian) Christianity is a reformed Jewish faith displaced by the clergy's pagan Trinitarianism; second, this ancient religion resists a corrupted gentile-Pauline theology, especially during Emperor Constantine's fourth-century reign; and third, Islam restored the Nazarene religion to the tolerant conditions existing under Noachic laws, the foundation of all true religions. Toland does not include a biographical account about the prophet-legislator, because, unlike *The Rise and Progress of Mahometanism*, his published work is vulnerable to government scrutiny under the 1710 Copyright Act.[43] However, Stubbe's presence is implicit in his work. Thomas Mangey, the chaplain to the Bishop of London and one of the first to criticize *Nazarenus*, refers to this presence when he compares "Mahometan Christianity" to *The Rise and Progress of Mahometanism*.[44] Almost fifty years later, many Britons continued to read and debate Stubbe's radical position on Islam.

The first letter of *Nazarenus* reworks the anticlerical polemic found in Toland's *Christianity not Mysterious* (1697), a deist manifesto that became an instant best seller when the Irish Parliament ordered it to be publicly burned and called for the author's arrest. This work proposes that the original primitive Christianity was propagated as a natural theology devoid of irrational "mysteries," and that Trinitarian Christianity is nothing more than a derivative paganism concocted by crafty priests. Over time, pagan Trinitarianism displaced the original Christianity, a tolerant and pluralistic civic religion. In this context, Toland's discovery of the Gospel of Barnabas (a Christian forgery) in Amsterdam in 1709 has profound theological implications: even though he admits that this apocryphal text is as corrupted as the canonical Gospels, it could help reconstruct an alternative historical narrative in which primitive Christianity is incompatible with—and antithetical to—doctrinal disputes over revealed "mysteries."

Accordingly, the early Nazarenes' natural religion is the Ebonite model of the tolerant apostolic church. Toland trivializes the theological distinction between James's emphasis on salvation through work, the practice of Levitical rites, and Paul's emphasis on salvation through faith, the dispensation of Mosaic law. For him, the Gospel of Barnabas shows that this much-disputed distinction is a practical, not a doctrinal, concern involving two different types of Christians: the Jewish ones, who observe Mosaic law, and the gentiles, who do not observe the same laws (117–18, 176–77). Like Stubbe, Toland aligns the Judaizing Christians with the Nazarenes, and the gentiles with St. Paul, "an enemy and imposter," and the Church Patriarchs, "a damning crew the *Fathers*" (150–54, 159, 173–75). The paganized theology of the Trinitarian gentiles is therefore a perversion of the Jewish-Nazarene system. Toland's historical reconstruction satirizes the "Apostolic Tradition and Succession," a theological invention concocted by "English High-church Pharisees" and "mercenary Priests" to further their narrow ecclesiastical interests at the expense of religious pluralism (190–93, 126). For him, Jewish and gentile Christians originally coexisted in a "Union without Uniformity" in which true religion is about inner virtue rather than outward ceremony (117). Mahometanism returns to this ancient tolerationist ethos.

Not adhering to any specific doctrine, Mahometan Christianity uncovers the civil constitutional basis for reforming Anglo-Protestant toleration. Toland is interested in the naturalization of English Jews under a reformed English civil order, a position that he carefully outlines in *Reasons for Naturalizing the Jews* (1714).[45] As his appendix to *Nazarenus* makes clear, the question of the Jewish nation and the *Respublica Mosaica* is central to his concept of the civil Erastian legislator (235–40). In *Letters to Serena* (1704) and *Origines Judicae* (1709), he describes Moses as a wise Egyptian legislator who founded a natural religion, a republican commonwealth. In this regard, he was responding to a well-established republican-Harringtonian tradition on the *Respublica Mosaica*, a prescriptive model in which the church, subsumed under the state, extends toleration to antitrinitarians and other Protestant dissenters.[46] Toland's stance in *Nazarenus* furthers this agenda. From his deist perspective, Nazarene Christianity is restored, and thereby supplemented, in Mahomet's reestablished *Respublica Mosaica*. The Prophet is a wise and just Mosaic-Nazarene legislator who deserves Christian respect and admiration. Insofar as Muslims tolerate Christians and Jews in their countries, reasonable Christians should likewise grant full toleration and citizenship to Jews and Muslims living in England and elsewhere. For Toland, English Mahometans should be entitled to property, public office, and legal protection. Otherwise, intolerant Christians will seem barbarous compared to the "generous and human treatment" granted to Christians living in Muslim nations. Because Muslims are a type of Christians, he argues that they should be "allow'd Moschs in these parts of Europe . . . as any other sectaries" (176, 135). Toland recasts Mahometanism as a Mosaic-constitutional ideal that is opposed, in principle, to the strictures of the Toleration Act, a piece of antidissenting legislation that never repealed the Test and Corporation Acts.[47]

Toland's radical approach to Islamic toleration is encoded in his anonymous publication, *A letter from an Arabian physician to a famous professor in the University of Hall in Saxony, concerning Mahomet's taking up arms, his marrying of many wives, his keeping of cuncubines, and his paradise* (London? 1706?).[48] As the title implies, Toland's defense of Islam recalls Stubbe's account: Mahomet the prophet-legislator instituted social policies necessary for salvaging the virtuous Christian commonwealth. Toland's tract is written as a satiric letter that features an "Arabian Physician" from Paris who, based on a previous conversation with a "famous professor" in England, argues against the charge that Mahomet is a "vile impostor" (4–5). This fictional character likens Mahomet to a Machiavellian prince who adopted the sword according to his "hereditary and Divine Right" to the conquered lands. To avoid civil strife in his republican empire, he offered toleration to all sects and religions, including Christians and Jews (5–6). As such, the Prophet is more merciful and tolerant of his enemies than Trinitarian Christians, who engage in trivial disputes over doctrines and rituals: "The *Mahometans* tolerate all manner of Religions . . . the Christians do nothing but persecute, wherever the Clergy's Power prevails over that of the Magistrate, or where their Dictates are look'd upon to be sacred and infallible Oracles, tho their Gospel forbids all manner of Persecution for Conscience sake" (8).

This passage reiterates *Nazarenus*'s central thesis: Islam recaptures the tolerant civic spirit formerly vested in Christianity, whereas historical Christianity is contaminated with the persecuting zeal of crafty priests who have hijacked "the

Magistrate." In this case, Mahomet's "hereditary right" does not refer to clerical privilege or aristocratic lineage but to a prophetic claim emanating from Moses' (and Christ's) social covenant with the Hebrews, as renewed by Abraham. Islam is the *Respublica Mosaica*, the "Union without Uniformity" that England urgently needs if it is ever to resolve the problem of toleration. To avoid government persecution, Islamic republicanism's radical politics—too dangerous to recount in *Nazarenus*—can be articulated only in an anonymous publication, a fictional letter ascribed to a visiting Muslim critic.

Nazarenus' satiric playfulness is not about doctrinal disputes but about the "Clergy's power" over the "Magistrate." For Toland, primitive Christianity thrived as a tolerant civic religion that did not impose a uniform doctrine on its citizens, rendering an independent ecclesiastical church obsolete. In his defense of Occasional Conformity—the taking of the Anglican sacrament to qualify for office while remaining part of a dissenting congregation—he implies that Anglican toleration cannot be reformed until England adopts the Erastian scheme of the Nazarene Christians:

> I am as much as any man for *Occasional Conformity*. Among Churches not differing in essentials; which was evidently the practice of the primitive Church most properly so call'd, and founded upon unanswerable grounds. *Toleration* also . . . is no less plainly a duty of the *Gospel*, than it is self-evident according to the Law of Nature: so that they who persecute others in their reputations, rights, properties, or persons, for merely speculative opinions, or for things in their own nature indifferent, are so farr equally devested both of Humanity and Christianity. (emphasis original; 161)

For Toland, the deist reduction of Christianity to a universal natural religion requires a healthy religious pluralism, a radical policy that has been negated by Tory-motivated efforts to prohibit Occasional Conformity. As part of their revenge on the Whigs for excluding them from office through the Association Act of 1696 and the Abjuration Act of 1702, the Tories persuaded Queen Anne in 1711 to pass an act outlawing Occasional Conformity. This act criminalized dissenting Whig Lords and MPs who evaded the Test and Corporation Acts by taking the sacrament. After the passing of this act, the defense of Occasional Conformity became the target for the Whig opposition to the Toleration Act and other such bills that disfranchised nonconformists for their religious beliefs.[49] For Toland, an Erastian model of Nazarene toleration will not merely protect Occasional Conformity. It can keep in check High Churchmen who "persecute others in their reputations, rights, properties, or persons, for merely speculative opinions." As restored in Mahometanism, the tolerant Nazarene system reflects the "Law of Nature"—the ancient Noahian and Mosaic constitution, a "duty of the *Gospel*"—and counters the clergy's persecuting zeal.

His observation on Occasional Conformity in a deist work that vindicates the "Mahometan Gospel" is radical. Through the influence and patronage of Robert Harley, elected to Parliament as an "Old Country" Whig in 1689, Toland's work voiced radical commonwealthean opposition against High Anglicans, Tories, and oligarchic Whigs, all of whom compromised the 1688 revolutionary settlement by supporting royalist agendas.[50] In their opposition to antidissenting legislation (such as prohibiting Occasional Conformity), he and the "Old" commonwealthean Whigs sought to redress ministerial corruption, public finance, soaring deficits, expensive wars, and standing armies—a republican program first articulated through Stubbe's neo-Harringtonian Mahometanism. Given this political tradition, Toland's writings on "Mahometan Christianity" reformulated ancient (Islamic) constitutionalism as promoted by Stubbe and other deists in the 1670s and the First Earl of Shaftesbury in the 1680s. In other words, *Nazarenus* can be read as an attempt to accommodate Islamic republicanism in the new polemical debates of the early Georgian period. Indeed, Toland supported Bishop Benjamin Hoadly, a Whig Churchman who, in his sermon, "The Kingdom of Christ," defended Occasional Conformity in Hobbesian and Erastian terms. This sermon ignited a fierce controversy that led to the dissolution of convocation for suppressing dissenters in 1718, the same year Toland published his work. Robert Rees Evans speculates that *Nazarenus*'s timely publication contributed to the dissolution of convocation by calling for the citizenship of dissenters and other religious minorities (mainly Jews) when parliamentary debate over toleration was at its height.[51] This precise timing would suggest that Toland's reformulation of Islamic republicanism was responsible, in part, for furthering the tolerationist agenda championed by the "Old" Whig opposition. Mahometan Christianity offers hope for a Whig-Erastian toleration policy bent on protecting the Commonwealth from antidissenting Tory legislation and corrupt Whig-oligarchic policies.

Toland's work marks the continuity of an Islamic-constitutional tradition that helped refashion post-1688 Whig politics. Partly through the Third Earl of Shaftesbury's patronage, he and the "Old Country" Whigs redefined themselves in opposition to the "New" Whigs who, in their eyes, had betrayed the Glorious Revolution.[52] Under this "New" Whig administration, England ("Britain" with the Act of Union between England and Scotland in 1707) was developing into a formidable military and commercial empire in a world where the Ottomans

no longer posed as the primary threat and Teckely was dead. England's involvement in protracted Continental wars—the Nine Years' War (1689–97) and the
War of the Spanish Succession (1702–13)—rendered French-Austrian rivalry for
the Spanish throne the greatest threat to Protestant England. Arranged in part
through William III, the 1699 Treaty of Carlowitz undermined French expansionist efforts to seize the Spanish throne by preventing the sultan, a key French
ally significantly weakened by this point, from attacking Austria's eastern front.
This treaty deprived France of a much-needed Ottoman distraction and, consequently, strengthened the anti-Bourbon League of Augsburg formed by England,
Holland, and Austria. Owing to these events, anti-Islamic polemicists projected
the Titus-Turk figure onto King Louis XIV and Jacobite defenders of the old (Stuart) Pretender. Many Britons saw them as a threat to English liberty and the Protestant succession.[53] As a result, anti-Catholic sentiments became pervasive in the
English court. Under these altered conditions, Mahometan Christianity became
acceptable among some gentile Whigs even as it remained radically opposed to
royal and ministerial policies. Whereas *A letter from an Arabian physician* would
have been too dangerous to publish under Toland's name during Queen Anne's
combined Whig-Tory ministry, the more cautious Islamic republicanism implicit
in *Nazarenus* would have found a favorable reception in 1718, a year that witnessed the dissolution of Convocation, England's increasing dependence on the
economic and military aid of Muslim North African, and a renewed British-led
alliance against Catholic Spain.[54]

   In Islamicizing the *Respublica Mosaica*, Toland in *Nazarenus* sought to secure
the 1688 revolutionary principles during an era undergoing sweeping political and
social transformations. This satiric work deconstructs Anglican universal history
and constructs an alternative narrative that legally vindicates an Erastian toleration policy. In this case, discussions about Islam are filtered through national
debates on the legal status of dissenting antitrinitarians and the redistribution
of rights, property, and privilege among all citizens despite religious affiliation.
References to "Jews," "Nazarenes," and "Mahometans" are codes for disfranchised
nonconformists who deny the "Papist" doctrine of the Trinity and reject some
or all Anglican sacraments. As such, Mahometanism caters to an anti-Catholic
discourse in which fear of "Popery" defines English nationalism and indirectly
justifies Hanoverian imperial rule.[55] Toland's burlesque theology is distinctly
radical not for what it says—playful ideas that the author may not believe—
but for turning biblical hermeneutics against its orthodox practitioners. What
remains radical are the rhetorical techniques through which scripture—biblical
and Qur'anic, canonical and apocryphal—is used to mock the antidissenting

strictures of the Toleration Act.[56] Orthodox writers recognized this radical literary mode when they blamed Mahometan Christianity for inciting opposition to
Anglican toleration.[57] Toland concurs by shrewdly noting that "I am not the first
who put *Christian* and *Mahometan* together."[58] Neither was he the last writer to
defend Britain's revolutionary settlement in Islamic-constitutional terms.

Coda: Islam and English Constitutional Thought

Whether in Tory satiric broadsides or deist mock-theologies, the burlesque mode
suggests that the "True Protestant Mahometan," a master trope for discussing
sensitive domestic problems, gave shape to the debates of the radical Enlightenment. In other words, I argue that polemical burlesques offer a crucial site for
investigating how Islamic republicanism lent narrative coherence to a series of
national crises that, in historical hindsight, erupted into the Glorious Revolution.
Many radical Protestants deployed Mahometanism for rewriting Christian prophetic history in tolerationist and constitutionalist terms; it provided them with
a convenient ideological framework with which to make sense of national crises
as they arose, supplementing a deficient and ailing Christian monarchy in England (and Europe) with rival prophetic stories about the just republics founded
by Noah, Abraham, and Moses.

In linking civic republicanism to the Mahometan cause, Tory and deist burlesques were, in effect, publicizing Islam's ubiquitous role in national and religious politics. Melinda Alliker Rabb has argued that late Stuart and Augustan
satire guarantees that "secrecy informs what is most precious and what is most
dangerous to the survival of the social order."[59] Likewise, Mahometan-themed
burlesques guarantee that secrets about Islamic republicanism are both precious
and dangerous to Restoration England's survival. Without Stubbe's defense, the
reformist opposition would have been deprived of a constitutional idiom necessary for reinterpreting and overcoming the political upheavals of the Exclusion
Crisis and the Glorious Revolution. By analyzing these upheavals as a transnational response to Ottoman-Hungarian affairs, I have recast the 1688 "Whig Triumph" as an Islamic-inspired event that prevented the counterreformation from
spreading into England. As such, my thesis questions progressivist Anglocentric
accounts that exalt John Locke as the revered "Whig" founder of British constitutional thought, uninfluenced by events across the English Channel.[60] Restoration
satires obsessed with Teckelite politics point not only to the Mahometan—rather
than Lockean—inspiration behind England's revolutionary settlement but also
to a common misunderstanding of Locke. As Nabil Matar has argued, Locke

relied on existing models of Islamic toleration to formulate his philosophical model.[61]

In the next chapter, I examine how Lady Mary Wortley Montagu's *The Turkish Embassy Letters* (1763)—deist letters written during her travels to the Ottoman empire between 1717 and 1718—reinvents Mahometan Christianity. These carefully crafted letters, I argue, register her encounter with Islamic republicanism following the failed siege of Vienna and unresolved tensions among Catholic Austria, Protestant Hungary, and the Ottomans that continued to demand Britain's attention. In her satiric mode of epistolary letter-writing, Islamic republicanism ceases to be a discourse about the constitutional balance between the monarchy and Parliament. Instead, it becomes a constitutional idiom for defending women's relative autonomy in marriage, inheritance, divorce, and property ownership, redefining gender and sexuality in an inclusive model of Anglican (female) citizenship.

CHAPTER TWO

Letters from a Female Deist

Lady Mary Wortley Montagu, Muslim Women, and Freethinking Feminism

I doubt not I shall be told (when I come to follow you thro' those Countries) in how pretty a manner you accommodated yourself to the Customs of the True Believers. At this Town they will say, she practiced to sit on the Sofa; at this village she learnt to fold the Turban; here she was bathed and anointed; and there she parted with her black Fullbottome. . . . Lastly I shall hear how the very first Night you lay in Pera, you had a Vision of Mahomet's Paradise, and happily awaked without a soul. From which blessed instance the beautiful Body was left at full liberty to perform all the agreeable functions it was made for.

Alexander Pope's letter to Lady Mary Wortley Montagu, Nov. 10, 1716

Written between 1717 and 1718 while traveling to the Levant with her husband, the English ambassador Edward Wortley, Lady Mary Wortley Montagu's *The Turkish Embassy Letters* (1763) is usually read as a feminist text obsessed with one emblematic episode: her eroticized encounter with the Turkish women of the hammam (private bathhouses off-limits to men) as described in an April 1717 letter. Ignoring interrelated questions about gender, sexuality, and genre, most critics read this letter in isolation, taking her "private" letter-writing for granted and remaining silent about her radical Protestant approach to elite Muslim women's sexual and sociopolitical agency.[1] But this lopsided view fails to recognize in Montagu the "female deist" who appropriates the deist epistolary genre to redefine Anglican citizenship in the gender-inclusive language of Islamic virtue, rather than in the gender-exclusive language of contractual rights.[2] Her writings thus belong to two divergent yet overlapping traditions: the lingering deist debates of the late seventeenth century as embodied in John Toland's controversial works (see chapter 1) and an early modern feminism as articulated by Tory free-thinkers Mary Astell and Delarivier Manley.

In a November 1716 letter addressed to Lady Montagu, Alexander Pope satirizes his correspondent as a libertine feminist who, while traveling across the Continent, gradually converts to Islam by discarding her "black fullbottome" wig (part of her English traveling attire) for a life of sexual promiscuity, Oriental luxury, and female enslavement. This insidious parody of her journey to the Ottoman world is an example of patriarchal Orientalism at work: the mistaken Western assumption that Muslim women are essentially oppressed and that they have no souls according to the Qur'an. For Pope, this doctrine allows Montagu to enjoy bodily pleasure without worrying about carnal sins. Anticipating the scurrilous remarks he would hurl at her years later, Pope's bawdy sarcasm targets the libertinism that undergirds her feminist fascination with Islam.[3] He wants to scandalize her eagerness to adopt the dress, customs, and sexual practices of "the true Believers" while forfeiting her national identity as a "freeborn" Englishwoman. Pope's satire suggests that her letters contain a buried critique of English sexual politics. But rather than reading her letters as a private expression of feminine desire, I read them as an ethnographic account of the socioeconomic agency that defines Muslim women's "feminotopia," an idealized female autonomy that contests a male social and sexual economy.[4] Montagu's feminotopia criticizes contract theory's false universals, which include democratic terms such as "freeborn Englishmen" that falsely include both genders when in practice women were excluded.[5] Montagu's appropriation of the deist epistolary letter as an effective genre for criticizing false universals enables this complex discursive.

Building on the work of Bernadette Andrea, I foreground Montagu's deist fascination with Islam in order to expand the genealogy of a British feminism that contested the terms of a hegemonic (predominately male) anti-Islamic discourse during the early eighteenth century.[6] I interpret her often-quoted proclamation— "I look upon the Turkish women as the only free people in the empire" (72)—in two complementary senses: first as a feminist motto that emerged earlier in the century among freethinkers who criticized England's false universals, and second as an imperialist idealization that refers only to slave/property-owning, "white-skinned" female citizens.[7]

As Felicity A. Nussbaum and Kathleen Wilson have argued, Montagu's feminotopias offer alternative female pleasures that resist "the emerging national imperative to control women's sexuality and maternity." Indeed, Montagu's freethinking philosophy accords with Mary Astell's and Delarivier Manley's Tory feminist stance on Islamic domesticity, maternity, and veiling as virtuous models for Englishwomen's sociopolitical agency. But even though Montagu's identification with elite Ottoman women can "counteract imperial tyranny," this cross-cultural process also contributes to what Srinivas Aravamudan sees as the Anglicization of a Levantine discourse on the East, indirectly inspiring projects of empire-building in late-eighteenth- and early-nineteenth-century Britain.[8] This complex historical trajectory is reflected in the oscillating discourse of Montagu's letters, which deflates patriarchal Orientalism while it consolidates feminine forms of national and imperial identity.

Turkish Spies and Arabian Physicians

After the publication of Henry Stubbe's *The Rise and Progress of Mahometanism,* some writers reread Islam's successful propagation as inaugurating the unfolding of Protestant providential history rather than marking a perverted hybrid of Christianity and Judaism. Positive accounts of Islam by Henri Comte de Boulainvilliers, George Sale, and Gottfried Leibniz retell the history of Protestantism from the perspective of the "Arabian legislator," suggesting that the Reformation took place nine centuries before Martin Luther nailed his famous Ninety-five Theses to a church door.[9] These accounts are, in part, a culturally diffused response to the deist controversy, which framed national debates in Restoration England as prompted by the converging events of the Hungarian Civil War, Exclusion Crisis, and Glorious Revolution (see chapter 1). Inspired by deist travel genres such as *Letters Writ by a Turkish Spy* and John Toland's *A letter from an Arabian physician,* Montagu's letters recast elite Ottomans as fictional Muslim characters in order to launch a disguised satiric assault on the Anglican order. Thus, as they mimic (and even parody) the deist epistolary letter, the letters link theologically to contemporary national debates on Islam.

Published after her death in 1762, Montagu's letters were not literally written to friends and relations between 1717 and 1718. Rather, they were written after her return to England based on notes she kept in her travel diaries, which were later destroyed by her daughter. As Cythnia Lowenthal has shown, her "familiar" letters were carefully crafted and rewritten in a dramatic epistolary form.[10] As noted, throughout the eighteenth century, deist publications on Islam usually relied on this form for reasons that will be discussed shortly. For example, a 1712 published version of Leibniz's private epistolary letter casually calls Mahometanism "a kind of Deism" that restored the "natural" Christianity practiced by the Nestorians and the Eutychians. However, his published scholarship never included these potentially heretical views on Islam.[11] For similar reasons, Montagu's radical claims about the wise effendi Achmed Bey's deism had to be written in the genre of the private epistolary letter if, like Leibniz, she ever expected to gain public access into the republic of letters.

Imaginary letters by Muslim characters are part of an eighteenth-century semijournalistic literary genre. Before Montesquieu's *The Persian Letters* (1730) achieved acclaim in England and Europe, Giovanni P. Marana's *Letters Writ by a Turkish Spy living in Paris* was the first popular multivolume work to fictionalize a deist account of Mahometanism. Published in Paris and translated into Dutch, German, Italian, and Russian, the eight volumes of the *Turkish Spy* appeared in English translation from 1692 to 1801, in thirty-one editions in total.[12] This satiric work centers on a fictional Muslim character—a Turkish spy living in Paris who criticizes, among other things, Christian rituals and doctrines. But unlike *The Persian Letters*, Marana's work satirizes not only Roman Catholicism but Christianity, which the Turkish spy describes as a "reformed" Judaism based on the primitive Nazarene model, corrupted by the "politheism of the Gentiles" (6:212–19).[13] He further adds that the Trinity is a blasphemous doctrine invented by the gentiles to further their ecclesiastical power (6:341). Given this antitrinitarian account of monotheistic history, the Turkish spy concludes that Christians should not disparage Mahomet, the "Holy Lawgiver," because "some ancient writers among the *Nazarenes* . . . make Honourable mention of *Him* and his family" (7:232; 5:145). An English translator notes that the Turkish spy is a "Deist rather than an Atheist. . . . and it is well enough known, to those who travel in *Turkey*, and Converse with Men of sense there, That there are abundance of Deists among the Mahometans, as well as among us Christians: and our Arabian demonstrates, that he is one of these" (8: "To the reader"). The satiric and indirect writing style of the Turkish spy letters renders Mahometan Christianity more "rational" than its Trinitarian counterpart.

Montagu adopts the Turkish spy motif in the guise of a wise Islamic scholar, an "effendi" from Belgrade named Achmed Bey who practices "plain deism" (53, 62).[14] Her letters are strongly fixated on the virtuous character of this "extraordinary scribe." She describes Achmed Bey as a well-educated aristocrat who avoids "mysteries and novelties" and all religious disputes, schisms, and rituals. He instead preaches a "natural" religion (or atheism), "whose impiety consists in making a jest of their prophet" (62). According to Montagu, the effendis "have no more faith in the inspiration of Mohammed than in the infallibility of the pope. They make a frank profession of deism amongst themselves. . . . [They] never speak of their law but as of a politic institution, fit now to be observed by wise men, however at first introduced by politicians and enthusiasts" (110–11). Islamic-

Ottoman law is deist in the sense that it is a flexible natural law that avoids the superstition practiced by vulgar politicians and fanatical religious leaders. Even though Montagu's view of the Prophet's "enthusiasm" and "inspiration" is more closely aligned with Anglican anti-Islamic (and anti-Catholic) polemic than with radical Protestant views, her positive characterization of Achmed Bey faithfully follows the fictional conventions of the deist-familial letter. As in the Turkish spy letters, the ostensibly private form of Montagu's epistolary letters allows the English reader to enter a transculturation zone that, in effect, establishes a one-to-one identification between Mahometanism and Protestantism but *without* explicitly upholding the deist tenets of the Islamic faith or elevating Muhammad to the status of a republican legislator.

Montagu's negative approach to early Islamic history compares Muhammad to an infallible pope. Nevertheless, Montagu uses Achmed Bey as a mouthpiece for deist ideas associated with English freethinking. Her characterization of the effendi probably derived from Sir Paul Rycaut's account of Muslim elites who professed atheism, blasphemy, and libertinism. In *The Present State of the Ottoman Empire*, Rycaut, the English consul to the Ottoman empire in the 1660s, notes that the Islamic sect of the "Muserines" secretly believes that a theistic God does not exist and that, if anything, God is in nature. He reports that their pseudo-deist or atheistic doctrine has prevailed in the sultan's court, especially among the effendis and "the apartments of the ladies and eunuchs."[15] Even though "Achmed Bey" has no known historical referent, Montagu would have had prior knowledge about the clandestine freethinking circles through Rycaut's work, which she references and corrects: "Sir Paul Rycaut is mistaken, as he commonly is, in calling the sect *muserine* (i.e. the secret is with us) atheists, they being deists." (62). Despite Montagu's reservations, this work may be presenting historically accurate information about a prevailing freethinking skepticism among Muslim elites. As evident in the Turkish spy letters quoted above, radicals in England and Europe used Rycaut's work as key evidence for an extended genealogy that traces the freethinking legacy to early Islamic and Ottoman history.[16] By criticizing Rycaut's views, Montagu is contributing to ongoing debates about this extended genealogy while attempting to steer away from any potential controversy.

According to Montagu, Achmed Bey is a deist freethinker who, as "a lawyer and a priest," controls all religious and civil matters (61). Writing to Abbé Antonio Conti, a Catholic and closet antitrinitarian, Montagu explains that the effendi's anticlerical deism reveals a theological affinity between Muslims and Protestants (63). Only English Protestants, Montagu suggests, could easily convert the Muslims:

I explained to him the difference between the religion of England and Rome, and he was pleased to hear there were Christians that did not worship images or adore the Virgin Mary. The ridicule of transubstantiation appeared very strong to him. Upon comparing our creeds together I am convinced that if our friend Dr. Clarke had free liberty of preaching here it would be very easy to persuade the generality to Christianity, whose notions are already little different from his. Mr. Whiston would make a very good apostle here. (62)

Achmed Bey's deism is comparable to the freethinking antitrinitarianism espoused by Samuel Clarke and William Whiston, two Arian Whig Churchmen who Montagu knew from her attendance in the Hanoverian court. She thoroughly approved their latitudinarian position on natural religion.[17]

By drawing a comparison between Arianism and Mahometanism, Montagu's letter subtly alludes to radical writings that realign the tradition of Protestant freethinking with the history of Islamic heresy. More specifically, she references the heretical writings of William Whiston, whose outspoken anticlerical views and challenge to Athanasius's Trinitarian creed ignited a fierce controversy that led to his ejection from the Cambridge professorship in 1710. Like his teacher Sir Isaac Newton, he used an Arabic manuscript to reinterpret the Apostolic church and to question the scripture's canonical authority.[18] Whiston's findings were culled from the research of Simon Ockley, an Anglican divine and respectable Orientalist who in his *The History of the Saracens* (1718) praised the Arabs as "great men" whose "considerable actions" are as virtuous as "any other nation under heaven."[19] Whiston used Ockley's scholarship not to convert Muslims to Anglican Protestantism but to write subversively "against [the] canon of scripture."[20] His heretical crime is that he ascribed more authoritative clout to a new work found in an Arabic manuscript than to the scriptures. In this regard, Whiston—like Newton, an Arian—is a disguised deist who admires Near Eastern monotheisms and shares the methodological agenda espoused in Toland's pro-Mahometan work *Nazarenus: or, Jewish, Gentile, and Mahometan Christianity* (1718).[21] Montagu alerts her readers to this Islamic-deistic alliance when noting that Achmed Bey acknowledges Toland: "[H]e seemed to have some knowledge of our religious disputes and even of our writers, and I was surprised to hear him ask, amongst other things, how Mr. Toland did" (111). Her witty allusions to notorious English theologians render the Anglican proselytizing rhetoric deployed in her letters a thinly veiled disguise for conveying firsthand confirmation on the Islamic roots of the radical freethinking legacy and its current preservation among Ottoman elites.

Furthermore, by referring to Clarke's freedom to preach and Whiston's status as a "good apostle," Montagu insinuates that a toleration policy for antitrinitarian dissenters is socially and politically feasible under Ottoman-Islamic law. In other words, she offers a corrective to the restrictive and oppressive atmosphere fostered by the 1689 Toleration Act, which did not repeal the Test and Corporation Acts. She notes that Protestants find more protection in the Ottoman empire than in Catholic Europe (46). Throughout her letters, she frequently attacks Roman Catholic and Greek Orthodox priests for, among many reasons, severely and relentlessly persecuting Hungarian Protestants (12, 15, 27–28, 46, 51). She suggests that once Christendom (including England) adopts the effendi's Erastian policy the problem of toleration will be resolved (63, 109). In this sense, her letters are responding to the English anti-Catholic sentiments spurred by the Hungarian Civil War, the 1683 siege of Vienna, and the Exclusion Crisis, major events that were (temporarily) resolved by the 1688–91 revolutionary settlement (see chapter 1).

Montagu's letter on Achmed Bey's deism is dated February 1718, the year in which Toland published *Nazarenus*. It was not included in the 1763 publication but was published anonymously as a separate letter in 1718 and 1719 under the title *The Genuine Copy of a Letter Written from Constantinople by an English Lady . . . no less distinguished by her Wit than her Quality; To a Venetian Nobleman, one of the Prime Virtuosi of the Age*. Mostly an attack on the Christian clergy (including the Anglican church), the letter was written as a response to a series of questions on Islam posed by a "Venetian Nobleman" in a previous conversation with an "English Lady of wit and quality." The Venetian nobleman is meant to be one Abbé Conti. Without Montagu's permission, he published her letter in the French original accompanied by an English translation, concealing the name of the letter writer and the recipient to evade prosecution under the seditious libel act.[22] However, family and friends knew the author's identity. Indeed, this letter conferred on her a notorious reputation as a "female wit."[23]

The title layout and narrative setting of Montagu's letter mimics *A letter from an Arabian physician to a famous professor in the University of Hall in Saxony* (London, 1706?), the deist tract published anonymously by Toland.[24] His fictional letter features an "Arabian Physician" who systematically responds to a series of objections against the Mahometan religion that were raised in a previous conversation with the recipient, an English scholar whom he met at a university in Paris. This fictional writer first wants to prove that Islam is more tolerant of religious dissent than any sect in Christianity and that Protestants share more with Mahomet's antitrinitarian faith than with Catholicism (6). Second, he uses this radical deist theology to support a libertine argument: namely, that the Muslim notions of a sexual paradise and polygyny are not inherently sinful because there is no primordial evil inherent in sexual pleasure. He maintains that sexual propagation was divinely sanctioned by the Old Testament injunction to breed and multiply and ridicules original sin:

> If you say there is [sin in the sexual act], then the Propagation of Mankind even in the most perfect State would have been vile and sinful; then a Man's enjoying his own Wife (which all Men take to be not only lawful, but a Duty) must needs be sinful; then Mankind (which is contrary to God's own Appointment) ought not to be propagated, and the World should be left desolate of Inhabitants of the Human Kind; the Absurdity of all Which is, I think, evident to all rational men. (14)

By employing the voice of the Arabian physician, Toland safely conveys his libertine views on sexuality while disavowing authorial responsibility. Disguised as a Muslim critic, he assaults the legal sanctity of men's marital duty as understood by orthodox (Anglican) Christianity. As such, the genre of the familial letter provides a cautious technique through which Toland ironically distances himself from his heterodox arguments in print. The casual private letter absolves the deist writer from assuming authorial liability, should a seditious lawsuit be filed, which could result in hefty fines or long prison sentences.

Montagu's letter on Achmed Bey deploys the same cautious technique of ironic self-distancing when addressing controversial topics such as human pleasure, original sin, and marriage. She describes him as "a man of wit and learning" who indulged in wine-drinking despite the Islamic prohibitions against consuming alcohol. Achmed Bey does not adhere to Qur'anic law in this case and even discounts the Prophet's authority. In reply to Montagu's question about wine-drinking, he argues that all human beings are meant to take pleasure in the world because God would not have created a world of sensual pleasure if it were sinful. As in Toland's letter, this libertine argument dispenses with the biblical narrative of "the fall" and the doctrine of original sin: the prohibition against wine-drinking is nothing more than a secular law meant to control the vulgar people, who drink in excess, and not people "of quality," who drink in moderation (111). Achmed Bey adopts deism's two-tiered system for categorizing "religion": a secular, rational ideal practiced solely by elites and a superstitious faith associated mainly with uneducated, lower-class commoners.[25] For Montagu, this distinction between the rational monotheism of "people of quality" and the gross enthusiasm of "the vulgar people" allows her, an aristocratic Englishwoman, to sympathize with a Muslim nobleman despite the gender restrictions she would have normally encountered in English courtly society. She makes this last point clear in an earlier letter addressed to Pope (her main satiric target in this case): Achmed Bey is a polite Mahometan who, unlike his English counterparts, treats women as his intellectual equals—"I pass for a great scholar with him." In response to Montagu's inquiries, he maintains that the confinement of Muslim women is completely false, except that "we [Ottoman Muslims] have the advantage that when our wives cheat us nobody knows it" (54). She uses the deist letter form not only to dispel Western myths about Muslim women's oppression, but also to satirize the hypocritical, back-biting Anglicanism that defines elite society's patriarchal mores in early-eighteenth-century Britain.

In this respect, the English feminist, too, assumes the rational voice of the "Arabian physician." Through this technique of ironic self-distancing, Montagu's letters adopt the fictional character of the female deist who finds greater freedoms in the laws of elite Ottoman Muslims than in those of aristocratic Anglicans. The satiric genre of the deist-familial letter thus allows an aristocratic Englishwoman to claim agency. And yet she was reluctant to publish these letters during her lifetime. She shied away from doing so when urged by Mary Astell, a Tory feminist who admired her views on Islamic culture and wrote a laudable preface that appeared in the 1763 publication of *The Turkish Embassy Letters*.[26] Perhaps Montagu was wary of being issued a seditious libel, given that eighteenth-century English readers were not fooled by fictional Muslim characters. For example, Bishop William Warburton notes in his *The Divine Legation of Moses demonstrated* (1742–58) that "modern freethinkers" are notorious for employing "personated character[s]," so the author is "now a dissenter, then a Papist, now again a Jew, and then a Mahometan; and when closely pressed and hunted through all these shapes, at length starts up in his genuine Form, an Infidel confess'd."[27] Muslim, Jewish, and Pagan characters ventriloquize ideas that are too dangerous to convey otherwise. The popularity of this form of satiric writing might explain, in part, why the *Turkish Spy* letters achieved international notoriety and why Montagu chose not to publish her letters during her lifetime.

Freeborn Harem Women

I have shown thus far that Montagu appropriated the deist-familial letter genre for developing a gendered critique of male-dominated, upper-class English society. In this section, I argue that her feminist opposition to English patriarchy also applies to contract theory's false universals. Championed by many (although not all) male writers, the notion of contractual rights neglects to address how the inequalities of the marriage contract underwrite a gender-exclusive view of Anglican citizenship. Montagu's critique of contract theory entails a reevaluation of elite Ottoman women's domestic spaces—such as the imperial harem—as symbolic sites from which women can reclaim socioeconomic agency. Mohja Kahf has examined how harem discourse "rationalizes for European women and men the kinder, gentler suppressions of patriarchy at home," while it can also be used to deconstruct this patriarchal logic. Indeed, Billie Melman argues that the harem discourse featured in many early modern women's writings avoid the ideological opposition between "freeborn" Englishwomen and "enslaved" Muslim women.[28] Building on Kahf's and Melman's insights, I support situating *The Turkish Embassy Letters* in a deist freethinking tradition. For Montagu, heterodox Turkish women acquire citizenship by virtue of owning their bodies—the means of sexual, economic, and political reproduction in (male) civil society.

Montagu claims to be the first Christian to visit the Ottoman empire in centuries and the first woman who has had access to the Ottoman women's household (55, 60, 72, 86). Although recent scholarship on the early modern period has shown that these claims to exclusivity are an exaggeration,[29] Montagu, as an English ambassador's wife, would have had firsthand knowledge of Ottoman court life and the harem that previous European male travelers lacked. In fact, she frequently chides them for their ignorance of Muslim women's socioeconomic conditions. For instance, she sharply criticizes Aaron Hill and his "brethren voyage-writers" for their "lament on the miserable confinement of the Turkish ladies, who are, perhaps, freer than any ladies in the universe, and are the only women in the world that lead a life of uninterrupted pleasure, exempt from cares, their whole time being spent in visiting, bathing, or the agreeable amusement of spending money and inventing new fashions" (134). Rejecting the Oriental-patriarchal discourse used by male travel writers, Montagu insists that Turkish ladies have agency in pursuing pleasures, experiencing physical mobility, managing their wealth, and "inventing new fashions." It is this agency that makes them "freer than any ladies in the universe" (134).

Contra Pope and others, Montagu also corrects the mistaken patriarchal assumption that women have no souls under Islamic doctrine: "Our vulgar notion that they do not own women to have no souls is a mistake. 'Tis true they say they are not so elevated a kind and therefore must not hope to be admitted into the paradise appointed for the men, who are to be entertained by celestial beauties, but there is a place of happiness destined for souls of the inferior order where all good women are to be in eternal bliss"(100).

Montagu's notion of a separate and inferior paradise for women is also mistaken, because the Qur'an states that spiritual salvation is equally available to both men and women.[30] In this case, her view of Muslim women rests on a Qur'anic understanding of the biological and social inequality between the sexes despite their spiritual equality. The Qur'an sanctions unequal economic and sociopolitical distribution, especially in gender relations. Her description of a female-only paradise also sanctions this inequality: the freedom of "Turkish ladies" is based solely on their capacity for pleasure, mobility, wealth, consumption, and (as I will argue below) procreation; they never assume men's roles in the Ottoman state, and Montagu never claims anywhere in her letters that men and women are socially equal. On the contrary, her notion of liberty depends on the sharp dissimilarities between the sexes. Reflecting a communal Islamic virtue rooted in a spiritual egalitarianism without class and gender equality (a legal-civil notion suitable to her hierarchical class biases), the "freeborn" harem women experience a liberty that is an alternative to the (male) egalitarian ideals promoted in rights-based contract theory.[31]

In this respect, her letters avoid the gender-blind perspective espoused by many male deists who, rejecting Calvinist original sin and bodily corruption, exalted sexual pleasure based on travel accounts on polygamous religions that experience "free love" without sin, guilt, or jealousy. Islam was usually singled out by Henry Stubbe and other male deists as an example of such a religion, which, in contrast to the degenerate Catholic church's celibate ethos, tolerates nonmonogamous marriages.[32] Stubbe notes that Islamic polygyny is based on the ancient laws of "Jews and Judaizing Christians," who believed "that all men were absolutely obliged by that first precept of increasing and multiplying, which could not be fulfilled by the steril, or those who left no tissue behind them" (174). However, he was more interested in the egalitarian distribution of male property rights under Mahomet's hypermasculine, Machiavellian republic than with women's sexuality under Islamic law. Montagu, by contrast, does not ignore the civic virtues of sexual reproduction.

In her letter to Abbé Conti (the same one published anonymously in 1718), she describes Muslim women's sensual paradise as follows:

> the virtues which Mahommed requires of women to merit the enjoyment of future happiness are: not to live in such a manner as to become useless to the world, but to employ themselves as much as possible in making little *musulmans*. The virgins who die virgins and widows who marry not again, dying in mortal sin, are excluded out of paradise. For women, says he, not being capable to manage affairs of state, nor to support the fatigues

of war, God has not ordered them to govern or reform the world but he has entrusted them with an office which is no less honourable, even that of multiplying the human race. (110)

Adopting the libertine argument found in heterodox works such as Toland's *A letter from an Arabian physician*, Montagu argues that Muslim women fulfill the Old Testament injunction to be fruitful and multiply. She then ridicules Catholic (and implicitly Protestant) notions of virginity and chastity: "What will become of your saint Catherines, your saint Theresas, your saint Claras and the whole bead roll of your holy virgins and widows, who, if they are to be judged by this system of virtue will be found to have been infamous creatures that passed their whole lives in a most abominable libertinism"(110).

Moving beyond Toland's limited critique of men's marital "Duty," Montagu ascribes promiscuous sexuality exclusively to women, refusing to acknowledge men's libertine sexuality or condemn sensual women as "rakes." By describing orthodox Christian women as libertines, Montagu's transvaluation of Christian sexual mores marks a twofold assault against the Catholic sacrament of marriage and, more covertly, the questionable double standards embedded in radical Protestant views on gender and sexuality. The former conveys a standard critique of Catholic corruption, whereas the latter extends this critique in order to challenge a male deist view that bars women from libertine pleasures. In other words, her letters cleverly reveal that patriarchal modes of political rationality deceptively deploy the generic category "freeborn Englishmen" to ensure men's libertine pleasure while implicitly holding women accountable to an Augustinian-Pauline doctrine of the monogamous family.[33]

For Montagu, the procreation of "little *musulmans*" is a virtuous public "office." As odd as this feminist position may initially appear, it is worth recalling Gale Rubin's insight into how the subordination of women in a marriage contract requires that they repress their sexuality so men can freely exercise their "right" to own the female kin of their choice: the "exchange of women is a profound perception of a system in which women do not have full rights to themselves."[34] Montagu's deist views on female sexual agency counteracts patriarchal rationality—the "trafficking of women"—because male property "rights" to female bodies requires that women's sexual needs remain repressed. In this case, Christian virginity and chastity marks women's exchange value within a political economy in which the childbirth process is strictly subsumed under the demands of patriarchal gift exchanges.

Montagu's childbirth experience in Turkey is not subsumed under this political economy. In a letter to her younger sister, Lady Mar, Montagu describes her daughter's birth in Constantinople as "not half so mortifying here as in England." She notes that in accordance with Turkish custom her lying-in period after child-birth was shortened to three weeks rather than the required four weeks practiced in England (113). For her, elite Ottoman women are better off than their English counterparts because Turkish childbirth practices do not observe a "rites of pas-sage" Anglican ceremony in which the mother cannot be with her child until she has completed her one-month period in isolated confinement. Adrian Wilson argues that the lying-in period, a communal female-oriented event, "inverted the conjugal relation of individual male property," so "the wife's bodily energies and sexuality now, for the space of 'the month,' belonged to her; what marriage had taken from her, the childbirth ritual temporarily restored."[35] Montagu locates this inversion of the patriarchal marriage contract in Turkish childbirth practices. She repaid the visits made to her soon after her three-week lying-in period, leaving on a sea voyage a few days thereafter. When she referred to her childbirth years later, she told her daughter that "there was a mutual necessity on us both to part at that time, and no obligation on either side."[36] For Montagu, Turkish childhood practices grant women ownership over their bodies permanently, allowing some choice over their children's welfare without "obligation."

In *The Sexual Contract*, Carole Pateman elaborates on Rubin's insight. She argues that democratic contract theory entails a male sex-right agreement that excludes women from citizenship by symbolically assuming their childbearing reproductive capacities. Supposedly, men are naturally endowed with political reproduction, whereas "physical birth symbolizes everything that makes women incapable of entering the original contract and transforming themselves into civil individuals" (95–96). According to Pateman, seventeenth- and eighteenth-century English contract theory "refuses any acknowledgment of the capacity and creativity that is unique to women. Men appropriate to themselves women's natural creativity, their capacity physically to give birth—but they also do more than that. Men's generative power extends into another realm; they transmute what they have appropriated into another form of generation, the ability to cre-ate new political life, or to give birth to political right."[37] Sexual reproduction is metaphorically displaced onto men's political "right," effectively depriving women of their socioeconomic agency in the public civic sphere. Montagu re-sists this patriarchal logic first by ascribing female ownership to sexual reproduc-tion (Ottoman women are responsible for their bodies and children) and second by positing a domestic sphere in which women can exercise their sociopolitical power separate from a male-dominated public sphere. In Montagu's hyperbolic imagination, procreation in the Ottoman world functions as a public "office" in which sexually overactive mothers continually give birth to civic virtue.

Patriarchal marriage, in this case, is not the natural telos to women's socioeconomic existence. In contrast to marriage under English contract theory, Muslim marriage entails nothing more than a formal agreement. In one of her letters, Montagu refers to the marriage of the Grand Signor's eldest daughter as a "contract" rather than a "marriage," because this Muslim wife (unlike English wives) chose not to live with her husband and yet owns "the greatest part of his wealth" (65). Socioeconomic and sexual agency is not allowed in English common law views on marriage and inheritance, which became more severe in the eighteenth century due to a process of legal rationalization meant to ensure that the constitutional "right" to private property applies only to men.[38] By contrast, the Ottoman legal system continued to protect wives and daughters under Islamic law. This legal protection would have been impossible under English common law from the sixteenth century through the late nineteenth century.[39]

Indeed, Montagu is aware that Islamic law grants some legal protections for Muslim women that would have been unfathomable to their English counterparts. Women living in the Ottoman empire are entitled to full control of their assets; some power to initiate a divorce, inherit property and wealth; recognition of sexual claims in marriage; and other civil protections. In other words, they have economic and political control over their sexuality, even as second-class subjects of the Ottoman empire.[40] Shari'a court records and personal status laws in early modern Islamic societies confirm Montagu's observations: despite their seclusion in a patriarchal society, Ottoman women participated in reforming marriage, divorce, and inheritance. This participation is unprecedented in the Western democratic reforms that have occurred in the Middle East throughout the twentieth century.[41] In contrast to Islamic law, the English common law of coverture in marriage transfers the wife's claim to wealth and private property to her husband, because she is legally considered *femme coverte* (an infant) in need of a man's protection. That is to say, her legal identity is subsumed under her father's or husband's "rights." Thus, English marriage laws rob women of their legal, sexual, and economic entitlements, not to mention their national identity as "freeborn" English citizens.

Montagu dramatizes her liability as an English wife while visiting a Turkish bathhouse in Andrianople (Sophia). She portrays the women of the hammams living in a prelapsarian "state of nature" that is preferable to the "disdainful smiles or satirical whispers" of any "European court" (58): "[They] are without any distinction of rank by their dress, all being in the state of nature, that is, in plain English, stark naked, without any beauty or defect concealed. Yet there was not the least wanton smile or immodest gesture amongst them. They walked and moved with the same majestic grace which Milton describes of our general mother"(59).

By comparing these women to Milton's Eve—"our general mother"—Montagu ties libertine sexuality to a Miltonic understanding of innocent female pleasures and, conversely, dissociates carnal pleasure from original sin.[42] As a female deist, she eroticizes Muslim women's bodies to foreground the socioeconomic agency that defines their Islamic feminotopia. Resisting the male voyeuristic gaze, she refuses to present herself as a pornographic object for male consumption. Instead, she presents herself as incapable of undressing because English patriarchal norms prevent her from joining the naked Turkish ladies:

> The lady that seemed the most considerable amongst them entreated me to sit by her and would fain have undressed me for the bath. I excused myself with some difficulty, they being however all so earnest in persuading me, I was at last forced to open my shirt, and show them my stays, which satisfied them very well, for I saw they believed I was so locked up in that machine, that it was not in my own power to open it, which contrivance they attributed to my husband.(59–60)

Montagu's letter demystifies Christian patriarchal beliefs about modesty and chastity: her "stays" metaphorically represent a "machine" signifying a husband's right to own the female body. She describes herself as male property under the English law of coverture in marriage, despite her status as a wealthy aristocrat.[43] Patriarchal slavery is rendered an English, rather than Turkish, institution. Through this subtle satiric critique, the hammam scene exposes cherished conceptions of "freeborn Englishwomen" as founded on a false universal in which English "freedom" pertains only to property-holding, orthodox Anglican husbands.

Read together, her views on Muslim women's reproductive powers and her critique of the marriage contract in the hammam scene represent a notable effort to carve out an autonomous site for feminine publicity, defined as both a Habermasian sphere of public debate/consumption and as a Bakhtinian form of the carnivalesque. She compares the Turkish bathhouse to a women's coffeehouse: a private, female-dominated space that parodies a male-dominated public sphere in England (59). In Habermasian terms, London's coffeehouses symbolize a public sphere off-limits to genteel women in the eighteenth century. It is the primary locus for deist debates and subversive clandestine activities as well as an urban center for modern (male) sociability, a place for news, gossip, discussion, and debate.[44] Montagu may have experienced something akin to this public sociability in her visits to the imperial women's harem, a domestic sphere of female communion that involved discussion, consumption, and scandal. She recast this experience as the "perpetual masquerade" of veiled Muslim women: a permanent, carnival-like atmosphere that, in Bakhtinian terms, enables a dialogical public reasoning that is free to transgress social, political, and religious norms/laws (71).

The sanctity of this domestic sphere cannot, as Montagu rightly observes, be violated by the sultan and his ministers (72). Moreover, the female community created by gender segregation is conducive toward a productive engagement with politics, as exemplified in the *valide sultan*: powerful mothers of the Ottoman sultan.[45] According to Montagu, the public world of the sultan and his men, by contrast, is composed only of war and strife, a Hobbesian "state of nature" where men's lives are nasty, brutish, and short (51, 66). She endorses this view when discussing Ottoman political corruption but not when describing Turkish women's prelapsarian "state of nature" in the hammam. Nonetheless, the freedom of the so-called women's coffeehouse is racially and class coded: Ottoman women's natural beauty is determined by royal lineage and "shiningly white" skin color (59), whereas in her later travels to North Africa the ugly nakedness of dark-skinned, Tunisian Muslim women symbolizes a human subspecies of "baboons" (151).[46] For Montagu, the hammam exemplifies a Qur'anic egalitarianism that dispenses with contract theory's false universals but not with classism and racism.

As such, Montagu's alternative female publicity should be read as a strategy for constructing an exclusive national and imperial identity. In her letters, she sympathizes with elite Muslim women's capacity to own other female bodies—slaves. The egalitarian state of nature attributed to the hammam is therefore a false universal that excludes the naked slave girls inaccurately portrayed as living "without any distinction of rank by their dress" (59). Adam R. Beach has argued that her casual references to servant girls remain eerily silent about the violent exploitation involved in the Ottoman (and British) empire's slave trafficking. Despite her critique of marriage as slavery, she ignores the socioeconomic inequalities that define domestic slave women in the imperial harem.[47]

Veiled Tory Women

Montagu's appeal to "freeborn" harem women recasts women's national and imperial identity in terms of economic inequality, social subordination, and royal distinction—ideas that were inherited from Tory feminism. Her deist critique of false universals relies on a Tory oppositional language that she, as a staunch Whig, opposed throughout her lifetime. In fact, many early modern feminists were High Tories who shared a general suspicion of Whig republicanism, which protected only men's rights. They preferred to treat the political theology of the absolute monarch—the divine rights of kings—as a model for an autonomous female subjectivity that is empowered by virtue of its self-seclusion. This political theology is enshrined in an idealized account of the Anglican state: a divinely sanctioned institution that ensures both men's *and* women's *equal* subjection, the necessary precondition for securing liberty regardless of gender.[48] The reign of Queen Anne (1704–14) embodied the identity between the absolute monarch and autonomous femininity, not only because she symbolized renewed Tory values but also because she promised to reform the Whig republicanism that had suppressed women's civic identity as equal subjects of the crown. In the long run, Tory feminism lost its ideological appeal with Queen Anne's death, especially after the failed Jacobite attempts to restore the Stuart succession in 1715 and 1745. And yet, as Catherine Gallagher argues, the "absolutist imagination" endured in British feminism well into the century.[49] This paradigm would serve useful to Montagu's vision of imperial Ottoman women's self-seclusion as a model for a liberated female subjectivity in eighteenth-century Britain.

I define "Tory feminism" as a malleable political theology that employs the language of royal prerogative, passive obedience, and hierarchal privilege to articulate biblical precepts about gender equality from within a diffuse tradition of English freethinking. Hailed as "the first English feminist,"[50] the Tory Mary Astell relied on this freethinking tradition when criticizing the marriage contract. As Sarah Ellenzweig has thoroughly documented, freethinking skepticism was not incompatible with a Tory defense of the Anglican church, especially among heterodox Tory women such as Aphra Behn.[51] This Tory freethinking enabled Astell—despite her orthodoxy and party loyalty—to admire Montagu's writings; Astell's preface to the letters extolled her "skill to strike out a New Path" (234). By reading Montagu's writings in the context of Astell's *Reflections upon Marriage* (1700), I situate Montagu's critique of false universals within a freethinking feminist tradition that recasts Muslim veiling practices in Christian terms.

Astell's laudatory preface betrays an interest in Montagu's deist critique of English marriage laws as contrasted to equitable Ottoman-Islamic laws. Deeply admired by Montagu, she was requested to write a preface in 1724, noting that the writer originally lent her a manuscript of her letters "to satisfy my Curiosity in some enquirys I made concerning her Travels" (234). In her preface, Astell praises Montagu's stylish epistolary letters for avoiding the bland anti-Islamic stereotypes typically displayed in "Male Travels," written "in the same Tone, and stuft with the same Trifles" (234). In a cautionary note, she implores women to abstain from imposing English prejudices when reading about Montagu's travels in the Ottoman world: "Lay aside diabolical Envy, and its Brother Malice with all their accursed Company, Sly Whisperings, cruel backbiting, spiteful detraction, and the rest of that hideous crew, which I hope are very falsely said to attend the *Tea Table*, being more apt to think they frequent those Public Places where Virtuous Women never come"(235).

Traditionally associated with women's domestic spaces, the vices of envy, malice, gossip, and spite are personified as brothers—masculine prejudices. Astell not only inverts English patriarchal values but also relocates civic virtue in women's "Tea Table" rather than men's coffeehouses, "Public Places where Virtuous Women never come." Her cautionary note to female readers reinscribes Montagu's literary conventions: virtue belongs only to the secluded female communion of the "Tea Table," which finds its analogue in Montagu's hammam as a women's coffeehouse. Because the domestication of tea in eighteenth-century Britain was congruent with the domestication of the fluid female body, the "Tea Table" served as a metonymy for an autonomous upper-class "white" femininity based on uninhibited consumption, civic virtue, and bodily self-discipline—a mode of sociability that parallels the masculine subjectivity formed in the coffeehouse.[52] Astell deploys the positive metonymic significance of the tea table—freed from misogynist stereotypes about female domestic vices—to redefine female civic virtue in contrast to men's "Public Places" rather than Muslim women's domestic spaces.

The theme of female empowerment through domestic self-seclusion runs throughout Astell's feminist oeuvre. She writes against women's social liabilities under English coverture and encourages women to protect their autonomy by entering tightly knit female communities. Her *Serious Proposal to the Ladies* (1694) outlines this alternative to the marriage contract's sexual and socioeconomic inequalities as understood in English common law. This controversial work proposed a model for Protestant England's first female-only college, a feminist educational commune that Montagu enthusiastically champions. In 1752, she confessed to her daughter an admiration for Astell's "English monastery" and wished that she could assume the role of "lady abbess."[53] Although her use of the terms *monastery* and *abbess* recasts Astell's utopian scheme in Catholic rather than Protestant terms—implying a standard Whig critique of Tory cryptopapism—her letters transpose this liberating secluded space onto the Turkish bathhouse and the imperial harem. As such, her defense of imperial Muslim women's domestic agency is enabled by the Tory language of God-given privileges and prerogatives. This language is crucial for early modern feminists because it critiques the Whig republican citizenship that had elevated male contractual rights since the mid-seventeenth century.[54]

Astell's *Reflections* is primarily a Tory assault on the biblical justifications for the social contract, in which wives who enter the marriage contract are analogous to "free" and "equal" individuals who enter a political contract with the sovereign. She dismisses the biblical precedent for male superiority and argues that the marriage institution was founded on faulty customary laws rather than on divine command. The preface to the *Reflections* subversively deploys the controversial arguments of two male theorists to argue that prelapsarian men and women were created equally before God. She cites the *Leviathan* as proof that "in the Original State of things the Women was the Superior, and that her Subjection to the Man is an Effect of the Fall" based on Hobbes's case that the mother's claim to her child trumps the father's authority in premarital conditions: "[W]here there are no Matrimoniall lawes, it cannot be known who is the Father, unless it be declared by the Mother: and therefore the right to Dominion over the Child dependth on her will" (11). Likewise, Astell refers to William Whiston's heretical views on gender equality in the antediluvian period to show that "before the Fall there was a greater equality between the two Sexes" (11).[55] Astell's critique of marriage as a fallible social institution hinges on an egalitarian account of Adamic history. Her views anticipate the paradisal lifestyles of elite Ottoman women as featured in *The Turkish Embassy Letters.* In other words, Astell and Montagu share a radical scriptural hermeneutics that seeks to recuperate women's political agency using William Whiston—a pseudo-Islamic Arian whose freethinking views are indirectly vindicated in their works.

Astell's feminist appropriation of Hobbes and Whiston reflects a seventeenth-century tradition in which Englishwomen reread the scriptures in women-friendly and antipatriarchal terms.[56] As a radical extension of this earlier tradition, Astell is invested in salvaging Christian-Pauline female modesty from the marriage contract. In the preface to the *Reflections,* she marshals an impressive lineage of biblical women to argue against those who justify women's "natural" inferiority based on a patriarchal reading of St. Paul's letters. Astell writes that his letters prove, "The Relation between the two Sexes is mutual, and the Dependance Reciprocal, both of them Depending intirely upon God, and upon Him only; which one wou'd think is no great Argument of the natural Inferiority of either Sex"(13).

According to Astell, women's "natural" inferiority cannot be inferred from St.

Paul's demand that women be modest, remain socially subordinate to men, and observe proper dress codes while in church. She supports this argument through a feminist interpretation of Pauline veiling practices. According to her reading of St. Paul's 1 Corinthians, 11:3–10, "*Praying and Prophecying in the Church* are allow'd the Women, provided they do it with their Head Cover'd, as well as the Men; and no inequality can be inferr'd from hence" (11) (emphasis original). For Astell, Christian modesty applies equally to both genders. Moreover, St. Paul does not forbid women from speaking in church "but only takes care that the Women should signifie their Subjection by wearing a Veil" (20). As understood by Astell, the veil is a sign only of equal subjection to God. It does not prove women's inherent inferiority or their lack of intellect and spirituality. From her Tory perspective, "subjection" to God and king does not necessarily entail gender inequality and veiling is not essentially a Muslim practice. On the contrary, modest dress enables women's religious autonomy according to a primitive Pauline code of piety that, for Astell, differs from a historically imposed Augustinian understanding of patriarchal marriage.

In this case, Astell's feminist reading of Pauline veiling is closely aligned with Qur'anic injunctions on women's modest dress, which are not negatively tainted with gender inferiority, original sin, or demonic influence as traditionally propounded in orthodox interpretations of Pauline veiling practices.[57] As such, her hermeneutical approach is potentially heretical, if not outright radical. Her feminist investment in the Bible is historically rooted in the early-seventeenth-century querelle des femmes, from Rachel Speght to Margaret Fell Fox. However, her reliance on contemporary radical sources departs from this earlier tradition of trying to historicize alternatives to the misogynist interpretation of the Pauline letters.[58] Unlike preceding feminists, she readily exploits the writings of controversial male heretics Whiston and Hobbes to reconcile women-friendly representations in the scriptures with an egalitarian-prelapsarian state that predates divisions among Judaism, Christianity, and Islam.

Her appropriation of radical sources is not unusual. In fact, Astell's theological and philosophical writings brought her into conflict with High Church clergymen, mainly because her unwavering support of church and state authority did not prevent her from strategically incorporating radical pantheistic ideas when they proved expedient for scoring polemical points against her opponents.[59] In this respect, the idea that her reading of the scriptures shares certain anticlerical tendencies with Montagu's deist views, or that Montagu's description of Ottoman veiling practices could be read as an ethnographic application of her Pauline exegesis, is not particularly paradoxical or problematic.

As in Astell's vindication of Christian veiling practices, Montagu does not equate the veil with women's inferiority. For her, veiling is a "perpetual masquerade" offering Turkish women "entire liberty of following their inclinations without danger of discovery" (71). It allows for a feminine mode of physical mobility that is denied in English patriarchal society, in which women must always be escorted by a male chaperone. She notes that "'Tis very easy to see they have more liberty than we have, no woman, of what rank so ever being permitted to go in the streets without two muslins, one that covers her face all but her eyes and another that hides the whole dress of her head" (71). In this case, veiling symbolizes Muslim women's sexual, economic, and physical mobility in the public sphere, allowing them to engage in illicit and extramarital love affairs without being detected by their husbands or any other men: "You may guess then how effectually this disguises them . . . 'tis impossible for the most jealous husband to know his wife when he meets her, and no man dare either touch or follow a woman in the street" (71). Yet during Montagu's trip to the mosque, the anonymity of this "disguise," in which she is clothed as an upper-class Muslim woman, paradoxically renders her public identity visible to others. In Bakhtinian terms, the veil's "perpetual masquerade" offers a transgressive fantasy of private anonymity that constitutes a dialogical public sphere for women.

Even though Astell and Montagu share positive views about the veil's feminist potential, they do not share a theological position on female modesty. Unlike Astell, Montagu ascribes libertine freedoms to veiled, "faithful wives":

> You may easily imagine the number of faithful wives very small in a country where they have nothing to fear from their lovers' indiscretion, since we see so many that have the courage to expose themselves to that in this world, and all the threatened punishments of the next, which is never preached to the Turkish damsels. Neither have they much to apprehend from the resentment of their husbands, those ladies that are rich having all their money in their own hands, which they take with them upon a divorce with an addition which he is obliged to give them. Upon the whole, I look upon the Turkish women as the only free people in the empire. (71–72)

Whereas Astell locates the freedom of Christian veiling practices in a Pauline tradition of modesty, Montagu locates the freedom of Islamic veiling practices within a libertine tradition of immodesty. For her, the veil allows women to *own* their bodies, because they receive a secular Islamic education that teaches them to believe in the pleasures of "this world" rather than in the salvation of the afterlife. It is this anti-Pauline theology that renders them "the only free people in the empire." However, Montagu and Astell want to recover the veil's feminist significance beyond the marriage contract's gender inequality. Despite their opposing theologies, Astell probably would have been amused with Montagu's sympathetic assessment of veiled Muslim women: "As to their morality or good conduct . . . the Turkish ladies don't commit one sin the less for not being Christians" (71). Understood from Astell's theological perspective, Montagu's writings cast these ladies as more accurately following Pauline prescriptions than their Anglican counterparts, who have exchanged the biblical veiling practices that would have guaranteed their spiritual gender equality for the false universals of English (Whig) liberty.

Montagu locates the veil's freedom exclusively within an Islamic (male) political economy. In contrast to Astell's theology, she refuses to ascribe agency to Christian veiling practices. Her May 1718 letter to the Countess of Bristol describes Christian-Armenian marital ceremonies as "odd and monstrous" when discussing the oppressive "silken veil" worn by the brides. According to her, these women are forced to wear a cap on their head while carried to church, where the priest pressures them into accepting an arranged marriage despite their choice. On arriving home, her "veil [is] never lifted up, not even by her husband, till she has been three days married"—a Christian veiling custom that Montagu equates with a living death worse than "slavery" (139). Even though she acknowledges that the Armenians "seem to incline very much to Mr. Whiston's doctrine," the Greek church's pseudo-Arian faith does not render the veil a symbol of women's "perpetual masquerade" (138). In other words, deist-Islamic theology enables veiled women's socioeconomic agency, whereas Arian Christian theology prevents this agency. For Montagu, veiling practices signify "slavery" only for Christian cultures.

However, this negative association does not imply that Muslim veiling is not bound to patriarchy. Montagu realizes that the veil could trigger men's violence. She notes that the sexual promiscuity of veiled Muslim women is punishable, as it is "very fully in the power of their husbands to revenge them if they are discovered, and I don't doubt but they suffer sometimes for their indiscretions in a very severe manner" (135). As described in her letter, she notes the discovery of a murdered "young woman": "About two months ago there was found at daybreak not very far from my house the bleeding body of a young woman, naked, only wrapped in a coarse sheet, with two wounds with a knife, one in her side and another in her breast. She was not yet quite cold, and so surprisingly beautiful . . . but it was not possible for anybody to know her, no woman's face being known"(135–36). Anonymous physical mobility does not always protect Turkish women. Even though she glosses this tragic incident as "extremely rare," she implicitly recognizes that Muslim veiling practices reflect a political economy in which the Turkish wife's body is subject to her husband's sexual violence. Hence, Montagu's letters do not idealize the veil as they do the hammam and the harem but instead uses the image as a symbol for a patriarchal Muslim order that is, relatively speaking, preferable to England's Christian-based false universals.

Despite their opposing positions on orthodox Christianity, Astell and Montagu share a scriptural hermeneutics that enables them to sympathize with veiled Muslim women, albeit for very different reasons. For Astell, veiling practices within the Christian (and Islamic) tradition render women subordinate subjects who nonetheless acquire spiritual equality by virtue of their modesty; for Montagu, only veiling practices in a deistic-Islamic (anti-Pauline) tradition can guarantee women's socioeconomic and sexual (libertine) agency, though it cannot offer women protection from patriarchal violence. At any rate, they equally rely on the political theology of the absolute monarch—Astell locates it in the Pauline church and Montagu in the imperial harem—and refuse to treat the veil as a negative foil for "freeborn" Englishwomen. Their Tory-inflected and heterodox interpretations of the veil represent an early feminist attempt to redefine Anglican citizenship in the prophetic language of Mahometanism (primitive monotheism) rather than in the post-Lockean language of (Whig) false universals.

Delarivier Manley's *Almyna; or, the Arabian Vow*

Montagu's epistolary letters accomplished what other "feminine" genres could not: a rationalist critique of contract theory vis-à-vis the female deist.[60] And yet her critique was first developed not in Astell's writings but in Delarivier Manley's *Almyna; or, the Arabian Vow* (1707): a play in which a freethinking Muslim heroine, Almyna, defies the sultan's violence against women. Montagu deeply admired Manley's plays and her Tory fiction, *The New Atlantis* (1709), which led to the arrest of Manley along with her printer and publisher. Montagu eagerly sought to obtain this "secret history" of the corrupt lives of powerful Whig politicians during the reign of Stuart kings and queens.[61] Thus, Manley warrants special attention as an influential feminist. Indeed, her interest in Islam and the Ottoman empire was probably inherited from her father, Sir Roger Manley, one of the earliest writers to refine the genre of the deist letter as the possible author of the first two volumes of the *Letters Writ by a Turkish Spy*.[62] Instead of reading *Almyna* as a straightforward Tory (or Jacobite) allegory on the divine rights of monarchs under Queen Anne's reign, I argue that the play's politicized language of female sexual reproduction reflects radical feminist concerns that cut across party lines. As Rachel Carnell has argued, many Whig historians label this play retrospectively "Tory propaganda" and thereby ignore the "multiple and conflicting political ideologies within the play."[63] These multiple and conflicting ideologies may be located in the heterodox rationalizations articulated by the play's outspoken Muslim feminist. Variously understood by literary critics as an appropriation of the ironic narrative style of Antoine Galland's *Arabian Nights Entertainment* (English translation in 1705–6; French translation from the Arabic, 1704), such viewpoints disregard *Almyna*'s self-conscious co-option of deist freethinking discourse.[64]

Bernadette Andrea, Ros Ballaster, and Bridget Orr argue for an identification between Manley's heroine and the character of Scheherazade, who uses her storytelling abilities to postpone, and thus effectively resist, the sultan's sexual and political violence.[65] In many ways, *Almyna*'s main plot is modeled after the Scheherazade narrative. Set in eleventh-century Muslim Spain, the seat of the Umayyad caliphate after its defeat in Damascus in the eighth century, *Almyna* dramatizes the tension between a misogynist sultan who has corrupted Islam and a loquacious Muslim woman who seeks to reform the prophetic faith. Almyna, "the Eldest daughter to the [Grand] Vizier," the highest-ranking official in the court, is to marry Abdalla against the wishes of his brother the Caliph Almanzor, the "Sultan of the East" who has vowed to murder all women (103).[66] His misogynist views are a product of his marriage to his first queen, who committed adultery with one of his slaves. Ever since, the sultan uses the Qur'an to justify his views on women as sensual beings without souls. Thus, the sultan marries a virgin every night only to later murder her. The Grand Vizier's decision to prevent the marriage between Abdalla, the sultan's successor, and Almyna—a decision prompted by the discovery of Abdalla's secret love for his other daughter, Zoradia—leads to Almyna's vow to marry the sultan and end his tyranny. Despite her father's warnings, she persists in her "Enthusiastick" revelation, in which she is the chosen one who will rescue all the "virgin-daughters" in the sultan's kingdom (131). She calls herself a "Prophetick Maid" inspired by the Prophet: "sure our great Prophet, has enlarg'd my Soul; / I speak from him inspir'd" (131). By the end of the play, the love-stricken Almanzor marries Almyna and converts to her reformed faith. As Bernadette Andrea has argued, the near-anagram Almyna/Manley suggests that the playwright's sympathetic identification with the Muslim heroine marks the triumph of Scheherazade's sentimental romance over Tory feminists' rationalist discourse.

However, this interpretation does not imply that Almyna's prophetic mission "veers from the rationalist focus of the 'first feminists.'"[67] On the contrary, Almyna's triumph is made possible through the scriptural hermeneutics employed by "first feminists" such as Astell. As Ros Ballaster admits, Almyna is unlike Scheherazade in her use of "philosophy and history rather than narrative to charm her suitor/husband."[68] As such, Almyna-Scheherazade is a female deist who employs her oratory and argumentative skills to persuade the sultan to end his patriarchal tyranny. In act 3, scene 2, Almyna appeals to classical philosophy and literature to argue for the exemplary virtue of historical women: Semiramis, Judith, Virginia, Lucretia, Portia, Clelia, and Cleopatra. She also adopts a freethinking deist argument: the sultan has corrupted the prophetic faith with irrational "mysteries" to justify patriarchal notions about women's apolitical and inferior nature on Qur'anic grounds. During her first confrontation with the sultan, Almyna deduces two materialist arguments to prove the existence of women's soul:

Cast but thy Eyes around the fair Creation,

And say what Beings challenge such perfection.

Are we not made for the most perfect work,

And therefore surely, the most perfect Creatures?

Besides, be not the Means, the Joys, the Pains the same,

In the production, of the Females, as the Males

If from the Parents, you derive the Soul,

When they beget Immortal, feel they no Distinction.

Or if, the Soul, be with the Life infused,

Wou'd not the Womb that holds 'em, find a Difference,

Since then their Beings, and their Birth's the same,

They dye the same, and the same Way shall rise,

And to Immortal Life adjudged as you be,

Dost thou not tremble; Sultan, but to think?

How fatal to thee, the Mistake may prove?

What will our Prophet say, at thy last day?

When all thy Queens, shall urge him, to revenge 'em? (4.1.146–47)

Offering a teleological argument on divine perfection followed by a biological argument on sexual reproduction, Almyna strategically deploys the radical language of deism while strictly avoiding the creationist story of Adam and Eve and the doctrine of original sin. Similar to the rhetoric used in *A letter from an Arabian physician*, Almyna argues that women must be perfect, because they are a part of the perfection manifested in the divine creation; she uses Qur'anic scripture to prove that men and women, physically produced from the womb of their mother, must be equally endowed with the same soul.[69] If the sultan rejects this conclusion, then he must agree to a ridiculous absurdity: mothers who produce men without souls, monarchs without political agency. As does Montagu in her deist letters, Manley ties men's symbolic reproduction of political power to women's physical procreation.

In this regard, Almyna's freethinking philosophy seeks to undercut the Sultan's prime justification for women's inferior reproductive capacity. For him, the "drudgery ... of propagation" is what renders women animalistic beings "without a Soul." Because of female sexuality's "glittering Ills," men have been led astray into the "Mother-vices," the fallen world of sin: "Had she not produced those glittering Ills,/We had like Trees and Plants, from Sun, and Earth:/Our Common Parents rose; masculine, and wise,/Free from the Mother-vices, folly, dotage,/Enervate softness, and destroying Passions" (113). The sultan's botanical conception of Adamic history vindicates men as the natural procreators, sinless fathers who give birth asexually (botanists did not consider the reproduction of plants to be a sexual process until the late eighteenth century), and debases women as unnatural procreators, mothers who give birth sexually. According to the Sultan's misogynist argument, the prelapsarian condition of Adam and Eve, "Our Common Parents," would have continued uninterrupted had not women introduced the sinful act of physical procreation. In this twisted account of biblical-Qur'anic history, *reproduction* belongs only to men. In fact, the sultan firmly believes that female sexuality, led by a base instinctual drive "to Multiply," has unnaturally assumed men's reproductive "Prerogative": "Instinct to them, as to their fellow Brutes,/Goads on, to Multiply, 'tis true, indeed,/(In imitation of our Sexe's Charter,/With a Prerogative usurpt from Man)" (116). By usurping men's natural ability to reproduce asexually, the sultan argues, women have violated the original Adamic contract of men, "our Sexe's Charter." They have robbed men's "high born Reason" (116). Alymna combats this patriarchal view of the social contract by arguing that female reproduction is central to spiritual life according to the Qur'an and that therefore men, as the sources of vice, have unnaturally usurped women's ability to reproduce civic virtue.

The sociopolitical significance of female sexual reproduction frames the play's dramatic conclusion. According to Almyna's interpretation of the Qur'an, if all women lack souls and should be murdered, then patriarchal monarchy cannot reproduce itself—it cannot give birth to the next male heir to the throne. Ruth Herman argues that *Almyna* demystifies the Hanoverian monarchy by questioning the symbolic act of oath-taking and patriarchal inheritance, namely, the 1689 oath of allegiance to William and Mary.[70] Likewise, the play demystifies the wedding vow—the patriarchal "right" that underwrites the royal vow. The sultan's brother, Abdalla, never marries due to his mistreatment of Zoradia, which results in the loss of patriarchal succession. In a rash effort to save Almyna from the sultan's wrath, Abdalla accidentally dies on the Grand Vizier's sword and Zoradia on Abdalla's sword. The sultan's concluding speech ends with a pun on the folly of "unlawful Oaths": "His [Abdalla's] Life, repay'd his falseness to *Zoradia*/ By me, let 'em avoid unlawful Oaths./ (Nor think that Provocation's an Excuse,) / Robb'd as I am, of my Succession here" (168). From a Tory perspective, "unlawful Oaths"—in marriage and monarchy—result only in the dissolution of the social contract through a civil war rivalry between the sultan and his brother, who fought for Almyna's feminist cause (ironically by betraying his "oath" to Zoradia and inadvertently killing her). In this case, Almyna, as the new sultana, is the only one in the position to reproduce the political power of the Umayyad caliphate.

Although Almyna embodies Tory hopes for Queen Anne's matriarchal reproduction of the next Stuart heir, the play also stages a gendered account of English republican virtue that cannot be confined to partisan politics. Spoken by the English actor-manager and playwright Colley Cibber, the play's prologue defends the heroic tradition of English drama from the harmful effects of Italian operatic music. English drama is a "chaste wife" whose virtuous reputation has been unjustly slandered by the foreign Italian opera, "a Strumpet by her Price" (100). The prologue argues that the English must remain loyal to their native genre if they are to retain their national character as other nations have done: "*Let* Frenchmen *Dance; th'* Italians, *Sing*" (100). The epilogue reiterates this argument in the language of anti-Catholicism: Italian opera's "Monastick Alters" and "Hyming Train" will plunge England into the dark ages, "Where Faith, not Reason, does the Rule maintain" (102). These xenophobic and religious fears were first expressed in John Dennis's *An Essay on the Opera's After the Italian Manner* (London, 1706). He argues that Italian opera's effeminate proto-Catholic passions threaten to destroy England's manly virtue as championed in heroic drama's rationalist tradition: the cultural foundation of English liberty, Protestant values, and maritime commerce since the golden age of Queen Elizabeth. He hyperbolically concludes that, owing to Italian opera's "effeminate airs," "the Declension of Poetry should portend the fall of Empire."[71]

In her preface, Manley writes that she modeled her play after Dennis's definition of English republican virtue: "The Character of *Almyna* was drawn (tho' faintly) from the that excellent Pen of Mr. *Dennis*, who, in his *Essay upon Opera's*, has given us a View of what Heroick Vertue ought to attempt" (97–98). Manley, relying on his views, blames the Italian opera for the play's poor attendance when it was first staged on December 8, 1706: she writes that the play, although "admirably Acted," failed to attract attention because it was performed at "so ill-fated a time, viz the immediate week before Christmas between devotion and *Camilla*" (97).[72] The allusions to "devotion" and "Camilla" possibly refer to the earliest productions of the Italian opera at Drury Lane, most notably Giovanni Bononcini's *Il trionfo di Camilla, regina de' Volsci.* This opera witnessed an almost unrivaled popularity when it was staged several times in London from 1706 to 1728.[73] For Manley and Dennis, English drama has a civic responsibility to protect republican virtue from the aesthetic corruption of a foreign Italian culture that Britons have seen traditionally as the pinnacle of Catholic tyranny. Symbolizing the republican virtue that abolished the patriarchal rights of Catholic kingship under Queen Elizabeth, Manley's new sultana hails the restoration of Protestant England's golden age under Queen Anne. But unlike Dennis's hypermasculine golden age, the ending of *Almyna* radically suggests that this restoration can be fulfilled only when misogynist men, Whigs and Tories, learn to practice the free-thinking philosophy of gender equality.

Thus, the Toryism implicit in *Almyna*'s dramatic action is thoroughly radical-ized across party lines, especially when considering the feminist careers of the star actresses who performed this play. Almyna's role was played by the famous and professionally astute Elizabeth Barry (1658–1713), an actress who acquired financial independence as a theater comanager. In 1695, she helped establish the Lincoln's Inn Fields Company, in which she unofficially assumed the position of theater comanager with her partner, the famous actor Thomas Betterton. In this position, Barry was one of the first actresses to exercise business management on an equal footing with men, sign a contract in her name, negotiate benefits, choose the best dramatic roles, and control the company's payment distribution.[74] An-other partner and power broker in the company, the actress Anne Bracegirdle (1663–1748), who played the role of Zoradia, was paid a salary equal to that of male actors, including Betterton. Because of her rivalry with a young actress, she quit the theater during the 1706–7 season.[75] As Manley explains in the preface, this decision hampered plans to restage *Almyna* (97). Indeed, Manley deeply admired these actresses' performances, which she saw as essential to the female roles spe-cifically tailored for they alone to play.

In *Rival Queens: Actresses, Performances, and the Eighteenth-Century British Theater*, Felicity Nussbaum argues that these "actresses … were among those who constituted the first female subjects in the public arena."[76] In their unprecedented access to the wealth and property that pertained only to men's "rights" under English common law, eighteenth-century actresses lived according to the first feminists' philosophy. On stage, their bodies served as national icons of "exceptional virtue" not incompatible with their sexually promiscuous lives offstage. They self-consciously embodied the classical republican idea of *virtú* although they were notorious for choosing an unorthodox life of sexual transgression and neglecting the Christian patriarchal values of female chastity.[77] In the context of these star actresses' professional, financial, and sexual autonomy, Almyna's freethinking philosophy acquires radical feminist connotations: Barry's performance of an alternative British womanhood translates the past republican virtue of a foreign Muslim culture into national debates about heroic drama and gender equality during Queen Anne's reign. On a performative level, *Almyna* codes Englishwomen's sexual and socioeconomic agency as quintessentially Islamic.

This feminist adoption of Muslim culture reflects the libertine values associated with elite freethinking culture. An informed audience pondering the heroic virtue of Almyna on stage would have known that Barry had a daughter, out of wedlock, with John Wilmot, the second Earl of Rochester. Notorious for his subversive authorship of bawdy and blasphemous poems, Rochester—who allegedly trained the young Barry for the theater—was involved in a secret sexual affair with her that resulted in an illegitimate offspring in 1677. This affair prompted many satiric assaults against her character, equating her financial success in the theater with libertinism, blasphemy, and prostitution. After *Almyna* premiered, her reputation as Rochester's mistress would continue to inflect the female roles she performed as well as her reception among the audience.[78] Indeed, Rochester's name looms over this play. In the title page to the play's printed edition, Manley dedicates her work to "the Countess of SANDWICH," Elizabeth Montagu (1674–1757): the second daughter of Rochester, she married into the Whig Montagu family, which was once connected to Oliver Cromwell's republican cause. According to Rachel Carnell, Manley sought patronage from the wealthy Earl of Sandwich through his wife, infamously known for her cruel and unusual treatment of her husband.[79] Manley's interest in polite Whig culture explains why she omitted "the Ceremony in the first Act . . . upon the dislike of that incomparable LADY, to whom this *Play* is inscrib'd, who is Mistress of a Genius not be deriv'd from a less glorious Original, than the immortal Earl of *Rochester*" (97). A possible allusion to the 1689 oath of allegiance, "the Ceremony" was omitted from future reproductions to appease the countess's Whig sensibilities. But without compromising the play's radical feminism, Manley strategically aligns her work with the royalist and libertine politics of the countess's Tory father, a favorite of the old Stuart court. In this symbolic gesture, Manley relies on Rochester's "immortal name" to negotiate her conflicting political and feminist allegiances within an elite freethinking culture that encompasses Whig and Tory camps.

As evident in Barry's role as Almyna, Rochester's name also recalls, indirectly, radical Protestant sympathy for Mahometanism. A "radical royalist," Rochester was attracted to an interregnum freethinking Protestantism that did not conflict with his unequivocal loyalty to the late Stuart Anglican regime. For example, he enthusiastically read excerpts of Henry Stubbe's republican account of the virtuous Islamic monarchy from Charles Blount's deist letter.[80] Royalist admiration for the Prophet's restored Christian monarchy constitutes the context in which Barry, as Almyna, could embody the heroic republican virtue of the Umayyad caliphate and, in effect, supplement Anglocentric accounts of Christian liberty. By casting republican virtue in feminist and Islamic terms, the play defamiliarizes the sacramental marriage "vow" as understood in English common law.

Indeed, the play never insinuates that patriarchal violence is a problem rooted in Islam. On the contrary, the sultan's misogynist theology—the doctrine that women are "without a Soul" as revealed by "our Prophet"—is exposed in the play as a groundless absurdity alien to Islamic teachings (112). Not only do Almyna and Abdalla dispute this crude patriarchal stereotype, but even the Grand Vizier condemns the sultan's fallacious reasoning. At the opening of the play, he cries "horrid Murther!" regarding the sultan's rage against women "Under the sacred Name and veil of Marriage" (106). Inferring his misogynist doctrine from "the faults of One," the sultan's Adamic account of human sexuality dramatizes Christian theological arguments that cast women, starting with Eve, as evil based on limited empirical and scriptural evidence (107). Far from representing Islam, the sultan's obsession with female original sin satirically parodies misogynist Christian views. In Brechtian terms, the play stages—via the actresses' iconic performance—an alienation effect that compels Englishwomen in the audience to confront their "slavery" as a product of a corrupt political theology that unlawfully sanctifies the marriage/social contract's gender inequalities. Contrary to Manley's moderate Toryism and political allegiances, the play proposes that Englishwomen could acquire liberty only when they use their independent reasoning to rebel against all patriarchs—fathers, husbands, priests, and kings.

In conclusion, *Almyna* offers a model of oppositional politics that does not marginalize the rationalist freethinking rhetoric that informs the writings of Tory feminists.[81] Indeed, Tory opposition between 1717 and 1760 is a crucial part of the untold story of English radical expression, in which freethinking Tory writers formulated many methods of protest that would be used by Whig republicans decades later.[82] Feminist admiration for freeborn harem women's privileges and prerogatives is rooted in intertwined republican and royalist discourses about Mahometanism, as evident in Rochester's brand of Tory freethinking. In the case of Astell, Manley, and Montagu, British feminism needs to be understood holistically as a mix of discourses in which the political theology of the absolute monarch, a deist philosophy of libertine sexuality, and the antiauthoritarian ideals of contractual rights played equally prominent, if ultimately divergent, roles in fashioning the skeptical critique of a male-dominated church and state order. Ultimately, Astell and Manley established the theological terms for a Tory critique of Whig false universals that came into fruition in Montagu's polemical ethnography. Only in this limited sense can critics consider these three writers pioneer feminists who fostered a freethinking approach to the self-secluded lives of imperial Muslim women to contest gender-exclusive conceptions of Anglican citizenship at the moment of their discursive formation.

Coda: Gender, Nation, and Empire

The genealogy of eighteenth-century British feminism remains incomplete if critics continue to fetishize Montagu's erotic experience in the hammam, ignoring the complex intersection between a deist epistolary letter genre that championed Islamic virtue and a Tory feminism that contested contractual right's false universals. These two intellectual traditions cross paths in *The Turkish Embassy Letters*, producing a sustained critique of English marital laws. Hence, the Tory-freethinking idea that "Turkish women [are] the only free people in the empire" implicitly grounds women's identity in gender-inclusive notions of property/ slave ownership, social subordination, racial hierarchy, and royal distinction. In short, Montagu's deist critique of men's false universals results in the consolidation of another false universal: (elite white) Englishwomen who are the only free people in the British empire. Even though British imperial claims to global domination were an elusive aspiration in the early eighteenth century, the feminist and imperialist ideologies implicit in her understanding of elite Ottoman women converge in a series of "embassy" letters that were written in the context of a diplomatic mission to resolve tensions between Austria and Turkey, a key strategy that promoted British commercial interests in the Mediterranean, eastern Europe, and parts of the Ottoman mainland.[83] As Srinivas Aravamudan has cogently argued, her cross-cultural encounter with elite Muslim women ultimately grounds female subjectivity in an Anglocentric paradigm, signaling Englishwomen's emerging imperial and national self-definition. In this regard, Islamic republicanism is a form of symbolic inoculation that protects the English body politic from foreign eastern contagions.[84]

Yet Montagu's writings also signal a subversive feminist disruption in England's fantasy of eastern empire-building. Her embassy letters are a testament to the short-term failure of English diplomatic efforts to secure a trading monopoly in the Levant. Much to her disappointment, her husband, Edward Wortley, was recalled by Joseph Addison, the English secretary of foreign affairs, because his pro-Turkish sympathies would endanger the prospect for a European peace between Austria and Turkey, a prerequisite for protecting the Levant Company's Mediterranean shipping routes from maritime conflicts. In other words, Edward Montagu failed to fulfill his consul duty. He could not represent his country's national interests: to protect the trading privileges exclusively recognized under the royal charter of the Levant Company, his private employer. On the strong recommendation of Hapsburg emperor Charles VI, he was replaced by Sir Robert Sutton, who successfully negotiated the Treaty of Passarowitz on July 1718. Engineered by English and Dutch diplomats, this treaty not only brought the Austro-Turkish and Venetian-Turkish (1716–18) wars to an abrupt end but also resulted in ceding Ottoman territories in the Balkans to Austria in exchange for awarding the Levant Company with lucrative markets and safe transit in Eastern Europe. This treaty promoted English commercial domination in the Levant.[85] In this context, *The Turkish Embassy Letters* should be classified as an antiembassy narrative—an annoying glitch in British imperial ambitions for global trade.

In the long run, Montagu's freethinking feminism lost momentum in the late eighteenth century and was eventually replaced by the figure of the immured harem woman as epitomized in Mary Wollstonecraft's *Vindication of the Rights of Woman* (1792). However, this shift does not imply that the Islamic republicanism championed by Astell, Manley, and Montagu was short-lived. The impeachment trial of Warren Hastings, the governor-general of the East India Company (see chapter 3), would remobilize deist-feminist accounts of imperial Muslim women. In February 1788, Edmund Burke gave a sensational public speech in Westminster Hall condemning Warren Hastings's colonial abuses in India and casting the Mughal empire as an Islamic republic that protects men and women equally under an ancient constitution. From Burke's Whig perspective, Hastings has not only ignored the universal natural law and morality practiced in England

and India but he has also raped a virgin country renowned for its time-honored commitment to civic virtue, which Burke describes as a veiled Muslim woman whose privileges and prerogatives have been unjustly violated. Montagu's disruptive feminist legacy resurfaces as British imperial guilt—the patriarchal-imperial dispossession of Bengal's freeborn harem women.

CHAPTER THREE

In Defense of the Ancient Mughal Constitution

Edmund Burke, India, and the Warren Hastings Trial

To name a Mahometan Government is to name a Government by
law. It is a law enforced by stronger sanctions than any law that
can bind an European Sovereign, exclusive of the Grand Seignior.
The law is given by God, and it has the double sanction of law and
of religion, with which the Prince is no more to dispense than any
one else. And, if any man will produce the Khoran to me, and will
but shew me one text in it that authorizes in any degree an arbitrary power in the Government, I will declare that I have read
that book and been conversant in the affairs of Asia to a degree in
vain. There is no such a syllable in it; but on the contrary, against
oppressors by name every letter of that law is fulminated.

Edmund Burke, "Speech on the Opening of Impeachment,"
Feb. 16, 1788

In February 1788 in Westminster Hall, Edmund Burke condemned Warren Hastings, the East India Company's governor-general from 1773 to 1784, for com-
mitting worse injustices in India than his Muslim counterparts in the Mughal
empire. According to Burke, Hastings should be impeached for importing tyranny to Hindustan, a nation protected by the long constitutional rule of a "Mahometan Government." In the epigraph, he challenges contemporary stereotypes
about Oriental despotism: he argues that the "Khoran" does not contain a "syllable" authorizing "arbitrary power." Seeking to undermine Hastings's defense—
that he ruled according to Muslim arbitrary law—he upholds Islam as a civic
religion that embodies the Whig principles of a limited parliamentarian monarchy. He casts Hastings's colonial abuses in India as a threat to both British
and Mughal governance, a shared constitutional history defined by "the double

sanction of law and of religion." Building on the work of Robert Travers, I argue in this chapter that Burke recruited Islamic republicanism for redefining British constitutional liberty.[1] Stemming from a republican tradition that cast the Qur'an in common law terms, his defense of the ancient Mughal constitution rendered a pro-Mahometan reformist ideology the standard by which the nation is to be morally judged, even as the trial concluded with Hastings's acquittal in 1795 and the subsequent discrediting of Indo-Islamic politics.

In an effort to recover a progressive version of Burke, recent scholarship has shifted its attention to his pre-1789 views on America, Ireland, and India, reassessing his overall contribution to English political thought without confining his Whiggery to the counterrevolutionary politics that typify his later writings;[2] and yet much remains to be said about his radical Enlightenment approach toward Islam, which is part of the larger discourse I identify that shaped prevailing attitudes about England's ancient constitution. Before the publication of *The Reflections on the Revolution in France* (1790), he was an active spokesperson for the Second Marquis of Rockingham's oppositional Whig party, which gathered information about the East India Company's unconstitutional practices in order to critique the crown's overreach. By the 1780s, Burke became suspicious of Warren Hastings. The Anglo-Irish parliamentarian tried to curtail his power through Charles James Fox's India Bill, which sought to place the EIC under a parliamentary commission. The House of Lords defeated this bill only to later pass William Pitt the Younger's India Act, which ensured that crown ministers were solely responsible for overseeing Company affairs instead. Ultimately, information about Hastings's colonial policies in India, along with Burke's growing condemnation of EIC corruption, became entangled in British constitutional debates, precipitating national anxieties about the king-in-parliament during King George III's turbulent reign. In retaliation to crown power, Burke, Fox, and Richard Brinsley Sheridan, the dominant faction of the Rockinghamite Whig opposition, resorted to impeaching Hastings (whom the king favored) and persuaded the House of Commons to send him to trial before the House of Lords in 1787. For Burke, the impeachment was an urgent issue that will determine "the nature of our constitution itself," the need to protect civic virtue from moneyed interest, secret influence, and arbitrary rule (6. 271). In this political context, the trial's aim was not simply to convict one man but to present a public forum in which the ancient constitution could be staged as a cross-cultural appeal to England's national past *and* India's Muslim history. An imaginative Whig living under the radical Enlightenment, Burke relies on this highly publicized impeachment scandal to recast imperial Britain as a virtuous Islamic republic.[3]

My analysis of Burke's thought contributes to literary and historical debates about the need for an "imperial turn" in eighteenth-century scholarship. Making transnational and global connections is important because, as Antoinette M. Burton puts it, empire abroad is a "fundamental and constitutive part of English culture and national identity at home."[4] Peter J. Marshall, H. V. Bowen, and Sudipta Sen have shown that eighteenth-century British India does not exist apart from the metropolitan political and legal context. Imperial myths, idioms, and tropes are deeply implicated in national anxieties pertaining to balanced constitutional governance in Britain and India.[5] These myths, idioms, and tropes evolved through cross-cultural alliances between Muslim India and Protestant England.[6] Rather than treating the Mughal empire as a monolithic "other," the colonial discourse of British India accommodated itself to Indo-Islamic sovereignty as a political expediency that reshaped British national culture. Although these accommodations fostered a cosmopolitan ethos among East India Company officials, some who subscribed to a deist universal religion and even married, converted, and settled among elite Indian Muslims, the defense of the ancient Mughal constitution does not mark a bygone preracial stage in Anglo-Indian coexistence. Rather, this defense models imperial Britain's deist-inflected "rhetoric of benevolence" after the Mughal empire's Timurid-Islamic idiom, a legalistic process that lent ideological coherence to a Whig oppositional agenda and imperialist program in 1780s Britain.[7]

I qualify Robert Travers's claim, in *Ideology and Empire in Eighteenth Century India: The British in Bengal* (2007), that the Warren Hastings trial represents a belated defense of the ancient Mughal constitution that "proved highly unstable and ultimately short-lived in the official discourse of British India" as it yielded to entrenched stereotypes of Asiatic tyranny in the 1780s and 1790s.[8] Although this assertion accurately characterizes British colonial discourse, it does not account for the figurative strategies deployed by Burke and the trial Managers to reinvent the Mughal-Timurid imperial myth in the metropolitan context of late-eighteenth-century English radicalism. By the 1780s, Muslim India served as a source of constitutional legitimacy for the oppositional Whig response to the king-in-parliament crisis. In the sections to follow, I argue, first, that Burke interprets Indo-Islamic law through a post-1688 common law lens; and, second, that during the seven-year Hastings trial, he relied extensively on the memorable figures of Tamerlane, India's republication legislator, and the virtuous Begums of Oude, politically powerful Indo-Muslim women—to defend constitutional liberty in terms of Indo-Islamic republicanism: a Whig political project that lost its ideological appeal by 1788–89 owing to his mishandling of the prosecution.

The Qur'an and the Common Law Tradition

Burke's sweeping account of Indian constitutional history, from its remote Hindu antiquity to the Muslim conquests, dominated his first-day speech on the opening trial proceedings.[9] In order to prove that past Muslim conquerors ruled in accordance to Hindustan's religious laws and customs, he describes the virtuous republics instituted by Tamerlane, Akbar, and the semi-independent Nawabs of Bengal as a heroic restoration of Hindu constitutionalism. Against Hastings's claim that he ruled according to Mahometanism's arbitrary laws, he defends Indo-Islamic sovereign legitimacy by selectively citing the *Institutes* of Timur Khan, the *Code of Gentoo Laws*, and the "Khoran," which he reads as a Whig text that condemns "oppressors" by name and renders arbitrary power unconstitutional by law. As J. G. A. Pocock first argued, Burke's ancient constitutionalism derives partly from the English common law tradition and partly from the eighteenth-century application of this tradition to Mughal (and pre-Mughal) India's political institutions.[10] The Hastings trial presents him with an opportunity for redefining the 1757–65 Bengal revolution as a decisive event within British constitutional history.

Eighteenth-century lawyers, constitutionalists, and parliamentarians typically used the ancient constitution for limiting the crown's prerogative discretion and protecting the rule of law from arbitrary power. In other words, ancient constitutionalism functioned as an advocacy tool for defining liberty in Georgian Britain and, later on, the nascent American republic.[11] The EIC conquest of Bengal, Bihar, and Orissa between 1757 (the Battle of Plassey) and 1765 (the acquisition of the *diwani*, revenue collection rights) ignited debates about British constitutional liberty abroad. In response to this legal dilemma, British officials and Orientalists in India frequently appealed to the ancient Mughal constitution as a political expediency aimed at legitimizing the English presence in Bengal. Warren Hastings's patronage of Oriental learning and Sir William Jones's founding of the Asiatic Society of Bengal in 1784 fed into an imperial need to acquire indigenous local knowledge for ruling according to an Islamic version of the British constitution.[12] In this regard, Burke's defense of the ancient Mughal constitution is not unique; nor is his approach to Indo-Islamic institutions through a common law lens fundamentally different from those practiced by his contemporaries, including Hastings. The conflict between Burke and Hastings is about the ancient constitution's meaning and not about the legitimacy of Mughal political institutions and legal customs.

Unlike Hastings, EIC officials, and MPs, Burke placed the Mughal constitution on a par with the British constitution, occasionally exalting Islamic limited governance above tyrannical European (and British) monarchies. During the trial, he drew elaborate analogies between the common law tradition and Mughal legal systems. From his cosmopolitan perspective, the Islamic law that has traditionally protected the "provincial constitutions of Hindoostan" is "a law as clear, as explicit, and as learned, as ours" (6:314). To prove this point, he establishes certain equivalencies between Islamic and English constitutional governance and customary law:

> The first foundation of their law is the Koran. The next part is the Fetfa [fatwa], or adjudged cases by proper authority, well known there. The next is the written interpretation of the principles of jurisprudence; and their books are as numerous upon the principles of jurisprudence as in any country in Europe. The next part of their law is what they call the Kanon [*kanun*, regulations that supplement the *Sharia*, the cumulative tradition of Islamic law], which is equivalent to Acts of Parliament, being the law of the several powers of the Country, taken from the Greek word which was brought into their country, and it is well known. The next is the Rage ul Mulk [*Ravaj al Mulk*, or custom of the ruling state], the Common Law or Custom of the Kingdom, equivalent to our Common Law. Therefore they have laws from more sources than we have, exactly in the same order, grounded in the same authority, fundamentally fixed to be administered to the people upon these principles. (6. 364)

For Burke, the Qur'an and Shar'ia, like the Bible and Thirty-nine Articles of Anglican Faith, are taken as the binding source of legal authority; Islamic jurisprudence is as advanced as that in Europe and England; the *kanun* "is equivalent to Acts of Parliament"; and the *Ravaj al Mulk* is likened to "the Common Law or Custom of the Kingdom." According to him, the high degree of legal sophistication exemplified by Muslim countries, particularly in South Asia, not only demonstrates beyond a doubt that "any Mahometan Constitution" cannot be despotic by nature but also suggests that, at least in India, the Mughal constitution is a more binding, authoritative, and superior source of law than the British constitution (6:469). Although English and Islamic laws share the same constitutional principles of equitable justice, Islamic customary law has "more sources than we have."

This emphasis on custom's prescriptive authority reinforces Burke's main argument against Hastings's misconduct in India: that he has violated the united sovereignty of India and England, because the EIC is accountable to the British governing body under its 1600 royal charter and to the Mughal emperor under the "dewan" (*diwani*) of Bengal as granted by the 1765 Treaty of Allahabad. Given this dual legal context, the servants of the EIC must adhere to the Mughal charter. By accepting the treaty's terms, they "were bound to observe the laws, rights, usages, and customs of the Natives" (6:281). Burke's legal argument is unique and potentially controversial in treating the Mughal constitution's prescriptive authority as equally binding as, if not superior to, the British constitution.

In order to lend authoritative clout to the ancient Mughal constitution, Burke defends "the principles of the Mahometans" as embodying a limited parliamentarian monarchy by virtue of its origins in God's natural law:

> The principles of the Mahometans . . . are binding upon every person from the Crowned Head to the lowest being that creeps upon the earth, as being supposed to be formed upon the law of God himself, and indeed, so far as it is agreeable to the law of nations, it is formed upon the Law of God himself, and afterwards interwoven by a long series of the wisest, the most learned and most enlightened Jurisprudents that ever were in the world. ("Speech in Reply 30 May," 7:284)

Speaking in a declarative tone, he describes constitutional liberty as emerging from Islamic customary laws (Shar'ia): the dynamic historical interplay between natural law—"the law of God himself"—and Muslim judicial practice (*fiqh*) ensuring that centralized power is kept in check (6:353, 364–65). For Burke, even the Ottoman Sultan cannot exercise arbitrary power—such as unfair taxation or the absolute right to dispose of his subject's life, property, or liberty—without "*the men of Law*" issuing a proper "Fetfa" (fatwa). He thus concludes that the "Mahometan Sovereign . . . is the person who is by the constitution of the country the most fettered by law" (6:354), and that he is "nothing and that the people are everything, as they ought to be in the true and natural order of things" (7:284). Mahometan governments embody the (Lockean) principles of the 1688–91 revolutionary settlement, because they are "in some degree republican" by protecting life, liberty, and property (6:464). Burke envisions the commonwealth of virtue as an ideal that India and Britain share.

His Whig interpretation of the ancient Mughal constitution is a legalistic strategy for undermining Hastings's defense. Hastings claims to derive his unrestrained governance from the arbitrary power vested in the ancient Mughal constitution, defined by him as an example of Oriental despotism: "The whole history of Asia is nothing more than *precedents* to prove the invariable exercise of arbitrary power."[13] In terms of Indian legal precedent, he claims that he has not violated his duty by launching aggressive wars, conquering foreign territories, and confiscating property, because these extreme policies were, by his account, necessary for the EIC's survival in a lawless nation such as Mughal India. From his perspective, English common law cannot be binding in cases where Asiatic lawlessness presents a state of emergency that requires the governor to assume unrestrained power.[14] In retaliation, Burke posits an Asiatic republicanism that disqualifies Hastings's extraconstitutional claim to an Indian state of emergency: "[I]n Asia as well as Europe the same Law of Nations prevails, the same principles are continually resorted to, and the same maxims sacredly held and strenuously maintained" (6:67). He condemns Hastings's defense as "Geographical morality," a non–legally binding moral relativism that fails to acknowledge natural law's universality as recognized globally. For Burke, "the laws of morality are the same every where," so that an immoral act of "extortion, of peculation, of bribery, and of oppression in England" has the same illegal status in "Europe, Asia, Africa, and all the world over" (6:346).

Hastings's Oriental despotism argument derives from Charles-Louis de Secondat Montesquieu's *L'Espirt des Lois*, which argues that laws and political institutions have to be suited to the people to whom they are applied (a premise shared by Burke and Hastings), and that enlightened European monarchies must be defined in contradistinction to Hindu and Mahometan lawlessness.[15] Although Burke recognizes that governments in India have often practiced despotism, he rejects the Oriental despotism thesis on legalistic grounds: "[E]very word that Montesquieu has taken from idle and inconsiderate Travellers is absolutely false" (7:265). For him, most travelers' accounts of eastern countries display "all those wild, loose, casual and silly observations on government" (7:263). Even though he adopts the Oriental despotism thesis in other political contexts,[16] he emphatically refutes Hastings's appeal to this thesis in an effort to dismiss his evidence as faulty and nonlegal—the fictional work of "idle and inconsiderate Travellers." He is not the first to reject the Oriental despotism thesis: during the last quarter of the eighteenth century, Voltaire and Abraham-Hyacinthe Anquetil-Duperron contested the stereotype that Asia is the land of lawlessness.[17] But he is the first to discredit Montesquieu's Eurocentric views by arguing for Mughal India's Whiggish constitution in theoretical and legalistic rather than historical and literary terms. Unlike his contemporaries, he appeals to the Mughal constitution only as an advocacy tool meant to hold Hastings accountable to an Indo-Islamic version of British (Whig) liberty.

In this legal context, the Muslim conquest of India serves as a focal point for staging competing interpretations of the ancient constitution, not as a historical topic centered on truth claims about the social, religious, and political state of India before and after the fourteenth-century Mongol invasion.[18] According to Hastings, Indian sovereignty has always entailed despotism since the "Maho-

metan Conquests," which dissolved and obliterated Hindustan's ancient constitutional rights.[19] He relies on a widely accepted imperial account that stresses
English-Hindu cooperation against the backdrop of Muslim despotism: the English arrived in India as liberators rather than colonizers. They freed the innocent
Hindus from Muslim tyranny and restored their ancient constitution and land
ownership.[20] His defense is a variant of this triumphalist story, claiming legitimacy in the executive prerogative that was constitutionally established after the
Muslim invaders abolished Hindu customary law.

In response to Hastings's account of the Muslim conquest, Burke posits
a tolerant phase of Muslim-Mughal rule after forced conversion by the "prophetic sword" failed to quell rebellious Indian subjects. He insists that "the Mahometans, during the period of the Arabs, never destroyed the native nobility,
gentry or landlords of the country" (6:308) and ruled in accordance with the
Hindu laws and customs. Like most of his contemporaries, he describes Mahometanism as a despotic religion: the early Arab-Muslim conquest in India is
"an era of great misfortune to that country and to the world in general," during
which the Prophet's fanatic followers encouraged tyranny and the innocent Hindus suffered under Muslim bigotry, cruelty, and oppression (6:307). However,
he provides a very different spin to Hastings's triumphalist story: despite their
initial ferocity, the Muslim conquerors contributed to India's national welfare in
the long run, whereas English rule has introduced corruption and avarice into
the otherwise peaceful and virtuous rule of the Mughal empire. Hastings's colonial administration has replaced the fierce yet tolerant rule of a constitutionally
based Islamic republic with an arbitrary "system of peculation and bribery." As
such, he is solely responsible for defacing Hindustan's Edenic paradise (6:373,
305–57).[21] According to Burke's reasoning, the English are brutal colonizers rather
than tolerant liberators and Hastings is the true Oriental despot. Although the
Muslim conquest brought despotism to India, Indo-Islamic governments have
the capacity—unlike the misruling EIC—to reform their institutions in accordance with customary forms of constitutional liberty.

Throughout the Hastings trial, the Muslim conquest was important for understanding the ancient constitution in the legalistic terms of conquest theories,
used for defining, debating, and contesting common law interpretations of constitutional restoration. Contra Hastings, Burke insists that "conquest" does not
entail arbitrary power, because "the conqueror only succeeds to all the painful
duties and subordination to the power of God which belongs to the Sovereign
that held the country before." As such, arbitrary power cannot be legally granted
through "succession," "compact," or "covenant," given that "Law and arbitrary

power are at eternal enmity" (6:351). In a draft that was not included in his speech, Burke claims that the Muslim invaders restored the ancient Hindu constitution under the "title of conquest," through which the succeeding conqueror has the right to assume "the duties, offices and functions of him he has displaced just as if he had come in by the positive law of some descent or some election." According to Burke, "the title of conquest makes no difference at all" in Indian history, because he defines "conquest" as a legally sanctioned enterprise only if it preserves property rights and prescriptive constitutional authority (6:470).

By insisting that the Muslim conquest should be defined by the law of "descent" and "election," he is contributing to seventeenth-century legal debates about the vexed relationship between the Norman conquest of England, typically associated with the establishment of arbitrary power, and Saxon liberty, the mythic origins of England's ancient constitution. In an effort to protect liberty from an unrestrained monarchy, common law lawyers and constitutionalists went at great lengths to prove that William of Normandy did not conqueror England by the sword, abolishing Saxon law and instituting a new constitution, but rather conquered by right of descent: he restored the constitution of Edward the Confessor, who based his rule on the republican government first practiced by Saxon and Germanic tribes (Gothic liberty). This "conquest-was-not-a-conquest argument" became crucial for interpreting William III's "elective succession" and James II's "abdication" in the constitutional idiom that inaugurated 1688–91 as a "Glorious Revolution" rather than a bloody invasion.[22] Likewise, Burke's account of the Muslim conquest (read: Norman yoke) as a restoration of the old Hindu (read: Anglo-Saxon) constitution recasts Hastings's arbitrary policies in India as a defining moment in British constitutional history that deserves as much, if not more, legal attention than the 1688–91 revolutionary crisis.

In this regard, Burke's cosmopolitan approach to British constitutional history shares more in common with Scottish Enlightenment historians—such as Edward Gibbon and William Robertson—than with English common law thinkers. In his unpublished "An Essay towards an History of the Laws of England" (c. 1757), the young Burke notes about England's legal history: "The present system of our laws, like our language and our learning, is a very mixed and heterogeneous mass; in some respects our own; in more borrowed from the policy of foreign nations, and compounded, altered, and variously modified, according to the various necessities, which the manners, the religion, and the commerce of the people, have at different times imposed."[23] England's ancient constitution is not a unique nationalist legacy that originated solely in "Saxon liberty" or in the 1688–91 settlement. Writing in response to Mathew Hale's *The History of the Com-*

mon Law of England (1713), Burke approaches English legal history from the comparative perspective of "foreign nations," whose "manners," "religion," and "commerce" shaped British constitutionalism. This global perspective is indebted to Scottish Enlightenment historiography, which deploys cosmopolitan narratives that complicate Anglocentric accounts of national and imperial histories.[24] Like William Robertson, who wrote favorably about Mughal India's immemorial past, he situates English law within a transnational framework.[25] In the long run, his cosmopolitan sensibility fostered the kind of cross-cultural perspective that he adopted during the Hastings trial. For him, eighteenth-century India represents an ongoing debate about the mixed heritage of British liberty.

Without his Muslim conquest theory, Burke could not defend post-1688 concepts of constitutional restoration in India and, by legal analogy, in Britain.[26] And yet a decade prior to the Hastings trial, he possessed a different legal opinion on Indian affairs. In his *Policy of Making Conquests for Mahometans*—a pamphlet that served as propaganda for his brother, William Burke, who was the London agent for the Raja of Tanjore—Edmund Burke argues that the EIC should not provide military aid to the Nawab of Carnatic, a despotic Muslim ruler who sought to depose the independent and benevolent Raja. The Nawab is an arbitrary conqueror rather than a tolerant republican. To prove this claim, he argues that Mahometan governments have "no settled law or constitution, either to fix allegiance, or to restrain power," and that these "Clans of Mussulmen" are "infinitely more fierce and cruel" than their English counterparts, the legitimate restorers of ancient Hindu liberty (5:113). This truncated history of Anglo-Hindu cooperation is almost indistinguishable from Hastings's anti-Islamic account of the Muslim conquest. For Burke in 1779, the Oriental despotism thesis presents a viable legal framework for understanding the English imperial situation in India. His position on Indian affairs changed dramatically by the 1780s, a decade in which he discovered the republican text par excellence: the English translation of the Qur'an by George Sale, a law practitioner and a pivotal Enlightenment figure in the eighteenth century.[27]

Tamerlane, the Republican Legislator

I have argued that Burke reinterprets the 1757–65 revolutions in Bengal as another version of 1688–91. By legal analogy, Hastings's arbitrary rule in Mughal India repeats King James II's tyrannical (Catholic) rule and, by legal precedent, Tamerlane's (Timur Khan's) Muslim conquest of India (1398–99) anticipates William III's constitutional restoration. These constitutional crises may be examined within two overlapping contexts: Burke's legalistic engagement with the English translation of the Qur'an and his political ties to the Rockinghamite Whigs and Philip Francis, a member of the Bengal Supreme Council from 1774 to 1780 and an avowed enemy of Hastings. Burke's speech on Timur Khan's virtuous republican rule reflects an eighteenth-century tendency to shroud radical deist accounts of Mahomet in the common law's prescriptive authority. His Indo-Islamic republicanism thus compensates for the failed Fox-North ministerial coalition by relocating the 1688–91 revolution in the Mughal-Timurid imperial legacy.

In his speeches, Burke reconstructs an alternative account of Timur Khan's Indian conquest that avoids the crude Orientalist stereotypes mobilized by Hastings's defense. Burke portrays Timur Khan as a virtuous republican legislator who instituted justice, equality, and toleration (6:309–10). Accordingly, his reign accommodated itself to the rule of the "principle Rajahs . . . [who] often assert[ed] their natural liberty and the just constitution of the country" (6:310). This Tartar conqueror restored and preserved customary Hindu liberty. Following the example of his great grandfather, the Mongol emperor Genghis Khan, Timur Khan assembled "a great Parliament" that established an elective monarchy by right of descent. From a post-1688 Lockean standpoint, the Tartar sovereign cannot institute "Ancient laws or new ones which he suggested himself, without the consent of the Assembly of his Parliament; that he could not have ascended the throne and he made it a Law for his Successors that none could ascend the throne without being duly elected; that they were to preserve the great in all their immunities, the people in all their rights, liberties, privileges and properties" (7:270–71).

Burke's Timur Khan reflects the revisionist historiography of Montesquieu, Voltaire, and Gibbon. They provided a more ambivalent, and even sympathetic, account of Timur Khan and the Tartar conquests than previous writers.[28] In this respect, Burke is heavily indebted to William Davy's and Joseph White's English translation of the *Institutes Political and Military . . . by the Great Timour* (1783), a work that he frequently cites during the trial as indisputable proof of Indo-Islamic virtue. Contrary to traditional depictions of Timur Khan as a violent barbarian, this work justifies his character as an ardent defender of "humane and liberal virtues" who granted equality to the nations he conquered and as a republican lawgiver who protected liberty and property.[29] Accounts about Tamerlane's enlightened reign were becoming very fashionable in the eighteenth century among those who speculated that the Tartars and the Goths were once the same people, since the Goths were thought to have originated from Central Asia, and that consequently some vestiges of Gothic liberty survived intact among the Tartars' descendants.[30] Burke mobilizes these synchronized accounts of Tartar-Gothic liberty to legally interpret Indo-Islamic conquest as constitutional restoration.

Ultimately, Timur Khan is a "great Reformer" who restored Islam to its core egalitarian principles, eliminated Muslim tyranny, and established a "Republic of Princes" in late-fourteenth-century India:

> For Tamerlane, coming into that Country as the great Reformer of the Mahometan Religion, to succeed to the rights of the Prophet upon a divine right and divine title, he struck at all the Mahometan princes who were there at that time as persons who were Tyrants abusing their power in the several countries; and he came often into a composition with the people of the Country upon the ruin of those Tyrants. He had neither time, means nor inclination, to dispossess the ancient Rajahs of the country. (6:308)

In Burke's account, Timur Khan replaced arbitrary and despotic Muslim tyrants with an elective monarchy of "ancient Rajahs." Reading aloud from the *Institutes'* twelve maxims, Burke maintains that Tartar sovereignty protects "the lower ranks," delivers "the oppressed from the hand of the oppressor," and learns from and tolerates all religions (6:356–61). Unlike past Muslim rulers, Timur Khan is also famous for having repealed the poll tax (*jizya*) traditionally paid by non-Muslims who acquired legal protection under *dhimmi* status, "freeing the Hindoos for ever from that tax which the Mahometans have laid upon every Country over which the sword of Mahomet prevailed, namely a capitation tax upon all who do not profess the religion of the Mahometans. The Hindoos by profess Charter were excepted from that. They were no conquered people" (6:309). Protected under their chartered rights, the indigenous Hindu people became free citizens—and not "conquered people"—under Timur Khan's Islamic republic, which exemplifies the civic virtues that Burke passionately defended during many points in his long political career: constitutional equilibrium among the king, Parliament, and the people, the slogan "no taxation without representation," the customary privileges of the landed gentry and nobility, the protection of property and charter rights, and the need for granting religious toleration to secure state power. In his imagination, these civic "Hindu" virtues were restored in Mughal India three hundred years before England's Glorious Revolution, perhaps predating Gothic liberty in ancient Germany. In a fit of republican fervor, he confesses that "there is no book in the world, I believe, which contains nobler, more just, more manly, more pious, principles of Government than this book called the Institutions of Tamerlane" (6:356).

By making this hyperbolic claim, Burke is appropriating the official imperial idiom through which Mughal sovereignty claimed Islamic legitimacy in the

Timurid myth. Indeed, he models Timur Khan's virtuous republic after Akbar's late-sixteenth-century reign. Akbar was the first Mughal emperor to reform the Shar'ia by repealing the poll tax imposed on non-Muslim subjects, extending religious toleration to his subjects, and incorporating powerful indigenous lineages such as the Rajputs. According to Burke, the story of the Rajput leader, Ajit Singh of Jodhpur (d. 1743)—typically ascribed to Akbar's stipulation that succeeding "[e]mperors should marry a daughter of Rajah Jeet Singh's house"— relates to Timur Khan's reign (6:309). Likewise, Burke locates events that took place after the reign of Mughal emperor Jahandar Shah (1663–1713)—such as Ajit Singh's seizure of Ajmer in 1721—within the short time span of Timur's reign in India (6:10). Rather than treating these false attributions as signs of ignorance or lapsed memory, I read his "confused" history as an effort to seek legitimacy in Mughal imperial historiography. This unique political idiom grounds Islamic legal concepts in Persian, Mongol, and Hindu traditions originating as far back as Brahman Chānakya's *Artháshastra* ("Science of Material Gain"): a third-century political textbook written for princes that anticipates Niccolò Machiavelli's philosophy on virtuous governance.[31] In *The Languages of Political Islam: India, 1200–1800*, Muzaffar Alam has shown that in pre-Mughal and Mughal India Shar'ia was redefined using non-Muslim terms. Because successful Islamic rule of non-Muslims required crucial modifications of traditional Muslim rule, Indo-Islamic polities adopted a more syncretist definition of Shar'ia and jurisprudence than any of the period's Muslim empires. As a result, the Timurid myth served as an eclectic and highly accommodative imperial discourse for seventeenth- and eighteenth-century Mughal regimes.[32]

Throughout the trial, Burke monopolizes this imperial discourse to delegitimize Hastings's definition of Mughal despotism. In contrast to Timur Khan's enlightened republic, the EIC, according to Burke, ruled under the *Esprit du Corps* (Kingdom of corporate magistrates)—"a Nation of placemen" and "a Republic . . . without a People" (6:285–86, 290). As such, Hastings modeled his colonial administration after "the Dey of Algiers" and "the Mahrattas," Oriental despots who abandoned constitutional checks and balances for increased revenue gains (6:279, 287). Hence, the unconstitutional confiscation of the estates belonging to the ancient Hindu nobility, landed gentry, and "all the freeholders of the Country" resulted from Hastings's unjust reformation of *zamindar* (tax collector) property, which has no precedent in Timur's virtuous conquest-as-reformation (6:382). In republicanizing the Timurid imperial myth, Burke indirectly contests the self-representational politics enacted by EIC officials who used Persian histories and chronicles to justify sovereign rule in Eastern India.[33]

His republicanized Timurid myth could only have been enabled through his imaginative engagement with a "Mahometan" strain of English radical thought that culminated in George Sale's 1734 English translation of the Qur'an. As discussed in chapter 1, the idea that Mahomet is a wise "Arabian legislator" emerged from the deist controversy and national anxieties about constitutional degeneration during the Exclusion Crisis and the Glorious Revolution. Beginning with Henry Stubbe's manuscript, deist polemics read the Prophet's restored Abrahamic covenant with the Jews and primitive Christians as the institution of toleration, equality, and liberty. Republican accounts of Mahomet's life shaped radical thought, especially after Henri Comte de Boulainvilliers' *Vie de Mahomet* (1730; English translation in 1731) was published in Europe and Britain. According to the English translator, this deist-inspired biography praises the Prophet as "a wise Politician, and a renowned Legislator."[34] But the thesis that Mahomet is an "Arabian Legislator" became an established mainstream discourse on Islam thanks, in major part, to Sale's groundbreaking translation—a polemical work of scholarship that, as Ziad Elmarsafy cogently argues, made possible "a project with distinct freethinking and republican . . . sympathies" through a scriptural exegesis that places the individual rather than the institution as the agent of political engagement.[35] By reading Sale's translation, Burke would have discovered that Muslim "legislators" are not essentially despotic and that the "Khoran" does not contain one "letter" or "syllable . . . . that authorizes in any degree an arbitrary power in the Government."

Prefixed to his translation, Sale's "Preliminary Discourse" depicts Mahomet as a civic legislator who introduced the Qur'an, a republican text "not unworthy even [of] a Christian's perusal."[36] In his dedication to Lord John Carteret, a Tory member in the Privy Council who opposed the Walpole administration, Sale describes the Prophet as an impostor who nonetheless accomplished a noble deed by founding a civic republic, giving "his Arabs the best religion he could, as well as the best laws" (vii). Although Mahomet cannot be equated with the divine stature of Moses and Jesus, he is superior to the pagan civil legislators of antiquity. For Sale, there is nothing wrong with an "impostor" who fabricates a new religion based on a monotheistic faith; better to have an impostor abolish idolatry than support paganism (vii–viii). According to the "Preliminary Discourse," Mahomet initiated a "great reformation" in the Arab-Christian world (28). This shrewd politician took advantage of the disputes between and among the Greek orthodox Christians and the Roman Catholics to restore Christianity to its original monotheistic roots (27–28). He propagated his religion through a toleration policy rather than violent conquest (ix). According to Sale, the Prophet came to

punish schismatic Christians' decadent morality, reform church and state corruption, and reaffirm Abraham's and Moses' covenant (23–24, 26). Despite his
professed faith in the Trinity and Anglican dogmas, contemporary critics accused
Sale's translation of placing Islam on a par with Christianity, whereas some freethinkers exploited his "Preliminary Discourse" for subversive purposes.[37]

In order to establish the legality of Mughal constitutional liberty, Burke re-
frames the Timurid myth in the republican language popularized by Sale's well-
known translation, rendering Timur Khan a wise proto-Protestant reformer who
assumed the Arabian legislator's prophetic mantle. In this respect, Burke's legalistic use of the Qur'an does not contradict Sale's primary justification for translating this republican holy book. Invoking the anti-Walpolean Toryism of Lord
Carteret, his dedicatory addressee, Sales writes that "to be acquainted with the
various laws and constitutions of civilized nations, especially those who flourish
in our own time, is, perhaps, the most useful part of knowledge: wherein through
your lordship, who shines with so much distinction in the noblest assembly in
the world, peculiarly excels" (vi). Islamic "laws and constitutions" offer a valuable
resource of legalistic knowledge that can be "useful" to astute oppositional politicians such as Lord Carteret. Given that Sale was a law student of the Inner Temple
in 1720 and a practicing lawyer throughout his life, his interest in the Qur'an and
Oriental languages contributed to his lifelong fascination with legal histories of
ancient constitutionalism. Just like his Roman republican counterparts, Minos
and Numa, Mahomet the lawgiver deserves the admiration of English constitutional lawyers and parliamentarians. Even after Sale quitted his legal career, he
treated the Prophet and the early Muslim conquests in the same light in which
common law lawyers approached classical legislators and Roman imperial conquest: as an advocacy tool used to protect the foreign and ancient heritage of
constitutional liberty from the unauthorized encroachments of arbitrary power.
By transposing the Arabian legislator onto Timur Khan, Burke's defense of the
ancient Mughal constitution renders Sale's translation useful for redefining England's constitution.

And yet the republican implications of Sale's translation became politically
useful for Burke as a direct consequence of his close relationship with Philip
Francis, a staunch reformist Whig who served as an appointee to the Bengal executive council and first convinced him to pursue Hastings's impeachment. After
having arrived in Bengal in late 1774, Francis became paranoid of Hastings's Indian policies, which, in his mind, extended the secret ministerial influence and
unregulated executive power that dominated the court of King George III. In
short, Francis exported oppositional Whiggism to Bengal, where the rise of the

EIC as a fiscal-military state recalled Walpolean ministerial corruption: unfair taxation, inadequate parliamentary representation, a growing national debt, private profiteering among government officials, widespread bribery, an unsustainable professional army, and secret royal patronage. While living in India, he consistently opposed Hastings's administration in the republican-country idiom of the ancient Mughal constitution. After having been injured in a duel with Hastings, Francis returned to England in 1780. This event marked a major turning point for Burke, who as a member of the Select Committee of the House in 1781 was beginning to learn about EIC abuses in India. They first met in that year and thereafter became close confidants. As Robert Travers has argued, Burke's Mughal constitutionalism as an ideal form of "Country government" was inherited from Francis's oppositional Whiggism: "Francis' impassioned defense of the ancient rights of Indian princes and landlords was picked up by Edmund Burke and fed back into the new flowering of reformist Whiggism in London."[38]

However, Travers's argument does not explain why republican interpretations of the Timurid imperial legacy captured Burke's political imagination and propelled reformist Whiggism in the 1780s. In other words, what would have led him, Francis, and other Whig associates to identify so passionately with Indo-Islamic law? The answer is that the older language of Islamic republicanism, as transmitted via Sale's translation, served as the ideological impetus for the Rockinghamite Whigs during critical junctures in the 1770s and 1780s when Indian affairs, especially after the American war, demarcated the constitutional battle line between Parliament and the crown.

The territorial acquisition of Bengal in 1765 and the near financial collapse of the EIC in 1772–73 encapsulated acute constitutional crises that tested King George III's prerogative and allowed Burke and the Rockinghamite Whigs to adopt the antiministerial stance that came to define their party.[39] In managing the "Indian Problem," a Whig coterie led by the Second Marquis of Rockingham switched tactics from court patronage to crown opposition. As the party's principal spokesman, Burke employed information on Indian affairs for consolidating Rockinghamite single-party rule and developing an opposition strategy that initially lacked ideological rigidity.[40] Thus, Francis's opposition to Hastings in the country rhetoric of the ancient Mughal constitution was instrumental for defining the Rockinghamite position on the need for constitutional equilibrium among the crown, the Parliament, and the people. Robert Travers rightly argues that Francis was the chief conduit through which country opposition—as grounded in John Bolingbroke's older Toryism and John Wilkes's popular radicalism—legitimated the oppositional antiministerial politics the Rockinghamites championed.[41] Travers does not mention, however, that this country opposition was partly formulated in dialogue with Islamic republicanism since the late seventeenth century. Between the Exclusion Crisis and the Glorious Revolution, some oppositional Whigs defended an egalitarian toleration policy by appealing to Ottoman constitutional precedent (see chapter 1). After the political fiasco surrounding John Wilkes, an elected MP who was expelled from the House of Commons in 1768 for having published an antigovernment libel, Burke, Francis, and the Rockinghamite Whigs (who cautiously supported his cause) sought to bolster their Wilkite oppositional credentials. They solicited the support of extra-parliamentary radicals who have tended to defend the civic virtue practiced by independent freeholders in pro-Mahometan terms.[42]

Thus, Burke's radical interpretation of the Mughal-Timurid myth lent ideological coherence to an otherwise poorly defined country-party opposition. Borrowing their tactics from previous radicals, he and his Whig associates identified with Indo-Islamic law to legitimize an oppositional agenda that lost most of its credibility after the collapse of the North-Fox coalition in 1783–84. In open defiance of the king's wishes, the formation of a shared ministry between the Whig Charles James Fox and the Tory Lord North marked a major crisis over rival interpretations of the British constitution comparable in scope to 1688. This new constitutional crisis culminated in Fox's 1783 India Bill, a document drafted by Burke (with Francis's help) that includes his legal theories on Islamic-Timurid republicanism. This bill sought to place the EIC under a parliamentary commission in which ministerial MPs, mainly the Rockinghamites, had first priority. Needless to say, the bill precipitated the king's dismissal of the Fox-North coalition in 1784. After the bill passed the House of Commons on a majority vote, it did not pass in the House of Lords due to the king's swift intervention. Consequently, the king formed a new ministry under William Pitt the Younger, who passed the India Act, ensuring that crown ministers would have the right to appoint a board of control to oversee Company affairs and that the governor-general would have unrestrained executive power. In Burke's paranoid imagination, the defeat of Fox's bill signaled a royalist conspiracy to abolish England's ancient constitution.[43] Like their disenfranchised republican counterparts in the 1670s and '80s, the Foxite Whigs pursued a radical "Mahometan" agenda as part of a last-ditch effort to attack the perceived powers of a tyrannical king and undermine the reformist pretensions of a corrupt minister. When legal appeals to classical Rome and the Anglo-Saxon past were ideologically exhausted, Burke turned toward Indo-Islamic republicanism as an alternative source of constitutional (Whig) legitimacy.

Even though the ancient Mughal constitution lost its appeal as the source of British colonial rule in India post-1784, it retained its legal-political currency during the opening trial proceedings. Ultimately, the Muslim imperial idiom helped revitalize Fox's country-party politics and legitimize Burke's rival definition of empire as a benevolent social contract between ruler and ruled. Supplementing traditional accounts of Anglo-Saxon and Gothic liberty, Timur Khan's constitutional restoration of the landed gentry's estates acquired renewed mythic significance for a resurgent Whig anticolonialism—an extension of Burke's lifelong indictment of English colonial abuses against Ireland's native nobility.[44] And yet this antiministerial, anticolonial politics, ironically wedded to benevolent colonial rule, is fraught with contradictions. Indeed, the Managers' later speeches on Hastings's mistreatment of secluded Indo-Muslim women overdramatize these contradictions, inadvertently depreciating Indo-Islamic republicanism's Whig constitutional virtues.

The Begums of Oude

In charging Hastings with "high crimes and misdemeanours," Burke and the Managers were committed to defend British liberty from the false patriotism of the Pitt ministry and the renewed despotism of the king by relocating the 1688–91 principles in Timur Khan's late-fourteenth-century Indo-Islamic republic. The "Begums of Oudh," the Muslim women who politically dominated the Nawab of Oudh (Awadh)'s court, served as another source of constitutional legitimacy for the Foxite Whigs during the 1788–89 trial session. Indeed, the charges leveled against Hastings's confiscation of these imperial women's treasure and property constitutes the bulk of impeachment articles one, two, and six. Burke and Richard Brinsley Sheridan defined contractual obligations between the benevolent imperial state and its indigenous Indian subjects in reference to Indo-Muslim women's seclusion, a positive symbol for sexual propriety, familial piety, and gender subordination.

A look at the Managers' conflicting interpretations of Indo-Muslim femininity is key to reading the sexual politics of the Begum charges, which most critics have read only in reference to imperial tropes. The Managers' conflicting interpretations point to the false egalitarianism embedded in Whig patriarchal versions of the social-sexual contract, in which the unequal relationship between husband and wife, or son and mother, stands for the equitable union between ruler and ruled.[45] Reading contract theory's "sexual metaphorics" in terms of feudal property rights[46] highlights the Begums' allegorical significance for defining the role of constitutional liberty in the domestic sphere. According to Burke's prosecution, Hastings had violated his guarantees to the Begums as specified under the Treaty of Chunar, in which he promised to protect the mother and grandmother of Nawab Wazir of Oudh from any attempts to confiscate their *jagirs*, a temporary land tenure granted by the Mughal emperor for local tax-collection purposes. To raise immediate revenue for funding his military counteroffensive against Chait Singh's 1780 revolt in Benares, Hastings convinced Asaf-ud-daula, the puppet Nawab of Oudh, to repay the Company debts of his deceased father, the Nawab Shuj' al-Dawla, by confiscating the inherited treasure belonging to his widowed mother, Bahu Begum, and her mother-in-law, Sadra al-Niśā. On January 1781, the Company army surrounded the Begums' palace, searched their private quarters (which are off-limits to men), arrested two chief eunuchs, and took more than fifty-five lakhs from their treasury (an immense fortune worth over £550,000). Hastings justified this contractual breach by arguing that the Begums had forfeited their guarantees by aiding Chait Singh's rebellion and inciting anti-Company revolts in Oudh's rural countryside. In response, Burke and the Managers maintained that this explanation was a false pretense. Accordingly, Hastings's true intension was to increase Company revenues by whatever means possible, even if this required violating treaty and chartered rights. Therefore, his aggressive invasion—and not the Begums' actions—incited the revolts. Burke portrays Hastings as a dangerous revolutionary and sexual predator whose only goal was to confiscate the noble Begums' *jagirs*, symbolically coded in English (non-Mughal) terms as hereditary private property belonging to the landed gentry and aristocracy.[47] From his gendered perspective, Hastings's confiscation of the Begums' *jagirs* violates masculine chivalric virtue, capitalist exploitation cast as prostitution. In which case, Hastings's failure to abide by the ancient constitution represents "a scandalous prostitution of the sacred character of *British Justice* in India" (6:155).

In order to expose Hastings's "scandalous prostitution," Burke reinterprets the Begums' *jagirs* in the legal idiom of feudal tenures as formulated by common law theorists. In his "Speech in Reply," he compares the *jagirs* to medieval fiefs that possessed customary and prescriptive property rights, analogous to the landed property that historically emerged from the theory and practice of feudal tenures in Europe. He claims that "a Jaghire signifies exactly what the word fee does in the English language or feodem [*feudum*] signifies in the barbarous Latin of the Feodists" (7:436). He defines "Feod," or "fee," as landed property paid as "salary" to maintain "the people" (tenants) for services rendered to the Lord. In his *An Abridgment of English History*, he specifies that these "feuds" or service grants eventually became inheritances, which "gave rise to the whole feudal system" in Europe (7:436, note 3).

Burke's definition of "Jaghire" contributes to legal debates about the history and nature of feudal tenures. Since the mid-seventeenth century, legal historians had reinterpreted the English common law strictly as the evolution of the *feudum* from a precarious land grant to a hereditary property right, a historical process imported from Europe via the feudal military tenures introduced by the Norman conquest. By the eighteenth century, the notion of feudal tenure—sanctified through institutionalized inheritance and marriage—was used as key evidence by those who argued that the Norman conquest was a legal enterprise that protected England's ancient constitution from the arbitrary power associated with feudalism.[48] Likewise, Burke employs the Begums' "Jaghire" as key evidence for sanctifying customary hereditary property in India, as protected by the ancient Mughal constitution. By contrast, Hastings's confiscation of the *jagirs* has, argues Burke, destroyed the private property system. By stripping the Begums of their personal belongings—the "very ornaments of the sex foully purloined"— Hastings is guilty of treating "the persons of women of the highest rank . . . worse than common prostitutes" (5:465; 6:77). Burke accuses Hastings of transforming the Begums into a piece of exchangeable property among male feudal tyrants. Hence, Hastings's disregard for hereditary property rights violates the social-sexual contract.

By having the Begums metaphorically stand for hereditary landed property in India, Burke portrays Hastings as a vile revolutionary whose arbitrary policies for reforming the *zamindar* tax-collection system was part of a wicked plan to dispossess the landed gentry and the independent freeholders. Burke and Philip Francis were at pains to prove that the *zamindars*, the local tax collectors whom they portrayed as hereditary landholders, were predominantly women who, like the English gentry, cannot be stripped of their property once they ceased serving office.[49] According to their argument, tenants (regardless of gender) cannot surrender their fee to the lord as payment for services due to him because, under customary law in India, feudal tenures are a perpetual grant passed down through hereditary succession and marriage. Burke defends property-holding women's rights in Mughal India: "[T]he sex there is in a state certainly of imprisonment, but guarded as sacred treasure under all possible attention and respect. None of the coarse male hands of the law can reach them" (6:415). Hence, the confiscation of *zamindar* property is analogous to the violation of feminine "sacred treasure," so ultimately "all the principal gentry, all the second rate gentry, and all the women and the minors of that country were cruelly destroyed" only by Hastings's "coarse male hands" (6:416). In other contexts, Burke deploys this analogy between landed property and elite Indian women when condemning Hastings for having pillaged the property and treasure of Raja Chait Singh's mother during the EIC attack on Benares (6:143–44). He also accuses him of unjustly depriving "Maha Ranny Bowannee" (Rani Bhawani) of the *zamindari* of Rajshahi title in order to pass her land on to her son on the condition that he be excluded from the succession (5:435; 6:448–50, 453). From the Managers' standpoint, Hastings, the archenemy of the "landed interest," is an unmanly revolutionary who has undermined the age-old foundations of aristocratic rule: hereditary succession, marriage rights, and landed property (6:457).

One could argue that Hastings's violation of the social-sexual contract prefigures Burke's later diatribes against the plebian radicals who invaded Marie Antoinette's sacred bedroom chamber during the French Revolution. However, his condemnation of Hastings's "revolution" does not defend the English conservative establishment. On the contrary, he uses the Begums scandal to legitimize a radicalized Timurid-Islamic republicanism. In *Scandal: The Sexual Politics of the British Constitution*, Anne Clark argues that radicals used sexual scandals as a strategic tactic for demanding drastic changes in the application of England's ancient constitution.[50] Of course Burke did not support extra-parliamentary radicalism during the trial, but as an oppositional Foxite Whig he was willing to borrow radical tactics to revise English coverture, in which married women's wealth and property is legally subsumed under their husbands' contractual "rights." He knows that the secluded Begums of Oudh, major power brokers in the region, were not confined by English marital laws. Between the fragmentation of the Mughal empire and the EIC sovereign rule, they were exerting greater influence over hereditary succession, the state treasury, and political alliances. As caretakers of the Nawab heir, the Begums controlled a huge administrative apparatus from their private quarters in Faizabad, the capital of Awadh, and acted as the civic custodians of Timurid dynastic values and Islamic piety.[51] Burke, in defending their honorable femininity, is therefore laying claim to the Timurid republican legacy as protected by these imperial women. By casting female socioeconomic autonomy as indispensable for male political rule, he redeploys (perhaps unknowingly) Lady Mary Wortley Montagu's freethinking feminism, which sympathizes with property-owning imperial Muslim wives in the Ottoman empire (see chapter 2). Far from advocating a conservative agenda, his freeborn Begums radically envision aristocratic female agency as a binding source of constitutional legitimacy.

This feminist defense is dramatized in Richard Brinsley Sheridan's popular speech on the "Princesses of Oude." Dubbed by Burke off-record as "a sort of love passion to our Begums,"[52] the speech casts Foxite Whigs as chivalric feminists and Hastings as a Gothic villain in a picaresque novel:

> A knowledge of the customs and manners of the Mussulmen of Turkey, would not en-able one to judge of those of Mussulmen in India: in the former, ladies went abroad veiled, and although not so free as those in Christian countries still they were not so closely shut up as were the ladies professing the same religion in Hindostan. The con-finement of the Turkish ladies was in great measure to be ascribed to the jealousy of their husbands; in Hindostan the ladies were confined, because they thought it contrary to *decorum* that persons of their sex should be seen abroad: they were not the victims of jealousy in the men; on the contrary, their sequestration from the world was *voluntary*; they liked retirement, because they thought it best suited to the dignity of their sex and situation: they were shut up from liberty, it was true; but liberty, so far from having any charms for them, was derogatory to their feelings; they were *enshrined* rather than *im-mured*; they professed a greater *purity* of *pious prejudice* than the Mohamedan ladies of Europe, and other countries; and more zealously and religiously practised a more *holy* system of *superstition*. Such was their sense of delicacy, that to them the sight of man was pollution; and the piety of the nation rendered their residence a *sanctuary*. What then would their lordships think of the tyranny of the man who could act in open defiance of those prejudices, which were so interwoven with the very existence of ladies in that country, that they could not be removed but by *death*? What . . . would their lordships think of the man who could threaten to profane and violate the sanctuary of the high-est description of ladies in Oude, by saying that he would storm it with his troops, and remove the inhabitants from it by force?[53]

Sheridan argues in favor of the Indian custom of purdah ("curtain"), female concealment. In contrast to Turkish women, who are victimized by their hus-band's "jealousy," Indo-Muslim women's self-seclusion symbolizes an agency enabled by a distinct and purified Islamic doctrinal error—oxymoronically por-trayed as a "*holy* system of *superstition*." Although he subscribes to the anti-Turk-ish, anti-harem discourse that Lady Mary Wortley Montagu refutes in her *The Turkish Embassy Letters*, he nonetheless describes the Begums' cloistered agency in the Mughal political idiom of feminine moral piety rather than in the language of contractual rights and masculine public liberty; purdah signifies the imperial sanctity bestowed on these noble women as custodians of Islamic-Timurid val-ues. In this civic capacity, the Begums' empowered domesticity metaphorically embodies the ancient Mughal constitution.

The Managers appropriated this freethinking feminism for the same reason

they adopted Timur Khan's Islamic-Timurid myth: to bolster a Foxite-Whig plat-
form that, in their paranoid imagination, was endangered by Hastings's unconstitutional support of male monarchs. Hastings argues that the Begums' treasure
constitutes public funds to which Asaf-ud-daula, the legitimate ruler, has right
of use without the Begums'consultation or approval. Moreover, he claims that,
in accordance with orthodox and patriarchal interpretations of the Qur'anic law
stance on marriage and inheritance, they are entitled only to a small percentage
of the deceased Nawab's wealth.[54] Unlike Burke and Sheridan, Hastings refuses
to acknowledge the influential role played by Indian mothers in educating the
young Nawab heir, directing his household, and determining dynastic struggles.
He also ignores the Begums' appeal to heterodox interpretations of the Shari'a
as justification for their claim to power.[55] In reaction, the Managers adopted an
earlier radical feminism that highlights elite Muslim women's customary right to
interfere in state affairs and own hereditary property and wealth.

As chivalric defenders of women's rights, the Managers reevaluate the Begums'
zenana (the imperial women's private quarters) as offering parliamentarian limitations on executive (male) power. The zenana not only housed the ruler's wives,
widowed mother, and concubines but also contained a bureaucratic storehouse
for valuable property, jewelry, regalia, treasure, imperial seals, and state documents.[56] In Sheridan's imagination, this fiscal-administrative role renders the
zenana a consolatory branch of government that enforces the social-sexual contract between mother and son, ruler and ruled. For him, the zenana is necessary
for an Indo-Islamic republic to administer justice. Defending the prescriptive authority of filial obligations, he relates the heroic story of Bahu Begum's domestic
intervention to save her young son, the heir-in-waiting, from the arbitrary will of
"the crown": "[F]or one day his savage father in a rage attempted to cut him [her
son] down with his scymeter, the Begum rushed between her husband and her
son and saved the latter, through the loss of some of her own blood . . . A son so
befriended and so preserved, Mr. Hastings had armed against such a mother—
he invaded the rights of that prince, that he might compel him to violate the
laws of *nature*, by plundering his parent; and he made him a *slave*, that he might
afterwards make him a *monster*" (66). Hastings's contractual breach threatens
the familial contract, "the laws of *nature*." Sheridan interprets Bahu Begum's maternal intervention as a republican-parliamentary restraint on the crown's pa-
ternal rage. Expanding this conceit, Sheridan delivers a passionate apostrophe to
"FILIAL PIETY," which he hails as "the primitive bond of society," and interprets
Hastings's sacrilegious attack on the Begums' zenana as a vile disregard for "the
sacredness of the ties" (117). Subverting "filial piety" is tantamount to overthrow-

ing the ancient constitution's two republican pillars: respect for private property and the rule of customary law.

In this case, the Managers' defense of the Begums' rights should not be read in the same manner in which Lady Mary Wortley Montagu saw the empowered domestic lives of imperial Muslim women in Turkey. Ultimately, women in "christian countries" are more "free" according to Sheridan. Whereas Montagu treats women's freedom in the Ottoman harem as a foil for criticizing marriage property rights in England, the Managers, by contrast, invoke the zenana's feminine sublimity to displace English patriarchal violence onto Hastings's administration. This displaced feminist politics would only exacerbate the public-private tension implicit in traditional Whig accounts of the social-sexual contract.

Sublime Trash

Not everyone was impressed by Sheridan's defense. In particular, Englishwomen in the Westminster audience, and the Begums themselves, were not moved by the Managers' sexual politics.[57] Burke's and Sheridan's conflicting position on Muslim domesticity in the separate contexts of Ottoman Turkey and Mughal India raised doubts about traditional Whig accounts of the public-private divide. Mostly due to the regency crisis in 1788–89, the Managers' problematic interpretations of the sexual contract in India became vulnerable to ridicule. Anti-Burke satires mocked their "secret" fascination with Oriental despotism, coded as a royalist and patriarchal propaganda for the Prince of Wales's hereditary right to Hanoverian rule in lieu of George III's madness. In these satires, Burke's sublime panegyric on Indo-Islamic republicanism is comically demoted to the vulgar sexual exploitation of female slaves.

The Managers' opponents attacked Sheridan's cultural distinction between the Turkish seraglio (the site of male sexual pleasure) and the Indian zenana (the site of constitutional female virtue) to expose their Whig feminism as legally untenable.[58] In *An Elucidation on the articles of Impeachment preferred by the last Parliament against Warren Hastings* (London, 1790), Ralph Broome, an EIC army officer and Hastings supporter, claims that the Managers' idealization of Indo-Muslim women has resulted "not only [in] a linguafactory of characters, but a linguafactory of laws also."[59] He criticizes Sheridan's "zenana doctrine":

> To say that the *Mother* acquired, and that the *Son* lost, a right to the treasure from its being deposited in the *zenana*, is the strangest idea that ever was started. Were I disposed to animadvert on that gentleman's speech, there would be much room for it in that part

where he tells the Lords, that they must not argue from the Turkish Mahommedans, they being of a mean and degenerate race. He was aware of there being no law or custom in Turkey that would warrant his *zenana* doctrine; and he therefore made a new species of Mahommedans for India.[60]

According to Broome's reasoning, Sheridan needs to posit a false distinction between the seraglio and the zenana because otherwise he would be forced to derive legal "rights" from a "mean and degenerate race" (Ottoman Muslims) who treat women as slaves. Without Sheridan's "zenana doctrine," the Managers would have to confront directly, without any hypocrisy, the sexual inequalities underpinning their Whig interpretation of the Indian social contract. In short, resexualizing the Begums would only delegitimize the zenana as a symbol for constitutional female agency and, in the process, transform the Indian sublime into a grotesque self-parody. As Broome satirically points out, Sheridan's feminist speech is equivalent to "Mulnahs" reading "chapters of the *Coran*, a recital of sublime trash."[61]

Attempting to avoid this criticism, Burke sexualizes the zenana by citing Ottoman imperial women as evidence. In his April 1788 speech (two months before Sheridan's speech), he argues that the Islamic protection of mothers in the Ottoman harem is equally applicable in all Muslim countries and that, by legal analogy, "women of great rank" in the zenana live under "the security, retirement, and sanctity" secured by the ancient Mughal constitution (6:475). Appealing to the Qur'an as a "public notoriety," he argues that Muslim nations' "Constitution" protects imperial mothers, who "are under the peculiar jurisdiction of their own Officers and their own Magistrates, and that in short their power is great, vast, unlimited" (6:478). Unlike Sheridan, he points to the legal precedent set by the *valide sultan* (powerful mothers of the Ottoman sultan) to convince the Lords that Muslim rulers always have had customary reverence for politically powerful women in their society. As evidence, he uses the "reveries" of an Ottoman prince of Moldavia as his prime source. After reading a passage from Demestrius Cantemir's *The History of the Growth and Decay of the Ottoman Empire* (London, 1734–55), translated into English by Nicholas Tindal, the nephew of the notorious deist Matthew Tindal, Burke explains to the Westminster audience,

> The dominion of the Grand Seignior's Mother within the Seraglio (where concubinage is established and a multiplicity of women permitted) so much differs from our customs that it seems with us to indicate some looseness of character, but I believe it will be found that the sanctity of a Convent is not greater than the chastity of those Seraglios. So that there is nothing light in the idea of it and that it is the Marriage of that Country. And

when you hear that the Grand Seignior cannot take a Virgin without the consent of his Mother, and ever since the reign of Bajazet, the grand Turk has had no other. It was not read with a view to any effect of that, knowing that in novelty the first effect is ridicule, but it is to shew the respect paid to her and her authority, interfering in the matters of State. (6:278–79)

Like previous deists, particularly Lady Mary Wortley Montagu, Burke sanctifies Muslim sexual practices in Turkey as a "Marriage" contract, equating the seraglio to "the sanctity of the Convent." Appealing to Ottoman legal precedent, he argues that Indo-Muslim mothers have a right to interfere "in the matters of State." He recognizes the sacred title of mother as employed in Mughal imperial discourse. But in doing so, he incites disbelief and ridicule: he defends the Indian social contract in reference to the sexual politics practiced by the *valide sultan*, an Ottoman concept that is not applicable to the nonhierarchical relationships existing among imperial women in the zenana.[62] In misapplying this concept, he indirectly invokes preconceived European notions about the tyrannical rule and sexual excesses of the seraglio, the locus of Oriental despotism. In *The Sultan's Court: European Fantasies of the East*, Alain Grosrichard has shown that throughout the seventeenth and eighteenth centuries the seraglio was a symbol for the sexual-political transgressions perpetuated by the Ottoman sultan's domineering mother, a dangerous female sovereignty. In the long run, Burke not only contradicts Sheridan's desexualized zenana but also reduces Indo-Islamic republicanism to a tyrannical fantasy—the dishonorable sexual exploitation of elite Muslim women in India. Burke's bold attempt to reevaluate the seraglio's sexual politics ultimately undermines the Managers' prosecution, because he has inadvertently made himself and the Managers vulnerable to the Oriental despotism charge by defending the *valide sultan's* prerogative rights as legally binding.

To insist that Cantemir's gloss on "The Valide-Sultana" be read as an example of "chastity" must have seemed outlandish to the Westminster audience. Burke's quotation of this Muslim work stresses that the Sultan is "forbidden by the laws, to lye with any of the women kept there, without his mother's consent" and that "[e]veryday during the feast of *Bairam*, the sultana-mother presents a beautiful Virgin, well educated, richly dressed, and adorned with precious stones, for her son's use."[63] This passage implies that Muslim state affairs are managed by a brothel of immoral prostitutes rather than by a nunnery of chaste mothers. According to the court transcripts, the Lords were "somewhat shocked" by Burke's Muslim sources and the "whole Court [was] in a convulsion of laughter, while the *young ladies* around, behind their fans, were tittering applause."[64] This observation records the unintended comic effects that Burke had on English men and women in the audience, testifying to the troubled sexual politics that plagued his understanding of contractual rights. During his speech on Fox's India Bill, he encountered similar laughter when he accused Hastings of directing "the pious hand of a son" to plunder "the ancient household of his father." Alert to the sexual-political despotism associated with the seraglio, the Parliament's "younger members" mocked his rhetoric (5:11). As low comedy, the Indian sublime loses its political ability to elicit moral sympathy for dispossessed Muslim women. To borrow Broome's phrase, Burke's speech is "sublime trash"; he chose to sexualize the zenana only to elevate it to the seemingly absurd status of divine law.

James Sayers's political cartoon *A Reverie of Prince Demetrius Cantemir, Ospidar of Moldavia* (fig. 5) exploited this comic mode of failed sublimity for satiric purposes. The cartoon is visually split between a foregrounded sleeping/dreaming Burke lying on a chair underneath a Mahomet bust and a background in which the Sultan's elderly mother presents a distressed virgin to her son, who is lying on a divan underneath an open Qur'an. "I have procured another Lamb for my Son." Near Burke stands an open book featuring Cantemir's gloss and a quote from Burke's speech: "I have observed that the greatest degree of respect is paid to Women of Quality in the East and that the strongest instances of Maternal Affections & filial Duty prevail there." Visually and verbally, the cartoons stress an ironic contrast between Cantemir's/Burke's sublime maternal piety and the *valide sultan/*Begum's oppressed female concubines. The parallel between Burke and the Sultan reveals the public-private contradiction implicit in Indo-Islamic republicanism: that Burke's enlightened Mahometanism—symbolized in the Mahomet bust and illuminated lamp pairing—remains blind to the sexually devious practice that Qur'anic law sanctions in the seraglio/zenana. With eyes shut and spectacles overhead, he fails to see that the "Koran," the republican text par excellence, justifies a despotic political economy in which imperial mothers fulfill the unrestrained sexual desires of their emasculated and lustful sons.

But the aim here is not simply to discredit Burke's Ottoman source. By mobilizing preconceived notions of the seraglio's despotic sway, Sayers hints at a male voyeuristic fantasy in which the sexual trafficking of female slaves is emblematic of an unconscious Whig desire for unlimited political power. In Burke's wet-dream "reverie," the social-sexual contract between ruler and ruled, mother and son, is coded as a royalist defense of what he calls the Begums' "great, vast, [and] unlimited" rule—in short, monarchal hereditary rights. In this case, his use of Cantemir's work participates in a despotic sexual fantasy in which the *valide sultan*'s "Maternal Affections" describes, figuratively and literally, Whig contractual

Figure 5. James Sayers, *A Reverie of Prince Demetrius Cantemir, Ospidar of Moldavia,* 1788. © Trustees of the British Museum.

obligations between ruler and ruled, even as Sayers's use of this trope suggests that the filial bond between mother and son is incestuous. He diagnoses Burke's perverted sexual politics: Indo-Islamic republicanism is plagued by an unresolved ideological contradiction between the convent of chaste mothers (parliamentary rule and constitutional virtue) and the seraglio of immoral prostitutes (royalist rule and commercial vice).

This contradiction surfaces in Burke's speech against the EIC appointment of Munny Begum, a lower-class Indo-Muslim woman who managed state affairs in Bengal. As the favorite concubine of the deceased puppet Nawab of Bengal, Mir Jaffir, Munny Begum was appointed by Hastings in 1772 as guardian to the Nawab's son, the young heir Mubarak-al-Daula. In his "Speech on Sixth Article: Presents," delivered in April and May 1789, Burke expressed outrage at this appointment. He accused Hastings of having accepted bribes from her—allegedly twelve lakhs of rupees (equivalent to several thousand pounds)—in exchange for granting her a privileged position in the Nawab's court that she, as "dancing girl" and "prostitute," was not entitled to inherit (7:52). Hastings admitted to having received "presents" from her, but only for "entertainment" purposes.[65] Burke used this confession to convince the Lords that Hastings was involved in a political and sexual transaction with a "prostitute" whom, by assuming stewardship over the heir, he placed in charge of Company revenues in Bengal. For him, she is a usurper who has discarded the hereditary rights of the Nawab's son and instead elected her illegitimate lower-class son for the succession. Literally and figuratively, Hastings has prostituted the British constitution in India: "Here is such an arrangement as I believe never was heard of, a secluded woman in the place of a man of the world, a Fantastic dancing girl in the place of a grave Magistrate, a Slave in the place of a woman of quality, a Common prostitute made to superintend the education of a young prince, and a stepmother, a name of horror in all countries, made to supersede the natural mother from whose body the nabob had sprung" (7:54).

Having violated the natural bonds of family and state, Hastings established a sham elective monarchy, raising a "Slave" and "prostitute" to public office, and appointing "a woman in a country where no woman can be seen, where no woman can be spoken to without a curtain between them" (7:1). For Burke, this shameful situation is different from that of the Begums, upper-class noble mothers who lawfully obtained their office by hereditary right. In this case, freethinking feminism eventually yields to his misogynist views on Munny Begum.

For many British contemporaries, Burke's argument about women and their domestic role in the public sphere became self-contradictory. Major John Scott, Hastings's agent and chief propagandist, accused the Managers of hypocritically forsaking their radical feminist position. In *A Letter to the Right Honourable Charles James Fox, on the extraneous matter contained in Mr. Burke's Speeches* (London, 1789), he points to Burke's earlier description of Munny Begum. He exposes inconsistencies in his political representation of Indo-Muslim female agency: printed in 1783, the *Eleventh Report of Select Committee* records Burke's observation that Munny Begum was unfit to be appointed guardian because she was a secluded woman; he does not mention a word about her villainous vocation as a "prostitute" and upstart usurper (5:362).[66] From the perspective of the Managers' opponents, the zenana represents an insurmountable problem for Burke, who continues to secretly harbor Whig reservations about women's intrusions into state affairs despite his self-serving feminism. Sayers and Scott understand what is at stake in these conflicting Whig interpretations: the constitutional rights that define royal power as implicit in the Tory feminism championed by Mary Astell and Montagu (see chapter 2). Burke's condemnation of Munny Begum is ironically coded as a backhanded defense of hereditary monarchy and the executive prerogative, royalist ideals that he and the Rockinghamite Whigs confidently claim to have always opposed in Parliament.

The self-contradictory account of Munny Begum is mocked in another Ralph Broome print. In his satiric *Letters from Simpkin the Second, to his dear brother in Wales; containing a humble description of the trial of Warren Hastings* (London, 1789), Broome deflates Burke's sublime speech in mock heroic couplets jam-packed with tantalizing sexual innuendos:

> MUNNY Begum, the object of HASTINGS' Election,
>
> Sole Regent was made, without any *Restrictions*.
>
> *No Restrictions, my* Lords, she was perfectly free,
>
> As *Regents*, I think, *should in general be.*
>
> But the powers of Regent alone would not do,
>
> ARCHBISHOP he made her, and CHANCELLOR too.
>
> The NABOB's *dear Person*, his armies and treasure,
>
> Were all at *this* BEGUM's, the dancing Girl's, pleasure.
>
> And here let me ask, can your LORDSHIPS suppose
>
> That he was not paid for it—*under the Rose?*
>
> Was it likely that HASTINGS these offices gave her
>
> Without *some return* from the PRINCESS's *favor?*

Beginning with the near rhyme "Election/Restrictions," Broome's poem suggests that there is something askew in Burke's "Regents," who "should in general" possess unlimited power yet should be restricted if they are elected, acquiring the throne through nonhereditary means. The unlimited power of regency only pertains to the royal heir, a constitutional legality that Hastings has ignored in succumbing to "the dancing Girl's pleasure." In Broome's anti-Burke lampoon, the insinuation that Hastings was involved with a prostitute is ironically recast in the chivalric language of romantic courtship as deployed by the Managers in their speeches on the Begums. By referring to Hastings's bribery "under the Rose" in granting "the PRINCESS's favor," this riveting burlesque mirrors the contradictions embedded in Burke's sexual politics: that his romanticized portrayal of Indian imperial women as "ARCHBISHOP(S)" and "CHANCELLOR(S)" is inconsistent with his fierce condemnation of Munny Begum.

Broome's repetitive references to regents' unlimited power allude to Burke's crypto-royalist defense of kings' hereditary rights during the regency crisis, a national event that sparked urgent questions about the constitutional ramifications of the social-sexual contract. During the winter of 1788–89, George III lapsed into a severe case of dementia, leaving Pitt and Fox with an unprecedented opportunity for reweighing the constitutional balance between Parliament and the crown. In their contentious debates about who would fill the regent position in the king's household, Pitt opted to install Queen Charlotte, an elected monarch who awakened misogynist Whig fears about the sexual and political prowess of sovereign temptresses.[67] In retaliation, the Whigs defended the regency of the Prince of Wales on the grounds that he had a hereditary right as the king's son. This defense was part of strategy to secure party leadership for the Rockinghamites under the prince's reign. After Fox's careless appeal to kings' inherent rights, which Pitt seized on to cast himself as the true defender of female sovereignty and parliamentary restraint, Burke was placed in the awkward predicament of having to offer historical precedents for the unlimited power vested in hereditary male regents.[68] As registered in Broome's satire, he therefore adopted a patriarchal stance on the fundamental incompatibility between an unrestricted kingship and elected female regency during his speech on Munny Begum.

On December 1788, he defended Fox and attacked Pitt in Parliament, disassociating himself from the current ministry's petty factionalism and court patronage: Burke claims to know "as little of the inside of Carlton House, as he did of Buckingham House," the London residencies respectively of the Prince of Wales and the King of England, but could not name any historical precedents for a male regency beyond a general appeal to the noninnovative "spirit" of the ancient constitution.[69] This legal blunder was prompted, in part, by scandalous allegations that the Foxite Whigs were involved in the private life of the Prince of Wales, notoriously known as a selfish, eccentric, and pleasure-loving libertine who was ostracized from his father's court. Despite his personal dislike of the prince, Burke was caricatured in print as a Papist who arranged the prince's sham wedding with Anne Fitzherbert, a Catholic widow. She was embarrassing for the Whigs given that the prince's clandestine marriage was nullified by the 1701 Act of Settlement and the 1772 Royal Marriages Act, which bar Roman Catholics from the succession.[70] In the context of these allegations, Broome's anti-Burke satire parodies the sexual rhetoric shared by the impeachment trial and regency debates. He exposes the Whig hypocrisy of those who charge Hastings with establishing an elective monarchy of Muslim female prostitutes in regency India and yet uphold a hereditary monarchy of Catholic male libertines in regency Britain.

Exacerbated by the regency crisis, the Managers' conflicting views on Indian sexual politics resulted in a series of irresolvable contradictions: the dubious distinction between the seraglio and the zenana; ideological friction between Burke's sexualization of Turkish maternal love and Sheridan's desexualization of Indian "filial piety;" Burke's fierce condemnation of Munny Begum in contrast to his sublime panegyric on Muslim imperial mothers; and his political flip-flop from ardent defender of Timur Khan's parliamentary laws and elective monarchy to chivalric admirer of the Begums' executive prerogative and hereditary rights. In their satires, Broome, Sayers, and Scott dramatize how these contradictions have mutated the lofty sublimity celebrated in Indo-Islamic republicanism into the seraglio's sexualized comedy. They expose Burke's cryptoroyalist rhetoric to mock his failed parliamentarian intervention, which precipitated the Rocking-hamite party's disintegration after the king's unexpected recovery in February.[71] Consequently, the ancient Mughal constitution lost its political-legal currency.

Coda: Burke's Counterrevolutionary Turn

To argue that "the idiom of the ancient Mughal constitution fell into imperial disuse" because Burke's defense of Indo-Islamic law "was a conceptual leap too far for a British audience" stubbornly committed to the Oriental despotism ste-reotype[72] is to ignore how quickly this imperial idiom lost favor in the consti-tutional fallout following the regency crisis, which discredited the oppositional politics deployed by Burke and the Foxite Whigs.

During the 1788 opening proceedings, many in the Westminster audience were spellbound by Burke's sweeping account of Timur Khan's and Akbar's virtuous Islamic republics. Captivated by his sublime rhetoric, they were willing to suspend temporarily their anti-Islamic prejudices and sympathize, even if reluctantly, with the Whig principles enshrined in the ancient Mughal constitution. A year later these principles were ridiculed in Westminster Hall and satiric prints. With the Managers' conflicting accounts of the Begums, Indo-Islamic republicanism failed to lend ideological coherence to the Rockinghamites' country-party agenda. Burke's shift from a republican champion of Timur Khan's elective monarchy to a royalist defender of the Begums' hereditary monarchy created a permanent rift within his party that anticipated his break with Fox over the French Revolution's constitutional significance for Georgian Britain. A few months before the con-vening of the French National Assembly in June and the fall of the Bastille in July, Burke's common law interpretation of Mughal history and the Qur'an had laid the legal foundation for his counterrevolutionary turn in 1790.

Despite his lifelong suspicion of deism and antitrinitarian theology, Burke's creative engagement with Mahometanism propelled the evolution of his political thought from republican to royalist.[73] His radical enlightenment approach to the Indo-Islamic republics provided a viable legal model for imagining what the sovereign rule of a benevolent imperial state might mean for a small island nation that was to administer justice in the Indian subcontinent for the first time. As such, the Warren Hastings trial represents the closest that the British imperial nation had come to officially adopting the Mughal empire's Islamic idiom.

The French Revolution forever extinguished this possible political fusion, however unimaginable the possibility might seem to twenty-first-century readers. Having abandoned the Whigs after publishing the *Reflections*, Burke's prosecution of Hastings shifted from a republican obsession with the "Republic of Princes" to a royalist assault on arbitrary plebian rebels.[74] In his "Speech in Reply," Burke ceased to emphasize the parliamentary restraints sanctioned by Qur'anic law, and, although he continued to cite the *Institutes*, he refused to quote Timur Khan's twelve maxims aloud (7:271–73). The year 1794 was very different from 1788–89: given events in France, the EIC no longer appeared as a source of constitutional corruption. With Hastings's acquittal in 1795, the English public hailed the ex–governor-general as a martyred hero and stigmatized the aged parliamentarian as a despicable villain. Furthermore, the 1799 battle of Seringapatam in Mysore marked Indo-Islamic republicanism's fallibility: the British defeat of Tipu Sultan, nicknamed "Citizen Tipu" owing to his alliance with revolutionary France and adoption of French republican idioms, suggested to many Britons that Indo-Islamic republics are attracted by nature to a failed Jacobin politics.[75]

And yet Islamic republicanism did not die with Burke. After publishing his counterrevolutionary writings, he lauded the chivalric history of European kings and queens and turned his back on the republican legacy of Asian princes and princesses. This avowal and disavowal would become a dominant motif among Romantic poets as they lost faith in the French Revolution. Despite (or rather because of) its unpopular association with French Jacobinism, Burke's anticolonial vindication of Islamic republics acquired renewed constitutional legitimacy for a young generation of English radicals who never forgot the political lessons of the Hastings impeachment trial.

CHAPTER FOUR

Ali Bonaparte in Hermetic Egypt

The Colonial Politics of Walter Savage Landor's *Gebir*

From hence, under the idea of the instrumentality of the French
Revolution, in the fulfillment of prophecies, religion itself became
accessary to deism and atheism! Prophecies, relative to the destruction of almost every kingdom and empire in the world, teemed from
the British press, some of them in weekly numbers, till government,
perfectly aware of the tendency of these inflammatory means, pru-
dently transferred the prince of prophets to a mad-house.

William Hamilton Reid, *The Rise and Dissolution of the Infidel
Societies in this Metropolis*, 1800

Infidelity is served up in every shape that is likely to allure, surprise,
or beguile the imagination; in a fable, a tale, a novel, a poem; in
interspersed and broken hints; remote and oblique surmises . . . in a
word, in any form, rather than the right one, that of a professed and
regular disquisition.

William Paley, *The Principles of Moral and Political Philosophy*, 1786

One of most subversive moments in Walter Savage Landor's epic poem *Gebir*
(1798) occurs in book 6, when Tamar, a poor shepherd and Gebir's brother, falls
madly in love with an Egyptian nymph who takes him on a magical flight over
Europe. In the middle of this episode, Landor inserts a provocative vision about
the coming of an egalitarian social utopia: passing over the island of Corsica,
the nymph prophetically announces the fall of all tyrannical monarchs—which
includes the tragic lovers of this epic, Gebir, the king of Spain, and Charoba,
the queen of Egypt—and the coming of a "mortal man above all mortal men"
who will usher in a Golden Age of justice that spreads from Europe to the East.[1]
Landor's footnote to the 1803 edition of *Gebir* identifies this passage as an allegory about the French Republic and Napoleon Bonaparte (Corsica being his

birthplace) in which this charismatic general becomes the redeemer of world history (349).[2] What is particularly subversive about this use of political allegory is the context of its articulation: the principles of the French Revolution are placed in the mouth of an Egyptian nymph, who is not only a symbolic figure of hermetic magic and enthusiastic prophecy but also, given the French occupation of Egypt in 1798–99, a champion of Bonaparte's messianic promise to restore egalitarian justice in Ottoman Egypt under an Islamic republic based in Cairo. This chapter argues that the French revolutionary context undermines Landor's repeated attempt to draw a political distinction between republican liberty and imperial tyranny in an Islamic-hermetic poem that, by 1800, had become ideologically compromised due to the failure of the French colonization of Egypt and Bonaparte's rise to dictatorial power.

Before the end of 1798, most Britons would have known about Bonaparte's July proclamation to the Egyptians, in which he grants toleration to all religions, accepts Islamic beliefs and practices, repudiates Catholicism, and dubs republican Frenchmen "the friends of the true mussulmen."[3] It first appeared in England in *Copies of Original Letters from the Army of General Bonaparte in Egypt, intercepted by the Fleet under the command of Admiral Nelson* (London, 1798), a collection of French dispatches and correspondences that were confiscated by the British navy and published as antiradical propaganda by the government. In the English translation of the proclamation, originally published in Arabic, Bonaparte usurps the authority of the Mamluk Beys in Egypt by adopting an Ottoman-Islamic idiom that pays homage to the "Empire of the Sultan" and the egalitarian laws of "the Prophet and his holy Koran" (235). Inserted in a government-sponsored tract set against "opposition writers," the proclamation would have confirmed British suspicions that "Jacobin" republicanism was founded on Islamic principles: "The French are true Mussulmen. Not long since they marched to Rome, and overthrew the Throne of the Pope, who excited the Christians against the professors of Islamicism (the Mahometan religion). Afterward they directed their course to Malta, and drove out the unbelievers, who make war on the Mussulmen. The French have at all times been the true and sincere friends of the Ottoman Emperors, and the enemies of their enemies" (236).

In an effort to conciliate the Egyptian population while securing French colonial power in the region, Bonaparte tried to persuade the ulema, the Muslim clerical class, that his Italian campaign of 1796–97 and attack on Malta were waged on behalf of the Sultan and the Muslim faith against the corrupt forces of the Pope and Christian "unbelievers." His diplomatic rhetoric relies on an earlier anti-Catholic strain of Mahometan deism that was held in contempt in eighteenth-century Britain, especially during the turbulent years of the 1790s. After Sultan Selim III declared war on France in September, Bonaparte became more desperate, issuing a second proclamation in which he assumes the occult persona of the Mahdi—a Muslim folk figure who hails the millennial return of Islamic justice in the same way in which Landor's Egyptian nymph prophesizes the coming of a republican utopia in the East.[4] Although Landor could not have known about these proclamations when he published *Gebir* in June, I argue that both admirers and critics, including Landor himself, read this poem retrospectively as radical propaganda in support of the French-Islamic "Directory" in Egypt.[5]

While Bonaparte was promoting the study of Arabic and Islamic literature in Ottoman Egypt for his political campaign, Landor, coincidently, was incorporating Islamic, occult, and hermetic material from medieval Egypt for his literary campaign—*Gebir*. Indeed, the main plot structure of this Oriental tale derives from a thirteenth-century Arabic-Islamic work from Egypt. Published as an English translation in 1672, Murtada ibn al-Khafif's *The Egyptian History* contains a section on the romance of Gebir and Charoba that Landor knew via Clara Reeve's work. In the 1803 preface to *Gebir*, Landor admits to having borrowed the plot of *Gebir* from Reeve's Oriental tale, "The History of Charoba," which contains a readaption of Murtada's romance located in the last section of *The Progress of Romance* (1785) (343). Not much is known about the life and works of Murtada ibn al-Khafif, except that he was an Islamic historian from Cairo who lived between 1154/55 and 1237. His only known book, *The Egyptian History*, survives in the French and English translations.[6] Its use of cyclical stories and religious epics promote a syncretistic account of "Universal History," a medieval Islamic tradition of writing history that relies on the romance narrative genre in order to tie together the mythic pasts of the pre-Adamites and the descendants of Noah with the rise of Muhammad in the early seventh century. Egyptian historians such as Murtada promoted this "Islamic Humanism," and like Bonaparte and Landor, looked toward pre-Islamic Egypt as the home of hermetic wisdom and esoteric science.[7]

Given Landor's initial sympathy for the French Revolution, the political significance of esoteric and Islamic motifs in *Gebir* needs to be contextualized in relation to the radical tradition of the Oriental tale. By the late eighteenth century, some English writers read obscure tales about the East as a sign of infidelity; in the epigraphs that begin this chapter, William Paley and William Hamilton Reid imagine that prophetic Oriental fables such as *Gebir*—a poem of "interspersed and broken hints . . .[and] remote and oblique surmises"—is an "inflammatory means" of fomenting a revolution against the British empire. The indirect language of tales and fables is a site of ideological resistance, particularly in the case of the genre of the Oriental tale.[8] And yet some literary critics have insisted that *Gebir*, a quintessential Oriental tale of the Romantic period, reproduces Eurocentric stereotypes that render it incapable of articulating an anticolonial discourse.[9] Moving beyond this postcolonial interpretation, I argue that *Gebir* offers a salient Islamic-hermetic critique of a resurgent Anglican imperialism in which, as Rowan Strong points out, "the Church of England was now seen as a support for British colonial rule."[10]

As noted in chapter 3, radical accounts of Islamic republicanism had lost their political currency by the end of the Warren Hastings trial in 1795, the year in which Edmund Burke abandoned a Whig anticolonial politics inspired by Indo-Mughal ideals for a counterrevolutionary pro-Anglican politics that recast radical dissenters as Muslim despots (partly in reaction to the anti-British alliance between revolutionary France and the Indian state of Mysore in the 1790s). Nevertheless, Islamic republicanism did not simply disappear. Rather, it moved underground among English radicals who, like Landor, saw Islam as the pinnacle of a long tradition of seventeenth-century hermetic thought that located the "light" of the original Christian republic in Arabia. To demonstrate this point, the first section of this chapter explores the hermetic context of the primary source for the Gebir-Charoba romance plot, the 1672 English translation of Murtada's *The Egyptian History*, while the second section compares Landor's investment in Islamic hermeticism to Bonaparte's politicized deist theology. In the last section, I conclude that Landor's 1803 edition of *Gebir* reinvents an anticolonial politics that ideally, yet problematically, salvages egalitarian republicanism from the imperial clutches of Napoleonic tyranny in the Near East.

The Arabic *prisca sapientia*

Written in blank verse, Landor's heroic poem begins with the invasion of Egypt by Gebir, the King of Gades (Spain), in the name of an ancestral feud fought for his dead father. In Egypt, he falls in love with Queen Charoba and is betrayed by the sorcery of her nurse, Dalica, and her sister, Mythyr, dying after donning a poisoned robe on his wedding feast. So the question naturally arises: how is this tragic romance plot related to an obscure Arabian book that aligns the Mosaic account of creation with both the mythical history of ancient Egyptian hermeticism and the tradition of Islamic prophecy? An answer to this question is worth considering despite Landor's emphatic assertion that only "the shadow of the subject" came from this "wild and incoherent, but fanciful, Arabian Romance"

and that "[n]ot a sentence, not a sentiment, not an image, not an idea, is borrowed from that work"(343). This cautious disclaimer does not preclude the pervasive impact of the Islamic-hermetic legacy in English literary culture.

I propose that an answer to the above question lies in the late-seventeenth-
and eighteenth-century English interest in the hermetic wisdom of the *prisca
sapientia*. This pristine mystical knowledge was supposedly buried in Arabic-
Islamic texts that had circulated among Rosicrucians, alchemists, and Quakers in
London's underground world since the 1650s and '60s. Between the eighteenth
and early nineteenth century, these texts served as a rich source of poetic inspiration for British authors such as Christopher Smart, John Keats, and Percy Shelley, all of whom drew heavily on the imagery, symbolism, and rituals found in
the hermetic mythologies of alchemically inclined Freemason and Rosicrucian
secret societies.[11] Even though Landor's membership in these clandestine orga-
nizations remains a mystery, *Gebir* clearly reflects the kind of Masonic, hermetic,
and alchemical concerns that would later whet Robert Southey's and Percy Shelley's intellectual appetite for uncovering ancient and heretical genealogies of the
Islamic Near East (to be discussed in chapters 5 and 6, respectively). Murtada ibn
al-Khafif's *The Egyptian History* played a more prominent role in defining *Gebir*'s
literary contours—and Romantic perceptions of Islam in general—than Landor
could possibly have anticipated or would have been willing to concede.

The hermetic romance of Gebir and Charoba first appeared in John Davies's English translation of *The Egyptian History* (1672). Born in Kidwelly, Car-
marthenshire, in 1625, Davies was trained as a Presbyterian at St. John's College in
Cambridge. With the patronage of John Hall of Durham, one of the leading republican propagandists, Davies set out to France, mastering the French language,
before returning to London, where he made his living translating French books.
In his translation of Murtada's work, from Pierre Vattier's French translation,
Davies includes a dedication to his uncle, John Griffith, in which he describes
his fascination with the "Genius of our earliest Predecessors" and asks his uncle
to "reflect on the Actions and Apophthegmes of those who have Inhabited the
World many Centuries of years before us."[12] Davies does not mention how he
came across the French translation of Murtada's work, offering only a brief reit-
erated account of Vattier's discovery of this Arabic text, nor any clues about his
intended reading audience besides his uncle. In his biography, Anthony Wood is
silent about Davies's political affiliations before and after the Restoration, simply
stating that he died in 1693 as "a genteel, harmless and quiet man."[13]

Nevertheless, Davies may not have been as innocent as Wood portrays him.
In Chalmers's biographical dictionary, Davies is described as having adopted the

"professions of the republican party" while he was at St. John's college during the English Civil War.[14] His relation to John Hall seems to confirm this view. In his pamphlet *Considerations upon the Resignation of the Late Parliament* (1654), Hall was one of the first to call for the dissolution of parliamentary control before it took place, a significant event that led to the establishment of the Lord Protectorate in January 1655.[15] Moreover, Hall left with the revolutionary army to invade Scotland and was afterward distinguished with favor by Oliver Cromwell himself.[16] Hall also played an active role in the circulation of mystical literature from abroad. Closely collaborating with Hall, Davies was the main middleman in the trafficking of subversive literature after the Restoration, translating a great number of French works on medieval alchemy, Christian heresies, and divine prophecies.

Among the translated works Davies published for Hall, Johann Valentin Andreae's *The Right Hand of Christian Love Offered* is of great theological and political significance. Hall was the first to translate and publish this popular hermetic-Rosicrucian work in 1647, followed by a second edition in 1655 coedited with Davies.[17] This work mostly derives from Andreae's *The Reipublicae Christianopolitanae Description*, first published at Strasburg in 1619, a classic hermetic work that describes the construction of an ideal Christian city based on scientific knowledge and principles passed down from ancient Arabia. A Lutheran pastor and mystic from Wurttemberg, Andreae wrote this work as a guide to the establishment of "Societas Christiana"—Rosicrucian communities that he founded between 1618 and 1620.[18] In *The Right Hand of Christian Love Offered*, Andreae offers a mystical vision of an egalitarian community based on the wisdom of the ancients; only the principles of the *Respublica Mosaica*—the pristine commonwealth founded by Moses and based on esoteric Egyptian knowledge—can overcome abusive class hierarchies and eliminate economic exploitation. In Andreae's imagination, the Christian Republic is in opposition to the sinful world of "hard bondage" and "many unwelcome labours . . . paying no wages." Only *labor* for Christ will lead to "Christian liberty" on Earth.[19]

Hall published *The Right Hand of Christian Love Offered* along with an opening piece titled *A Modell of a Christian Society* for Samuel Hartlib, the puritan reformer and mystic who, after having read Andreae's work and witnessed the "Societas Christiana" in Germany, immigrated to England in the 1640s with the intent of setting up egalitarian communities and "schools" of science. The parliamentary England of the 1640s provided the kind of intellectual firmament in which Puritan reform and scientific advancement seemed possible. Thus, Hartlib, after having escaped the Catholic conquest of Elbing in Polish Prussia, founded the Office of Address in England through the financial support of Parliament.[20] The objective of this state-sponsored organization was, ideally, to arrange a system of intellectual correspondences with international scholars and scientists who could supply rare books and manuscripts from remote libraries. In this context, the aim of the Office of Address was, according to Hartlib, to increase information on "matters of Religion, learning, and all Ingenuities." With these goals in mind, Hartlib commissioned John Hall to translate two documents relating to Andreae's "Societas Christiana," which were used as a means of promoting the Office of Address.[21] Hartlib's organization also supported the kind of radical scientific ideals that profoundly influenced Robert Boyle and the latter establishment of the Royal Society; in fact, Boyle maintained a close correspondence with Hartlib and was very enthusiastic about Hall's translation of Andreae's works, going so far as to praise one of Hall's works, *Leucenia*, a mystical romance that features the coming of the Christian Republic.[22] Even though Hartlib was not acquainted with Boyle and his "Invisible College" until they met in 1647, Hartlib, whom Boyle dubbed as the "Midwife and Nurse" of the Invisible College, encouraged him and other radical scientists, including future members of the Royal Society, to study alchemy and hermeticism under the care of the Protectorate.[23]

Because alchemists and radical scientists had more freedoms under Protestant protection than under Catholic rule, the late-sixteenth- and mid-seventeenth-century mystical-hermetic movement was deeply entrenched in the reform politics of radical Protestantism. From the second decade of the seventeenth century onward, the study of spiritual alchemy—as conveyed through key Rosicrucian manifestos such as Andreae's *Fama Fraternitatis* (1614) and *Confessio Fraternitatis* (1615)—was associated with an antiroyalist politics that sought economic, educational, and religious reform. With the English Commonwealth's relative freedom of the press, the 1650s witnessed an explosion of hermetic and alchemical writings attacking the church and allied to the cause of political and religious radicalism.[24] Within the English hermetic movement, Hartlib and Hall were two of the most prominent collectors of rare books and manuscripts on alchemical knowledge; besides its significance for the scientific study of experimental chemistry, this esoteric knowledge was primarily used as a way of defining Protestant republicanism through the study of religious histories. In *A Humble Motion to the Parliament of England Concerning the Advancement of Learning* (1649), a tract opposed by bishops in the Anglican church, Hall argues that social, religious, and educational reform of Protestant England requires that the universities implement the study of alchemy, anatomy, medicine, and world religions into their general curriculum. He also advocates thorough research into the history of various non-European cultures, as he later argued in *Of the Advantageous Reading of History* (1657), and calls for the establishment of a library dedicated to the acquisition of rare books and manuscripts on religious histories from around the world.[25]

Hall's activities were of vital importance to the growth of the Hartlib circle: he served as Hartlib's link to the Cambridge neo-Platonists, particularly to Henry More, and their huge collection of Arabic and alchemical works.[26] More visited Hartlib in 1655 and met other members of his circle in 1659, a period in which many Arabic books and manuscripts were in heavy circulation. Like Hartlib and his circle, More believed that ancient knowledge from Egypt and Arabia was crucial in an era of scientific discoveries and political changes; More, in other words, was devoted to the alchemical tradition of the *prisca sapientia* supposedly buried in eastern texts that predate the Mosaic account of creation. For More and other Cambridge neo-Platonists, these mystical, non-Christian sources, mostly hermetic and Arabic works from the twelve and thirteenth centuries, can be reconciled with the basic monotheistic tenants of the true apostolic Christianity.[27] In the hopes of attaining esoteric knowledge passed down from Noah and Moses, Hartlib studied ancient alchemical works on Jewish antiquity and Egyptian science, not only to learn more about the secrets of medicine and transmutation but, like More, to discover a means of restoring the golden age. In this context, Hartlib's unique collection of Arabic manuscripts—made possible through substantial parliamentary grants[28]—reflects a theological-political agenda in which the eastern sciences were the key to restoring Christianity to its primitive egalitarian condition, that of the *Respublica Mosaica,* in Cromwell's England.

From the perspective of dissenting radicals, particularly Quakers, the Arab-Islamic legacy became indistinguishable from the *prisca sapientia*, making knowledge from "Araby" central to a Protestant understanding of hermetic, Rosicrucian, and alchemical texts. By the mid-seventeenth century, a huge surge in the popularity of the Arab-Islamic esoteric sciences resulted in the English translation of the hermetic corpus from its primary linguistic medium, Arabic. For instance, English scientist and theologians were eager to obtain the works of Arabian alchemists, primarily those of Jabir ibn Hayyan, known in England as "Geber" (a possible derivation for "Gebir"). Moreover, Edward Pococke translated Ibn Tufayl's *Hayy ibn Yaqzan*, a twelfth-century allegorical tale that fuses Islamic and Aristotelian doctrine into a "rational" monotheism. This work was especially popular among the Hartlib circle, Quakers, and radical freethinkers.[29] George Keith, a Quaker apologist, translated this Oriental tale as *An Account of the Oriental Philosophy, the Wisdom of some Renowned Men of the East* (1674), praising its philosophical rationalism and mystical knowledge. For him, Ibn Tufayl's work is not only agreeable with "Christian principles" but also reveals God's true "inner light" without the aid of the church and orthodox dogmas.[30] The hermetic genre of the Eastern romance allegorizes a heretical Quaker ideology. Not surprising, orthodox Anglicans directly equated the hermetic and mystical philosophies of the Quakers—mainly those of George Fox—with a "Mahometanism" construed as a revolutionary civic religion that poses a major threat to the Anglican establishment.[31]

Partly due to his radical interest in Oriental tales and partly because of his connections to the parliamentary regime of the 1650s, Hartlib's scientific agendas were condemned during the Restoration.[32] Terminating his relation with Robert Boyle, the Royal Society, and its Anglican latitudinarianism, Hartlib and his circle continued to practice a form of spiritual alchemy that High Anglican authorities viewed suspiciously as a covert attempt to undermine ecclesiastical and civil law. Thus, the study of hermetic and Arabic texts was a subversive activity primarily practiced by radical scientists and republicans throughout the late seventeenth century.[33] Indeed, this radical literary and scientific context serves as the backdrop to the Mahometan-deist views of Henry Stubbe, whose policies on social, educational, and religious reform are reminiscent of the Hartlib circle, and John Toland, whose defense of the *Respublica Mosaica* are indebted to the Arabic-hermetic tradition of *prisca sapientia* (see chapter 1).

Given the wide circulation of radical hermetic texts in the late seventeenth century, the polemical bent of an alchemical text like Murtada's *The Egyptian History* becomes easier to decipher. Indeed, Murtada's work is full of praises for the "divination," "astrology," and "occult sciences" taught by the ancient Egyptian priests; it even includes a section dedicated to the story of a reputed Egyptian priest, Hermes (Hermes Trismegistus), who was extremely knowledgeable of ancient science and foretold the coming of the Deluge.[34] Alongside his fantastic renditions of Mosaic history, Murtada also includes extraordinary narratives that trace the origins of primitive Christianity—in this case, an antitrinitarian Coptic monotheism—to a utopian, scientific city modeled after the predeluvian, Egyptian civilization. Like many of his contemporaries, Murtada sought to anchor the Islamic tradition within earlier, Coptic histories that predate the Arab conquest of Egypt in the seventh century; hence, he is primarily invested in aligning glorious myths about the pre-Islamic history of Egypt with a Qur'anic metanarrative about the life of the Old Testament prophets.[35] Given Davies's association with Hall and the Hartlib circle, Murtada's Coptic account was perhaps seen as reconfirmation of the supposed truth behind hermetic history. In other words, the *prisca sapientia* buried in this Arabian text reveals the past existence of an Islamic-Christian republic, an early attempt to restore the Christian faith to its pristine Mosaic condition. Like most Arabic-hermetic works imported to England, *The Egyptian History* was most likely read as a Rosicrucian Oriental tale that reconciles primitive Christianity with the "inner light" of Near Eastern monotheism.

In extracting the Gebir-Charoba romance plot from a medieval Arabian book, Landor aligns his writings (and politics) with the Islamic-inspired hermetic tradition of Rosicrucianism, alchemy, and Quakerism. His earlier writings support this view. *The Poems of Walter Savage Landor* (1795) includes a long poem in three cantos titled "The Birth of Poesy," in which Landor traces the origin of poetry to ancient Greece and Egypt, as well as to Judaic history. In canto 1, Orpheus recites a palinode in which, after singing about the Divine creation, he proclaims that only Moses has truly seen God: "Yet one, one only, hath his visage / seen: / One of Chaldea, from an ancient / race, / Who knew the planets, knew their / name and place. / How all the system moves around / the poles, / And how the sphere upon its axis / rolls."[36] The footnote to these verses is especially revealing:

> Moses is the Chaldean: so called, perhaps, from a long residence there, or in Egypt, where, like Orpheus, he had acquired the knowledge of *many mysteries* . . . many have been so absurd as to reduce most of antiquity to a Judaic origin. Hence, they have dreamed that Orpheus and David were one and the same person. There is not a period of their lives in which they resemble each other, though in their writings there is often a striking similarity. Still, the pieces attributed to Orpheus are more correct than the Psalms of David. (314)

In claiming that Moses is a Chaldean who learned science and astrology while in Egypt, Landor attributes a purer Judaism to the Egyptian "mysteries" than to the Old Testament. His revisionist account of Mosaic history carves out a pivotal role for eastern esoteric science within the metanarrative of Old Testament prophecy.

Faithful to Murtada's unorthodox account of biblical-Islamic history, Landor explores the motif of Moses' Egyptian wisdom. Book 5 of *Gebir* begins with a description of the ruined city of Masar, known as "Missr el Kahira" in Arabic, or "Cairo" in English:

> Once a fair city, courted then by kings,
> Mistress of nations, thronged by palaces,
> Raising her head o'er destiny, her face

Glowing with pleasure, and with palms refreshed,

Now, pointed at by Wisdom or by Wealth,

Bereft of beauty, bare of ornaments,

Stood, in the wilderness of woe, Masar. (32, lines 1–7)

This description of the mythical city of Cairo, which historically was the capital of the Fatimid caliphate between 909 and 1171, strikes the chords of eighteenth-century ruin sentiment to remind readers of a specific event in the Old Testament: the biblical account of the Tower of Babel. This association between Babylon and the ancient Egyptian city of Cairo is crucial in the Qur'an. The fall of Egyptian imperial power is there attributed to the Pharaoh's impious treatment of Moses: upset over Moses' defiance of the Egyptian gods, the Pharaoh asks Haman, his chief minister, to build him a great tower out of clay bricks on which he may ascend to heaven and kill the God of Moses. As a result, the God of Moses demolishes the tower, killing most of the Pharaoh's army.

In George Sale's translation of the Qur'an (1734), Moses' liberation of the Hebrews is associated with the downfall of corrupt Egyptian tyranny and magic (320). Landor employs this Qur'anic motif even as he deviates from the Islamic and biblical accounts; Queen Charoba's nurse, Dalica, takes a journey to Cairo with the purpose of concocting a magical potion to poison Gebir and save Charoba from the foreign conquerors. Among the ruins she meets her sister Mythyr, and the reader discovers that Dalica and Mythyr are the descendants of an accursed "ancient race" of magicians who fought against Moses during the Hebrew exodus:

Still were remaining some of ancient race,

And ancient arts were now their sole delight.

With Time's first sickle they had marked the hour

When at their incantation would the Moon

Start back, and shuddering shed blue blasted light.

The rifted rays they gather'd, and immersed

In potent portion of that wondrous wave

Which, hearing rescued Israel, stood erect,

And led her armies through his crystal gates. (32, lines 14–22)

In this dense passage, "rescued Israel," or Moses' liberated people, fought at the city of Cairo as they made their way out of Egypt. Considering the references to "ancient arts" and "Time's first sickle," the "ancient race" possibly refers to an accursed race of Egyptian magicians who survived the Deluge and later failed to defeat the Hebrews. This account deviates from the Old Testament story of the exodus and the Qur'anic treatment of Moses as described in Sale's translation. Following Murtada's unorthodox account of biblical history, Landor is suggesting that Moses and the Israelites defeated the Pharaoh and his accursed evil magicians with the help of esoteric knowledge passed down from the predeluvian Egyptian priests. Indeed, this account of the Hebrew people is explicitly outlined in Murtada's hermetic interpretation of Mosaic history, which deviates from the Qur'anic account: Moses inherits science and alchemy from the descendants of the predeluvian Egyptian priests, whereas the Pharaoh misuses this ancient knowledge to persecute Moses and his people.[37]

The literary parallels between Landor's poem and Murtada's account do not prove that the plot of *Gebir* was borrowed from an "Arabian Romance" or invalidate Landor's claim to originality. More often than not, he deviates from Murtada's and Clara Reeve's versions in favor of peculiar innovations. And yet these parallels point to an Arabic-Islamic legacy that, after its transplantation in Restoration England, offered a vast repertoire of occult hermetic material— plots, motifs, themes, rituals, and symbols—with which Landor could rewrite the biblical account of universal Mosaic history. Whether he knew it or not, he drew inspiration from the "wild," "incoherent," and "fanciful" aspects of Murtada's strange stories while writing his idiosyncratic and confusing Oriental tale about ancient Egypt. In fact, he was deeply committed to the study of Arabic culture and literature and read many European works on Muslim religious practices, occult Arabian lore, and Egyptian magic as evident in a footnote from his 1800 publication, *Poems from the Arabic and Persian*.[38] Like Bonaparte, he sought hermetic wisdom in the literary relics of the Islamic Near East.

The Jacobin Mahdi

My historical survey of Arabic hermeticism in the long eighteenth century constitutes the primary social context from which to understand English republicanism in the 1790s and, congruently, Bonaparte's colonial project in Egypt—an unprecedented literary, philological, and scientific undertaking that for Edward Said inaugurated modern Orientalism. Indeed, Landor claims to have read Arabian and Persian poems from a French translation in which he discovered a preface that he considered compelling enough to append to *Poetry by the Author of Gebir* (1800) but later removed due to its treasonable contents. His supposed translation of the "Extract from the French Preface" voices outspoken support for Bonaparte's Egyptian campaign. It also contains a hermetic subtext that celebrates the search for the *prisca sapientia*:

> No nation pursues with an equal alacrity the arts which embellish life. In the midst of a
> foreign, roused and resuscitated at the unextinguished beacons of a civil, war, while ca-
> lamity constantly kept pace, and sometimes struggled with, glory, her general meditated,
> and at once accomplished, the eternal deliverance of Egypt. Men of learning and men of
> science were the proper companions of Buonaparte. They are engaged at this moment in
> presenting to Europe the fruits of their several discoveries. Conquerors like him, poster-
> ity will declare it, have never been the enemies of the human race.[39]

Reiterating the nymph's prophetic vision, Landor depicts Bonaparte as the mystical hero who travels to Egypt in search of the ancient arts and sciences; he rejuvenates a decadent European civilization with his "vast intellectual treasures" from the Arabian East, thereby fulfilling the republican vision of equality and fraternity on earth. The Masonic-hermetic tradition figures very prominently in this narrative. Hermes Trismegistos once ruled over a utopian city in Egypt, which, according to Freemason lore, is the origin of an egalitarian society that housed all the arts and sciences, and at one point included the inventors of all sciences and laws: mainly, Osirius, Jupiter, Mercury, Moses, and Mahomet. In fact, Bonaparte himself was interested in Masonic affairs in France and was convinced that Egypt was the center of world civilizations, as evident in his attempt to transcend Christianity by championing the cause of Judaism and Islam during his occupation of Egypt.[40] Not surprising, Landor removed the "Extract from the French Preface" to avoid a sedition charge during an era in which the British government was cracking down on radical authors and publishers. This section argues that this self-censoring decision partly reflects a fear that his work on Arabic and Persian poetry—including *Gebir*—could be publicly perceived as propaganda in support of the Islamic republic instituted by "Ali Bonaparte," the self-styled Jacobin Mahdi.

Casting himself as a Muslim convert, Bonaparte adopted the name of Ali, the cousin and son-in-law of the Prophet, to appease the elite Egyptian clerics and quell any revolts among Cairo residents who resented foreign occupation under Christian infidels. Supposedly, the French came as deist liberators rather than colonizing crusaders. Their mission was to overthrow the Egyptian ancien régime, the despotic Mamluk Beys—descendents of enslaved Christian soldiers from Circassia and Georgia who rose to power in Egypt under the nominal rule of the Ottomans—and not to convert the population to Christianity, to eliminate the Ottoman administrative infrastructure, or to disown the Sultan's authority. In order to convince the ulema of his benign intentions, Bonaparte founded a "Directory" composed of French officials supervising a governing council of Muslim clergy and Cairo elites, which functioned independently of the Ottoman sultanate. He also patronized local mosques and Qur'anic studies, protected pilgrim caravans to Mecca and Medina, presided over Muslim holidays and Egyptian festivals, and even tried converting the French army to Islam legally without undergoing the Muslim practice of circumcision and imposing the wine-drinking prohibition (an un-Islamic proposition that was rejected by the Muslim clerics of the Al-Azhar Seminary in Cairo).[41] Marriages between Frenchmen and Muslim women were common, accompanied by formal conversion to Islam. Indeed, French general Jacques Menou, governor of Rosetta, married a notable Egyptian woman of the Sharif caste and changed his name to "Abdullal" (Servant of God).[42] Inspired by a deist fascination with Islamic doctrine, these French policies concealed an ambitious colonial project in Egypt and Syria: a covert military operation to undermine British wealth in India by dominating vital trade routes between the Near East and Central Asia. By laying claim to the Sultan's power and the Prophet's progeny, Bonaparte sought to consolidate his imperial power in a key geopolitical region that the British navy, under the command of Admiral Horatio Nelson, had only partially saved from French incursions after Nelson's famous naval victory at the Battle of Aboukir (Abu Qir) Bay in July 1798. Situated in this international and colonial context, Bonaparte's proclamation to the Muslim inhabitants of Egypt is an attempt to pass off French deists as professing Muslims for propagandistic purposes only.

After the Sultan declared a defensive jihad against France in September 1798, joining the anti-French coalition with Britain and Russia, Bonaparte was forced to revise his propaganda. Because he could no longer convince the Al-Azhar clerics that he was a viceroy acting under express orders from Istanbul, nor could he persuade them to disown their loyalty to the Sultan, he held a diwan (Muslim council) in December 1798 to proclaim himself a Mahdi, a Muslim messiah. Bonaparte assumed the occult prophetic status of the "awaited one" who is to usher a perfect Islamic society on Judgment Day based on peace, justice, and equality. Originating in radical Shi'ite eschatology, the belief in the returning Mahdi became widespread in Egypt during the Shi'ite Fatimid dynasty, between the tenth and twelfth centuries (the era during which Murtada wrote *The Egyptian History*). This imperial state theology was opposed to the Sunni Abbasid caliphate. Ever since, the concept of the Mahdi became part of an Egyptian folk occultism shared among Shi'ite and Sunni Muslims and was deployed periodically by rebels who wished to replace the existing order with a just Islamic polity. Unlike Christianity and Judaism, this occult strand of Islamic messianism focuses on the active historical responsibility of its followers to establish an ideal religio-political community (a reconstituted and reformed *umma*) rather than on a returning "savior" who redeems a passive humanity in need of spiritual regeneration.[43] In an effort to revise his colonial rhetoric, Bonaparte treated Mahdihood as an eschatological version of French *égalitare*—a convenient piece of propaganda for prophesying the imminent collapse of the sultanate (and all monarchal rulers) without alienating the Egyptian ulema and Muslim population or offending the republican morale of an exhausted French army that was becoming increasingly restless. Ultimately, Bonaparte's strategic switch from deist Muslim to occult prophet did not secure his power. In August 1799, he fled to France undetected, only to obtain the absolutist title of "First Consul for Life" after launching a successful coup in October. Combined British and Ottoman military forces eventually drove the abandoned French Army out of Egypt in 1801.

Notwithstanding his self-serving propaganda, Bonaparte's admiration for the Prophet and Islamic civilization was genuine enough to displace the anticlerical rhetoric that he had previously deployed in Europe. In his private memoir, he treats Muhammad as his imaginary alter ego, a republican "prince":

> Muhammad declared that there was only one God, who had neither father nor son and that the Trinity imported an idea from paganism. . . . Muhammad was a prince; he rallied his compatriots around him. In a few years, his Muslims conquered half the world. He rescued more souls from false gods, overturned more idols, and pulled down more pagan temples in fifteen years than adherents of Moses and Jesus Christ had in fifteen centuries.[44]

Pursuing this deist strain of thought, Napoleon also praises the enlightened rule of the Abbasid Caliphs of the eighth and ninth centuries for their patronage of the arts and sciences, particularly for promoting the translation of Greek and Latin works into Arabic, encouraging the development of poetry, philosophy, chemistry, and mathematics, and transmitting this Arab-Greco legacy to future generations in Western Europe.[45] In Napoleon's case, the iconoclastic history of Islam feeds into a personal imperial fantasy of worldwide republican domination and enacts a hermetic-mystical quest for Eastern Enlightenment, the Arabic *prisca sapientia*. As I have noted, these two currents of thought constitute the cultural life of the radical Enlightenment in England and Europe. As manifested in Bonaparte's occult status as Mahdi, Egyptian hermeticism, broadly defined, is the guiding leitmotif of his deist-Islamic policy. This synchronized vision of Islam, paganism, and occultism can be seen, for example, in his participation during the Festival of the Nile. In this ceremony, Bonaparte, appareled in Oriental dress, the tricolor flag of revolutionary France flown from minarets throughout the city of Rosetta, was visually juxtaposed with Egyptian architectural themes: wooden obelisks, ringed columns, ancient pyramids, and looming arches. This public spectacle not only served to promote Franco-Egyptian solidarity but also—as a ritualized performance that recalls Masonic imagery and symbolism—to emphasize the affinity between French egalitarian principles and Shari'a law.[46] The political ideal of liberty, equality, and fraternity was fused with a hermetically tinged Islamic messianism, which, in a time of change and uncertainty, temporarily served as the de facto state idiom of France between 1798 and 1799. As Juan Cole aptly notes in his study on the Egyptian campaign, "The French Jacobins," having turned away from European affairs, "were now creating Egypt as the world's most modern Islamic Republic."[47]

Needless to say, this Jacobin investment in Islamic republicanism alarmed British government officials and Tory conservatives to the point of hysteria. In a desperate bid to ward off any possible revolutions in England, the William Pitt ministry decided to shame oppositional writers by printing an English translation of the French proclamation to the scorn of the English reading public. Appearing in a total of eight editions, the popular publication of the *Copies of Original Letters from the Army of General Bonaparte* was used as a beating stick with which to deprecate Bonaparte's Islamic republic—his "new solon"—and, closer to home, to condemn radical authors and deist freethinkers allegedly implicated in a Franco-Ottoman conspiracy to eradicate Christianity (xi).[48] This publication printed the entire proclamation in English in an accompanying appendix, supplying indisputable evidence of French admiration for Islam. It also referenced "Jacobin" English newspapers—*The Morning Chronicle* and *The Courier*—as unreliable sources of news information. Supposedly, these newspapers had misled the British public into believing that the original Arabic proclamation did not profess Mahometanism.[49] Part of the agenda of this antiradical work, the *Copies*, is to get the record straight: English "Jacobins" want to cast doubt on the authenticity of the proclamation to conceal their despicable sympathetic support for the establishment of an anti-Christian republic in Ottoman Egypt. As I have demonstrated, the late seventeenth and eighteenth centuries abounded with this negative type of paranoid propaganda, no matter how outlandish and groundless. Five months after the publication of *Gebir*, most English readers would have identified any Egyptian-themed tale steeped in republican allegories with a Jacobin-Mahometan plot to undermine British national interests at home and abroad.

Indeed, this identification between Islamic Egypt and French republicanism was so deeply ingrained in British national culture that a new biography of Mahomet acquired the following suggestive title: *The Life of Mahomet, or the history of that imposture, which was begun, carried on, and finally established him in Arabia . . . To which is added, an account of Egypt* (London, 1799). Besides offering yet another standard attack on the Prophet, this anonymous publication appends to the history of Islam a descriptive account of ancient Egypt, which is "now the theatre of war."[50] According to the "Author's Apology for Subjoining An Account of Egypt," the biographer felt compelled to include this material because, having fallen short of his projected page limit, the remainder of the work needed to be filled with useful information that contextualizes Mahomet's life in light of contemporary events. As such, *The Life of Mahomet* speaks more to Bonaparte, the deist "impostor" of Egypt, than to Mahomet, the false prophet of Arabia. It is peppered throughout with political allusions to the Egyptian campaign, invoking an anti-Christian Jacobin-Mahometan plot. This hyperbolic rhetoric erupts in the midst of a sermonizing subsection that exalts the destined triumph of the Gospels and the British Constitution over Muslim global expansion:

> I have heard that in France there are no less than fifty thousand avowed atheists, divided into different clubs and societies throughout that extensive republic, which I believe as firmly as that there are fifty thousand devils around the throne of God; but supposing it were true, and by no means a piece of British manufacture, I do boldly assert that their united endeavors, though assisted by four hundred thousand libertines, atheists, and deists from England, will neither keep Mahometanism from the grave of oblivion, nor the HEALER OF THE NATIONS from universal triumph.[51]

For this biographer, the "united endeavors" of republican French atheists who proselytize "Mahometanism" involves the massive mobilization and full cooperation of "libertines, atheists, and deists from England." These disproportionate numbers—"fifty thousand" French atheists and "four hundred thousand" English heretics—suggest that there are many more sympathizers of Bonaparte's Mahometan policies in Britain than in France. Unrealistic as these staggering numbers may be and however much this biographer self-consciously acknowledges the propagandistic status of this "British manufacture," *The Life of Mahomet* is meant to inflame public resentment against domestic radicals. Due to their deist leanings, they are automatically branded enemies of the British Constitution and friends of Islamic republicanism. As in *Copies of Original Letters*, the agenda here is to demonize Islam in order to stoke nationalist and counterrevolutionary zeal.

To further this anti-Islamic, antiradical agenda, the appended "account of Egypt" casts Ottoman-Islamic political rule as republican in spirit. Sprinkled with remarks on Bonaparte's invasion, this ethnographic account looks at the climate, geography, and societies of ancient Egypt, which includes Pharaonic and Ptolemaic religious beliefs, superstitious practices, and magical rites, examines the pre-Islamic virtues of Egyptian political and legal institutions, and concludes with a warning on the inherent dangers of absolutist monarchies in ancient and modern Egypt. Halfway through, the author brings up "an important topic for political discussion":

> It ought, however, to be remembered, that the Reis Effendi or principal secretary, to-gether with some other ministers of state, are said to have been banished from the Ottoman Porte, on the supposition of being friendly to French principles of government. May not the Bassa of Grand Cairo be likewise tinctured with republican sentiments, in which case all the opposition made to Buonaparte would be merely a feint to save appearances. I do not offer this as a fact, but its being a circumstance far from impossible, affords an important topic for political discussion.[52]

This loaded passage exploits radical Enlightenment theories that imagine Ottoman state officials as the true custodians of a clandestine freethinking tradition—a submerged intellectual legacy originating in the medieval Islamic era and passed down to Europe and England. These theories were frequently deployed by those who, like Lady Mary Wortley Montagu, wanted to legitimize their political opposition to the Anglican state (see chapter 2). By referring to the Bassa's secret "republican sentiments," this biographer employs these theories as proof of the ideological affinity existing between French republican rule and the Ottoman government, insinuating a possible conspiracy that is not based on "fact" but is "far from impossible." Supposedly, Ottoman opposition to Bonaparte's conquest is feigned for the purpose of misleading the British government. Again, this self-conscious use of propaganda not only seeks to discredit the Egyptian campaign but also to treat egalitarian republicanism as a corrupt political theology imported from the Muslim world. The fact that this "important topic" is never discussed but only briefly mentioned encourages paranoid readers to indulge in conspiratorial fantasies regarding the anti-British alliance among French republicans, Ottoman officials, and English infidels.

Although far from being representative of the late 1790s, the antiradical publications of the *Copies of Original Letters* and *The Life of Mahomet* serve as an immediate backdrop to Landor's anonymous Egyptian-themed poem, packed with radical Islamic, hermetic, and deist connotations that contemporary readers could have easily recognized. In February 1800, the *British Critic*—a periodical "intended to uphold the tenets of the Established Church and the Tory politics of the ruling government"—attacked *Gebir* for its blasphemous views on Christianity.[53] Indeed, while studying at Trinity College, Landor wrote a scathing satire on the Anglican church that mocked the kind of conspiratorial fantasies I have noted; his *To the Fellows of Trinity College* (1800) offers a humorous portrayal of the church hierarchy and rituals, especially when the Anglican clergy is confronted with the prospect of a French invasion of vulgar atheists and infidels.[54] This type of seditious writing prompted Robert Southey to dub Landor a "mad Jacobin," one of the most wholehearted enthusiasts for the French Revolution he had ever met.[55] *Gebir*, written two years before *To the Fellows*, also engages in a radical critique of church and state by lending itself retrospectively to Bonaparte's Muslim-deist quest for hermetic knowledge in Egypt.

This provocative mode of radical critique becomes strongly pronounced in book six of *Gebir*, in which the Napoleonic Republic is figured as the emergence of a worldwide utopian community firmly rooted in Egyptian egalitarian ideals: "The Hour, in vain held back by War, arrives / When Justice shall unite the Iberian hinds, / And equal Egypt bid her shepherds reign" (45, lines 225–27). The references to "hinds," "Equal Egypt," and "shepherds reign" suggest that Landor's utopia transcends social and economic hierarchies and is based on an antimonarchical, egalitarian form of government. This social vision is especially significant given that Tamar is the poor shepherd who, as the nymph prophesizes, will become the ultimate hero in the future, superseding the epic grandeur of King Gebir and his doomed people. Only the descendants of Tamar and the Nymph shall enjoy the pleasures of the golden age. These ideas first took shape in Landor's "The Birth of Poesy," a poem that anticipates *Gebir* in its thematic structure. In his introduction to this poem, Landor claims that the origins of poetry can be traced back to a utopian age of shepherds "perhaps before labor was known on earth" (312). In their songs, the shepherds of the fallen world of tyranny nostalgically evoke the "simplicity in *former* times" (emphasis original) and hail the coming of the New Jerusalem (234, line 225).

The New Jerusalem trope reemerges as an integral part of the utopian vision found in *Gebir*. Canto 1 of the "Birth of Poesy" concludes with a "Solymean chief" who proclaims that monarchy will come to an end when a new republic arises in Sion (235, lines 272, 283–84). The principles of this political and spiritual redemption were first taught by Moses, who, after having been initiated into the ancient Egyptian "mysteries," conveyed his knowledge in "two stone-tablets for his native land" (239, line 472). A similar theme pervades in the sixth book of

Gebir. In the nymph's vision, Bonaparte's "New Jerusalem" is heavily tinged in esoteric imagery:

Time,–Time herself throws off his motly garb
Figur'd with monstrous men and monstrous gods,
And in pure vesture enters their pure fanes,
A proud partaker of their festivals.
Captivity led captive, War o'erthrown,
They shall o'ver Europe, shall o'er Earth extend
Empire that seas alone and skies confine,
And glory that shall strike the crystal stars. (47, lines 301–8)

The personified Time casting away a corrupt monarchical and ecclesiastical history—the "monstrous men and monstrous gods"—recalls images of the "temple of Virtues" erected in Masonic lodges; these secret festivities mostly involved symbolic rituals celebrating the coming of a new egalitarian utopia throughout Europe (the "New Jerusalem"). As Margaret Jacob has shown, pagan rituals and festivities became fashionable among Masonic lodges during the early phase of the French Revolution.[56] A Mason who witnessed an Egyptian ritual at a lodge describes a Masonic ceremony: "Our brother orator ascended the chair and entertained us with the customs of the ancient Egyptian Priests to transmit the heroic deeds or the histories of the country to posterity by way of metaphorical symbols. . . which makes us notice how necessary is silence, virtue and the sociable love of mankind."[57] Allegorical narratives about ancient Egypt encapsulate the principles of the French Revolution: virtue, equality, and fraternity. As in Landor's poetics, freemasonry frequently made use of Egyptian-hermetic myths to convey their enthusiasm for the French Revolution and their total dislike of the ancien régime, the monarchical and clerical establishment. During Bonaparte's occupation of Egypt, these Egyptian-themed Masonic ceremonies and rituals acquired renewed political vigor by serving as the official idiom of the Islamic Directory in Cairo.

But why was Landor so invested in Egyptian Masonry? In a footnote to the "Birth of Poesy," Landor cites William Warburton's *The Divine Legation of Moses demonstrated* (1738) as his primary source of information on Mosaic history. Warburton was an Anglican theologian and clergyman of the mid-eighteenth century who defended Orthodox Christianity against the twin threats of Hermeticism and Spinozism; in his lengthy two-volume work, he argued that the implementation of Mosaic law must be based on divine revelation because it is not supported by an ancient pagan legality necessary for the moral welfare of society. For him, the Eleusinian mysteries of antiquity, particularly their doctrine on the afterlife, were essential in ossifying the moral belief of society and supporting the legal authority of the political establishment.[58] Although Moses dispenses with the necessity of instituting the doctrine of an afterlife (and thus, Mosaic legation must be supported by supernatural means), he bases the religious practices of the early Israelites on the Egyptian mysteries. Landor promotes this view when he states that the palinode of Orpheus was uttered by "other great Solemnities" (314).

But what would attract Landor to Warburton's historiographical outlook on the role of prophetic revelation in pre-Mosaic Egypt? In section four of *The Divine Legation of Moses demonstrated,* Warburton argues that it is plain hypocrisy for the early church fathers to speak of the mysteries as "gross impieties" when it is obvious that these esoteric doctrines held a pure, spiritual morality that influenced the course of Mosaic history and early Christian doctrine (2:175). Moreover, the Pagan mysteries contain divine moral teachings that were altered and corrupted by the early Christian church: "[the Fathers] . . . so studiously and affectedly transfer the Terms, Phrases, Formularies, Rites, Ceremonies, and Discipline of these *odious Mysteries* into our holy Religion; and thereby, very early viciate and deprave, what a Pagan Writer could see and acknowledge, was ABSOLUTA & SIMPLEX as it came out of the Hands of its divine Author" (2:177). Even though this is mostly an attack on the tradition of Catholic corruption, Warburton acknowledges that the Mosaic tenets of Christianity have existed in embryonic form among Pagan teachings of the Eleusinian mysteries before the early Christian church defiled these simple and pure teachings. Although Warburton took his work to be a condemnation of Catholicism and a defense of orthodox Anglicanism, it prompted accusations of infidelity and sparked controversies among clergymen in England and France. In giving precedence to Egyptian culture over the Hebraic, Warburton's work seriously compromises the exceptional truth of Judeo-Christian history in the same fashion in which hermetic and deist works set out to do. In the preface to his second edition of *The Divine Legation,* Warburton rigorously refuted those opponents who claimed that his defense of Christianity was a false pretense used to support atheism, deism and Arianism (x–xi). However, Warburton's work became very influential among radical Protestants who made use of its dense historical research on antiquity but discarded its orthodox Christian stance on divine revelation. This occurred for one primary reason: Warburton exclusively locates prophetic revelation in the pre-Mosaic antiquity of Egypt, prolonging the biblical chronology beyond the orthodox time span of six thousand years.[59]

Landor seized upon the subversive tendencies in Warburton's controversial views. As in the case of deist freethinkers and dissenting radicals, Landor deploys duplicitous rhetoric and ironic self-distancing in order to read against the grain of orthodox Anglican discourse. After citing Warburton's views on early Christianity in a footnote to the palinode of Orpheus, he adds that "the *honest Fathers* may be said to have possessed at least as much zeal as information or fidelity" (313). According to Landor, the church fathers were immersed in ancient Egyptian "mysteries." In an obscure gloss on a footnote in "The Birth of Poesy," he states that

> The Priests at Eleusis enjoined the strictest secrecy; and probably not without reason. Even the Christian piety could not keep its temperament in these nocturnal and subterraneous assemblies. But the mysteries in question may more aptly be compared to those of the *Free Masons*. Such mummeries are prodigies in our enlightened days; though formerly they might have been useful to their Institutors. It is Religion whose name they have generally used–Religion, who is equally amiable and simple in herself, but embarrassed and confused by those who have embraced her. (314)

On the one hand, Landor looks down upon the secrecy and outward ceremonies of the freemasons, whom he compares with the ancient "mystery" religions, but on the other hand he suggests that the freemasons have played a decisive role in the initial formation of civic and religious law. This ambivalent anti-Masonic view sheds light on Landor's theological and political affiliations. His views follow a deist trajectory laid out in late-seventeenth-century speculative mythologies that give exclusive prominence to ancient Egyptian religion over Judaism (Moses is a Chaldean who learns science and magic from Egyptian priests), contradicting the biblical chronology that accepts, given the Archbishop James Ussher's calculations, 4004 BC as the authoritative date the world was created.[60] Despite his explicit anti-Masonic stance, Landor's enthusiasm for Masonic Egypt basks in the French republican spirit that he wholeheartedly celebrates in his self-suppressed "Extract from the French Preface."

The Masonic City of the East

The failure to colonize Egypt and Syria followed by Bonaparte's absolutist control of republican France compromised the utopian egalitarianism of *Gebir*, an Oriental tale that—in historical hindsight—records a Masonic celebration of France's Islamic republic. By 1803, Landor had a change of heart. He ceases to glamorize Bonaparte's hermetic-mystical quest in Egypt and describes his duplicitous politics in a language that recalls Edmund Burke's critique of the French Revolution. In his footnote to "A mortal man above all mortal praise," Landor writes,

> Bonaparte might have been so, and in the beginning of his career it was argued that he would be. But unhappily he thinks, that to produce great changes, is to perform great actions: to annihilate ancient freedom and to substitute new, to give republics a monarchal government, and the provinces of monarchs a republican one; in short, to overthrow by violence all the institutions, and to tear from the heart of all the social habits of men, has been the tenor of his politics to the present hour. (349)

Despite the pervasive Burkean sentiments raised in this passage—references to "ancient freedom" and "social habits"—Landor's cautious qualification should not be read as a conservative retreat from his radical investment in Islamic hermeticism. Although he acknowledges that his praise of Bonaparte is misplaced in the post-Egyptian campaign period, he continues to pursue a republican politics that, in his mind, distinguishes constitutional liberty from colonial tyranny. This section argues that *Gebir*'s anticlerical egalitarianism appropriates Thomas Paine's "Egyptian" account of Mosaic history in order to reconstitute a republican mythos that, ideally, transcends the tragedy of Napoleonic empire-building.

The distinction between constitutional liberty and colonial tyranny become blurred in the hermetic motif of Gebir's splendid city. According to Landor, Gebir seeks to invade Egypt because he wants to avenge the "primeval wrongs" suffered by his ancient Gadite people, who were previously driven out of Egypt. In honor of their ancient ancestors, Gebir and his Gadite men spend their time excavating the ruins of an ancient city they have come to rebuild. Upon exhuming the fragments of the city, a utopian past comes to life: "again the sun / Shines into what were porches, and on steps / Once warm with frequentation—clients, friends, / All morning, satchel'd idlers all mid-day, / Lying half-up, and languid, though at games" (8–9, lines 3–7). The inhabitants of this ancient city resemble eighteenth- and nineteenth-century pictorial depictions of lazy Orientals lounging around ruins, whereas Gebir's men resemble a team of careless and overworked archaeologists:

> Some raise the painted pavement, some on wheels
> Draw slow its laminous length, some intersperse
> Salt waters thro' the sordid heaps, and seize
> The flowers and figures starting fresh to view.
> Others rub hard large masses, and essay

To polish into white what they misdeem
The growing green of many trackless years.
Far off, at intervals, the ax resounds
With regular strong stroke, and nearer home
Dull falls the mallet with long labor fringed. (9, lines 8–17)

Ironically enough, the violence with which the city's remains are excavated and the stringent manner in which the heaps of fragments are polished suggest that Gebir's workers are not preserving the ruins of antiquity; instead, they are literally defacing them. If anything, the striking contrast between the idle and labor-free inhabitants of the ancient city and the hard labor of the Gadite men draws attention to an uneasy parallel between a utopian society buried in the past and a dystopian society that disavows or erases its own history. In other words, Gebir and his scientific army represent a parody of the Masonic-hermetic tradition: the mystical hero of the East recovers special wisdom from a utopian city in Arabia, whereas Gebir and his army disfigure, if not obliterate, the sacred aura of their ancestral city. From a post-1798 standpoint, this passage could be read allegorically as an emerging critique of the Egyptian campaign: Bonaparte and his team of savants are not interested in preserving ancient liberty but instead want to distort Egypt's hermetic past for self-serving and corrupt political ends.

But who are the Gadite people and why are they rebuilding a city in the deserts of Egypt? Although Landor does not faithfully adhere to Arabian history—for him, the name "Gebir" etymologically derives from the word "Gibralter"—he deploys certain motifs from the Islamic account of prophetic history. Gebir sends his army to restore "a city [that] stood/ Upon that coast, they say, by Sidad built,/ Whose father Gad built Gades" (2, lines 43–44). This reference to the Gadites and King Sidad is an allusion to Ad and his people in chapter 89 of George Sale's English translation of the Qur'an: "Hast thou not considered how the LORD dealt with Ad, the people of Irem, adorned with lofty buildings, the like whereof hath not been erected in the land .... who had behaved insolently in the earth, and multiplied corruption therein? Wherefore thy LORD poured on them various kinds of chastisement."[61] Sale's footnote on the legendary city of Iram is also worth noting:

For they say Ad left two sons, Sheddad and Sheddid, who reigned jointly after his decease, and extended their power over the greater part of the world: but Sheddid dying, his brother became sole monarch; who, having heard of the *celestial paradise*, made a garden, in imitation thereof, in the deserts of Aden, and called it Irem, after the name of his great grandfather: when it was finished, he set out, with a great attendance, to take a view of it; but when they were come within a few day's journey of the place, they were all destroyed by a terrible noise from heaven.[62]

Gebir and the Gadites refers to the Qur'anic account of the descendants of Gad (Ad), the "Adites" or "the people of Ad," a powerful tribe of the post-Noahatic era. In Landor's syncretist account, they built the Spanish city of Cadiz (referring to the Latin name Gades). Ad's son, Sidad (or Sheddad), modeled Iram after the "celestial paradise," which he built in the desert near Aden according to Arabian legend and not, as Landor would have it, in the northern coast of Egypt. As Mohammed Sharafuddin rightly points out, the Qur'anic context suggests that Gebir's attempt to rebuild the ancient city of Iram is an impious affront to God's will.[63] What needs to be emphasized, however, is not only that Gebir challenges divine authority but that he is imitating God's role in the biblical story of creation: he rebuilds the city in six days, only to despair on the seventh day when his city is destroyed by supernatural forces (9, lines 35–37). Gebir, in other words, is assuming the role of a false prophet or antichrist figure.

For Landor, Gebir and his people are emblematic of the political and ecclesiastical authorities who corrupt the truths of religious history. Intent on "treasure," Gebir's men uncover a chamber among the ruins where they are confronted by a hostile serpent, which Landor interprets as a warning against arrogant men who violate the sanctity of ruined cities: "Go mighty men, and ruin cities, go—/ And be such treasure portions to your heirs" (9, lines 33–34). This sarcastic commentary serves as an allusion to original sin (the serpent as a symbol of the biblical fall), but equally significant is that the sarcasm reinforces the didactic message of eighteenth-century ruin sentiment: the vanity of all human wishes. In repeating the tragic mistakes of his ancestors, Gebir overlooks Qur'anic warnings about the futility of establishing absolute political power on earth; he simply adopts the blind hubris of those responsible for corrupting the historical sanctity of a pristine, sacred religion. This Qur'anic myth underscores the lessons to be drawn from an abusive monarchical power that exploits religion for the purpose of legitimizing the growth of a great world empire.

Landor incorporates the political lessons of the Qur'anic mythos into the third book of *Gebir*. Having discovered that "Egypt is a land / Of incantation," (14, line 205) Gebir decides to follow the nymph's advice on how to put an end to the supernatural destruction of his city; he completes an elaborate sacrifice in front of seven ancient pillars and then descends into an Egyptian tomb. It is there where he meets Aroar, who tells him that he was sent by the Gods to show Gebir the divine punishments that his father and "the race of Sidad" have undergone in Hell

(17, line 36). Stephen Wheeler provides a convenient gloss showing that "Aroar" is an Old Testament allusion to an ancient city in *Deuteronomy* 2:36; Moses and the Israelites defeated a great king and his people in the city of Aroer by the river Arnon (17). In fact, Landor states that "[Aroar's] name is heard, no more by Arnon's side / the well-wall'd city, which he rear'd, remains" (17, lines 27–28). Moreover, Gebir discovers that Aroar is afflicted by divine punishment for his sinful associations with the ancient Gadites: "I myself / Bore, men imagined, no inglorious part; / The Gods thought otherwise!" (17, lines 39–40). Landor is providing an extra-biblical account of the Hebrew exodus in linking together the Old Testament account of Aroar with the Islamic account of the Gadites. Again, Landor rewrites Mosaic history in a way that is reminiscent of how radical Protestants deployed Arabic-Islamic sources to revise scriptural history: in conflating the institution of monarchy with an accursed race of ancient Egyptians (the "race of Sidad"), the ideals of republicanism are firmly grounded in the teachings of Moses.

Landor's Islamic rewriting of the Old Testament figures prominently in his political allegory on the British monarchy. The hellish underworld primarily includes monarchs who "tortured Law / To silence or to speech" and loved their country only for its wealth and "glitt'ring merchandize" (24, lines 283–84, 286–88). Aroar explains to Gebir that this is why his ancestors are suffering in Hell, and that if they had one more chance in life they would gladly embrace poverty and labor instead of raising "trophies, tributes, and colonies" abroad as they did in their previous lives (18, lines 67–73). Gebir also encounters famous historical figures among his ancestors:

> "Aroar, what wretch that nearest us? what wretch
> Is that with eyebrows white, and slanting brow?
> Listen! Him yonder, who, bound down supine,
> Shrinks, yelling, from that sword there, engine-hung;
> He too amongst my ancestors? I hate
> The despot, but the dastard I despise.
> Was he our countryman?"
> "Alas, O King!
> Iberia bore him, but the breed accurst
> Inclement winds blew blighting from north-east." (21, lines 184–92)

Thomas De Quincey, who bought a copy of Landor's *Gebir* when it was first published, was alert to Landor's political allegory: the wretch with the white, slanting eyebrows "is our worthy old George III" and the unknown figure who is "engine-hung" is none other than the guillotined King Louis XVI. For De

Quincey, the message was obvious: if England insists upon its reactionary policy, then George III might end up like Louis XVI. As a conservative Tory who admired Landor's "audacity," De Quincey describes Aroar as being "too *Tom-Panish*" and "up to a little treason."[64]

De Quincey's reading implies that Landor's political allegory contains the same unorthodox tendencies that are associated with Paine's radical deist writings. In section 1 of *The Age of Reason*, Thomas Paine wrote a subversive tract that got him immediately arrested for treason upon its publication in 1793; he claims in this work that his attacks on the system of monarchy necessitate an ideological critique of the clergy, who according to Paine preach their theological mystifications as a way of duping the multitude into willingly submitting to the yoke of tyranny.[65] Paine makes a distinction between "Christianity" and "Christ": he dismisses Christian divinity in a couple of sentences, claiming that the doctrine of the Trinity was decided by majority vote at the council of Nicaea in AD 325 and that Jesus Christ was simply a "virtuous reformer and revolutionist" who preached "the equality of man."[66] Paine, an avowed deist, provides a subversive critique that repudiates the principal ideology of the British monarchy: orthodox Anglicanism and the divine rights of kings. De Quincey suggests that Landor was invested in a similar "Tom-Panish" critique of the British monarchy (it is worth noting that Landor was personally acquainted with Paine and dined with him in the company of Samuel Parr).[67] In the hellish underworld of the third book, there are other British monarchs besides George III: William III (lines 201–11), Charles II (lines 213–16), and Charles I (lines 219–22). In associating these monarchs with the "race of Sidad," Landor dislodges the history of the British monarchy from the Christian narrative of redemption and situates it within the Islamic narrative of damnation. Like Paine, he rewrites biblical history in order to strip the British monarchy of scriptural authority.

Most significantly, the third book of *Gebir* includes William III in the hellish underworld. Here he is denounced as a "tyrant" who withers "t'wixt the continent and isle." According to Landor, William III is the false *"Deliverer"* (21–22, lines 205–9). In articles he wrote for the Whig press, primarily the *Courier* and the *Morning Post*, Landor was rebuked for including William "the Deliverer" in his scathing attacks against the British monarchy and William Pitt's administration. In one of his letters to Landor, Robert Adair, a faithful Foxite Whig and associate of Samuel Parr, expresses his views on Landor's critique of William III: "I confess that I think better of King William than you seem to do."[68] Adair construes Landor's political position as an anti-Whig stance on parliamentary England. However, he is willing to help Landor publish his essays in the *Courier* (which never occurred), since Landor's writing has "resources for escap[ing]" the authorities by "stat[ing] the strongest truths, and to state them safely."[69] Nevertheless, Landor's political views—no matter how "safely" stated—were too radical for a moderate Whig such as Parr, who strongly advised Landor to avoid his "favourite and perhaps erroneous opinions" when writing speeches, newspaper articles, and political pamphlets against the Tory administration.[70] Landor's radical politics are very distinct from the reformist Whig tradition that emerged from the 1688–91 Revolution; and as in the case of Paine's *Rights of Man*—where William III is condemned as a tyrant and "the bill of rights is more properly a bill of wrongs, and of insults"[71]—Landor's *Gebir* should be read as an extreme indictment of both Tory conservatism and Whig reformist politics. In this case, his poem harps back to the egalitarian republicanism popular among radical hermetic circles in the late seventeenth century.

Paine is also interested in this hermetic legacy. In his *Origins of Freemasonry* (1805), Paine sought to vindicate the Freemasons as a special class of enlightened thinkers who derived their pure monotheistic faith from a pre-biblical, quasi-Oriental religion; for Paine, "Masonry . . . is derived and is the remains of the religion of the ancient Druids; who, like the magi of Persia and the priest of Heliopolis in Egypt, were priests of the sun." The reference to Egypt, Persia, and the "priests of the sun" has explicit hermetic overtones. According to Paine, Egypt is "the City of the Sun"—the origin of all the arts and sciences.[72] Of course, this raises an interesting point about Paine's views on Judeo-Christian history in parts 1 and 2 of *The Age of Reason*: if Moses, who "was not an Israelite," was educated by Egyptian priests skilled in science and astronomy, then his account of Mosaic history cannot be located within an exclusive Judeo-Christian chronology.[73] It appears that Paine's views on an "Egyptian" monotheism might have emerged from a larger hermetic-freemason tradition.[74] In this case, Paine's views are almost indistinguishable from Landor's; for Paine, the Christian priestly class has used the false doctrines of "revealed religion" to corrupt the original religion of the *Respublica Mosaica*, an "ancient system of theism" originating from the Near East.[75]

Paine's views are not only an attempt to discredit the church and state but also becomes the basis for his anticolonial, anticapitalist critique. As he makes clear in part 1 of *Rights of Man* (1791), the "truth" of the Mosaic account of creation is that *all* men are created equal without regard to social and economic distinctions, and thus (contra Burke) the British monarchy has no legitimate theological justification for maintaining class divisions or colonizing foreign nations.[76] A similar anticolonial rhetoric appears in the textual revisions and footnotes to the

1803 edition of *Gebir*. By this point in his life, Landor had become disillusioned with Bonaparte's dictatorship in France and recants the Nymph's utopian vision of Bonaparte and the French Revolution in an appended footnote: "Great hopes were raised from the French revolution, but every good man is disappointed. God forbid that we should ever be impelled to use their means of ameliora-tion ... internal and external subjugation" (47). As a compensatory narrative for Napoleon's failed utopian empire, the 1803 edition uses hermetic Islam to supplement republican politics. Landor includes a new hermetic vision in the seventh book, augmented with corresponding "arguments" clarifying the didac-tic message of the poem: "Against colonization in peopled countries. All nature dissuades from whatever is hostile to equality." Landor adds twenty lines describ-ing "the absurdity of colonizing a country which is peopled," which include his radical vision of the egalitarian utopia:

> The Nymphs and Naids teach Equality:
> In voices gently querulous they ask
> "Who would with aching head and toiling arms
> Bear the full pitcher to the stream far off?
> Who would, of power intent on high emprize,
> Deem less the praise to fill the vacant gulph
> Than raise Charybdis upon Etna's brow?
> Amidst her darkest caverns most retired,
> Nature calls forth her filial Elements
> To close around and crush that monster *Void*.— (47–48, lines 15–24)

As in most radical Protestant accounts, the equal distribution of labor is em-phasized; a truly egalitarian republic must overcome the economic and political *"Void"* that separates wealthy leaders from disenfranchised and exploited work-ers. Monarchy is a self-destructive political system that robs the poor workers of their liberty and equality at home and in the colonies, and it is this self-de-structive tendency that Landor exemplifies through the tragic death of Gebir in Egypt: "Mark well the lesson, man! And spare thy kind" (49, lines 29–30). This didactic lesson is gleamed from Napoleon's "internal and external subjugation" of peopled countries, in France, Europe, and Egypt.

By situating Paine's radical views on biblical history alongside Landor's use of hermetic motifs in *Gebir*, what becomes obvious is that Landor's disavowal of Napoleonic republicanism does not represent a swing toward Tory conservatism or a symptom of Burkean nostalgia for "ancient freedom" and the "social habits of men." By the 1803 edition of *Gebir*, the hermetic motifs of the Islamic republicanism become more strongly pronounced, in which case an Arabic-Islamic account of Mosaic history (rather than the secular myths of the French Revolution) serves as the basis for a larger critique of imperial Britain and Anglican evangelism. As De Quincey puts it, Landor's views on Christianity are "degrading" to the English nation, because he has the nerve to question the exceptional truth of the Bible by insisting that the Jews engaged in pagan practices.[77] Of course, radicals such as Landor and Paine would have no qualms with De Quincey's reproach. The purpose of my analysis, however, is not simply to argue for Paine's "influence" on Landor or to conflate the theological beliefs of two distinct thinkers but to uncover a hermetic tradition of Arabic Islam to which both Paine and Landor properly belong. In this respect, *Gebir* is so thoroughly permeated by the utopian-hermetic ideals of an earlier republican era that it cannot possibly adhere to the values of any centralized government, whether absolutist or Napoleonic, nor to the political principles of any economic system that exploits its subjects at home and abroad. However unrealistic these ideals must have appeared in 1803, Landor exalts Islamic hermeticism as if it were politically untainted by recent events in Egypt, Syria, and Europe.

Coda: Political "Gibberish"

By modeling the main plot of *Gebir* after Murtada's *The Egyptian History*, Landor's Oriental tale indirectly appropriates the Arabic-hermetic motifs commonly deployed in seventeenth-century radical Protestant historiographies. Hence, *Gebir* is "hermetic" in the two distinct yet complementary senses: it is a mystical romance that exemplifies what Charles Lamb calls plain nonsense, or "Gibberish," and a radical poem committed to the ideals of social, political, and economic leveling.[78] Although *Gebir* seems to remain aloof of historical realities, it participates in the revolutionary legacy that permeated the Hartlib circle between the 1650s and '70s, the subsequent movement of the radical Enlightenment and Bonaparte's pro-Mahometan deist project. Like his radical predecessors, Landor saw in the Islamic East the *prisca sapientia*—the story of a Protestant republic that circumvents the Anglican account of universal ("European") history and relocates the Mosaic principles of social and economic egalitarianism within the prophetic tradition of Arabic Islam. And like Bonaparte, he saw how this radical Islamic-hermetic legacy could be co-opted for the purpose of consolidating colonial rule abroad, but he also understood that without it there was no hope for a just future. Fraught with ideological contradictions, the 1803 edition of *Gebir* struggles to maintain the distinction between Islamic republicanism and French colonization during a period in which such a distinction was seen as a contempt-ible fiction among a paranoid English public. Because Gebir and his army ironi-cally play into an allegory about Bonaparte and his savants, post-1798, Tamar and the Egyptian nymph—like Gebir and Charoba—are destined to repeat the tragic cycles of revolutionary history.

Gebir's Islamic-hermetic qualities are an outgrowth of the larger prophetic tradition I have described. The poem's compensatory Islamic republic serves two purposes: to allay frustrated desires about Napoleon's betrayal of the French Revolution at home and abroad, and to supplement radical republicanism with an anticolonial politics. My reconfiguration of Landor's theological and political commitments accounts for the "Tom-Panish" anticolonial rhetoric embedded in the narrative of *Gebir*. In this context, the Oriental tale should not be treated as a transparent literary genre that encodes "Oriental exoticism," the moral pri-macy of Western Christianity, or the "manifest destiny" of the liberal British (or French) empire. Indeed, Nigel Leask's paradigmatic assessment of *Gebir* needs to be significantly revised: this poem is not just another narrative that reflects anxi-eties about Britain's imperial mission and it is certainly not a misnomer to speak about an anticolonial rhetoric in the Romantic period.[79] The hermetic legacy of Arabic Islam does not necessarily render an anticolonial rhetoric inoperative, or worse yet, nonexistent when it is deployed in *Gebir*. To argue that the poli-tics of *Gebir* possesses a "residual colonialist rhetoric" in which "to Europe alone belongs the present," as Alan Richardson does, is to read this poem (as well as its historical context) in a manner that ignores the prominence of the Oriental tale among deists, Rosicrucians, alchemists, and Quakers.[80] To accept Leask's or Richardson's verdict, in other words, is to read this genre as exclusively filtered through the lens of a liberal-Whig historiography that forgets Edmund Burke's passionate pro-Mahometan indictment of British imperial rule (see chapter 3) and the elevated status that Islamic republicanism held in the romantic imagina-tion of Landor's most loyal fans—Robert Southey and Percy Shelley.

CHAPTER FIVE

The Flight and Return of Mohammed

Plotting Samuel Taylor Coleridge's and Robert Southey's Unitarian Epic

> Since the beginning of the present century . . . the
> muse has become a very infidel. She has
> followed after strange gods; and become
> familiar with creeds, which would have
> astonished our forefathers. She has been heard
> to chaunt *suras* out of the Alcoran, and *storas*
> out of the books of light, the holy Puranas.
>
> Review of *Helga; A Poem* 1815

Robert Southey and Samuel Taylor Coleridge were enthusiastic about writing a grand Miltonic epic to be titled "The Flight and Return of Mohammed." In the months of July–August 1799, they drafted their plans for their collaborative project, which was to describe some of the historical events that shaped Muhammad's life (see appendixes). In their romantic imagination, the persecution of the Prophet under the idolatrous priests of the Koreish (or Quraysh, the Arab tribe that claims to be descendents of Ishmael, Abraham's son, and to which Muhammad belonged), his antagonism to the local Jewish community, the immediate conversion of his friends and enemies, his triumphant conquest of Mecca, and the expulsion of paganism from Arabia evoke a biblical archetype that reenacts the narratives of biblical monotheism: Noah's repopulation of the world, Moses' exodus from Egypt, David's theocracy in the Holy Land, and Christ's messianic mission in Jerusalem. Though Coleridge's interest in the project began to wane by the end of the year and Southey abandoned it by July 1800, the planned epic on the Prophet's life betrays a radical fascination with Islamic republicanism that, not coincidentally, came to an abrupt—although not final—end soon after Bonaparte left Egypt in August 1799 and deserted his Islamic-based "Directory" in Cairo.

Indeed, the envisioned epic reflects Coleridge's and Southey's youthful enthusiasm for the 1798–99 French campaign to bring Islamic liberty to Egypt. Besides the 109 lines that Southey composed, Coleridge's fragment poem "Mahomet" (1799), which serves as this book's epigraph, best summarizes the political and theological ideas that inspired these two "Jacobin" poets while contemplating recent events in Egypt. Despite the fact that Muhammad has brought about both evil and huge wasteful empires, he is both a Protestant Prophet destined to reform the religion of the idolatrous Christians and a Napoleonic hero intent on liberating the people from political and religious tyranny. Unlike Southey's sketch plan and his version of the epic, Coleridge's "Mahomet" explicitly echoes Napoleon's deist propaganda in Egypt: the republican Prophet destroyed "the Fane of the Idol," both pagan and Christian, and the "Priesthood." In verses recalling the natural and apocalyptic imagery "Kubla Khan," Mahomet leads "the People with mad shouts" in a revolution to liberate the sublime energy of "the ruinous River . . . all rushing impetuous onward." In deploying this enthusiastic rhetoric, Coleridge's poem invokes the Napoleonic politics described in chapter 4: to consolidate French colonial power among the Egyptian ulema or Muslim clerics, Bonaparte assumed the Prophet's mantle. He cast himself as the Mahdi, or "Guided One," who has arrived in Egypt to bring the apocalyptic fall of a decadent Trinitarian Christianity and hail the millennial return of a just Islamic republic.

Not surprising considering its recognizable Jacobinism, the epic on Mohammed's life was abandoned. The publication of the "Mahomet" fragment had to wait until later in Coleridge's life, and Southey's contribution was published posthumously.[1] As with most of the contemporary works that I have examined thus far, an epic on the flight and return of Muhammad would have been too risky and dangerous to publish during the draconian censorship restrictions of the late 1790s. Thus, very little is known about the circumstances that drove the poets to contemplate their Islamic epic. In his later recollections on "Mahomet," Coleridge frames the proposed epic project as introducing a theological "disputation between Mahomet, as the representative of unipersonal Theism, with the Judaico-Christian machinery of angels, genii, and prophets, an idolater with his gods . . . and a fetish-worshipper who adored the invisible alone" (*Anima Poetae*, 290). Interestingly enough, he treats Islam as the religion of "unipersonal Theism" and categorizes Judeo-Christianity alongside pagan idolatry and fetish-worshipping. This unorthodox interest in "unipersonal Theism" resonates with Unitarian polemics against Trinitarian (Anglican) Christianity, and, indeed, by 1794, Coleridge left Cambridge with a heterodox perspective on theology and

politics. He questioned the Trinity, the atonement, and original sin, going so far
as to consider becoming a Unitarian minister during the period of 1796–98. As
an epic celebration of "unipersonal Theism," the theme of the flight and return
of Muhammad embodies a Unitarian critique of the Anglican establishment that,
in defending Islam in Bonaparte's deist terms, would have been too seditious
to publish in the poets' lifetime, even as a fragment poem. Besides, Coleridge
and Southey would have never published this epic for the further reason that its
radical Islamic message was too closely bound up with the colonial failure of the
French occupation of Egypt.

Unitarians were widely perceived as supporters of French Jacobinism. Because
their heretical beliefs were not protected under the 1689 Toleration Act and further penalized by the 1698 Blasphemy Act, many Britons saw them as a political
affront to church and state. As a confirmation of this public resentment, the Birmingham riots of 1791 resulted in a "Church and King" mob burning two Unitarian chapels and several houses belonging to prominent Unitarians. Moreover,
their petitions in Parliament to remove legal disabilities were denied in 1792, only
to be recognized in 1813 with the enactment of the Trinity Act.[2] Given Unitarianism's (or Socinianism's)[3] notorious reputation, British loyalists could construe
a pro-Mahometan epic as a Jacobin-inspired dissenting conspiracy against the
establishment. By foregrounding Coleridge's and Southey's political investment
in the imagined epic, I argue for the historical continuity between a 1690s Unitarianism and the radical appropriation of Bonaparte's propagandistic rhetoric.
In response to this long and complicated history, Coleridge's changing attitudes
toward Islamic republicanism can be charted in three successive phases: an early
interest in Mohammed's life, the abandonment of this epic project in 1800 followed by enthusiasm for Southey's *Thalaba*, and the conservative disavowal of
the Mahometan-Unitarian link in the 1816 publication of "Kubla Khan."

Islam and the Unitarian Controversy

Over a century before Bonaparte landed in Egypt and Coleridge wrote his poem
"Mahomet," English Unitarians were implicated in schemes to institute an Islamic republic. In August 1682, two "single Philosophers," who "come as Orators
of those Unitarians," presented an Epistle to Ahmet Ben Ahmet, the Moroccan
ambassador who was visiting London on a diplomatic mission to renew Anglo-
Moroccan relations concerning the garrison city of Tangier (ix).[4] They praised
the ambassador, the emperor of Morocco, and the Muslim world and described
themselves as "your nearest fellow champions." The addressers deploy diplomatic

rhetoric to persuade the ambassador, as a representative of the "fellow worshippers of that sole supreme Deity of the Almighty Father and Creator," that because Unitarianism and Islam share a belief in God's unity they should form an alliance against "those backsliding *Christians* named *Trinitarians*" (iv–v, vii, ix). According to the Epistle, the ancient pre-Nicene Christianity teaches the oneness of God, which only modern-day Unitarians and the Mahometans continue to uphold. Thus, in the scheme of providential history, Mahometanism is a reformed Christian religion: Muhammad came with the sword as a "*Scourge* on those *Idolizing Christians*," the vile Trinitarians (vii). Ultimately, the addressers portray themselves as helpless victims under the persecution of "the inhumanity of the clergy" and as coreligionists who await their deliverance through the aid of Muslim military might (ix). In many respects, the Epistle not only confirmed Anglican suspicions about a Muslim-dissenter conspiracy but also redefined Unitarianism in early modern England.[5] As such, this Epistle, and the ensuing controversy that it helped to fuel, reveals the extent to which Islamic republicanism became the central organizing trope for describing the politics of Socinian dissent in the early English Enlightenment.

Needless to say, the Epistle caused a huge public uproar among orthodox Anglicans and became the primary target of anti-Unitarian polemics from the 1690s onward. Presented to the Moroccan ambassador and addressed to the Islamic scholars of Morocco, the anonymous Epistle was the work of English Unitarians.[6] Even though the Epistle was framed as a proselytizing work for converting Muslims to Unitarian Christianity (which may explain why the Moroccan ambassador refused to accept it), its central message remains focused on a synchronized monotheistic vision: "not only all the *Patriarchs* down from *Adam* till *Moses*, not only the *Jews* under the written Law, and the Old Testament, to this day, were still Worshippers of an *one only God* (without a *Trinity* of *Persons* :) but that also all the Primitive *Christians*, in and after *Christ*, and his *Apostles*' time" (ix). Primitive monotheists such as Jews and Muslims are closer to the prophetic spirit of Christianity than present-day Trinitarians.

Not surprising given its heretical message, a transcript of this Epistle is found in the orthodox work of a principal Anglican polemicist, Charles Leslie's *Socinian Controversy Discussed* (1708). In this work, Leslie characterizes Socinian proselytizing before the Muslim world as a false pretense aimed against the exceptional status of Christianity: "[I]f we shou'd Dwindle down the *Christian Doctrine* to what [the Unitarians] Believe, we shou'd soon Gaine [the Mahometans]: For then . . . we shou'd Cease to be *Christians* as well as they" (xxix). For Leslie, the Epistle is living proof that the English Unitarians, who, in his mind, believe the "Alcoran to preserve the true faith," have formed a secret political alliance with the Muslim world (ii). According to this conspiracy theory, Muslim Unitarians have forfeited their English identity by, "secretly and Under-hand," holding their government in contempt (xxvii). Conspiracy theories that lump radical Protestants and despotic Muslims together were commonly deployed by High Anglicans and Tories against radical Whigs who supported toleration of dissenters during and after the Exclusion Crisis (see chapter 1). Similarly, Leslie's critique of the Epistle is meant to raise doubts about the citizenship status of nonconforming Unitarians by linking them to "Mahometans."

Nevertheless, Leslie was not the first to link Socinianism to Islam. Ever since the 1609 English publication of what was known as "that Racovian Alcoran"— the Racovian Catechism, which Unitarians used as a propagandistic means of spreading their principles throughout England and Europe—the theological views of Unitarianism and Islam were almost indistinguishable for many Christians in England.[7] This connection was formed so tightly that, by 1670, Richard Baxter, the dissenting Puritan poet, hymn-writer, and theologian, could class the Socinians and Muslims in the same group without offering any elaborate explanations or risking any misunderstandings.[8] But even before the seventeenth century, orthodox Christian theologians stigmatized prominent founders of the Unitarian movement, such as Michael Servetus and Faustus Socinus, as disguised Muslims who derived their antitrinitarianism from the Qur'an through their favorable contacts with North Africans. Anti-Socinian propaganda was also fixated on the notorious legend of the late-sixteenth-century Italian Unitarian Paulus Alciatus, who converted to Islam during his trip to Constantinople.[9] Thus, Leslie's Muslim-Unitarian conspiracy theory has its antecedents in a much earlier tradition of anti-Unitarian propaganda, which his readers would have easily recognized in his polemical reading of the controversial Epistle.

In this earlier tradition, however, the link between Mahometans and Socinians was not construed as a civil issue pertaining to the exclusive concepts of English citizenship and national identity. Under the provisions of the Corporation and Test Acts, which were further reinforced by the 1689 Toleration Act, Unitarians were not treated as English citizens: they could not hold any public office, teach in schools, graduate from Oxford or Cambridge, sue or use any bill in the course of law, become guardians, executors, or administrators, or receive a legacy or deed of gift. Late-seventeenth-century debates that exploited the Muslim-dissenter analogy focused less on religious affiliation (who was Christian or not) and more on questions about the citizenship status of nonconformists, an issue that largely depended on the scope of Anglo-Anglican toleration: the distribution of rights, privilege, and property (see chapter 2). Thus, by the time Leslie published his views, the stigmatizing of Socinians as Mahometans possessed more nationalistic and socioeconomic overtones than previously: if Unitarians are more Muslim than Christian, then that justifies the legal reasons why the Toleration Act should exclude them from the social, economic, and political protections available to English citizens who adhere (in theory or practice) to the nationalist criterion as codified in the Thirty-nine Articles of Anglican faith.

This Anglican appeal to the Muslim-Unitarian connection does not imply that English Unitarians could not equally exploit the Muslim-dissenter analogy for their political gains. Like their deist counterparts, dissenting Unitarians employed Islam as an Erastian beating stick with which to condemn English toleration. In *Vindication of the Unitarians* (1690), for instance, William Freke, an Arian, subtly equates the Unitarian creed with Islamic monotheism and "the unity in the Alchoran," while maintaining that orthodox Anglicans, in their support of the corrupt pagan doctrine of the Trinity, are actually endorsing an oppressive "popery." Because of their belief in God's unity and their toleration of other non-Muslim religions, the Mahometans have experienced more prosperity, politically, economically, and spiritually, than have the adherents of Western Christendom, whether Catholic, Protestant, or Anglican.[10] Likewise, Arthur Bury, the rector of Exeter College and a latitudinarian, defended Islam on Socinian grounds. In *The Naked Gospel* (1690), a work that anticipates Toland's idea that the original Gospel was a simple text that was corrupted by speculative "mysteries," he argues that Mahomet's rise to power was enabled by divine Providence. Accordingly, this Arabian "impostor" was a great "Reformer" who sought to purify the Christian faith from Trinitarian idolatry and restore the Gospel's original "Unitarian" simplicity.[11] Freke and Bury used Mahometanism's Socinian tenets to criticize corrupt aspects of English toleration rather than fuel public resentment against church and state. Nonetheless, this polemical maneuver resulted in harsh persecution under the charge of blasphemy and sedition. Freke suffered at the hands of Parliament for his outspoken heresy: besides having his antitrinitarian tract burned by the public hangman, he was fined five hundred pounds and forced to recant publicly. Bury was fined the same amount, excommunicated, and his *Naked Gospel* was burned.[12] At the height of this Socinian witch hunt, Thomas Aikenhead, who was accused of having preferred Mahomet over Jesus, was executed in 1697.[13] English law criminalized these Mahometan sympathizers as the state's enemies.

The anti-Unitarian smear campaign was partly prompted by the publication of the Reverend Stephen Nye's *A Letter of Resolution concerning the doctrines of the Trinity and the Incarnation* (1691?). His propagandistic work not only offers an outright critique of Trinitarianism as Tritheism (the belief in three Gods) but also reinforces the heretical link between pre-Nicene Christianity and Mahometanism. For Nye, the Trinitarian doctrine is the "stumbling-block" that prevents the Jews and the Muslims from entering the Christian fold. In this case, Nye believes that the Muslims offer valuable lessons about toleration, since Muhammad, a "Unitarian" reformer, not only taught "that one truth in the *Alchoran*, the Unity of GOD," but also introduced civil protection to all the Christian nations he conquered.[14] Jews, Muslims, and dissenting antitrinitarians can become members of the church if Islamic toleration were legally adopted by the Anglican state. Nye portrays Muhammad as a radical Protestant hero who, as in Coleridge's enthusiastic account of the Prophet, reinstituted the original primitive Christianity: "*Mahomet* is affirmed by divers Historians, to have had no other Design in pretending himself to be a Prophet, but to restore the Belief of *the Unity of God*, which at that time was extirpated among the Eastern Christians, by the Doctrines of the Trinity and Incarnation. They will have it, that *Mahomet* meant not his Religion should be esteemed a new Religion, but only the Restitution of the true intent of the Christian Religion."[15]

Many Anglican polemicists hand-picked this particular passage as undeniable proof that the Unitarians have more in common with Islam than Christianity and that, consequently, this shared belief system is indicative of a clandestine Muslim-Unitarian alliance. As in Leslie's conspiracy theory, high Anglicans read Nye's account of Muhammad as a sinister sign that the Socinians do not merely want to reform the church but replace the Anglican state with an Islamic republic.[16]

The radical Protestantism embedded in Nye's account of Islam recalls the Whig-deist fascination with Islamic republicanism. The main clue lies in Nye's "divers Historians," a possible allusion to Henry Stubbe—the Restoration republican who wrote a manuscript that circulated among radical circles in the late seventeenth and early eighteenth centuries and became the target of many Tory satires. In his *The Rise and Progress of Mahometanism* (c. 1671), Islam is a reformed Protestant religion that restored the egalitarian republic of the ancient Nazarene Christians (see chapter 2). Although there is no evidence proving that Nye read Stubbe's account, his *A Brief History of the Unitarians* suggests that his understanding of Christianity and Islam is inflected by Stubbe's antitrinitarian historiography. This tract, dedicated to Thomas Firmin and Henry Hedworth, two prominent figures of the English Unitarian movement, was first published in 1687 and reprinted in *The Faith of One God* (1691), a collection financed by

Firmin. *A Brief History* argues that the Nazarenes, an early Jewish-Christian sect, are the legitimate ancestors of the Unitarians. The apostles, the early translators of the Old Testament from Hebrew to Greek, Theodotian and Symachus, and the early church fathers were professing Nazarenes who believed in God's unity and Christ's humanity.[17] With the ascendancy of the Nicean council, backed up by Roman imperial power and the consolidation of a paganized Trinitarian ideology, the Nazarenes became persecuted heretics. As a result they had to flee to "the Turkish and other Mahometan and Pagan dominions" in search of "liberty of Conscience."[18] Although Nye describes Arianism as the first corruption that led to Trinitarianism (a view that counters Stubbe's account), he insists, in a standard Stubbean move, that the Nazarenes are better off with the Mahometans than with the Catholics or Protestants, and that all primitive Christians, Muslims, and Jews equally acknowledge God's unity (180). Given this context, the Stubbean view of Islam presented in Nye's *A Letter of Resolution* evokes the radical regicidal politics of the English Civil War: Mahomet is a "Unitarian" revolutionary who overthrew kings and priests in an attempt to restore the egalitarian conditions of the early Nazarene republic.

Anglicans eager to expose the dangerous republicanism latent in the English Unitarian movement found a convenient explanation in the controversial Epistle and Nye's *A Letter of Resolution*, two works that, in their imagination, offer ample proof for the Mahometan-Unitarian conspiracy to overthrow church and state. Though Unitarians such as Bury and Nye were merely Anglican clergymen seeking institutional reform, they were branded as revolutionary outsiders by orthodox polemicists. By reading against the grain of Unitarian rhetoric, Edward Stillingfleet, John Edwards, William Sherlock, and Charles Leslie cast the Unitarians as foreign Islamic enemies who posed a republican threat to English national liberty.[19] This hyperbolic representation is not surprising given that the Moroccan ambassador's visit to England marked the end of British control of Tangier, an English garrison city in Morocco between 1681 and 1684. The loss of Tangier redefined English attitudes toward Islam and their allies. As Nabil Mater has argued, negative images of the African Moor as a diabolical enemy "had become completely grounded in colonial desire and religious difference" from 1684 onward.[20] With the deterioration of Anglo-Moroccan relations, the Barbary region ceased to play a positive role in the formation of England's national and colonial identity and instead Islam, which previously had been admired as a strategic military ally, was recast as absolute difference.[21] Under these altered circumstances, the Unitarian Epistle could easily be framed as a seditious affront to English nationalism and state power rather than as a lighthearted plea for institutional reform. In the eyes of their orthodox detractors, the English Socinians were likened to proto-republican "Moors" who sought to undermine British political, military, and commercial interests.

"There is one God, and Priestley is his prophet"

With the gradual formation of an Anglican nationalism in eighteenth-century England, orthodox polemicists used the image of Unitarians as "Mahometans" as a prime justification for their exclusion from citizenship. Once again orthodox polemicists panicked about a possible Muslim-Unitarian plot to thwart the state, especially after the French Revolution. The Epistle to the Moroccan ambassador and *A Letter of Resolution* continued to haunt the Unitarian psyche.[22] The most acute manifestation of this resurgence can be found in the polemical exchanges between Joseph Priestley, who converted to Socinianism during his ministry at Leeds and wrote prolifically in favor of Unitarian theology, and Samuel Horsley, the archdeacon of St. Albans who was elevated to Bishop of Rochester in 1793 for his defense of Anglican dogmas. In this eight-year controversy (1783–91), Horsley launched a smear campaign against the English Unitarian movement by maintaining that Priestley, a prominent philosopher and scientist of the age, was secretly preaching the Mahometan faith. To elucidate the subtle connections among antinationalist sentiments, dissenting politics, and Islamic republicanism, this renewed Mahometan-Unitarian conspiracy can be traced in the theological writings of Priestley, whose mind, as one late-Victorian historian puts it, charts "the mental pilgrimage" of late-eighteenth-century Unitarianism.[23]

   Horsley's attack on Priestley's heterodox views and his reputation as a biblical scholar resulted in an exchange of hostile letters between the two antagonists. This publicized confrontation is the chief theological debate for which Priestley is remembered among his contemporaries and marks one of the high points of his long career as a theologian.[24] Horsley's rhetorical strategy is to discredit Priestley's reputation as a Christian scholar rather than argue against his doctrine. To accomplish this, he stigmatizes Priestley as a disguised Mahometan who seeks to overthrow church and state. In one of his replies, Horsley alludes to Nye's *A Letter of Resolution* as evidence that the Socinians support Mahomet's anti-Christian mission: "In the Unitarian writings of the last century, it is allowed of Mahomet, that he had no other design than to restore the belief of the unity of God.—Of his religion, that it was not meant for a new religion, but for a restitution of the true intent of the Christian.—Of the great prevalence of the Mahometan religion, that it has been owing not to force and the sword, but to that one truth contained in the Alcoran, the unity of God."[25]

Horsley is savvy enough to exploit an earlier 1690s anti-Unitarian rhetoric for his polemical purposes: like their late-seventeenth-century predecessors, Priestley and his Socinian cohort are involved in a new conspiracy with Mahometan enemies intent on overthrowing England's Christian rule. To support this latest conspiracy theory, Horsley refers to the Unitarian Epistle printed in Leslie's earlier tract as indisputable proof, deploying an earlier polemical strategy bent on discrediting dissenting claims to Anglican citizenship and property rights.[26]

Of course, Priestley denies Horsley's incriminating charges. For him, the idea that Islam is advancing the Unitarian creed and that the Socinians will soon acknowledge the divine mission of Mahomet is absurd, because these "groundless calumnies" have no textual and historical basis. Ignoring the controversial claims made by English Socinians in the late seventeenth century, Priestley asserts that he has never encountered Unitarian writings in support of Mahomet's mission or known of any named Unitarians converting to Islam.[27] As for Leslie's publication of the Epistle, it is "probably an invention of his"—a forgery used to discredit the movement in England, then and now.[28] Priestley cites extensively from the work of an early-eighteenth-century dissenting minister and Unitarian, Thomas Emlyn, who denies the authenticity of the Epistle because the names of the addressers and subscribers remain unknown.[29] After having dismissed all the incriminating evidence, Priestley concludes that Horsley's charges are "another specimen of your *invention* of *facts*" meant to "throw an odium upon the unitarians."[30]

Priestley accurately points out that Horsley employs hostile and hyperbolic language. Oddly enough, however, given his extensive knowledge of Unitarian history, he quickly brushes away any evidence suggesting that Socinian and Islamic doctrine share some principles. Moreover, his sweeping assessment of the Unitarian Epistle's inauthenticity is mistaken; certainly his late-seventeenth-century predecessors did not disregard this work.[31] Priestley's hasty dismissal may be due to his strong anti-Islamic views: Mahometanism is not a "revealed religion," for it was fabricated by a vile impostor who succeeded in his mission through violent military means rather than divine initiative. For Priestley, the Muslims need to be converted to the true Protestant faith as expressed in the Unitarian creed, the only way of facilitating their entry into the Christian fold.[32] Obviously, Priestley has theological reasons for dismissing Islam as false, because to admit otherwise would undermine the exceptional truth of Christian revelation. For him, Islam poses a threat to providential history that can only be solved through Muslim conversion to the true prophetic faith as recovered in Unitarian teachings.

Priestley's unwillingness to entertain the possibility of a Unitarian-Islamic connection reflects other anxieties as well. He would have known that English Unitarians often appeal to Islam when attacking the Trinity: in fact, he endorsed the life and works of Edward Elwall, an eccentric Seventh Day Baptist and religious controversialist who was attacked as a Jew and a Turk and put on trial for, among other heresies, basing his Unitarian arguments on lengthy quotations from the Qur'an.[33] Priestley republished Elwall's *The Triumph of truth: being an account of the trial of Mr. E. Elwall, for heresy and blasphemy*—which went through ten editions between 1771 and 1794 in addition to four abridgments issued between 1788 and 1791—in a pro-Unitarian dissenting tract titled *An Appeal to the Serious and Candid Professors of Christianity.* In this propagandistic work sponsored by Priestley, Elwall explains that Muslims and Jews, unlike the superstitious Trinitarians, use their independent reason to comprehend God's unity (17).[34] In the long run, orthodox writers could have read Priestley's hasty dismissal of Horsley's evidence as an apprehensive rhetorical move, a sneaky attempt to draw attention away from a dangerous possibility that he is too afraid to face: that republican Unitarians may be joining the Muslims under the pretence of converting them.

Horsley was not the first and only one to accuse Priestley as a disguised Mahometan. Indeed, Priestley's *An history of the corruptions of Christianity* (1782), the controversial work that originally prompted Horsley's hostile attacks, argues for a radical iconoclasm that orthodox Anglican readers could potentially have construed as Mahometan. As in Stephen Nye's account, the first and most controversial section of Priestley's work on the early opinions on Christ argues that the primitive Nazarene Christianity preached God's unity and Christ's Jewish-messianic mission, two doctrines which were eventually corrupted by a gentile Trinitarian view of Christ's divinity and that became doctrinal law under the Athanasian creed. In this case, Priestley's work attacks the established church's most fundamental doctrines: the Trinity, the virgin birth, original sin, predestination, the atonement, and the plenary inspiration of the scriptures. Thus, many condemned his historical account not only for favoring the heretical Ebonite and Nazarene systems, but, as with Nye's tracts, for its Islamic monotheism. Quoting Thomas Howes's fourth volume to the *Critical Observations on Books*, Priestly complains that he has falsely cast his theological work as the "ravages" of the "Mahometan Unitarians," who, with "fire and sword," rather than the pen, de-

stroy the Christian faith.[35] Reverend James Barnard satirically states that Priestley
should acknowledge the Muslims as his "brethren" and include them in his next
edition of *An History of the Early Opinions concerning Jesus Christ* (1786).[36] Some
orthodox polemicists pointed out that Priestley's defense of Christ's prophetic
status must be proof that he accepts the revealed truth of the Qur'an and that
Islam is preferable to Christianity.[37] As one writer sarcastically puts it, "The real
creed of the Unitarian ... is—There is one God, and Priestley is his prophet;
and it is a matter of moonshine to a Christian, whether Priestley or Mahomet be
exalted in that honour."[38] In short, Priestley's Unitarianism is another version of
Islamic prophecy. By 1790, he self-consciously knew that his detractors considered him "half a Mahometan."[39]

Priestley was wary of being branded a Mahometan, a term that linked antinationalist views with Protestant dissent in late-eighteenth-century England. Like
his seventeenth-century Unitarian predecessors, he was depicted as an enemy
who has betrayed England's colonial and military interests and as one of the
principal spokesmen for the American and French Revolutions. As a result of
this public perception, he was forced into self-exile in the United States in 1794,
three years after having his home, library, and laboratory destroyed during the
Birmingham riots. Under these dire circumstances, Priestley could not have met
Horsley's charges head-on. To have done so would have revealed something that
Priestley's religious sensibilities could not tolerate but that the young Coleridge
and Southey might have embraced: that the reformist politics of Unitarian dissent potentially sheaths a seditious republicanism intent on deposing all kings,
priests, and noblemen.

"Th' enthusiast Warrior of Mecca"

The proposed epic on the flight and return of Muhammad articulates what remains politically repressed within Priestleyan Unitarianism: Islamic teaching
embodies an egalitarian form of Old Testament prophecy that can serve as a
practical guidebook for republican dissenters battling against eighteenth-century
state priestcraft. In many respects, Coleridge's poem "Mahomet" dramatizes this
politicized Unitarian fantasy. Indeed, Priestley's speculations shaped his early
ideas, rhetoric, and poetics.[40] Between 1794 and 1796, he became an avid enthusiast of Priestleyan Unitarianism, which, in his mind, revealed the true tenets of
democratic reform by interpreting primitive Christianity as an egalitarian religion. Coleridge was interested in the Priestley-Horsley controversy and even
proposed to write a review of both sides of the debate in which he would state his

own theological position.[41] Although this review was never written, his interest in the controversy serves as a reminder that Priestleyan Unitarianism provided Coleridge with a theological vocabulary with which to describe the Napoleonic radicalism that is employed in a poem such as "Mahomet."

Between February and May 1799, the period during which he was studying in Germany, he was thinking intensely about Islam: his notebook entries include mention of a German-translated Arabic manuscript that features an address by an "Iman" to a Muslim on his deathbed. This scene comes from Carsten Niebuhr's *Description of Arabia* and was translated into German by Johann Heinrick Welpler, a professor of Oriental languages at Cassel and later a professor of philosophy and theology at Marburg.[42] Coleridge's exposure to the German university led him to his acquaintance—either in his readings or in person—with Orientalist scholars specializing in the study of higher criticism and the Islamic faith. As in Goethe's fragment poem, "Mahomets Gesang," a dramatic piece written in praise of the Prophet's genius, Coleridge's "Mahomet" and the unrealized epic reflect what Elinor Shaffer identifies as the driving agenda of German higher criticism: to discover the key to all mythological systems by subsuming the Jewish and Islamic ethos within the Christian narrative of history.[43]

Coleridge eventually translated the "sublime passage" on the "Iman" into English and published it in *The Courier* on August 1811 under the title "A Death Bed or Funeral Address of an Iman to a Mussulman" (262). According to him, this religious scene demonstrates the cultural and political force of the Muslim worldview. By this time a sworn enemy of Napoleonic politics and a harsh critic of the French occupation of Egypt, he published the Iman's address as counterrevolutionary propaganda. His address suggests that Napoleon's conquest of Constantinople will only create a cultural backlash and revitalize Muslim resistance, because, for Coleridge, "the religion of Mahomet is . . . more adapted to call forth all the energies and practical enthusiasm of the human heart" (260). Mahomet's egalitarian teachings encourage the passions of "the People" in their fight against Napoleon's tyrannical colonial project. Because the Turks are not "semi-barbarians" and fiercely protect their liberty, according to Coleridge, the French colonization of their territories will only result in widespread revolts.

Despite the article's counterrevolutionary message, his Mahometanism remains as radical as when he first praised the "enthusiast" Prophet in "Mahomet." He asks his readers "to consider the Mahometans as rather sitting in the Twilight of Christianity, than in the utter darkness of paganism" (260). For him, the "languid influence" of paganism pertains more to the early corruptions of primitive Christianity ("the persecutions of the earlier Christians") than to the rise of Islam (261). In this case, he remains faithful to his earlier Unitarian and deist position on Islam. Indeed, by the end of the article, he proposes to write a follow-up essay on Napoleon's admiration of the Muslim faith and its possible political value for revolutionary France, though like most of Coleridge's projects, this essay was never written (262). Even after he abandoned Priestleyan Unitarianism and republican politics, he could not imagine a version of Unitarian Islam that is devoid of any traces of dissent. Although German higher criticism shaped his approach to non-Christian religions, his republican interpretation of Islam also owes a substantial debt to English Unitarian history, from the Epistle to the Moroccan ambassador to Priestley's controversial defense of Unitarian theology.[44]

Priestleyan rhetoric guides Coleridge's politicized account of Christian history. As part of his 1795 Bristol lecture series, which was supposed to raise funds for Coleridge's and Southey's Pantisocracy scheme, the published account of the "Lectures on Revealed Religion, its Corruptions, and its political views" rehashes many of the central motifs found in Priestley's *An history of the corruptions of Christianity* and *An History of Early Opinions concerning Jesus Christ* (1786): primitive Jewish Christianity, which professed Christ's humanity and God's unity, was first corrupted by Gnosticism and Platonic philosophy, a paganizing tendency that eventually resulted in the erroneous Trinitarian doctrine, the atonement, and original sin; and these forms of idolatry were responsible for the "mysteries" with which church and state governments continue to dupe the ignorant masses.[45] Grafted onto this Unitarian view of Christian history, Coleridge (unlike Priestley) explains how social and political decadence, the inequality of property, class distinctions, and commercial exploitation stem from the corruption of primitive Christianity. Accordingly, Jesus Christ was a "poor and uneducated" messiah who taught "Universal Equality" and encouraged common property.[46] Against the laws of kings and priests, Christ is a plebeian republican leader who wanted to abolish private property and the accumulation of luxuries.[47] From Coleridge's perspective, he was attempting to fulfill the egalitarian teachings of the Mosaic constitution: to restore the old Jewish "Federal Republic" in which Israel's twelve tribes shared land equally, interest and usury were outlawed, and the priesthood was eliminated.[48] Whereas historical Christianity is state priestcraft, primitive (Mosaic) Christianity offers hope for future democratic reform. Moreover, as outlined in Coleridge's "Religious Musings," the French Revolution marks Christ's millennial return, the end of priestly idolatry, social inequality, private property, and exploited labor. Coleridge uses Priestleyan rhetoric to further his radical political agenda.

His account of Mahomet as the new republican hero and messiah of the age unleashes the Islamic republicanism that is potentially embedded in Unitarian accounts of prophetic history, even as many heterodox writers, especially Priestley, refused to replace Christ with Mahomet. If Christ is a "Prophet," a revolutionary leader whose only goal is to recover a progressive Old Testament tradition, rather than a "Savior," then his role in the biblical narrative of history is not that different from the prophets who came *before* and *after* him. In other words, Christ's centrality in providential history is dispensable, and, as a result of this contingency, his role could be potentially supplemented by another prophet. As such, "Mahomet" is a poem that replaces Christ with the Islamic Prophet, because, in Coleridge's (and Priestley's) Unitarian account of prophetic history, these two Oriental Prophets are equally involved in the same project: to restore the primitive religion of Moses to its true pristine condition and bring about the downfall of state priestcraft. Thus, Coleridge's view of Mahomet as "th' enthusiast Warrior of Mecca" who "crush'd the blasphemous Rites of the Pagan / And idolatrous Christians" and "laid Naked and Prostrate the Priesthood" displaces his earlier vision of Christ as a radical iconoclastic teacher who dispelled the "floating mists of dark idolatry" and preached freedom and equality ("Mahomet," lines 4, 7, 9).[49] Unlike Priestley's negative treatment of Islam, Coleridge's "Mahomet" is willing to reframe Unitarian republicanism as a radical version of Islamic prophecy.

By conflating Christ with Mahomet in his poem, the Prophet symbolizes the Second Coming of Christ, a historical event that, as he enthusiastically proclaims in one of his speeches, is anticipated in the French revolutionary promise: the end of superstition, despotism, and the priesthood and the dawning of Christ's "truth, "love", and "EQUALITY."[50] As such, "Mahomet" mobilizes two overlapping Unitarian fantasies: modeled after Christ and Moses, the Islamic Prophet is a dissenting "Unitarian" republican who initiated the Protestant Reformation, and, within an eschatological scheme, he also marks the reincarnation of Christ's Second Coming. Rewriting the apocalyptic vision of rushing rivers that concludes the "Religious Musings" (lines 416–20), the "ruinous River" and "mazy uproar" in the last lines of "Mahomet" allude to the French revolutionary upsurge and anticipate the Christian millennium in the Prophet's radical movement—"the People with mad shouts . . . . all rushing impetuous onward" (lines 9–10, 14). In "Mahomet," the French Revolution signals a democratic world order that is neither strictly "Christian" nor "French." That is to say, this poem expresses a desire for a golden age without Christ or Bonaparte.

This unusual desire raises a question about the ideological work that is performed in Coleridge's Unitarian fantasy: is this poem a form of Romantic escapism that locates political solutions "outside of history"? Clearly, his Mahomet, an "enthusiast Warrior . . . . who scatter'd abroad both Evil and Blessing," closely resembles Robespierre. In *Conciones Ad Populum* (1795), Coleridge wrote,

> [E]nthusiasm in Robespierre was blended with gloom, and suspiciousness, and inordi-
> nate vanity. His dark imagination was still brooding over supposed plots against free-
> dom—to prevent tyranny he became a Tyrant—and having realized the evils which
> he suspected, a wild and dreadful Tyrant.—Those loud-tongued adulators, the mob,
> overpowered the lone-whispered denunciations of conscience—he despotized in all the
> pomp of Patriotism, and masqueraded on the bloody stage of Revolution. . . .I rather
> think, that the distant prospect, to which he was travelling, appeared to him grand and
> beautiful; but that he fixed his eyes on it with such intense eagerness as to neglect the
> soul-ness of the road. If however his first intentions were pure, his subsequent enormi-
> ties yield us a melancholy proof, that it is not the character of the possessor.[51]

Like Mahomet, who reformed the Pagan and Christian world at the cost of establishing "Huge wasteful Empires" ("Mahomet," line 3), Robespierre's dark imagination was originally intent on a prosperous revolution for the good of the people, only to result in tyranny and evil. By 1799, the period during which Coleridge began to have doubts about the French Revolution, his ambivalent attitude toward Robespierre is displaced onto the character of Mahomet. In short poems such as "France: An Ode" and "Fears in Solitude," written in March and April of 1798, Coleridge expresses dismay and confusion over France's imperial ambitions—Napoleon's invasion of Republican Switzerland and the looming threat of a French attack on England. These poems dramatize his turning away from "radical politics" by seeking comfort "outside of history": in the private world of the domestic affections and in the beauty of Nature. By substituting the Prophet for Robespierre (or Bonaparte), "Mahomet" deploys a compensatory narrative, supplementing the failed French Revolution with a triumphant Islamic republicanism. But unlike "France: An Ode" or "Fears in Solitude," the Mahomet narrative is not a "conservative" escape from history; on the contrary, it marks an imaginative engagement with history in which "Liberty, Equality, and Fraternity" are relocated in the Islamic Near East. As such, the Unitarian fantasy featured in "Mahomet" salvages radical politics by creatively appropriating the French revolutionary rhetoric that Bonaparte deployed during his Islamic rule of Egypt.

"Mahomet" registers a desire to find an adequate conclusion for the radical messianic politics of the "Religious Musings," or the incomplete epic "The Destiny of Nations: A Vision." Islam offered Coleridge the only alternative route toward imagining a Protestant millennium in a world that had lost hope in the Revolution after Napoleon's rise to absolute power. What Morton Paley calls "the apocalyptic grotesque" (an apocalypse without the millennium) became a dominant feature of Coleridge's poetry between 1798 and 1800, because it was no longer feasible for radical millennialists such as him to trace messianic politics in French events.[52] Within this context, the spectacular ending to "Mahomet" represents the limits of his political imagination, the closest approximation to a messianic utopia. Ironically and problematically, this anti–French Unitarian vision is articulated through the colonial language Bonaparte used to convince Egyptian clerics of his Islamic authority.

"Can the evils of the established systems be well allegorized?"

Like "Mahomet," Robert Southey's *Thalaba the Destroyer* (1801) provides a compensatory narrative that seeks to rescue radical politics by situating the Unitarian revolution in the Islamic Near East rather than Western Europe. Conceived and written during the same period that Coleridge and Southey were working on their Islamic epic, this Oriental tale exhibits a basic Unitarian plot structure: Thalaba, a radical Protestant-Muslim hero, defeats a seminary of evil magicians (the priesthood), destroys all forms of pagan idolatry, and fights for the true prophetic faith of Abraham, Moses, and Christ. In his book, Daniel E. White argues that *Thalaba* is not a story about "a rational Unitarian religion," as proposed by Nigel Leask, but rather a "Unitarian religion that is intuitive." Accordingly, Southey's view of Islam does not express the "rational Unitarianism" that Priestley and the young Coleridge subscribe to, because, according to White, Southey's nonsectarian Christianity is closer to the mysticism of Arianism and Quakerism than rational dissent.[53] But despite his deep-seated aversion to sects and denominations, Southey's approach to Eastern biblical history is filtered through a Unitarian sensibility. Building on White's insight, I argue that Southey rewrote the unrealized epic on the flight and return of Muhammad in the narrative of *Thalaba*, not merely because he disbelieves the Prophet, as many critics and biographers have argued,[54] but because he wants to accomplish what Coleridge's "Mahomet" failed to achieve: perfecting an allegorical account of Islamic republicanism that successfully distances itself from, yet supplements, the Napoleonic ideals of the Egyptian campaign.

Southey's 109-line poem "Mohammed" is a prime example of what he calls the "mythological imagination": the ability to write ambitious poems that capture "the manners and mythologies of different nations."[55] Penned by December 1799, this fragment was composed as book 2 of the Islamic epic; it describes the events surrounding the Prophet's flight from Mecca to Medina in AD 622. As an illustration of Islamic fatalism and submission to God's will, "Mohammed" retells the story of how the Prophet fled from his enemies by hiding in a cave with some of his close disciples, while Ali, his son-in-law, stayed in Medina and slept under covers pretending to be the Prophet. After discovering the deception, the soldiers of the Quraysh attempted to search for the Prophet's hiding place, but as they approached his cave, they decided to leave after seeing a pigeon flying out and a spider spinning a web over the entrance. Nature—and not a miracle—save the Prophet's life. Ali then comes to visit him and reminds him of his mission—the defeat of all evil, idolatry, and paganism–something more important than his personal life. Mohammed cannot return to Mecca to witness the death of his first wife, "Cadijah," because God, according to Ali, has prepared another path for him.[56] Southey highlights the power of nature and Ali's valor in contrast to Mohammed's lack of courage and even faith. For Southey, Islam, an iconoclastic natural religion, understands history as a series of predestined events that none-theless require human agency and faith, even in the case of the Prophet.

This heretical view of Islam possesses a radical iconoclastic element that Southey greatly admires. As evident in his *The Commonplace Book* and library holdings, his views on the Prophet were inspired, in part, by the writings of the eighteenth-century deists discussed in chapters 2 and 3: Stubbe, Toland, Boulain-villers, and Lady Mary Wortley Montagu, all of whom see the prophets of history as flawed humans.[57] In other words, Southey's fragment describes the Prophet's rise to power as a temporal affair inspired by the natural law inscribed in a semi-pantheistic world. In this regard, Mohammed's character is antiheroic, another "false prophet." In his preface to *The Curse of Kehama*, Southey claims that the representation of Islam offered in *Thalaba*

> required that I should bring into view the best features of that system of belief and wor-
> ship which had been developed under the covenant with Ishmael, placing in the most
> favourable light the morality of the Koran, and what the least corrupted of the Moham-
> medans retain of the patriarchal faith. It would have been altogether incongruous to
> have touched upon the abominations engrafted upon it; first by the false Prophet him-
> self, who appears to have been far more remarkable for audacious profligacy than for
> any intellectual endowments, and afterwards by the spirit of Oriental despotism which
> accompanied Mahommedanism wherever it was established.[58]

According to Southey, the teachings of ancient Islam, rooted in "the covenant with Ishmael," represent the "best features" of iconoclastic monotheism and the Qur'anic ethos. By contrast, the modern "abominations" that have corrupted this simple faith—beginning with the "false Prophet"—are not worthy of attention.

In his notes to *Thalaba*, he equates superstitious Islamic practices with Catholicism's "Monkish ingenuity," a tyrannical faith that he deeply abhors.[59] For him, institutional Islam "has been miserably perverted."[60] Nevertheless, his use of anti-Islamic polemic links institutional religion to state corruption only to praise the pristine simplicity of Islamic iconoclasm just as his "Mohammed" poem foregrounds the purity of Islam's natural law despite the Prophet's apparent lack of heroism.

Indeed, Southey's anti-Islamic prejudices do not prevent him from sympathizing with Ali's radical iconoclastic mission. In his February 1800 letter to the Unitarian reviewer and translator William Taylor, Southey admits that Muhammad is not the main protagonist of his epic; rather, "Ali is of course my hero."[61] This emphasis on Ali's heroism explains why Southey's plot outline to book 2 inserts the "*Fatima & Ali*" plot after the scene of "*Mohamed & Abu* in the cavern" (see Appendix B). Ever since Southey recorded his admiration for Ali in *Joan of Arc* (1796), he saw him as the revolutionary Caliph who transcended sectarian politics. In his imagination, Ali is the founder of the dissenting "Party of Ali" (*Shi'at Ali*) before its theological codification into a distinct "sect" by the middle of the eighth century.[62] By violently opposing the institutional establishment of the Umayyad caliphate, Ali's "party" embodies both a nonsectarian prophetic tradition and a brave fatalistic militarism in a way that Mohammed could never entirely fulfill due to his negative association with Oriental despotism. In elevating Ali above the Prophet, Southey seeks to promote a militant enthusiasm beyond sectarian conformity. As Daniel White has shown, Southey is "a kind of dissenter from Dissent" who, while writing *Thalaba*, had to remind himself, "I must build a Saracenic mosque—not a Quaker meeting house."[63] In his fragment poem, the young Southey subscribes to a Shi'ite version of Islam to sanction militant enthusiasm as a pure nonsectarian movement founded on religious intuition rather than theological strife.

But even though Southey privileges intuition, enthusiasm, and mysticism over sectarian forms of rational dissent, his heretical approach to Islam remains inspired by a radical Protestant historiography. Like Priestley and Coleridge, he interprets the Christian narrative of history as another version of Mosaic or Islamic prophecy. While reflecting on the major world religions, Southey asks in his *The Commonplace Book*: "why should inspiration be confined to Judea?"[64] For Southey, Hinduism, Judaism, Islam, Zorasterianism, and Confucianism, before their corruption as institutional state religions, taught the same prophetic truths as Christianity: the unity of God, the destruction of idolatry, and the fight against tyranny. In 1797, he expressed admiration for Priestley: he was honored to have "lived among the friends of Priestley," claiming that "no man has studied Christianity more or believes it more sincerely."[65] Like Coleridge, Southey claims that Christ disapproves of private property, class distinctions, and luxuries, and that these egalitarian teachings were practiced by the primitive Christians.[66] Even after Southey adopted a more conservative stance toward the Anglican church as he grew older, he was troubled by Athanasius's creed, could not adhere to all the Thirty-nine Articles, and abhorred the Test Acts.[67] Overall, his antisectarian approach to the history of monotheism displays certain Unitarian sensibilities, which initially enabled him to collaborate with Coleridge on the planned Islamic epic that celebrates God's unity, the fall of paganism, and the elimination of state priestcraft. For Southey, Muhammad's (or rather Ali's) radical mission occupies a pivotal place in the providential unfolding of Protestant history: Islam marks the beginning of the Unitarian revolution.

Shi'ite Islam may have intrigued Southey because of the historical parallels between the rise of a reformist militant movement in the Near East and the emergence of an aggressive widespread revolution in France: mainly, the toppling of church and state governments, the beginning of a new historical era followed by the adoption of a new calendar, the rise of a sovereign leader who represents the people, and the waging of massive military campaigns as a defensive strategy. In a letter to William Taylor in September 1799, Southey employs a military trope—a surprise French invasion of England—to describe his and Coleridge's hexameter poem on Muhammad: "Coleridge and I mean to march an army of hexameters into the country and it will be unfortunate to have all strong places in the hands of our enemies. We have chosen the story of Mohammed. . . . But remember this is a secret expedition, till the manifesto accompany the troops."[68] During the same period, Southey told Sir Humphry Davy that "we have formed the plan of a long poem to execute in hexameters, but this you had better not mention, as it will need a strong preliminary attack to bully people out of their prejudices against innovations in metre: our story is Mohammed."[69] Conceived in a time when a Napoleonic invasion of England was a possibility, Southey's hexameter poem on the Prophet's life poses as a "Jacobin" assault on the literary establishment. In this case, "Mohammed" offers a political allegory in which Ali's military genius represents Bonaparte's revolutionary fervor. This metaphorical association has its historical analogue in the 1798–99 French occupation of Egypt: casting himself as the nonsectarian defender of all world religions, Bonaparte renamed himself Ali and briefly considered converting to Islam.[70] As discussed in the previous chapter, he adopted folk forms of Shi'ite eschatology to pacify revolts in Cairo and maintain an aura of Islamic legitimacy in opposition to the Sunni sultanate in

Istanbul, which declared war against France in September 1798. During the time Southey was writing his Islamic epic, the name "Ali Bonaparte" was an object of derision among British loyalists who sought to discredit the "Jacobin" (reformist) cause at home.[71]

As a result, Southey may have felt the need to write another Islamic epic by the end of 1799 that resists Bonaparte's imperialist idiom. Instead, he wanted to sanitize republican politics from French excesses in his "Mohammedan fable," *Thalaba the Destroyer*, which was supposed to precede his unfinished poem on "Mohammed."[72] In principle, Southey remained a republican until 1812, even though prior to this date he expressed many doubts about the course of "Jacobin" politics and, by 1810, renounced his juvenile admiration for revolutionary France.[73] Unlike Coleridge, who in "France: An Ode" expressed disillusionment with French affairs, Southey's first doubts emerged in 1799 when Napoleon became sole dictator in the coup d'état of November 10.[74] During this unsettling period Southey's interest in completing "Mohammed" began to wane (he abandoned it by July 1800) and his obsession with what he then called "Thamama" began to occupy his time.[75] In his *Commonplace Book*, Southey raises the following questions about his plans for an Islamic poem on the "The Destruction of the Dom Danael," the preliminary title of *Thalaba*:

> Cannot the Dom Danael be made to allegorize those systems that make the misery of mankind?. . . .Can the evils of established systems be well allegorized? Can Thamama see them in the realms where Magicians govern? . . . How can the mental murder of half mankind be presented? Can the extremes of wealth and want be shown equally fatal to virtue and happiness[?] . . . I do not think this can be done in a manner fit for poetry.[76]

Southey wanted to write a political allegory in which "Thamama," the Muslim hero, defeats a cohort of tyrannical magicians, a degenerate institutional Islam that stands in for the kings and priests of the ancien régime. And yet Southey faced a literary challenge: the French revolutionary allegory must be undetectable in a writing mode that, for him, resulted in persistent questions about what is "fit for poetry." As stated in his outline, the allegory "must be nowhere naked."[77] He must avoid the near transparent political allegory employed in his "Mohammed" epic; given the links between Islamic republicanism and Unitarianism, any educated reader could detect the poem's French-Islam analogy. *Thalaba* was supposed to resist this easy detection. Therefore, this poem should not be read as a "complete political disengagement," as Ernest Bernhardt-Kabisch puts it, nor, as Carol Bolton argues, a transitional conservatism that exchanges radical politics for domestic quietism.[78] Rather, *Thalaba* is a republican-Unitarian allegory that rewrites "Mohammed" to deflect attention away from colonial and autocratic forms of Napoleonic governance while remaining committed to a politics of radical change that, ideally, cannot be compromised by recent events.

As such, *Thalaba* performs the same kind of ideological work as Coleridge's "Mahomet," or the unrealized collaborative epic project, but only more efficiently: the Oriental tale of Thalaba offers a compensatory narrative that rescues radical politics by situating the "Unitarian" Reformation in the Islamic Orient rather than Napoleonic Europe (or Egypt). In this case, radical Protestant politics is safely disassociated from the looming dangers of French revolutionary excess. As in his two famous epics, *Joan of Arc* and *Madoc*, Southey's *Thalaba* posits a militant proto-Protestant hero who destroys idolatrous worship under the conviction that he is restoring the ancient "covenant with Ishmael." The Unitarian-Islamic ethos of the tale foregrounds the antisectarian iconoclasm of dissenting Protestantism, but without the danger that the Ali-Bonaparte analogy will implicate Unitarian dissent in French imperialist ambitions, especially after the failed expedition in Egypt and the Holy Land.

Set during the Abbasid Caliphate of Harun-al-Rashid, *Thalaba* dramatizes the struggle of a race of sinister pagan magicians who dwell in the "Domdaniel" under the sea and seek to escape their prophesied downfall at the hands of a champion of God. At the beginning of this story, the magicians are on the verge of assassinating this divine champion, the young Muslim Thalaba whose family has been massacred. Thalaba becomes an orphan when his mother, Zeinab, dies while they are crossing the desert. He is adopted by the patriarch Moath, who raises him in pastoral simplicity. After consulting the powers of a demonic ring that he acquired from the dead body of the evil magician Abdaldar, the young Thalaba learns about his destined mission to destroy the Domdaniel and avenge his father's death. The next series of books record the various temptations and trials that, despite the many setbacks, reconfirm Thalaba's mission and his absolute faith in God's will: the magician Lobada, who, disguised as a sage, tries to lead Thalaba astray; the battle with the sorcerer Mohareb; the earthly but false paradise of Aloadin's garden; the splendid luxuries and power offered by the Sultan; Mohareb's Manichean speculations about Allah; and the hero's dramatic encounter with his father's murderer, the sinister magician Okba, whom he refrains from killing and learns to forgive. Set in the undersea cavern of the Domdaniel, the final dramatic scene culminates in the ultimate revolutionary act of Islamic-Protestant abjection: with his father's sword in hand, he destroys the magicians' evil idol, the "Living Image" of Eblis (Satan), resulting in the apocalyptic collapse of the cavern and Thalaba's rise to Muhammad's paradise (book 12, line 349). His martyrdom invokes a Christ-like sacrifice, a radical Protestant version of jihad. Regardless of its close ties with enthusiastic fatalism, Unitarian radicalism is removed from the public sphere of Western revolutionary politics and contained within the safety of an Islamic private consciousness.

Ironically, *Thalaba* narrates an allegory of revolution by diffusing its political content within a radical Protestant ethos, thereby avoiding any direct associations with the events of the French Revolution. Again, this poetic strategy is not a conservative sign of Romantic escapism. In *The Politics of the Imagination*, Nigel Leask has argued that the "ethic of retirement" in the poetry of Wordsworth and Coleridge is not an instance of Burkean conservatism; the Lake poets are not ideologues of the status quo or quietists simply because they have abandoned French revolutionary ideals and instead embraced the life of retirement, nature, and custom. Leask's analysis reveals that Wordsworth' s and Coleridge's "ethic of retirement" reflects a mode of Unitarian rhetoric and deist argumentation rooted in a seventeenth-century Commonwealthean tradition, from John Milton to John Toland.[79] In this context, the privileging of an Islamic private consciousness over radical political engagement in *Thalaba* articulates an "ethics of retirement" that is aligned with seventeenth-century Unitarian republicanism but without relying on the failed narrative of the French Revolution.

While Coleridge's and Southey's versions of an Islamic compensatory narrative perform this ideological function, they do run into a literary problem: because their French-Islam analogy supplements, and therefore potentially obscures, the attempt to recuperate an earlier Unitarian republicanism, their radical accounts of Unitarian Islam could be misread as another instance of Jacobin-inspired politics. And as Coleridge makes clear in his Bristol lectures, the aim of his dissenting politics is to revitalize a libertarian Christianity as opposed to championing an atheistic Godwinian radicalism or the failed revolution in France. One reason why the epic on the flight and return of Muhammad was abandoned may have something to do with the difficulty of writing an allegory that differentiates an earlier commonwealthean politics from a later Jacobin-style rhetoric.

Thalaba's use of allegory does not collapse these two related but distinct ideologies, allowing it to plot an alternative history that locates Unitarian dissent in the Islamic Near East. This literary achievement may explain why Coleridge was more eager to see *Thalaba* published than to complete the Mohammed epic; although he admits that *Thalaba* "is not altogether a poem exactly to my taste," he wrote a favorable review that features long excerpts that exemplify "the ethics of retirement": Thalaba and Moath's family practicing their evening Islamic prayers in a pastoral setting and the sentimental romance between Thalaba and Moath's beloved daughter, Oneiza.[80] But perhaps one of the most striking (and ironic) scenes in *Thalaba* occurs in book 5, which includes an account of the Islamic capital of Bagdad, a symbol for both the "Fallen" Babylon of the Old Testament and the corrupted Abbasid Caliphate of "Haroun":

> Thou too art fallen, Bagdad! City of Peace,
> Thou too hast had thy day!
> And loathsome Ignorance and brute Servitude
> Pollute thy dwellings now,
> Erst for the Mighty and the Wise renowned.
> O yet illustrious for remembered fame,
> Thy founder the Victorious, and the pomp
> Of Haroun, for whose name by blood defiled,
> Jahia's, and the blameless Barmecides',
> Genius hath wrough salvation; and the years
> When Science with the good Al-Maimon dwelt;
> So one day may the Crescent from thy Mosques
> Be plucked by Wisdom, when the enlightened arm
> Of Europe conquers to redeem the East. (5:73–86)

This passage describes the demise of the decadent institutional Islam that Southey so much despised. Beginning with sultan Almanzor "the Victorious," Oriental despotism needs to be "redeemed" by "the enlightened arm / Of Europe." This vision of Christian redemption represents a radical affirmation of preinstitutional, nonsectarian Islam rather than an imposition of a Western imperialist ideology, because in the long run *Thalaba* resists a Napoleonic enlightenment allegory even as it is inevitably conditioned by Anglo-French imperial rivalries in Egypt and Syria. Despite its apparent Eurocentrism, only an "enlightened arm" can "redeem" the iconoclastic sublimity of ancient Islam, announcing Europe's Second Coming as a Unitarian-style republic that replaces the cross with the crescent.

A Unitarian Vision in an Arabian Dream

Thalaba may have become the surrogate Islamic epic for a more practical reason. To avoid being seen as Unitarian conspirators who have forged a secret alliance with the Muslim world, Coleridge and Southey may have had to reject the Islam-French analogy. Indeed, to profess Unitarianism in the 1790s was to seek the opprobrium of a hostile English public. After Burke's fierce condemnation of the Unitarian petition in Parliament in 1792, many Britons portrayed Unitarians as seditious "Jacobin" conspirators against church and state for criticizing the Toleration Act.[81] Charles Leslie's 1711 tract would have reminded the public about the Muslim-Unitarian conspiracy: reprinted in 1799 as conservative Anglican propaganda by the Society for Promoting Christian Knowledge, his *The Truths of Christianity Demonstrated* stigmatizes the Unitarians as "much more Maho-metans than Christians," and to confirm this accusation he cites, once again, the Epistle to the Moroccan ambassador.[82] I argue that Coleridge's "Kubla Khan," the subject of intense source-hunting speculation,[83] not only registers anxieties about the Mahometan-Unitarian conspiracy but also severs its ties to Islamic radicalism and, more specifically, Southey's *Thalaba*. Opposed to the radical spirit of "Mahomet," the 1816 edition of "Kubla Khan" is a conservative act of political self-effacement.

Kubla Khan's unlawful construction of a "stately pleasure-dome" by a "sacred river" shares certain apocalyptic motifs with book 1 of *Thalaba*, in which the young Muslim hero and his mother, Zeinab, learn about a "stately palace" that was built (and destroyed) in violation of divine law (1:101, lines 1–2;). Staggering through the desert, they run into the ruins of the earthly paradise of Iram; the only survivor, Aswad, lives to tell an apocalyptic tale about divine wrath and failed imperial ambitions. According to Aswad, Sheddad, the king of the people of Ad, built the splendid city of Iram in defiance of the teachings of the Prophet Hud, who was sent by Allah to end the pride, vanity, and sinfulness of Sheddad and his people. One of the five Arab prophets mentioned in the Qur'an, Hud foreshadows the way Prophet Muhammad was treated with insolence and unbe-lief by the Meccans and members of his tribe.

Like Kubla Khan's pleasure dome built by a sacred river, the "Alpha" (the Tigris or the Euphrates), Sheddad's beautiful palace and sublime gardens attempted to surpass the splendors of Adam's paradise:

> A mighty work the pride of Shedad planned,
> Here in the wilderness to form
> A garden more surpassing fair
> Than that before whose gate,
> The lightening of the Cherub's fiery sword
> Waves wide to bar access
> Since Adam, the transgressor, thence was driven.
> Here too would Shedad build
> A kingly pile sublime,
> The palace of his pride. (1:227–36)

Southey describes the construction of this paradise as a work of ecological disaster that results from the accumulation of "luxuries": Sheddad's city required the exhaustion of his mines of gold and his caves of "gem," the deforestation of many acres of land, the large-scale gathering of silkworm from the East, and the hunting of "Ethiop" elephants for their precious ivory (1:237–51). The return to "Eden's grooves" to "re-create . . . whate'ver was lost in Paradise" is equated with imperial exploitation and the destruction of nature, unholy acts that, as Thalaba learns from Aswad, triggered God's vengeance: the apocalyptic destruction of Iram, King Sheddad, and his people, as foretold in Hud's prophecy (1:393, 399–400). This apocalyptic motif is also present in "Kubla Khan": a prelapsarian paradise of "luxuries," the violation of "sacred" nature along with the domination of the landscape, and the "Ancestral voices prophesying war" (line 30). These striking parallels are not coincidental. In fact, "Kubla Khan" was not written in 1798, as Coleridge later insisted, but in August 1799,[84] the same month when Southey wrote book one of *Thalaba*, the "Mohammed" epic was first conceived, and Bonaparte abandoned efforts to colonize Egypt and the Holy Land.

The legendary city of Iram and the people of Ad myth had been used as a vehicle for allegorizing republican politics in Landor's *Gebir*. As noted in chapter 4, Landor's use of the Qur'anic myth of Sheddad embodies an ecological critique of colonial politics: Gebir, a foreign conqueror of Egypt, meets a tragic end after reconstructing Iram, a sinful imperial project that exploited the labor of the people and exhausted the natural resources of the land. By aligning the Mosaic narrative of history with the story of Prophet Hud's mission to rescue the people of Ad from idolatry and luxuries, Landor, a republican who became disillusioned with the French Revolution, wrote an anticolonial allegory condemning William Pitt's reactionary policies and Bonaparte's false prophecies as "Grand Sultan" of Egypt. Even though the notes to *Thalaba* suggest that Southey learned about the Hud myth in the works of George Sale and Barthelemy D' Herbelot, the myth's radical associations most likely stems from Southey's close reading of *Gebir* (*Thalaba* 194–95). Between September and December of 1799, Southey frequently praised *Gebir* as a masterpiece.[85] He wrote an enthusiastic review of the poem in the September 1799 issue of the *Critical Review*, in which he quotes from the passage on the "Gaditte" excavation of the ancestral city.[86] He admired the poem so much that he took it with him on his trip to Lisbon in 1800, the period when he was writing *Thalaba*.[87] In the 1838 preface to *Thalaba*, Southey admits being "sensible of having derived great improvement from the frequent perusal of Gebir at the time" (4). In this case, Landor's poem accounts for Southey's interest in redeploying Unitarian Islam as an anti-imperialist allegory. Indeed, Southey's original plan was to make "the Mohammedan tradition of the Garden of Iram" the "ground work" for his allegorical epic on "the Destruction of the Dom Daniyel."[88]

Thalaba, the twin brother of *Gebir*, embodies a republican account of universal history that replaces Noahetic prophecy with the Islamic revolution. As a way of contending with ecological, demographic, economic, and political crisis in post-1640 England, universal histories seek to justify the deprived conditions of postlapsarian history by discovering the relationship between original sin and a pristine reorigination of nature and humanity. This euhemeristic historiography led to a great deal of speculation about the place of non-Christian chronologies and genealogies within the biblical account of Noah and the "second Fall" into sin and scarcity.[89] For instance, in a *Universal History from the Earliest Account of Time* (1740-65), a twenty-six-volume work that Southey and Coleridge would have known, the history of Islam is aligned with an Old Testament chronology that appeals to two biblical events as explanatory models: the Deluge and the fallen Tower of Babel. As such, this universal history accounts for religious, linguistic, and cultural diversity by tracing the rise of the "impostor" Muhammad to the corrupt branch of Ambrahmic-Noahetic monotheism, the descendants of Ishmael, and linking the legend of the Adites and the Garden of Iram to the story of the Deluge and Nimrod's Tower.[90]

In fact, Southey's original plan was to write the myth of all myths, an epic on Noah and the Deluge as a universal allegory that explains the French Revolution: Noah is the "young man" who will "revolutionize the world" only to die in an "Abbe Barruel-Bartholomew-massacre."[91] For Southey, the French Revolution is encoded as a Noahetic event, when "nothing was dreamt of it but the regeneration of the human race."[92] In his imagination, the "Noahchid" accounts for sin and scarcity in the late 1790s, displacing the tragic narrative of the French Revolution but without abandoning hope in republican politics. As in his depiction of Mohammed, Southey employs the trope of a Napoleonic invasion of England to describe his hexameter poem on Noah: "[I]f I march a regular army of some thousands into the country, well disciplined, and on a good plan, they will effect their establishment."[93] This poem was never executed because *Thalaba* initiates the Napoleonic invasion instead—the moment when, as Southey writes to his mother, "the Deluge [was] floating in my brain with the Dom Daniel."[94] In other words, the Islamic myth of Sheddad becomes the universal archetype that displaces the myth of Noah the revolutionary prophet. In Miltonic terms, Islam justifies the ways of the Noahetic revolution to man.

Thus, Southey's universal history deploys Unitarian Islam as an anti-imperialist allegory in which the trope of the Deluge ("the re-generation of the human race") and the Christian apocalypse (revolutionary rebirth) are juxtaposed in the character of an Oriental prophet—which, in Coleridge's imagination, is manifested in the enthusiasm of Mahomet and the sublime terror of Kubla Khan. In this regard, Islam is not only a religion that is grounded in the Abrahamic tradition of "Hagar & Ishmael" (see Appendix A) but is also a biblical archetype that reenacts the republican lessons found within that tradition. This cyclical model of the prophetic tradition is evident in "Mahomet" and "Kubla Khan," two poems in which the Oriental prophet is a product of what Freud describes as the dream-work process of condensation and displacement: a metonymic image of Noah, Moses, Christ, and Mahomet and a metaphorical substitute for Robespierre and Napoleon. In this dream-work process, the trope of the Deluge—the imagery of rushing water and flooding rivers in the last lines of "Mahomet" and in the "mazy . . . sacred river" of "Kubla Khan" (lines 24–25)—is synchronized with the apocalyptic rebirth of civilization.[95] Islam marks the Deluge-apocalypse as a single event that is to be repeated in a cyclical revolutionary history ("revolution" as both a leap forward in time and a recycling of the past). Thus, "Kubla Khan" is a miniature version of an Arab-"Islamic" epic in which the Garden of Iram myth is the master trope for plotting the French Revolution's rise and fall. Indeed, as early as 1794, Coleridge was interested in writing a Thalaba-like poem on an Asian city: "A Subject for a romance—Finding out a desert city & dwelling there / —Asia—."[96] Inspired by Landor's *Gebir*, Southey's *Thalaba* had far-reaching political consequences for imagining the Islamic East. Even in Wordsworth's "the Dream of the Arab" section in book 5 of *The Prelude*, prophetic history signals a Deluge-apocalyptic "revolution" in which the Arab knight, the Noah-prophet figure, rescues the stone (science) and the shell (poetry) from the "second" flood—a dream-vision that has its imaginative roots in *Thalaba*.[97]

By adopting Southey's Qur'anic trope of the Garden of Iram, "Kubla Khan" adopts the "fable of revolution" that Marilyn Butler locates in the allegorical narrative of *Thalaba*. In plotting this "revolution," the poem employs four poetic framing devices: one, a third-person description of the unholy construction of the imperial city of Iram, a "stately pleasure-dome" that encloses the beauty of the landscape within "walls and towers" (2, 7); two, "Ancestral voices prophesying war" as a result of Kubla Khan's (Sheddad's) attempt to refashion nature according to his will; three, the imaginative tension or paradox embodied in Kubla Khan's imperial project ("A sunny pleasure-dome with caves of ice!") (36); and four, the first-person, lyric poet who has an alluring yet dreadful vision of paradise rebuilt. For Butler, the abrupt transition from the third to the fourth poetic frame marks the historical move from the ancien régime to the French Republic, so "the overthrow of *this* garden by an undeluded outsider becomes . . . a version of the revolutionist's plot."[98] And yet this abrupt transition also suggests a return to the ancien régime in that the poetic "I" functions as a metaphorical substitute for Kubla Khan. In other words, the poet-persona rebuilds the city of Iram in his imagination—"I would build that dome in air / that sunny dome! those caves of ice!" (lines 46–47)—and thereby inherits the paradoxical tension implicated in Kubla Khan's imperial project (the third poetic frame). In short, the poet's imaginative vision is as despotic, idolatrous, and unholy as Kubla Khan's stately pleasure dome. To establish this connection, the final poetic frame concludes with a vision of the Abyssinian maid followed by a dire warning for intoxicated and enthusiastic poets who envision an "Islamic" paradise in their poems: "Beware! Beware! . . . / For he on honey-dew hath fed, And drank the milk of Paradise" (lines 49, 53–54). To qualify Butler's claim, "Kubla Khan" registers the *failure* of the revolutionist's plot: rather than playing the role of an "undeluded outsider," the lyric poet is a "deluded insider" who repeats the transgressive act of Kubla Khan (and Sheddad) in replacing the ancien régime with French republican liberty.

Even though Coleridge employs the myth of Sheddad's garden to allegorize the same political concerns expressed in *Gebir* and *Thalaba*—the dangers of imperial ambition in England and France—"Kubla Khan" differs significantly from these two poems and even "Mahomet": the poet-prophet does not offer a reassuring vision of the coming Islamic republic. Rather, he lies under "The shadow of the dome of pleasure" in that his poetic vision of a utopian paradise is as deceptive and fragmented as Kubla Khan's prophetic promise (line 31). In this case, the metaphorical substitution of the lyric "I" for Kubla Khan forestalls the employment of an egalitarian republican narrative that resolves the sociopolitical contradictions of the ancien régime. Consequently, the "failed plot" of the French Revolution is not replaced by a compensatory narrative about the rise of Unitarian Islam. On the contrary, "Kubla Khan" registers profound anxieties about this act of supplementation; the belief in the paradise of Islamic republicanism is another instance of the misplaced millennial hopes that the younger Coleridge expressed in his enthusiasm for the French Revolution. Mohammed's prophetic vision, he fears, might be as deceptive and despotic as Robespierre's dark imagination.

Yet this political warning or "doubt" is couched in a radical Qur'anic allegory that was suppressed in Coleridge's 1816 publication of "Kubla Khan." The fragment was first published at Lord Byron's request along with the addition of a cautious preface, an overarching framing device. Given that the trope of a rebuilt garden city possessed radical associations for young poets such as Byron, the editorial goal of the preface is to reframe "Kubla Khan" in order to deflect attention away from the radical influence of *Thalaba*: Coleridge calls the poem a "psychological curiosity" that is not to be judged "on the ground of any supposed *poetic merits*," misdates the composition of the fragment ("In the summer of the year 1797"), posits Purchas's *Pilgrimmes* as the main source of inspiration, and fails to mention Southey's company ("the Author ... retired to a lonely farm-house between Porlock and Linton") (511). This decontextualization of "Kubla Khan" reflects Coleridge's more mature and conservative stance toward the Islamic Orient. As Marilyn Butler has argued, his editorial preface is an example of a "quietist maneuver," a sign of religious orthodoxy and political conservatism: "In 1816 as much as in 1798, for Coleridge to *empty* the paradisal garden of people and of politics must also read as a political move."[99] Indeed, by 1816, *Thalaba* was a well-known poem, especially among second-generation Romantic poets, and provided the immediate political backdrop for "Kubla Khan." In this case, his refusal to acknowledge *Thalaba* as the source of inspiration for his poem is an act of political self-effacement. The preface includes a self-reflective poem that dramatizes this disavowal: his intention was to employ framing devices to achieve narrative coherence in "Kubla Khan"—"a thousand circlets spread / And each misshape the other" (1:30–31). But under the sway of opium he wrote a "fragment," recording a "dream of pain and disease" instead. By creating an ironic self-distance between his authorial intention and the poem's unorthodox message, the older Coleridge, who abandoned radical politics and theology, absolves himself from the embarrassing Unitarian beliefs he once held in his youth to conceal his earlier interest in Islamic republicanism.

The 1816 publication was therefore part of a rhetorical strategy that allowed him to disavow his earlier "doubts" about the collaborative Islamic epic and "Mahomet"; his editorial framing device obscures that "Kubla Khan" was written as a fragment within another fragment, shifting authorial responsibility away from his earlier investment in Islamic republicanism. Whereas the 1799 fragment expresses fears about the politics of Unitarian Islam, the 1816 edition recodes these anxieties as a pure psychological state divorced from the political sphere. And yet the fragment may have promoted the conservative publication of "Kubla Khan." During his later years, it served as the basis for his Anglican critique of God's "Unity" as upheld in Islamism and Unitarianism, two deist "religions" not even worthy of that name.[100] Coleridge writes "that prime article of Islamicism, the unipersonality of God, is one cause of the downfall ... of their literary age."[101]

By dramatizing fears about the "downfall" of the Islamic-Unitarian "literary age," "Kubla Kahn" is mobilized in support of the anti-Islamic conservative message of the 1816 publication. In this regard, the poem conceals Coleridge's lasting fascination with Islam. In fact, even after abandoning the project on Muhammad he continued to think about it in 1804 and, between 1812 and 1820, produced an unfinished Arabian play titled *Diadesté*, a disguised Unitarian tragedy tied to *Thalaba*.[102] Whether considering his Islamic epic, his political anxieties about this project, or his later refusal to acknowledge Unitarian Islam, his use of Oriental motifs is a prime example of rhetorical indirection, a radical writing style that evades blasphemy, sedition, and treason; or, as George S. Erving has shown, "a series of strategies for disseminating the ideas that most mattered to him in ways that carried the greatest effect with the least risk."[103] Unlike previous Unitarians (but not unlike Joseph Priestley), Coleridge took extreme precautions to avoid being identified as a dangerous Mahometan conspirator.

Coda: "A Sect of Poets"

In his 1802 review of *Thalaba* in the *Edinburgh Review*, Francis Jeffrey read Southey's Oriental tale as an encrypted "Jacobin" poem that embodies the heretical and republican principles of Wordsworth, Coleridge, and Charles Lamb, all of whom belong to "a *sect* of poets." Turning the tables against Southey's antipathy toward sects and denominations, Jeffrey casts him as the head "apostle" of a new sect of Protestant dissenters who seek to overthrow the established order of English poetry:

> The author who is now before us, belongs to a *sect* of poets, that has established itself in this country within these ten or twelve years, and is looked upon, we believe, as one of its chief champions and apostles. The peculiar doctrines of this sect, it would not, perhaps, be very easy to explain; but, that they are *dissenters* from the established systems in poetry and criticism, is admitted, and proved indeed, by the whole tenor of their compositions. Though they lay claim, we believe, to a creed and a revelation of their own.[104]

Based on his earlier review of Southey in the *Anti-Jacobin*, a Tory journal in which he stigmatizes Southey's literary circle as "a definite group of new poets with radical principles in poetry as well as in politics," Jeffrey portrays the Lake Poets as zealous Protestant conspirators who pose a major threat to church and state.[105] They "constitute, at present, the most formidable conspiracy that has lately been formed against sound judgment in matters poetical."[106] As both Robert M. Ryan and Daniel E. White have argued, Jeffrey's conceit is not misdirected or whimsical; his Tory smear campaign against early Romanticism reveals the importance of the language of Anglican nonconformity for radical poets such as Southey and Coleridge.[107] In addition, I propose that Jeffrey's use of *Thalaba* foregrounds the Islam-French analogy that Southey tried to avoid in writing a nonsectarian political allegory. According to my interpretation of English Unitarian history, Jeffrey may have chosen *Thalaba* for a strategic purpose: to showcase Southey's literary interest in Islamic myth as a sinister sign of the Mahometan-Unitarian conspiracy. By exposing this new conspiring "sect" as a cohort of Islamic prophets who preach "a creed and a revelation of their own," Jeffrey's review disgraces the "Jacobin" Lake poets in the eyes of a hostile English public who, after 1800, associate Islamic republicanism with both Napoleonic despotism in Egypt and anti-British nationalism at home.

Despite the best efforts to hide their tracks, Coleridge's and Southey's fascination with Unitarian Islam was frequently decoded as an allegory for republican politics. In line with Jeffrey's review, an anonymous reviewer from the 1815 issue of *The Edinburgh Review* recognized the subversive use of Orientalist mythography in poetry, noting that ever since Southey's publication of *Thalaba*, "the muse has become a very infidel. . . . She has been heard to chaunt *suras* out of the Alcoran." Though this comment refers to William Herbert's *Helga; A Poem* (1815), it also characterizes "the flights of Southey or Lord Byron."[108] Indeed, *Thalaba* helped radicalize the Oriental tale genre, such as Lord Byron's *The Bride of Abydos* and *The Giaour* (1813) and Thomas Moore's *Lalla Rookh* (1817). The heretical spirit of the Islamic epic on the Prophet's life reemerges in Thomas Carlyle's 1840 lecture on Mahomet as a "Hero-Prophet." By the second decade of the nineteenth century, *Islam* had become a well-recognized code word for radical republicanism and dangerous enthusiasm, ideas that Coleridge disowned in the 1816 publication of "Kubla Khan" and that Southey shied away from in *The Curse of Kehama* (1810) and in the 1838 revisions to *Thalaba*.[109] With the downfall of Robespierre, the failure of the Egyptian campaign, and the defeat of Napoleon at Waterloo, Coleridge and Southey lost hope in the myths of prophetic regeneration. They could no longer believe in a just Islamic republic that could redirect Western civilization toward the golden age. At any rate, "The Flight and Return of Mohammed" stands as a literary relic of a forgotten moment in the long and complicated history of Unitarian radical thought, an era in which, as I have argued throughout, Islam served as a beacon for some radical writers who felt betrayed by the secular values of their age.

CHAPTER SIX

A Last Woman's Eschatology

The Avenging Turks in Mary Shelley's *The Last Man*

> When the earth shall be shaken by an earthquake; and the
> earth shall cast forth her burthens; and man shall say,
> What aileth her? On that day *the earth* shall declare her
> tidings, for that thy Lord will inspire her. On that day men
> shall go forward in distinct classes, that they may behold
> their works.
>
> *The Koran*, "The Earthquake," chapter 101

Mary Shelley's interest in a syncretistic account of Judaism, Christianity, and Islam is best exemplified in Percy Shelley's *The Assassins: A Fragment of a Romance*
(1814–15), an unpublished work that she edited and transcribed.[1] This incomplete
"fragment" romance aligns the historical narrative of the Jewish diaspora following General Titus' sacking of Jerusalem in AD 70 with an Oriental tale about
an early antitrinitarian Christian community. The Assassins, a primitive Jewish-
Christian people named after a radical Gnostic sect in Islam, the Nizari Ismailis,
fled Jerusalem before it was sacked by the Roman armies. In the wilderness of
Lebanon, these nomadic people established an egalitarian commune. Lacking
magistrates and priests, their Islamic republic practices equal labor and mutual
love, and, "acknowledging no laws but those of God, they modeled their conducts
towards their fellow men by the conclusions of their individual judgment on
the practical application of those laws" (124). The Assassins are proto-Protestant
Muslims. They remained secluded from state priestcraft and gross superstition,
choosing instead to study the rational truth found in scripture and the esoteric
sciences without clerical mediation. By borrowing the name of an eleventh-
century radical Islamic sect, Percy and Mary Shelley provide an extremely unorthodox account on the origins of apostolic Christianity. Their synchronized
prophetic (Abrahamic) history not only indulges in the Gnostic heresy but also
implies that Trinitarian Christianity deviated from the natural religion of love.
Only "Gnostic" Islam remains faithful to primitive Christianity.

The Assassins' Islamic republicanism helps elucidate Mary Shelley's unusual eschatological portrayal of the Turks in *The Last Man*. Indeed, it is highly ironic, if not outright bizarre, that this novel posits an apocalyptic history in which the modern (Christian) millennium does not commence with Islam's fall. On the contrary, the defeat of the Turks dashes all utopian schemes, secular and religious. This event inaugurates a "feminine" Oriental infection—the avenging Turks in a metaphorical form—that spreads into Europe and England. For a novel that stages an apocalyptic clash between a "civilized" Christianity and a "barbaric" Mahometanism in Constantinople (Istanbul), I find it remarkable that *The Last Man* has not received as much attention as the Safie-Felix subplot in *Frankenstein*. Much has been written about the liberal feminist Orientalism informing the story of Felix's "sweet Arabian," Safie, who escapes the oppression of her father's Muslim faith for the feminist freedom found in European Christendom. However, literary critics have not investigated the feminist-Orientalist tropes employed in Shelley's other novels.[2] In examining representations of Islam in *The Last Man*, it is possible to move beyond *Frankenstein* and build on scholarship that treats Mary Shelley as an author in her own right—and not simply as Percy Shelley's alter ego or Mary Wollstonecraft's shadow-image.[3] Many critics have discussed "the Last Man" theme in the nineteenth century and offered countless attempts to read the novel's characters as allegorical portrayals of the author, Percy Shelley, and Lord Byron.[4] Unfortunately, these discussions limit the novel to biographical issues (Mary's tragic and lonely life) or to the preoccupations of a small literary coterie. Building on previous chapters, I explore how Mary Shelley's resistance toward Godwinian politics leads to an alternative feminist story about the Islamic republic within the eschatological framework of *The Last Man*. I contend that she, unlike her husband, never abandoned her commitment to the radical syncretism featured in *The Assassins*.

In a journal entry dated October 21, 1838, Mary Shelley describes her uneasy relationship to Godwinism, the feminist cause, and, implicitly, Mary Wollstonecraft:

> In the first place, with regard to "the good cause"—the cause of the advancement of freedom and knowledge, of the rights of women, &c.—I am not a person of opinions. I have said elsewhere that human beings differ greatly in this. Some have a passion for reforming the world; others do not cling to particular opinions. That my parents and Shelley were of the former class, makes me respect it . . . . For myself, I earnestly desire the good and enlightenment of my fellow-creatures, and see all, in the present course, tending to the same, and rejoice; but I am not for violent extremes, which only bring

on an injurious reaction. I have never written a word in disfavour of liberalism; that I have not supported it openly in writing, arises from the following causes, as far as I know:—That I have not argumentative powers: I see things pretty clearly, but cannot demonstrate them. Besides, I feel the counter-arguments too strongly. I do not feel that I could say aught to support the cause efficiently; besides that, on some topics (especially with regards to my own sex), I am far from making up my mind. I believe we are sent here to educate ourselves, and that self-denial, and disappointment, and self-control, are part of our education; that it is not by taking away all our restraining laws that our improvement is to be achieved; and, though many things need great amendment, I can by no means go so far as my friends would have me. When I feel that I can say what will benefit my fellow-creatures, I will speak: not before.[5]

Feminist critics have interpreted this key passage as Shelley's inability to express her feminist consciousness: Mary Poovey argues that she sought to articulate the ideals of her husband and mother but was constrained by the social conventions of female propriety; for Anne Mellor, Shelley is idealizing self-restrained women in the bourgeois family, but ultimately she "was a feminist in the same sense that her mother was"; and Jane Aaron argues that Shelley's apolitical stance is a symptom of patriarchal self-repression.[6] These readings assume that Shelley was never genuinely interested in critiquing liberal feminism. I would instead argue that Shelley's skepticism stems from the radical feminism championed by Lady Mary Wortley Montagu (chapter 2); like her, she was suspicious of any Whiggish position (including her mother's) that exalts "freeborn" Englishwomen at the expense of "enslaved" Muslim women.

As such, Mary Shelley's freethinking feminism is significantly different from that of Mary Wollstonecraft and the older Percy Shelley. Attending to the radical ideas entailed in speculative mythographies, such as Percy Shelley's *The Assassins*, reveals that the rejected anti-Islamic eschatology of *The Last Man* is enabled through Mary Shelley's investment in a mystical theosophy that christens "Gnostic" Shi'ite Islam the primitive Jewish Christianity. After considering the Shelleys' views on Gnostic Islam in the first section, I discuss Percy Shelley's revolutionary epic, *The Revolt of Islam* (1818), showing how he deserted his earlier views on Gnostic Muslims for the imperialist and anti-Islamic program outlined in Constantine Volney's eschatological tale, *The Ruins of Empire*. The final section argues that Percy Shelley's Wollstonestancraftian narrative on the Western liberation of Muslim women, inspired by Volney's Orientalism, is satirized in *The Last Man*. Mary Shelley's use of radical mythographies undermines the Eurocentric claims that underwrite a secular Volneyan eschatology. Consequently, the novel's "enslaved" harem woman, Evadne, marks a prophetic-revolutionary moment in which the racial, patriarchal, and imperialist ideas implicit in Mary Wollstone-craft's disparaging remarks about Muslim femininity are thoroughly repudiated as false ideologies.

"Illuminizing Jerusalemites" in Disguise

In his examination of women's feminist critiques, Eamon Wright has shown that British female writers from the late eighteenth century onward reworked im-ages of Mahometanism to articulate a racialized, feminist self-identity, a politi-cally correct concept of race that provided a common reference point in their writings.[7] In contrast to this tendency, I propose that, for Mary Shelley, Maho-metanism is not a foil against which an "Enlightened" (Christian) feminist posits her identity. On the contrary, the tragic romance between Lord Raymond, the enlightened Byronic hero, and Evadne, "The Sultana of the East," envisions a prophetic history in which the Western feminist project fails. This failure results from what Morton D. Paley calls a "negative apocalypse" (an apocalypse that re-sists the millennium) and what Steven Goldsmith dubs the "counterapocalyptic" (the Romantic mind's inability to transcend itself).[8] The novel's antimillennialist logic is strongly indicative of Mary Shelley's lifelong interest in nonbiblical myths about the Orient, as recoded in speculative accounts that exalt early Shi'ite his-tory and theology.

The author of the "Introduction" to *The Last Man* claims that the Sibylline leaves, the prophetic text that constitutes Lionel Verney's apocalyptic tale, are written in "ancient Chaldee, and Egyptian hieroglyphics, old as the pyramids. But there were ones in modern 'English' and 'Italian'" (7).[9] This fabulous account hy-perbolizes Mary Shelley's fascination with syncretistic mythographies that align seemingly disparate religious chronologies. Indeed, the entry on the "Sibyllae" in John Lempriere's mythographical work, the *Classical Dictionary* (1788) (listed in Mary Shelley's journal as part of Percy's reading list), states that the Sibyls' prophecies "speak so plainly of Jesus Christ, of his sufferings, and of his death, as to make it evident that they were composed in the second century by some of the followers of Christianity, who wished to convince the heathens of their error, by assisting the cause of truth with the arms of pious artifice."[10]

Whether the Sibyls' prophecies were fabrications concocted by early Chris-tians or authentic records that predate the Old Testament had been a controver-sial subject since the late seventeenth century. That Mary Shelley chose to focus on this aspect of syncretistic mythography testifies to her keen interest in extrabiblical chronology; the Sibylline oracles myth was at the center of theological debates that cast doubt on the Hebrew scriptures' authenticity by proposing that other non-Christian texts might enhance its meaning.[11] Shelley's novel does not engage explicitly with complicated debates about scriptural chronology. Instead, *The Last Man* portrays a nihilistic universe without redemption, a secular world that deemphasizes the place of religion in history. And yet biblical prophecy's universal significance is ever present in a novel that is obsessed with historical finality. The Sibylline prophecies hint at the unorthodox eschatological fantasies that lie at the core of *The Last Man.*

Speculative mythographic themes emerge in *Last Man* with the eccentric character of Merrival, a mystical astronomer. In his three-way conversation with Lionel Verney and the new Lord Protector, Ryland, Adrian insists that, despite the plague, the "earth will become a Paradise" (173). Ryland scoffs at this statement only to be corrected by Merrival, who maintains that "the poles of the earth will coincide with the poles of the ecliptic . . . an universal spring will be produced, and earth become a paradise." He remains fully confident that the plague poses no immediate danger, because, according to his calculations, there will be a peaceful millennium after a hundred thousand years (174). Of course, Merrival's prophecies are completely debunked by the end of the novel: he becomes so absorbed in his astrological theories that he remains completely oblivious of the real dangers that the plague poses to humanity. After his family dies from the contagion, he lost faith in "the system of universal nature," and he eventually dies embracing the earthly grave of his wife and children (225–26, 237). Like both Adrian and Verney, two characters who fail to discover paradise on a plague-stricken earth, Merrival is ironically portrayed as a foolish man who abandons his attachments to the domestic affections and familial domesticity for useless speculations on the end of history and worldly pursuits.

The irony of the Merrival subplot is a means by which Mary Shelley can safely introduce her readers to extrabiblical chronology. Her gloss on the passage on Merrival's calculations refers to an "ingenious Essay" written by the astronomer and Norwich shoemaker Sampson Arnold Mackey (174). The title of the essay alluded to his *The Mythological Astronomy of the Ancients Demonstrated, by restoring to their Fables & Symbols their original meanings* (Norwich, 1822–23), a heterodox work arguing that the Jewish accounts of history are astrological allegories pertaining to an ancient Zodiac system derived from more authentic Egyptian and Hindu sources. Accordingly, ancient Oriental knowledge regarding the pericyclical motion of the earth's pole, including the ecliptic, better explains the biblical "fall" from Eden (the decline of the golden age) than Christian original sin.

Nineteenth-century British reviewers saw Mackey as a mystic who spoke against Christian revelation, engaged in the astronomical speculations popularized by Drummond, Volney, and Dupuis, and dabbled in the ancient Egyptian, Chinese, and Hindu chronologies.[12] Unlike that of speculative mythographers such as Jacob Bryant, Captain Francis Wilford, Volney, and Dupuis, Mackey's work was seen as exceptional in its views on Hindu chronology: for him, Hindu astronomy cannot be reduced to the Christian mythos, as argued by Captain Wilford and Dupuis, because Hindu myths spans many thousands of years before Christianity. As a result, he concludes that there is nothing unique about the Jewish account of history; that is to say, the Pentateuch is a derivative Oriental work.[13] In this context, the Merrival subplot not only subtly criticizes hypermasculine millennial thought, but also creates a safe distance between the author's beliefs and a Mackeyan speculative mode not suitable for a proper Anglican woman to pursue.

Mary Shelley's interest in Mackey is not surprising: she was always interested in the arcane sciences, as evident in the story of Victor Frankenstein and his experiments in alchemy, and, of course, she was a key member of Percy Shelley's circle. Lord Byron, Thomas Love Peacock, and other Godwinian radicals shared an unorthodox interest in syncretistic systems built upon ancient astronomy, Near Eastern cosmology, and allegorical interpretations of scripture. They put syncretic mythographies to subversive uses to depict Christianity as simply one among many other equally viable mythological systems. As Marilyn Butler has shown, Romantic syncretism was closely allied to "French infidel mythography" and could serve as a radical tool for "isolating and belittling current religious orthodoxy."[14]

This impulse to reinterpret Christian history alongside other religious myths is the driving force behind *The Assassins: A Fragment of a Romance.* In this syncretistic mythographical tale, Jewish history is intertwined with the fate of the early Christians: after the destruction of Jerusalem in AD 70, an antitrinitarian Jewish-Christian group abandons the orthodox Jewish community and establishes an egalitarian community in "the solitudes of Lebanon" (151). These secluded nomads embody the true principles recuperated from a pristine egalitarian Christianity; they

> were remarkable neither for their numbers nor their importance. They contained among them neither philosophers nor poets. Acknowledging no laws but those of God, they modeled their conduct towards their fellow-men by the conclusions of their individual judgment on the practical application of these laws. And it was apparent from

the simplicity and severity of their manners, that this contempt for human institutions had produced among them a character superior in singleness and sincere self-apprehension to the slavery of pagan customs and the gross delusions of antiquated superstition. Many of their opinions considerably resembled those of the sect afterwards known by the name of Gnostics. They esteemed the human understanding to be the paramount rule of human conduct; they maintained that the obscurest religious truth required for its complete elucidation no more than the strenuous application of the energies of mind. (150)

The Shelleys' religion amounts to Gnostic theosophy. As someone who was invested in editing and transcribing *The Assassins*, Mary Shelley willingly adopts a Mackeyan syncretist mode while disavowing any responsibility as an author committed to heterodox beliefs. Through the Merival subplot, she puts forward a "Gnostic" repudiation of orthodox biblical chronology and then ironizes this repudiation by couching it within a larger gender critique of manly millennial thinking.

In her preface to the 1840 edition of Percy Shelley's complete works, Mary Shelley disavows any knowledge about Percy's purpose in writing *The Assassins*. However, she references the medieval legends about the Assassins: they "were known in the eleventh century as a horde of Mahometans living among the recesses of Lebanon,—ruled over by the Old Man of the mountain; under whose direction various murders were committed on the Crusaders."[15] In the twelfth and thirteenth centuries, European crusaders fabricated wild stories about an extremist Shi'ite Muslims led by the "Old Man of the Mountain," the Syrian leader Rashid Al-Din Sinan, among others, who was notorious for allegedly conducting secret conspiracies and "assassinations" (a word etymologically derived from the Assassins myth). European crusaders learned about these stories from Sunni polemicists' anti-Shi'ite propaganda. Feeding into western Orientalist stereotypes, these stories remained unchallenged in the eighteenth and nineteenth centuries.[16]

Mary Shelley's preface also reveals that the injured stranger saved by an Arabian family is "Shelley's old favourite, the Wandering Jew."[17] In chapter 3 of *The Assassins*, the Arab Albedir discovers the naked, bleeding body of an unnamed stranger, supposedly the Wandering Jew Ahasuerus, impaled on a tree branch. This symbolic parody of the Tree of Life and Christ's crucifixion points to the stranger's Gnostic credentials: he embodies humanity's Fall and Redemption, an interfusion of materiality and spirituality represented in the snake image (a commonplace Gnostic symbol that appears several times in this narrative). In radical prophecies written between 1786 and 1830, the Wandering Jew was a Cabalistic-hermetic symbol of the "last man," who is cursed to live until the apocalypse for having abused Jesus Christ.[18] *The Assassins* fuses this "last man" figure with the Old Man of the Mountain from Assassin lore. The identification of the stranger with both the Wandering Jew and the Old Man raises a pressing question about how the Shelleys could have concluded their truncated story: does the Wandering Jew find his home in an exiled community of proto-Muslim Christian Arabs, becoming, in effect, the next Assassin leader, another Old Man of the Mountain, the hidden Imam? Such a "last man" prophecy would have meant that history culminates in the revolutionary refusion of the Abrahamic faiths, and not in the conversion of the Jews or the defeat of the Turks.

In *Shelley and Scripture: The Interpreting Angel*, Bryan Shelley argues that the "Gnostic" Assassins reflect a larger concern in Percy Shelley's lifelong heretical interpretation of Christian revelation: namely, that orthodox Christianity needs to be supplemented with nonbiblical sources, because the canonical scriptures remain incomplete and flawed. Equating Christ's message with spiritual gnosis, Shelley's Christian Gnosticism, an esoteric doctrine known only among illuminaries, teaches that the spirit's emancipation from "fallen" materiality requires individual freethinking, and that Christ is a revolutionary prophet who revealed gnosis in his rational apprehension of God's oneness. Percy Shelley subscribed to this "Gnostic" creed throughout his life.[19] In *On Christianity* (1817), for instance, Shelley maintains that the orthodox church has failed to recognize the "rational" truth behind Christ's "revolutionary" message, and that the gospel account is "imperfect and obscure."[20]

But the Gnostic heresy found in *The Assassins* includes an additional twist: the first-century primitive Jewish Christianity is named after a radical sect in Islam. The historical Assassins are a mystical branch of the Ismailian Shi'ite Muslims; they study astrology and magic and are bent on replacing orthodox Sunni rule with an egalitarian social order. Also known as the Nizari Ismailis sect, these eleventh-century Shi'ite extremists propagated a Gnostic-dualistic creed in which only the Imam, Prophet Muhammad's heir and the "Perfect man" (Holy Spirit), can liberate the spirit from a "fallen" universe corrupted by the conflict of good and evil. For this Muslim freethinking movement, "the ultimate religious obligation is knowledge—gnosis—of the true Imam," and not strict adherence to Qur'anic law.[21] Adopting this Gnostic doctrine, the Nizari Ismailis drew on ancient Near Eastern prophecies—inspired by Judaic, Christian, Zoroastrian, and Manichaean myths—to reread the Qur'an as an allegorical text containing esoteric truths.[22] For them, the Prophet embodies universal reason and ancient occult wisdom; each successive Imam is a reincarnation of this Gnostic truth as conveyed in the poetic imagination.[23] In this belief in artistic creativity as the key to spiritual-political transformation, Percy Shelley self-consciously posits a historical congruence between Gnostic Christians' heretical ideas and the Assassins' freethinking philosophy, both predicated on the notion that art leads to divine knowledge.

Thus, Bryan Shelley's observation that Percy Shelley "confuses a community of primitive Christians with a radical Islamic sect" needs to be corrected.[24] On the contrary, Percy Shelley's "Gnostic" (antitrinitarian) Jewish Christianity entails an Islamic prophetic tradition that exalts creative gnosis. In *An Ecclesiastical History, Ancient and Modern* (1755), the most authoritative account of Gnostic Christianity in the eighteenth century, John Lawrence Mosheim argues that the Gnostic Christians rejected both the Trinity and the Old Testament, seeking instead recourse in the "secret" mystical writings of Abraham, Zoroaster, Christ, and other prophets.[25] Mosheim accuses the Gnostics of having corrupted "the doctrine of the gospel by a profane mixture of the tenets of the Oriental philosophy."[26] In volume 5 of *The History of the Decline and Fall of the Roman Empire* (a work that Mary Shelley references in a citation to European research on the Assassins),[27] Edward Gibbon establishes a possible theological connection between Islamic prophecy and Christian Gnosticism: according to his account of the Mahometan doctrine, Christ's original message was lost before it was recovered by the "Gnostic" Qur'an, which explains that Christ was not crucified but taken to heaven while another man died in his place. Even though Gibbon is skeptical of the Gnostic influence on Mahometanism, he provocatively writes that "Mahomet was instructed by the Gnostics to accuse the church, as well as the synagogue, of corrupting the integrity of the sacred text."[28] The Prophet's teachings preserved a primitive Jewish-Christian Gnosticism. Likewise, the story of the "Gnostic" Assassins is about a pseudo-Muslim idyllic community that, for almost six hundred years, lived beyond the "palaces of the Califs and the Caesars" and among "Arabians and enthusiasts" (Shelley, *The Assassins* 127, 125). In the Shelleys' syncretistic imagination, an Islamic-style Reformation was in effect long before Prophet Muhammad and Martin Luther.

This radical Protestant fascination with revolutionary Shi'ite doctrines predates the Shelleys' idealized Nizari Ismailis. Bonaparte consciously adopted the role of the Mahdi, a messianic figure central to radical Shi'ite creeds, during the 1798–99 French occupation of Egypt (chapters 4 and 5). This event had a tremendous impact on the Islamic-inspired writings of Walter Savage Landor and Robert Southey—two radicals who sparked Percy Shelley's interest in Shi'ite

myths about the Near East. Going back even further, radical enlightenment accounts about Gnostic Shi'ites have their roots in the late seventeenth century. In
*Enlightenment Contested: Philosophy, Modernity, and the Emancipation of Man,
1670–1752,* Jonathan Israel points out that Pierre Bayle, a notorious atheist whose
Dictionnaire historique Percy Shelley may have read, was deeply invested in tracing
European freethinking to ancient Greek Gnostic undercurrents existing among
early extremist Shi'ites, the *ahl al-haqq* or "men of truth," revolutionaries who
opposed the three revealed religions and sought to overthrow the Umayyad and
Abbasid Caliphates. Israel speculates that this extended freethinking genealogy
represents historically accurate information: that Gnosticism's anti-Christian
Greek philosophy was preserved and transmitted by clandestine radical Shi'ites
who defended reason, toleration, and equality.[29] Regardless of whether this information is historically accurate, the revolutionary implications of this Greco-
Arab Shi'ite legacy could only have inspired the Shelleys' mythographical project.
Like their radical predecessors, the Shelleys composed an Oriental narrative that
traces republican freethinking principles to the proto-Islamic Near East. Ideally,
this extended Gnostic genealogy avoids the travesties of the French Revolution
during a reactionary era in which progressive ideals were losing their appeal.

A revolutionary Gnostic narrative about "the last man" is precisely what the
Shelleys were interested in writing. On August 25, 1814, the day that they began
to "write part of Shelley's Romance" on the Assassins, they read Abbe Barruel's
work.[30] In fact, they first read Barruel's "histoire de Jacobinism" on August 23 and
then reread it on October 11, 1814.[31] That they were reading this work during the
same period they were composing their Oriental romance is not a coincidence. In
the *Memoirs, illustrating the history of Jacobinism* (1798), a popular work that went
through several translated editions in England, Barruel argued that French Jacobinism is part of a large international conspiracy headed by millennial prophets
and secret freemason societies. These "Illuminizing Jerusalemites," as he styles
them, pose a great danger because their main agenda is the "overthrow of every
religious and civil law, and at the downfall of every throne."[32] Emmanuel Swedenborg, a Swedish scientist and mystical prophet who died in London in 1772, is
implicated in this radical conspiracy by promoting what Barruel sees as a corrupt
Oriental doctrine: "Swedenborg tells us, that his doctrines are all of the highest
antiquity, and similar to those of the Egyptians, the Magi, and the Greeks; he
even asserts them to be anterior to the deluge. . . . Should any person be tempted
to seek [Swedenborg's revelation] elsewhere, he must go in quest of it among
those clans where Christianity and Political laws are not known."[33] Ultimately,

Swedenborg and his followers take "refuge in the dens of Rosicrucian Masonry": his prophecies invalidate Mosaic history by locating apostolic Christianity's pure "Jewish" monotheism in a pseudo-Gnostic Oriental culture in which the Jacobin ideas of "Equality, Liberty and independence" were first propagated.[34]

The same accusation can be leveled against *The Assassins*. Indeed, in the *History of the Assassins* (1818; translated into English in 1833–35), Joseph von Hammer, an Austrian Orientalist, made such an accusation: he compares the Assassins' dangerous enthusiasm to the freemason illuminati and the French regicides.[35] Writing against the grain of reactionary propaganda, the Shelleys put Barruel's work to subversive uses, framing their syncretistic account of the proto-Muslim "Gnostic" Christians within a revolutionary narrative about "Illuminizing Jerusalemites." In doing so, the Shelleys recast the Assassins as exemplary heroes fighting for republican liberty despite their initial defeat. They are a source of inspiration for English radicals living in a repressive era, although their romance would have been too dangerous to publish in its lifetime, even as an incomplete romance.

Given their investment in *The Assassins*, along with Mary Shelley's underhanded allusions to Mackeyan speculation in *The Last Man*, I have argued that the Shelleys treated Gnosticism in what Norman O. Brown describes as the "the middle term" linking Islam to primitive Jewish Christianity, enshrining the Romantic imagination of Ismailian gnosis as a Jewish-Muslim refusion.[36] As an "Illuminizing Jerusalemite" who wrote a completed sequel to an Oriental tale that could have been titled "the last man," Mary Shelley wanted to recover the repressed history of Europe's invisible enemy, the Arab Jew as recuperated in Gil Anidjar's historical assessment of Derrida's Abrahamic supplement. Hence, *The Assassins'* unnamed stranger is an unreadable cipher for the "Jewish-Muslim symbiosis": an unstable Abrahamic vision that Anidjar paradoxically describes as "the first as already the last, of the last and of the end, an explosive specter of uncertain and troubling existence."[37] Read as an addendum to this fragmentary vision, *The Last Man* exemplifies Mary Shelley's longstanding commitment to a unified Abrahamic monotheism, a supplementary faith in which Christian modernity does not determine global history. Although Percy Shelley holds similar views, his later writings on Muslim and Ottoman corruption betray his orthodox leanings, favoring an anti-Islamic eschatology over the freethinking Shi'ite republicanism that he exalted in his syncretistic account of the Arab Jew.

The Unacknowledged Legislator of the East

Composed during 1817, Percy Shelley's *Laon and Cythna*, also titled *The Revolt of Islam*, serves as the template through which Mary Shelley's *The Last Man* reimagines Islam's eschatological role. This poem therefore deserves attention. It reflects on a crisis over Parliamentary reform in Britain, but places it in a Muslim context. Parliamentary reform, a topic of great concern, presented Percy Shelley with the opportunity to create a literary work that salvages liberty, equality, and fraternity in post-Waterloo Britain. His poem resurrects the French Revolution's beau ideal, despite France's tragic and bloody course in the previous two decades. In a letter to his publisher, he claims that his primary interest is in the prospect of a future revolution in Western Europe, not in Muslim culture and religion: "The scene is supposed to be laid in Constantinople and modern Greece, but without much attempt at minute delineation of Mahometan manners. It is in fact a tale illustrative of such a Revolution as might be supposed to take place in an European nation."[38] His epic deploys negative stereotypes about Muslims to express subtle concerns about reactionary Europe and imperial Britain that could have resulted in a seditious libel persecution if presented explicitly.[39] This cautionary tactic explains why, among other changes, he renamed the poem "The Revolt of Islam" by 1818.[40] But this change does not imply that Islam is merely a red herring meant to evade the censors. Adopting the anti-Islamic polemic found in Constantine Volney's *The Ruins of Empire*, Shelley uses Mahometanism as the prototype of a despotic state religion—an eastern ancien régime that needs to be reformed, or colonized, by the Western poet-prophet—"the unacknowledged legislator of the world" as hailed in his *Defense of Poetry*. Prompted by the altered circumstances of post-Waterloo Britain, his version of tyrannical Islam marks a swift departure from Shi'ite Gnosticism.

   In canto 1 of Shelley's epic, the narrator describes at length "an Eagle and a Serpent wreathed in fight," followed by an unnamed female prophet-seer who interprets this cosmic battle (line 193). After the snake and eagle fall into the sea, the female prophet promises to disclose the meaning of this symbol to the narrator, who joins her on a boat journey to the Temple of the Spirit of the Good. Employing an Old Testament prophetic voice, she relates "a strange and awful tale" that reveals "the dark Future's ever-flowing urn," but, like the Cumaean Sibyl or the Priestess of Apollo, her vision can convey only a minute part of her divinely inspired foreknowledge (lines 334–35, 345). Looking at the stars and the planets for guidance, the female prophet interprets the two "Gods"—the Eagle (negative force) and the Snake (positive force)—as pseudo-Zoroastrian principles that operate within the never-ending, cyclical movements of revolutionary-prophetic history. These principles are not supernatural laws existing beyond history; they are laws of nature that dictate the ebb and flow of sociopolitical upheavals. The biblical monotheistic faiths do not determine the female prophet's cosmology: her vision of cyclical revolutions within a homogeneous temporal continuum without a beginning, middle, and end eschews a linear, biblical eschatology that divides the passage of time into heterogeneous segments, beginning with Eden, moving into the Fall, and terminating with salvation.

Nonetheless, once Shelley inserts Islam within his mythological poem, he lapses back into a linear biblical model. Canto 1 introduces the epic saga that awaits the two revolutionary protagonists, Laon and Cythna. Their plan is to spread the Godwinian "rights of man" to a world ruled by despots, beginning with Constantinople, the capital of the Ottoman empire. As secular prophets, they invoke historical *revelation* (removing the veil/cover of history)—as the moment in which political tyranny is unmasked and overthrown. Canto 5 describes this moment as the fall of Sultan Othman and the demise of Islamic civilization. By canto 10, the nonviolent revolution introduced by Laon and Cythna spreads to the surrounding nations, which forge a counterrevolutionary alliance against the rebel "atheists" just as British and European monarchies formed a coalition against revolutionary France. The tyrant Othman returns to power and executes many rebel "atheists." The plague soon emerges from the rebels' decomposing bodies, followed by widespread famine. The defeat of the revolutionary forces marks the apocalypse: "Too well/these signs the coming mischief did foretell" (10:3931–32). One of the tyrant's soldiers describes an "Angel bright as day" riding on a horse, recalling the angel on a horse from *Revelations* (10:3875-8). Mahometan tyranny's collapse and the subsequent backlash against the radical cause heralds the apocalypse. In representing Islam as anti-Christ, Shelley's cyclical mythos returns to the Christian eschatological time frame that the poem initially disavowed.

This eschatological view of Islam complicates the epic's ending. After the "blue Plague" fell "upon the race of man" (10:3964), the frightened masses congregate under a Christian priest (an "Iberian" priest in *The Revolt of Islam*), who forms a strategic alliance with the sultan and his Muslim followers to crush radical freethinkers. Cythna confronts all the kings and priests, and they (except for the "Iberian Priest") identify her as the apocalyptic angel: "All thought it was God's angel come to sweep / the lingering guilty to their fiery grave" (12:4522–23). Laon and Cythna eventually are captured and burned at the stake as heretics. The liberated ex-Muslim population remembers them as revolutionary martyrs. After death, Laon and Cythna return to their cosmic home in the Temple of the Spirit of the Good as described in Canto 1. Even though Cythna has failed to complete the Golden City's revolution, she has successfully unveiled the truth of "Liberty" within a secular eschatology that anticipates the fall of all world religions, beginning with Islam. And yet, for Laon and Cythna, prophetic revelation takes place within an ongoing cyclical time frame: there is no Judeo-Christian millennium after the apocalypse, only a return to a transcendental neo-Platonic universe. A linear biblical temporality that posits "the end of history" is displaced by a cyclical temporality without beginning or end, even though this moment of narrative closure is highly unstable and even tenuous: the next revolution can only be accomplished by the liberated ex-Muslim inhabitants, who will bring about an apocalyptic "end of history" once Islamic despotism is defeated. Incapable of assigning a positive function for Mahometanism in secular history, Shelley must rely on the anti-Islamism implicit in a teleological Christian eschatology fixated on historical finality.

Shelley voraciously read the works of syncretic mythographers such as Constantine Volney, Charles Francois Dupuis (active supporters of the French Revolution), Sir William Drummond, John Frank Newton, and Thomas Love Peacock. These writers believed that all myths derive from elemental natural phenomena and that religion gives narrative form to the heavenly bodies as represented in the ancient Zodiac of Persian, Chaldean, Hindu, and Chinese astronomy. Peacock's epic poem, *Ahrimanes*, a work that Shelley most likely read between the summer of 1813 and the autumn of 1815, presents a dualistic Zoroastrian cosmology in which history is described as revolutionary cycles. The work also contains notes citing Dupuis, Drummond, and Newton. The eagle and snake battle described in the first canto of *Laon and Cythna* is an archetypal ourobous image of a snake swallowing its tail, which Volney and Drummond describe as a cosmic symbol for the revolutions that occur within time.[41] Regardless of his official position on mythography, Shelley, and other members of his radical circle, had no reservations about using unorthodox myths to demolish an exclusive Christian history and discredit the monotheistic revelations. Indeed, the Assassins tale represents such an attempt to de-Christianize world history. But then why does his revolutionary epic resort to a Christian eschatological conception of Mahometanism?

Volney's *The Ruins of Empire* provides an important context for understanding Shelley's fascination with the apocalyptic collapse of an oppressive Islamic empire. Volney's mythographical work (the text from which both Safie and the creature in *Frankenstein* learn about history) reflects on the rise and fall of all great empires, with an obsessive emphasis on the decadent Ottoman empire's demise in the next revolutionary cycle. From the very first sentence, the narrator, posing as a traveler in the Ottoman domains, begins his tale on the "ruins" of past empires by referring to the current conflict between Russians and Ottomans in the late eighteenth century. All he witnesses while traveling through Egypt and Syria is "tyranny and wretchedness" (3). These opening descriptions set the tenor for the rest of the book: "the Genius" (akin to Shelley's female prophet) appears before the narrator and explains how Islamic despotism is doomed to follow all the mighty empires that have fallen throughout history. Thus, in the Genius's lengthy descriptions of Judaism, Christianity, and other world religions as tools used by crafty politicians, Mahometanism's theocratic rule is always invoked as the epitome of state priestcraft (43, 45-6, 48–49). The Genius teaches that fallen empires in Persia, Egypt, and China confirm the near-apocalyptic expectation that "war, famine, and pestilence" will eventually end Ottoman rule (10). Shelley imparts a similar view in his eschatological epic. As Filiz Turham has argued, the Ottoman empire is the metaphorical locus in British Romantic writings for literary representations of the end of empire (and, I should add, in Volney's *Ruins*); indeed, by the late eighteenth and early nineteenth century, the once-powerful Ottoman empire was in decline, economically, militarily, and politically.[42] In appropriating Volneyan history—wedded to a Christian eschatological framework—Shelley's view of tyrannical Islam runs counter to his earlier syncretistic revolutionary position on the Muslim world.

Volney's polemical target is Islamic civilization as a whole, not merely the Ottoman empire. Even though he is skeptical of all religious systems, he is particularly intent on discrediting Mahometanism. In his enthusiasm for Ottoman disintegration, he looks forward to the dismemberment of the entire Islamic body politic:

The decree is past; the day approaches when this colossus of power shall be crushed and crumbled under its own mass. Yes, I swear it, by the ruins of so many empires destroyed. The empire of the Crescent shall follow the fate of despotism it has copied. A nation of strangers shall drive the Sultan from his metropolis. The thrown of Orkhan shall be overturned. The last shoot of his trunk shall be broken off. . . . In this dissolution, the people of the empire, loosened from the yoke which united them, shall resume their ancient distinctions, and a general anarchy shall follow. . . until there shall arise among the Arabians, Armenians, or Greeks, legislators who may compose new states. (51–52)

This prophecy about the end of Muslim civilization and the subsequent rise of nation states not only anticipates Shelley's epic but also (especially in the last sentence) his grandiose vision of the poet-prophet as "the unacknowledged legislator of the world." As in Shelley's "Ozymandias" (1818), the sonnet about the "trunkless legs" belonging to a "colossal Wreck" discovered by a traveler in "an antique land" (lines 1–2, 13),[43] Volney's "colossus of power" symbolizes Islamic despotism as a fragmented ruin that will buckle under its unbearable weight. Most notably, "the Revolt of Islam" is written at the right angle to an earlier draft of "Ozymandias." Apparently, Shelley was engaged in Volneyan reflections on Mahometanism while he was editing his epic.[44] In a footnote to the paragraph that follows the above-cited passage, Volney states that the defeat of the Turks will politically transform the Mediterranean coast, and that "If . . . the French become important in proportion as they become free, and if they make use of the advantage they will obtain, their progress may easily prove the most honorable sort; inasmuch as, by wise decrees of fate, the true interest of mankind evermore accords with their true morality" (53). Islam's collapse is an event that revolutionary France should use to fulfill its manifest destiny, a golden opportunity to spread democratic reform abroad. Thus, the growth of French democracy and culture is synonymous with both Islam's collapse and the colonization of the Mediterranean Levant. Imperial ambition is the true gospel preached by the unacknowledged legislators of the East.

Anti-Islamic rhetoric is intrinsic to an imperialist Volneyan eschatology. In his earlier work, *Travels through Syria and Egypt* (1778), Volney declares that Mahomet's laws are the most "wretched" of any religion, and "that the convulsions of the governments, and the ignorance of the people, in that quarter of the globe, originate more or less immediately in the Koran, and its morality."[45] Mahometanism is the quintessential tyrannical religion that hinders revolutionary progress. Thus, in Volney's imperialist conception of world history, an enlightened republic requires the downfall of all Muslim regimes. Not surprisingly, Napoleon relied on Volney's researches on Islamic civilization to prepare for his invasion of Egypt in 1798. Indeed, Napoleon read the *Travels through Syria and Egypt* as an eschatological "bible" on how to defeat the Turks and reclaim the Holy Land, even though he willingly embraced many aspects of Islam while in Egypt. In this respect, *The Ruins of Empire* clearly articulates the secular eschatology inherent in French imperial ideology. As Edward Said succinctly puts it, Volney's Orientalist works were "effective texts to be used by any European wishing to win in the Orient."[46]

Shelley's shift from a radical Shi'ite perspective to a Volneyan imperialist program is indicative of a post-Waterloo political climate in which English radicals were losing faith in the revolutionary promise. Recalling "The Revolt of Islam," Shelley's unpublished *A Philosophical View of Reform* (composed between 1819

and 1820) reaffirms this promise by arguing that the quest for parliamentary reform in Britain is linked to other nations around the globe. For him, the apocalyptic fall of the Ottoman empire, along with other struggling nations suffering
from tyranny, will set into motion progressive history:

> The Turkish Empire is in its last stage of ruin, and it cannot be doubted but that the
> time is approaching when the deserts of Asia Minor and of Greece will be colonized
> by the overflowing population of countries less enslaved and debased, and that the cli-
> mate and the scenery which was the birthplace of all that is wise and beautiful will not
> remain forever the spoil of wild beasts and unlettered Tartars. In Syria and Arabia the
> spirit of human intellect has roused a sect of people called Wahabees, who maintain
> the Unity of God, and the equality of man, and their enthusiasm must go on 'conquer-
> ing and to conquer' even if it must be repressed in its present shape. Egypt having but
> a nominal dependence upon Constantinople is under the government of the Ottoman
> Bey, a person of enlightened views who is introducing European literature and arts, and
> is thus beginning that change which Time, the great innovator, will accomplish in that
> degraded country; [and] by the same means its sublime enduring monuments may ex-
> cite lofty emotions in the hearts of the posterity of those who now contemplate them
> without admiration.[47]

Shelley's political manifesto anticipates three major "revolutions" that will
weaken the Ottoman ancien régime: the 1821–29 Greek Revolt, a national independence struggle that allowed European imperial intervention and Russian
expansionist policies in the region; the Wahhabi reformist movement, a group
of Muslim rebels who, inspired by the scholar Muhammad Ibn 'Abd Al-Wahhab
(1703–1792), purged Mecca and Medina of iconic worship after conquering the
cities in 1803–4, only to be temporarily defeated by Sultan Mahmoud II between
1812 and 1818; and the "enlightened" Egyptian Pasha and viceroy Muhammad
Ali (1769–1849), who, following the withdrawal of French and British occupying
forces, defeated his Ottoman and Mamluk rivals and adopted Western methods
of military training and education in 1815. For Shelley, these revolutionary events
are apocalyptic signs. Not only is the Ottoman empire fated to collapse, but all
Western Europe and Britain is on the verge of major social and political transformations once these revolutionary events come to pass. In other words, Ottoman
tyranny's defeat will inaugurate a successful worldwide revolution, a positive and
much-needed change that will renew radical hope during a counterrevolutionary
era that has witnessed the return of repressive monarchies in Western Europe.

In Shelley's eschatological scheme, the collapse of the Ottoman empire promises to undermine the 1815 Concert of Europe, the Vienna peace settlement ar-

ranged by Britain, Austria, Prussia, and Russia. This peace sought to ensure that, after Napoleon's defeat, the restored monarchies of France, Spain, Naples, and Italy, as well as the Ottoman sultanate, remain secure. From the beginning of this settlement, the "Eastern Question" threatened the delicate balance of power in post-Napoleonic Europe. If the Ottoman empire were dismantled, a political vacuum would emerge in Eastern Europe, Asia Minor, and the Near East, setting the world stage for imperial rivalries among warring European nations. The "Eastern Question" presented complicated diplomatic problems that British politicians preferred to ignore: Britain needed to keep the crumbling Ottoman empire intact in order to forestall Russian expansion into the Mediterranean and the Near East, key regions that were in route to British India. However, Britain did not want to be viewed publicly as allied to a "despotic" Muslim state. Even as Anglo-Ottoman and Anglo-Russian diplomatic ties remained ambivalent and fluctuating during this period, British foreign policy mostly favored the sultanate over its rivals, avoiding a strategic alliance with Muhammad Ali in Egypt and failing to support the Greek cause in 1821 (a decision that outraged Percy Shelley and many English radicals).[48]

For Shelley, these diplomatic decisions confirmed Britain's tyrannical inclinations and exposed the Achilles' heels of the Concert of Europe: the ailing Ottoman empire. Therefore, the colonization of this decrepit empire, internally or externally, by Muslim reformers or Western liberators, is what will determine revolutionary global change as dramatized in his epic poem and, as I argue below, spoofed in Mary Shelley's *The Last Man*. During this critical juncture in eschatological history, Ottoman Islam is to be discarded as the oppressor's religion; the coming (millennial) utopia will be initiated by the Wahhabis, "who maintain the Unity of God, and the equality of man," rather than by the radical Shi'ite Gnostics. As such, Shelley abandoned the Assassins myth, not out of hatred for Islam but because, post-1815, this myth represents an outdated response to changing historical circumstances. Instead, Volney's apocalyptic views on the decadent Ottomans served as the most expedient explanation.

Hence, the anti-Islamic Volneyan discourse implicit in *The Revolt of Islam* needs to be qualified. Although Shelley's revolutionary epic is an imperialist manifesto that de-Islamicizes the Orient under the banner of Western secular humanism, the political goal here is not to attack Islam per se but to demonize British diplomatic efforts to secure the sultanate for the sake of promoting their imperialist aspirations in the Near East. In the post-Napoleonic context, his attack on Ottoman Islam is coded as a radical critique of British and European policies abroad and, therefore, the allied Christian priest represents a greater threat to revolutionary global change than the sultan himself. Yet the poem's religious politics remains thoroughly ambivalent, because the fight against Ottoman tyranny sometimes elides into a war against Islam as an irredeemable tyrannical faith. Certainly, this understanding of the Prophet's teachings is far removed from the noninstitutional and pristine teachings of Shi'ite Islam in *The Assassins*. By the time Shelley begins writing his epic, he had abandoned his earlier radical syncretistic romance, because he lost faith in an egalitarian Islamic republic that would serve as the engine of progressive history. During a transitional period where Mahometanism primarily manifested itself as Ottoman tyranny at the expense of reformist Muslim movements in Arabia and Egypt, Shelley chose to embrace the anti-Islamic eschatology embedded in Volney's imperialist vision. Since Mahometanism is drained of any positive political associations by the time Shelley composed his epic, this faith needs to be reformed—or synonymously, colonized—by the enlightened prophets of the West. Thus, Marilyn Butler's reading of Shelleyan optimism remains insightful: the poet-prophet as the "unacknowledged legislator of the world" reiterates an imperialistic Volneyan program, because Shelley's epic defines this world as, first and foremost, the Islamic Near East.[49]

The Feminist Revolt of Islam

Shelley's imperialist commitment to a Volneyan program is acutely evident in his feminist critique of Oriental patriarchy. E. Douka Kabitoglou has hailed his revolutionary epic a "feminist manifesto," taking its place between the works of Mary Wollstonecraft and John Stuart Mill.[50] Likewise, Nathaniel Brown calls this epic "the most powerful feminist poem in the language and . . . the most thoroughly grounded in the realities of the woman question."[51] Although Shelley's epic poem is undoubtedly about the liberation of repressed femininity at both the metaphysical and social levels (the political integration of the masculine and feminine psyche), their readings ignore how Shelley subordinates radical feminist concerns to the imperatives of a Western civilizing mission. Spreading the "rights of woman" in Constantinople, Cythna, the "enlightened" prophet, de-Islamicizes Muslim women when "liberating" them from their repressive veils. In this regard, feminism justifies a Volneyan imperialist program intent on defeating Islam. Mary Shelley, I argue, resists this secular program. Her "introduction" to the novel eschews Percy Shelley's radical feminism: instead of exalting the "feminist" prophet, she describes the female "translator" of the Sibylline leaves as a dispossessed prophet-figure (a widowed female novelist) whose writings are mediated by English patriarchal power.

Percy and Mary Shelley are writing in response to Mary Wollstonecraft's feminist representation of repressed Muslim femininity. In *A Vindication of the Rights of Woman*, Wollstonecraft argues that Western men are not as polite as they portray themselves, because they treat their women in the same barbaric manner in which Muslim men treat their women, as "weak beings [that] are only fit for a seraglio."[52] Like their Muslim counterparts, Western men deprive women of their rational autonomy and reduce them to sensual objects meant to fulfill their sexual needs. In this regard, the marriage practiced in England and Europe confines women within "an eastern harem."[53] All European and English male writers, she argues, have embraced "Mahometanism," including Milton: "though when [Milton] tells us that women are formed for softness and sweet attractive grace, I cannot comprehend his meaning, unless, in the true Mahometan strain, he meant to deprive us of souls, and insinuate that we were beings only designed by sweet attractive grace, and docile blind obedience, to gratify the senses of man when he can no longer soar on the wing of contemplation."[54]

The "true Mahomentan strain" is identified with an oppressive patriarchal system that is essentially un-English and non-Western; the despotism of the harem is "natural" to Islamic societies that cast women as having no souls, but not in an Enlightened Western civilization based on Christian values. Throughout the 1790s, the trope of the "naturally" oppressed Muslim woman prevailed among English feminist writers, from Catherine MacCaulay's *Letters on Education* (1790) to Mary Robinson's *Thoughts on the Condition of Women* (1799). Like Wollstonecraft, these feminist writers have distorted views on Muslim women's lives, asserting that under Mahometanism women have no souls and therefore no hope for a future state or afterlife.[55] The Muslim belief that women lack souls is, of course, incorrect. It was employed primarily as a rhetorical plea that England and Europe abandon its "Mahometan" ways and become more like themselves—rational and enlightened societies that treat women as independent persons invested with "rights." Only then will men and women be truly capable of eradicating tyranny in the state and at home. As Joyce Zonana succinctly puts it, Wollstonecraft "displaces the source of patriarchal oppression onto an 'Oriental,' 'Mahometan' society, enabling British readers to contemplate local problems without questioning their own self-definition as Westerners and Christians." Accordingly, 1790s feminism takes recourse in contractual rights theory in a "conservative effort to make the West more like itself."[56]

The ideological dichotomy between freeborn Englishwomen and enslaved Muslim women serves as the primary justification for inciting a revolution of female manners in the Ottoman empire. Under Laon's tutelage, Cythna plans on liberating the enslaved Ottoman women by teaching them about enlightened Wollstonecraftian feminism. For her and Laon, patriarchal oppression forestalls any possible improvement in human society: "Never will peace and human nature meet / till free and equal man and women meet" (2:994–95). Indeed, female bondage is at the root of all social evils, because "Woman, as the bond-slave, dwells / Of man, a slave; and life is poisoned in its wells" (7:3314–15). Enslaved to a tyranny sanctioned by religion, man in his turn enslaves women. According to Cythna, this tyrannical self-repression makes the woman question intrinsic to any political emancipation:

"Can man be free if woman be a slave?
Chain one who lives, and breathes this boundless air
To the corruption of a closed grave!
Can they whose mates are beasts, condemn to bear
Scorn, heavier far than toil or anguish, dare
To trample their oppressors? in their home
Among their babes, thou know'st a curse would wear
The shape of woman—hoary crime would come
Behind, and fraud rebuild religion's tottering home." (2:1045–53)

Women's freedom from domestic slavery's "curse" is a prerequisite for any effective politics that seeks to free humanity from despotic monarchies and repressive religions. Otherwise, this politics will reinscribe the same corrupt power it seeks to overthrow and "fraud rebuild religion's tottering home." For Cythna, the feminist battle begins in Constantinople, where she hopes to "lead a happy female train ... over the rejoicing plain" and where crowds of freed Muslim women "shall throng around / The Golden City" (2:1004–6).

Islam takes first priority in this feminist crusade. After making a grand escape from the sultan's subterranean seraglio in Canto 7, Cythna safely arrives in Constantinople. In Canto 9, she makes many converts after preaching Godwinian equality among the veiled women of the Golden city:

"Some said I was a maniac wild and lost;
Some, that scarce had risen from the grave
The Prophet's virgin bride, a heavenly ghost:—
Some said, I was a fiend from my weird cave,

Who had stolen human shape, and o'er the wave,

The forest, and the mountain came;—some said

I was the child of God, sent down to save

Women from bonds and death, and on my head

The burden of their sins would frightfully be laid.

    "But soon my human words found sympathy

In human hearts: the purest and the best,

As friend with friend made common cause with me,

And they were few, but resolute;—the rest,

Ere yet success the enterprise had blessed,

Leagued with me in their hearts;—their meals, their slumber,

Their hourly occupations were possessed

By hopes which I had armed to overnumber

Those hosts of meaner cares, which life's strong wings encumber.

"But chiefly women, whom my voice did waken

From their cold, careless, willing slavery,

Sought me: one truth their dreary prison has shaken,—

They looked around, and lo! they became free!

Their many tyrants sitting desolately

In slave-deserted halls, could none restrain;

For wrath's red fire had withered in the eye,

Whose lightening once was death,—nor fear, nor gain

Could tempt one captive now to lock another's chain." (9:541–58)

Cythna's speech can be read as an address to Western readers (particularly English women), and thus, "Her political speech seeks to renovate not only the Turkish Other, but the Western self as well."[57] Nevertheless, her speech is essentially anti-Islamic. The women of the Golden City are ready to overthrow patriarchal enslavement, which they (along with Cythna) identify exclusively with Islam. What is especially noteworthy is how these women see Cythna as both Mahomet's "virgin bride," Ayesha, who contributed to the *Ahadith*,[58] and a female Christ-figure who saves women from their patriarchal "sins." The prophetic tearing away of false religions is metaphorically equated with the "unveiling" Muslim women: through her powerful speech, Cythna "tore the veil that hid Nature, and Truth, and Liberty, and Love" (9:523–24). Unlike the radical feminist writings of Lady Mary Wortley Montagu and earlier Tory feminists, Percy Shelley associates the veil with Muslim repression.[59] Impeding the progress of Western liberal values, Mahometanism is a false covering that needs to be (forcefully) removed.

Thus, the "freedom" implied in this literal and figurative "unveiling" involves de-Islamicizing Ottoman women. In stripping them of their Muslim identity, Cythna's prophetic feminism prepares the way for western republicanism.

A radical "feminist" figure is also discernible in the mysterious female prophet of Canto 1, a spirit who has witnessed many political revolutions, from ancient Greece to modern France. Although she does not make any explicit declaration about women's rights, she, like Cythna, considers herself to be an "independent" woman who has lived through revolutionary struggles. Having walked through the desolate and bloody streets of Paris, the female prophet records her despair over the French Revolution: "How I braved death for liberty and truth,/And spurned at peace, and power, and fame; and when/Those hopes had lost the glory of their youth,/How sadly I returned" (1:519–22). Her disillusionment with liberty and equality recalls Mary Wollstonecraft's firsthand observations during her residency in revolutionary Paris between 1792 and 1795. In *Historical and Moral View of the Origin and Progress of the French Revolution* (London, 1794), Wollstonecraft writes, "The rapid changes, the violent, the base, and nefarious assassinations, which have clouded the vivid prospect that began to spread a ray of joy and gladness over the gloomy horizon of oppression, cannot fail to chill the sympathizing bosom, and palsy intellectual vigour."[60] A comparison between this passage and the above-quoted lines suggest that female prophet's independent character is modeled after Mary Wollstonecraft.

As the poem's outermost frame, the dedication to Mary Shelley establishes a strong affinity between Wollstonecraft (via her daughter) and the female prophet. Percy Shelley describes his wife as whispering "a prophecy." He compares her to spiritual virgin women in Rome who protect the state's prosperity by keeping a "lamp of vestal fire burning" (96, 99). Then he hails her as an "aspiring child," a living example of her mother's radical teachings:

> They say that thou wert lovely from thy birth,
> Of glorious parents, thou aspiring Child.
> I wonder not—for One then left this earth
> Whose life was like a setting planet mild,
> Which clothed thee in the radiance undefiled
> Of its departing glory; still her fame
> Shines on thee, through the tempests dark and wild
>   Which shake these latter days; and thou canst claim
> The shelter, from thy Sire, of an immortal name. (100–108)

Mary Shelley possesses a quasi-religious, prophetic stature as a result of her having been born from "glorious parents," particularly from Wollstonecraft (the "One" who "left this earth"). As such, Mary Shelley's character is synonymous with the "immortal name" of Godwin, a man Percy deeply admires. Mary Wollstonecraft's feminist views breathe life into his idea of the secular female prophet, as manifested in Cythna, the unnamed woman of Canto 1, and Shelley's wife.

In the author's introduction to *The Last Man*, Mary Shelley casts doubts on her husband's characterization of the female prophet; she questions the secular humanist basis of his epic, which she read and reread even before it was published.[61] While visiting the shores of Baiae on December 8, 1818, the author and a "companion" (presumably Percy Shelley) enter the mysterious cavern of the Cumaean Sibyl. Stumbling on a hidden chamber in the cave, they discover the legendary "Sibylline leaves," ancient prophecies supposedly written by divinely inspired women, the Sibyls. They gathered a collection of prophecies before departing. Throughout her subsequent studies, the author assumes the role of the secular prophet: a modern "translator" who interprets these "sacred remains" and reflects on "the immensity of nature and the mind of man." Her "translation" of these leaves constitutes the narrative of *The Last Man*. The author dedicates the work to her now-departed "companion," as commemorated in Petrarch's words: "Di mie tenere fondi altro lavoro / Credea mostrarte; e qual fero pianeta / Ne' nvidio insieme, o mio nobil tesoro?" ("From my tender leaves I expect to offer you a different work, and what fierce planet envied our being together, Oh my noble treasure?") (8). In choosing these lines, Mary's "dedication" to her husband resists praising him as a poet-prophet figure. Instead, her "companion" is a "noble treasure" to be possessed. Inverting the romantic topos of the "dedication" prefixed to her husband's revolutionary epic, Mary ironizes, in effect, the egotistical self-possessive nature implicit in his (patriarchal) exaltation of the "feminist" prophet. In this regard, the author's "tender leaves" represent a "different work" from that of Godwin-Shelleyan patriarchal politics.

Even though she is inspired by the Sibylline verses, the author does not portray herself as a heroic female spirit or an "independent" feminist, but as an abject and frail woman who writes only for day-to-day survival:

> I confess, that I have not been unmoved by the development of the tale; and that I have been depressed, nay, agonized, at some parts of the recital, which I have faithfully transcribed from my materials. Yet such is human nature, that the excitement of mind was dear to me, and that the imagination, painter of tempest and earthquake, or worse, the stormy and ruin-fraught passions of man, softened my real sorrows and endless regrets,

by clothing these fictitious ones in that ideality, which takes the mortal sting from pain. (8–9)

Although such a passage tends to be read as an expression of Mary Shelley's tragic life,[62] it also registers the economic hardships facing a widowed Englishwoman. The female author writes to support herself in a patriarchal society in which, according to the English common law of coverture (chapter 2), a woman's identity exists only through her husband's or father's name. In this context, "human nature," "imagination," and "the excitement of mind" are not transcendental terms that designate eternal joy and universal peace; they are fictional-psychological terms that compensate for the real sorrows of earthly life. The tragic story of a lonely man, Lionel Verney, who survives an apocalyptic plague that devours the human race, cannot express the agony of the female translator of these prophecies. Therefore, Mary Shelley's Sibylline myth is not an attempt to define an autonomous sphere of female artistic creativity, as proposed by Sandra Gilbert and Susan Gubar in *The Madwoman in the Attic*.[63] On the contrary, Shelley portrays her prophetic stature as cultural dispossession: under the guidance of her companion, the Sibylline "translation" is always-already a product of patriarchal power. Steven Goldsmith argues this point eloquently: "the Sibyl's oracles serve precisely to introduce a culturally mediated image of woman's writing, one particularly pertinent to a novelist laboring under the shadow of a sometimes idolized husband-poet."[64]

Mary Shelley's disempowered female prophet counteracts the (naive) optimism that informs her husband's exalted "feminist" prophet. In this regard, her writing does not participate in the imperialist-feminist crusade that undergirds *The Revolt of Islam*. Percy Shelley's Wollstonecraftian feminism encodes a colonialist discourse in the guise of revolutionary rhetoric.[65] Entailed in this rhetoric, the Ottoman empire's "feminist" revolt reflects a Volneyan imperialist agenda that undermines Muslim society from within, the "unveiling" of Muslim women. In resisting the feminist-prophetic role, the author of the introduction to *The Last Man* disavows Percy Shelley's imperialist agenda: she is not interested in reforming the world under the "enlightened" feminist, not to mention the project of "liberating" women in the Islamic East (even as the novel's main plot hinges on the utter failure of such a project, as I argue next). Instead, her "narration of misery and woeful change," as told by "the last man," Lionel Verney, exposes a dark imperialist ethos: a reversed historical "progress" that preempts any prophetic claims about female liberation (8).

The Sultana of the East

The Last Man introduces the nineteenth-century reader to a twenty-first-century British democracy. In this futuristic novel, "progress" culminates in a political utopia, resulting in Lord Raymond's election as England's new Cromwellian republican, the "Lord Protector." This moment brings about a new historical era in British political history (as it did in mid-seventeenth-century England), preparing the initial stages for a millennial golden age:

> [Lord Raymond] was continually surrounded by projectors and projects, which were to render England one scene of fertility and magnificence; the state of poverty was to be abolished; men were to be transported from place to place almost with the same facility as the Prince Housain, Ali, and Ahmed, in the Arabian Nights. The physical state of man would soon not yield to the beatitude of angels; disease was to be banished; labour lightened of its heaviest burden. . . . The arts of life, and the discoveries of science had augmented in a ratio which left all calculation behind; food sprung up, so to say, spontaneously—machines existed to supply with facility every want of the population. (85)

The allusion to the brothers who travel on flying carpets in *The Arabian Nights* is an extended metaphor that not only highlights Lord Raymond's unrealistic republican schemes, but also that this scheme is essentially "Oriental." Of course, Raymond's Orientalist politics drives the main plot: he is to liberate Greece from Ottoman despotism and seeks "to plant the cross on yonder mosque," the Christian dome of St. Sofia (154). In his crusading narrative against Islam, Mary Shelley undermines the feminist trope of harem-based slavery as deployed by her husband and mother. Her novel does not rehash the Safie-figure who "unveils" in the name of Western (Christian) liberty. Instead, her novel reverses the anti-Islamic eschatology propelling the "feminist" *Revolt of Islam*: the prophetic death of Evadne, the "Sultana of the East," culminates in the victorious Anti-Christ, a "feminine" infection (the metaphorical form of the avenging Turks) that punishes democratic men for their gender-blind hubris.

As a prototype of the Byronic hero (and even Lord Byron himself), Lord Raymond is interested only in defeating the "barbaric" Turks and restoring the Greek mainland to the "civilized" descendants of an ancient Hellenic people:

> in his hope of the conquest of Constantinople, he counted on an event which would be as a landmark in the waste of ages. . . when a city of grand historical association, the beauty of whose site was the wonder of the world, which for many hundred years had been the strong hold of the Moslems, should be rescued from slavery and barbarism, and restored to a people illustrious for genius, civilization, and a spirit of liberty. (140)

Following the lead of Alexander the Great and Napoleon, his dreams of conquest are motivated by his earlier imperialist ambitions to "take Constantinople, and subdue / all Asia" (48). Raymond is a Christian crusader, especially given that his name is an allusion to a crusading knight in Torquato Tasso's Italian epic.[66] His main goal is to eradicate Muslim civilization. He will not rest in peace until he sees "the cross on St. Sophia," a war waged "to decide the fate of Islam" (146, 127). This eschatological worldview, part of a militant theological program, looks forward to a Christian millennium after the fall of Islam. Christianity's comeback in the East compensates (or avenges) for Islamic supremacy in Europe since Muslims conquered Constantinople in the fifteenth century. Thus, recapturing the Byzantine dome of Sancta Sofia, a center of Christian worship that was converted into a mosque in 1453, is significant for Raymond, even though he is supposedly fighting a non-Christian battle for furthering Greek (pagan) liberty. Mary Shelley, a person deeply interested in the outcome of the Greek War of Independence, demystifies the Manichean-Christian world views that prop an eschatological Volneyan distinction between East and West.

To expose the "Christian" basis of philhellenic politics, Mary Shelley glosses Adrian's naive views on toleration. Although he is honored to fight for the Greeks, Adrian, akin to a Shelleyan pacifist, is disturbed by war's bloodshed. He warns against those who de-humanize the Turks because of their religion:

> But let us not deceive ourselves. The Turks are men; each fibre, each limb is as feeling as our own, and every spasm, be it mental or bodily, is as truly felt in a Turk's heart or brain, as in a Greek's. . . . Think you, amidst the shrieks of violated innocence and helpless infancy, I did not feel in every nerve the cry of a fellow being? They were men and women, the sufferers, before they were Mahometans, and when they rise turbanless from the grave, in what except their good or evil actions will they be the better or worse than we? (126)

The ethnocentric prejudice contained in this passage should not be read as an expression of the author's anti-Islamic sentiments. Ironically, despite his "toleration," Adrian is not willing to tolerate Muslims *as* Muslims. The Turks can be respected as fellow human beings precisely because they are *not* Muslim. This passage exposes the ethnocentrism embedded in this false multiculturalism, in which Turks will rise from their graves "turbanless" on a Christianized Judgment Day. In ironizing Adrian's humanism (or, more precisely, Percy Shelley's tolerant views), Mary Shelley distances her novel from her husband's anti-Islamic politics. She instead chooses to unearth the racial-theological precepts that permeate a secular philhellenic worldview.

The novel first establishes this critique when recasting Lord Raymond's relationship with women as Oriental despotism. Even though Perdita is a reclusive and free-spirited person in her youth, as the "Lord Protector's" wife she becomes a submissive and frail woman confined in her husband's royal palace. The novel describes her as "veiled" and imprisoned behind high walls, completely unaware of Raymond's whereabouts: "The veil must be thicker than that invented by Turkish jealousy; the wall higher than the unscaleable tower of Vathek, which should conceal from her the workings of his heart, and hide from her view the secret of his actions" (96). Perdita is the immured harem woman, and Raymond is a tyrant comparable to the evil sultan Vathek featured in William Beckford's gothic tale. Later in the novel, Perdita, out of sheer love, accompanies Raymond on his expedition to liberate the Greeks, only to be left behind in "a summer seraglio of the sultan" while he attends to military matters in Greece (147). But Lord Raymond is not satisfied with only one seraglio. Curious about the works of an anonymous Greek artist, Raymond follows the artist's messenger and discovers "a pair of small Turkish slippers" before the entrance of a secluded apartment. Much to his surprise, he discovers that the apartment's "inmate" is his beloved Greek, Evadne, living in poor and miserable conditions. Despite his repeated offers of assistance, she chooses, out of honor, to remain "impenetrably veiled from him" (91). Throughout the next few months, Raymond and Evadne continue to meet in private, and "they built a wall between them and the world" (93). Neglecting his duties as a republican governor, Lord Raymond becomes the ruthless Turk he detests; he oppresses his immured wife and indulges in the forbidden love of a secret seraglio. Keeping a patriarchal harem is as revealing about English democracy as it is about Ottoman despotism.

Princess Evadne is an Orientalized character infused with a zeal for female independence. However, she does not discover "feminist" freedom in the West. At first, she becomes Adrian's "beloved Ionian," a romantic symbol of philhellenist love: "Her country, its ancient annals,/ its late memorable struggles, were all made to partake in her glory and excellence" (30). However, Evadne never reciprocates his affections and instead falls in love with Lord Raymond, who eventually abandons her. Upon hearing that Lord Raymond married Perdita, Evadne returns to Greece, where her father, Prince Zaimi, the ex-Greek ambassador to England, dies after losing his fortune and reputation, and a heartless marriage is arranged between her and a wealthy Greek merchant at Constantinople. By seeking Russia's aid in her scheme for becoming the Princess of Wallachia, Evadne is misconstrued by both the Greeks and the Turks: she is accused of "bring the scythe of foreign despotism to cut away the new springing liberties of her country" (91). She and her husband flee to England, only to suffer more tragedy: her husband commits suicide and she falls into desolate poverty. Evadne's life records a story of female disempowerment that cannot be neatly categorized as "Occidental" or "Oriental." Evadne is not, properly speaking, affiliated with either "Greek" or "Turkish" culture; instead, she is a hybrid somewhere between the philhellenic woman of the Byronic mythos and the harem inmate of an "Arabian Nights" tale. Unlike Percy Shelley's secular female prophet, Mary Shelley's "liberated" mixed-race woman underscores the widespread social and patriarchal oppression equally prevalent in Greece, Turkey, and England.

After Perdita learns about his secret affair, Raymond resigns from his post as "Lord Protector" and decides to don the philhellenic mantle once more, abandoning his devastated wife and child in England and, once again, forsaking Evadne, who is left behind in her apartment extremely ill and almost starving (104). She eventually follows him to Greece. In the midst of a bloody battlefield, she appears before Adrian attired as a Greek soldier. Half-alive and in "wild delirium," she calls for Raymond, lamenting the "hard fate" of a women who, "driven by hopeless love and vacant hopes to take up the trade of arms," has suffered "beyond the endurance of man privation, labour, and pain." Before her death, she utters an apocalyptic prophecy about "Fire, and war, and plague":

> there is the end! there we meet again. Many living deaths have I borne for thee, O Raymond, and now I expire, thy victim!—By my death I purchase thee— lo! the instruments of war, fire, the plague are my servitors. I dared, I conquered them all, till now! I have sold myself to death, with the sole condition that thou shouldst follow me—Fire, and war, and plague, unite for thy destruction—O my Raymond, there is no safety for thee! (144)

The passage marks a major turning point in the novel: Evadne's prophecy accurately predicts both Raymond's death in Constantinople and the destructive plague that overtakes "man." She anticipates patriarchy's apocalyptic demise, and yet, her prophecy says nothing about the fall of Oriental despotism. Mahometanism is not the quintessential patriarchal religion. In this respect, Evadne's prophecy displaces the Volneyan obsession with Islam's collapse. In effect, Shelley's "liberated" female prophet supplements her husband's admiration for a Wollstonecraftian (imperialist) narrative with a reversed anti-Christian eschatology that, by comparison to Englishmen, renders the Turks favorable adversaries.

This denial of anti-Islamic eschatology is articulated by a hybrid Greek-Muslim woman, a "Sultana of the East" (144). The novel represents Evadne primarily as the evil Sultana Valide—the political odalisque, or the sultan's phallic mother who castrates men and wreaks havoc on the patriarchal political-religious order.[67] The novel also portrays her as a member of the sultanate of women, the powerful imperial women who have overthrown sultans and their male heirs on several occasions. These imperial women pose a threat to the patriarchal ideal of Christian domesticity in English histories and plays from the seventeenth century onward.[68] As such, eighteenth- and nineteenth-century British readers saw them as subversive harem women who embody political disorder. They are therefore potential "feminists" who turn the men's world upside down (see chapter 2). Evadne is a "sultana" who is literally equal to men, given that she is attired in military uniform, and yet, this bad equality symbolizes her hopeless love for an abusive man. Hence, the "Sultana of the East" prophesizes the fall of patriarchal rule, even those perpetuated under a republican democracy. In the long run, this apocalyptic fall involves a drastic rewriting of Volneyan-Shelleyan eschatology, to the extent that history ends with Lord Raymond's failed crusade and not with the apocalyptic defeat of the Turks in Constantinople.

After Evadne's death scene, the plague engulfs all Asia, overtakes Constantinople, moves into Europe, and finally enters England. As many critics have pointed out, this Oriental plague is personified as a feminine entity that overturns men's world (*The Last Man* 193, 229, 248, 330). The plague is a "She" who has usurped man's place in the Great Chain of Being, undermining the (patriarchal) God who, as Mary quotes from Psalms 8:5–6, gave "man . . . dominion over the works of his hands, and put all things under his feet" (248). The plague is a diabolical anti-Christ: in parodying the Christian incarnation, "she" becomes "incarnate in his flesh" and "has entwined herself with his being, and blinds his heaven-seeking eyes" (248). The feminine plague completely disrupts a male-dominated, commercial empire: "Of old navies used to stem the giant ocean-waves betwixt Indus and the Pole for slight articles of luxury. Men made perilous journies to possess themselves of earth's splendid trifles, gems and gold. Human labour was wasted—human life set at nought. Now life is all we covet. . . . We were sufficiently degraded" (248). In such passages Shelley literalizes Christ's teachings: "the first must be the last." In the novel, this teaching means that "man" must assume woman's "degraded" condition—a transvaluation of the Christian-patriarchal universe. In contrast to her husband's epic, the feminine principle in *The Last Man* does not succumb to the imperialist will-to-power driving a hypermasculine eschatology. Men's imperial domain must now face the feminine anti-Christ's avenging wrath.

Ultimately, the feminine principle determines men's revolution. As a parody of Shelleyan cosmology, the plague first emerges from Egypt as a serpentlike creature, an anti-Christ image: "this enemy to the human race had begun early in June to raise its serpent-head on the shores of the Nile" (139). This Oriental serpent is not a positive emblem of revolutionary self-generation, as it is for Percy Shelley and Volney. Instead, Mary Shelley restores this emblem to its Old Testament context: it represents the "fallen" history of egalitarian leveling, humanity reduced to a primitive degenerate state. The plague depopulates Britain, allowing for a classless society in which there is enough wealth and surplus for the poor. "Private property" is abolished, and thus, according to tenets of Godwinian philosophy, no "hideous poverty" exists. In order to emphasize the condition of this dystopia, Verney repeats twice in the same paragraph that "We were all equal now," but, of course, this phrase is ironic. The deadly plague, Verney reminds his readers, results in "an/equality still more levelling, a state where beauty and strength, and wisdom, would be as vain as riches and birth" (249). Inverting the patriarchal order, the "feminine" plague paves the way for a democratic revolution that is as devastating to men as it was to women.

Ultimately, Western women's patriarchal enslavement is "revealed" from the prophetic viewpoint of Evadne, a subversive harem woman who plays the role of a proto-feminist martyr. Islam, in this case, is not a degenerate Orient opposed to an unadulterated "western" Greece—an imaginary opposition in vogue during the philhellenic craze of the late eighteenth and early nineteenth century.[69] Insofar as Evadne, a Greek-Muslim hybrid, disturbs the racial ideology entailed in a "pure" philhellenic politics, the novel's plot rejects the anti-Islamic polemic associated with Volneyan eschatology. Whereas the *Revolt of Islam* de-Islamicizes the Orient in the name of Western feminism, *The Last Man* de-Christianizes the (Western) prophetic tradition under the name of a quasi-Islamic female prophet from the East. As speculative mythography, the novel recuperates a radical prophetic legacy rooted in the egalitarian Shi'ite Gnosticism of *The Assassins*. Evadne's fulfilled prophecy activates a visionary gnosis that recreates the world as an unrepresentable feminine unity—the plague. According to this ironic theosophy, *The Last Man* critiques the false universals of Shelley-Godwinian philosophy, showing how the last man's universal "rights" apply, literally and tragically, to only one gender not both. Inverting Mary Wollstonecraft's and Percy Shelley's feminist trope, Mary Shelley portrays Westernized women as victims who need to be rescued from the despotic yoke of English republicanism.

Coda: Wonderful Narrations

One of the greatest ironies of *The Last Man* is that the reader never encounters "the end of history," even on the last page. Only the cyclical return back to the secular origins of "man"—the progressive West's deevolution—is possible; hence, Verney, the uncouth savage compared to the "wolf-bred founder of old Rome," Romulus, returns to Rome by the end of the novel as a "wild-looking, unkempt, half-naked savage" (15, 352). Ironically, he is the "last man" who cannot find the "end of history," so he writes his own prophetic narrative, one that comprises the Sibylline leaves that the nineteenth-century author discovers, assembles, and retells. Mary Shelley's novel resists modern millennial finality in establishing three overlapping time frames: the mythical past of the Sibylline oracles, the nineteenth century present in which the author discovers the Sibylline leaves, and the late-twenty-first century future in which the story is set. Collapsing the distinction between a beginning, a middle, and an end, *The Last Man* posits a cyclical temporality—what Anne Mellor describes as "the possibility of alternative beginnings, of never-ending new births" and what Eve Tavor Bannet reads as women's eternal "now."[70] My aim, however, is not to argue for any essentialist claims about the relationship between cyclical temporality and women's time, but to argue that in *The Last Man* women's cyclical time is modeled after an Ismailian prophetic tradition.[71] As a result, Shelley's novel resists the anti-Islamicism championed in Percy Shelley's Volneyan-imperialist epic. Despite his Gnostic critique of Christian revelation, the older Percy Shelley fostered a Protestant obsession with the fall of Muslim civilization. Mary Shelley, on the other hand, is perhaps the first English eschatological writer since the Protestant Reformation to relish the Muslim anti-Christ.[72] Unlike *The Assassins*, a "fragmented" romance, her novel embraces this unholy reverence for the Muslim anti-Christ by writing in a safe genre, one that was typically construed as "feminine" and "apolitical" during the eighteenth and nineteenth centuries.[73]

But if Verney exemplifies the futile attempt to write a Volneyan prophecy, then what does Safie, the "liberated" Arabian woman from *Frankenstein*, have to say about men's mighty empires? The daughter of a treacherous Turkish merchant and a virtuous Christian Arab mother, Safie cherishes the Western liberty practiced in the De Lacy household. She refuses to return to Asia with her oppressive Muslim father to be "immured within the walls of a harem" (83). Felix's "sweet Arabian" receives her first lesson on language, politics, and history from Volney's *The Ruins of Empire*. Meanwhile, Frankenstein's creature observes this scene through a chink from behind the cottage wall. He benefits from Safie's western education:

> Through this work [*The Ruins of Empire*] I obtained a cursory knowledge of history, and a view of the several empires at present exciting in the world; it gave me an insight into the manners, governments, and religions of the different nations of the earth. I heard of the slothful Asiatics; of the stupendous genius and mental activity of the Grecians; of the wars and wonderful virtue of the early Romans—of their subsequent degeneration— of the decline of that mighty empire; of chivalry, christianity, and kings. I heard of the discovery of the American hemisphere, and wept with Safie over the hapless fate of its original inhabitants. (80)

For the creature (and implicitly Safie), these "wonderful narrations" do not inspire hope in the Ottoman empire's collapse, the opportunity to bring Western liberty to the "slothful Asiatics," or the prospect of Greek liberation. Instead, Volney's work only awakens distrust about progressive history. In contrast to Percy Shelley's interpretation, "the strange system of human society" outlined in Volney's history induces skepticism about the promise of revolutionary perfection. Nestled in the novel's inner-most narrative frame, this lesson not only prefigures the creature's doomed attempt to ingratiate himself within the De Lacy family and ultimately humanity, but also emphasizes the shallowness of Safie's Western education. This emphasis is important considering that she is named after the female student featured in Rousseau's educational treatise, which prompted Mary Wollstonecraft's feminist rebuttal. Safie, who can "speak" only through the creature's alienated narrative voice, weeps over western colonization's devastating effects in the Americas rather than rejoice in western liberty. Once the creature exposes himself to his companions' scorn (including Safie's), Felix's feminist teachings fail to define the West as rational, enlightened, and tolerant.

Ultimately, the Safie-creature dyad is a muted version of Evadne, a hybrid character whose tragic life invalidates anti-Islamic feminist idealizations. Skeptical concerns about the Godwinian "good cause" and liberal feminism, as recorded in Mary Shelley's 1838 journal entry, appear as early as *Frankenstein*. They re-emerge in an eschatological novel that ponders the republican past, of her nation and her family, with a mixture of nostalgia and bitterness. Unlike her husband, she could not embrace a Volneyan imperial history during a post-Napoleonic era marked by the death of revolutionary ideals as well as family and friends. Instead, she found consolation in cyclical Islamic myths, the repressed "Gnostic" story of the Arab Jew. After all, *The Assassins*—a "last man" story in which the Wandering

Jew joins Lebanon's Christian Arabs—culminates in Shelley's novel: history is fulfilled without the Second Coming, even as Lionel Verney is doomed to repeat the cursed life of the Wandering Jew. *The Last Man* supplements *The Assassins* in refusing to exchange Jewish-Ismailian gnosis for the Christian-Hellenic logos. Mary Shelley remains faithful to the Abrahamic vision that her husband abandoned: we were all Muslims before we were all Greeks.[74]

Epilogue
Postcolonial Reflections

> Our current hypothesis about Mahomet, that he was a scheming
> Impostor, a Falsehood incarnate, that his religion is a mere mass
> of quackery and fatuity, begins really to be now untenable to any
> one. The lies, which well-meaning zeal has heaped round this man,
> are disgraceful to ourselves only.... A false man found a religion?
> Why, a false man cannot build a brick house!
>
> Thomas Carlyle, *On Heroes, Hero-Worship, and the Heroic
> in History*

> [I]t seems that if we are to think intelligently about the relations
> between Islam and British Law, we need a fair amount of "decon-
> struction" of crude oppositions and mythologies, whether of the
> nature of *Sharia* or the nature of the Enlightenment.
>
> Rowan Williams, *Archbishop's Lecture-Civil and Religious Law in
> England: A Religious Perspective*

Archbishop of Canterbury Rowan Williams could not foresee that his reflections on the selective accommodation of the Shar'ia within the framework of
UK statutory law would erupt into an international controversy the day after
he delivered his foundational lecture at the Royal Courts of Justice on February
2008. The Anglican clergy, British politicians, and media pundits demanded his
immediate resignation because he speculated that the equitable principles shared
by British and Islamic law may allow competing jurisdictions in which Muslim
citizens could opt to have some cases heard in a Shar'ia rather than English law
court. Notorious for his liberal views, Rowan Williams had touched on a sensitive cultural nerve when—in the spirit of Derrida's Abrahamic supplement—he
called for the need to deconstruct the imaginary opposition between Islam and
the Enlightenment. He not only reawakened post-9/11 xenophobic fears about

Muslim immigrant communities living in the UK and abroad, but also recalled, unknowingly and ironically, the centuries-old arguments of radical freethinkers who saw Islamic law as compatible with English republican ideals. The Archbishop's critics repressed this alternative intellectual history, as emblematized in the Bishop of Rochester Michael Nazir-Ali's emphatic response: "English Law is rooted in the Judaeo-Christian tradition and our notions of human freedoms derive from that tradition. It would be impossible to introduce a tradition like Shar'ia into this corpus without fundamentally affecting its integrity."[1] Like Samuel Huntington and Bernard Lewis, the Bishop relies on the "clash of civilizations" story to explain why Islam is fundamentally antithetical to Western (Judeo-Christian) democracy.

In offering a counternarrative to the "clash of civilizations" story that has framed post-9/11 accounts of Islam, this book seeks to discredit the false Eurocentric assumption that English law and democratic thought are exclusively rooted in Judeo-Christian history. The eighteenth century abounds with remarkable British writers—such as Lady Mary Wortley Montagu, Edmund Burke, Walter Savage Landor, Robert Southey, Samuel Taylor Coleridge, and Percy Shelley—who treated Islam as a theological, legalistic, and philosophical framework for defining constitutional liberty. This epilogue considers how Islamic republicanism was reinvented in British India between Thomas Carlyle's belated defense of Mahomet and Rowan Williams' controversial remarks.

In terms of literary chronology, Carlyle's heroic Mahomet marks both the culmination and end of the discourse of Islamic republicanism that I have been tracing in this book. In his 1840 lectures, published as *On Heroes, Hero-Worship, and the Heroic in History,* Carlyle asks his British audience to imagine Mahomet as a "Prophet-hero" who belongs in the pantheon of virtuous republicans alongside Martin Luther, Oliver Cromwell, and Napoleon. This topic could be publicly addressed for the first time due, in part, to the 1828 repeal of the Test and Corporation Acts, which removed the civil and legal disabilities that had suppressed radical Protestant expression (chapter 1), and to imperial Britain's increasing interaction with Islamic universalism in South and Southeast Asia.[2] Carlyle casts the Prophet's universal teachings as an antidote to the secular age's social, economic, and political ills. He vindicates him from the "impostor" charge and instead praises him as a republican legislator who founded "a kind of Christianity" free from idol worship, capitalist greed, and an autocratic priesthood. The Prophet introduced "change and progress" in "the universal condition and thoughts of men" comparable to Martin Luther and the Protestant Reformation (54, 37).

Unfortunately for Carlyle, the Prophet cannot offer a viable remedy for mid nineteenth-century industrial modernity, because his portrayal of this "wild Son of Nature" consigns the Arab and Muslim world to an irrecoverable past—a stale Oriental primitivism that renders Islam unmodern in the context of a decaying Ottoman Empire and a flourishing British Empire in India (63).[3] Moreover, any political sympathy for Mahomet the "Prophet-hero" became impossible after the 1857–59 Indian Mutiny. This turning point in Anglo-Indian relations rendered post-Mughal religion and politics backwards from the perspective of Victorian self-confidence in the British civilizing mission.[4] And yet, after desacralizing the dethroned Mughal emperor in 1859, the British indirectly revived pan-Islamic nostalgia for the once-mighty Ottoman caliphate throughout South Asia and the Indian Ocean, creating (as I will argue below) the social conditions under which hope for a reformed Islamic republic could be rearticulated in the late nineteenth century.[5]

Should Carlyle's lecture therefore be read, post-1857, as a celebratory epitaph on Islamic republicanism? Is deconstructing the East-West binary, as the Archbishop calls for, impossible to perform today? These questions may be answered negatively by focusing on the publication of *The Rise and Progress of Mahometanism* (c. 1671). Henry Stubbe's work was the republican text par excellence for many Restoration and eighteenth-century radicals seeking to remedy the Anglican State's inequitable policies by appealing to Ottoman legal precedent (see chapter 1). Gathering dust in Unitarian library collections for centuries, a copy of his manuscript was finally published in London in 1911 by the Indo-Muslim Urdu linguist and philologist Hafiz Mahmud Khan Shairani (1881–1946), who praised Stubbe for refuting anti-Islamic stereotypes.[6] I argue that the "Prophet-hero" from Arabia is resurrected in Shairani's publication, which, unlike Carlyle's lecture, productively recovers Islamic republicanism on behalf of the Indian anti-imperial struggle and the pan-Islamic cause.

A dedicated collector of manuscripts on the Islamic sciences, theology, poetry, music, history, and literature, Shairani used Stubbe's manuscript as a political tool for bolstering Muslim nationalist sentiments, in the Indian Punjab and abroad, and opposing the anti-Islamic Orientalism that facilitated imperial rule in nineteenth- and twentieth-century British India. In his introduction, Shairani is explicit about his anti-imperialist political theology. Reflecting on Stubbe's political career and his historical account of how the Roman empire imposed the Trinitarian heresy on primitive Christians, Shairani writes, "To us, who are Muslims, these admissions are of deep significance, especially at the present time, when England is sending an army of missionaries to cajole us into accepting these very doctrines [Trinitarianism]" (xiii).[7] His appendix to the manuscript notes that Orientalism—which he calls "hostile propaganda"—is responsible for the Crusades, the expulsion of the Moors from Spain, and "last, not least, the modern attempt to rob the Muslims of their faith, in order to lure them to the belief in the doctrines of Trinitarianism" (238). In Shairani's imagination, the Trinitarian heresy enabled Western imperialism's missionary agenda in fourth-century Roman Europe and twentieth-century British India. Implicitly, he interprets Stubbe's account as a corrective to this repressive and faulty political theology, which was enshrined in late Victorian and Edwardian definitions of a progressive Christian modernity.

Shairani mentions that he prepared his publication "under the auspices of the Islamic Society" (founded as the "Pan-Islamic Society" in 1903 and renamed the "Central Islamic Society" in 1910) (v). According to this progressive Muslim organization, their stated objective is to combat "[m]isconceptions prevailing among non-Muslims regarding Islam and Muslims; disseminate information on Muslim issues, and involve powerful British people to influence in positive ways both public perceptions and official policy regarding the Muslim world."[8] Partly founded by the radical pan-Islamist Mushir Husain Kidwai (a name included among the subscription list to Shairani's publication), the Society's goal is to dispel racist stereotypes that cast Muslims as backward, barbaric, and unmodern—a post-1857 Victorian Orientalism that was further consolidated under William E. Gladstone's administration. The Society lobbied for Anglo-Muslim cooperation, especially with leaders in Ottoman Turkey and the Indian subcontinent.[9] In this pan-Islamic context, Shairani's publication aspires to synthesize Islamic theology, science, and culture with a modern vision of India, Egypt, Algeria, and other Muslim nations that does not conflict with Western civilization's democratic values.[10] Envisioning such a synthesis between East and West, *The Rise and Progress of Mahometanism* provided an ideological rationale for the early pan-Islamic movement.

Although Shairani insists that his work was not published by the Islamic Society and "that the opinions of the author should therefore not be construed as those advocated or advanced by the Society," the listed subscribers and named funders for his publication imply otherwise (v). Among the most prominent Indo-Muslim subscribers, Sayyid Amir Ali, Sayyid Ahmed Khan, Mustapha Khan, Abdul Haq, Sayyid Husain Bilgrani, and, as mentioned above, Mushir Husain Kidwai were political activists, in Britain and India, involved in progressive student-led campaigns for Indian independence from British rule; most of these subscribers were convinced that the cause for Indo-Muslim nationhood was inevitably tied to other liberation movements, especially in the Ottoman Empire—the only legitimate and last-remaining caliphate.[11] As the Islamic Society's president and secretary, Kidwai helped broker a transnational alliance between Indo-Muslim nationalists and the Young Turks, a new generation of Westernized Ottoman intellectuals who in 1908 peacefully coerced Sultan Abdülhamid II to restore the Ottoman constitution only to oust him from power a year later. Having witnessed this bloodless revolution firsthand, Kidwai assured his Indian compatriots that the Young Turks were preserving the caliphate—an Islamic republic—and fighting for oppressed Muslims around the world.[12] Contrary to Shairani's explicit statement, Stubbe's Islamic republicanism, framed by a preface, introduction, and appendix saturated in pan-Islamic rhetoric, conveniently feeds into the ideological program championed by Kidwai and other Indian subscribers.

In his preface, Shairani claims that publication funds were raised by "the Muslims resident in England" from Constantinople (Istanbul) through "the efforts of Halil Halid Bey (the author of *The Crescent* verses *The Cross*), and the courtesy of the directors of the Turkish newspapers, the Sabah and the Sirat-i-Mustaqim, two separate subscriptions were raised in Constantinople, which proved to be very handsome and substantial support to the Funds" (v). After writing an influential book that defends Islam from Christian prejudices, Halil Halid Bey was branded by British authorities to be "undoubtedly one of the most important emissaries of Pan-Islamicism."[13] Shairani acknowledges Halid's interest "in the progress of this publication," a comment suggesting that Stubbe's work furthers the anti-imperialist agenda of a high-profile Young Turk who condemned Orientalism (vi).[14] Shairani also points out that the Turkish press—a propagandistic organ for Muslim nationalism and radical pan-Islamism—provided "very handsome and substantial support." Late-nineteenth-century Turkish newspapers such as the *Sabah* voiced pro-Ottoman, anti-British sentiments and exerted an enormous influence over Indo-Muslim public opinion.[15] The *Sabah*'s and *Sirat-i-Mustaqim*'s financial sponsorship imbues Shairani's publication with a revolutionary message.

Shairani's reliance on radical support outside of India is not unusual for his time. Between 1900 and 1939, many progressive Muslims promoted national independence from Western imperial rule on a transnational scale. Whether defined in Ottoman, Indian, Egyptian, or Arab terms, idealized representations of the Islamic republic circulated widely across overlapping Muslim networks. According to Humayun Ansari, radical pan-Islamists (such as Kidwai), loyalists (who

supported British imperial rule), and national separatists (who sought to promote a separate Muslim homeland in India) coexisted, often peacefully, within
"distinct yet interconnected networks" that promoted the pan-Islamic cause in
Turkey. The British government homogenized their ideological differences by
categorizing them jointly as seditious revolutionaries who support the Ottoman
caliphate.[16]

Working from within these extensive transnational networks, Shairani was
affiliated with prominent members of the Aligarh movement, which rechanneled
the pan-Islamic cause away from Ottoman affairs and toward the nationalist
agenda for a separate Muslim homeland in India. Founded in 1875 by the Muslim
social reformer Sayyid Ahmad Khan, the Muhammedan Anglo-Oriental College
at Aligarh was the hub of pan-Islamic fervor, anti-British resistance, and Indo-
Muslim nationalist agitation. Indeed, by 1912, Viceroy of India Charles Hardinge
condemned the college as "a hot-bed of sedition."[17] Grappling with Islam's decline in an increasingly modernizing world, the college's professors and students
organized grassroots activism that promoted Islam's democratic ideals as superior to European and British colonialism. For example, Sayyid Amir Ali—an
Aligarh reformer from Calcutta whose name graces the subscription list—wrote
books vindicating Muhammad's "modern" teachings on equality, toleration, and
charity. An avowed loyalist who favored British rule (but supported the Young
Turks), he advocated to include Muslims in India's political process.[18]

The 1911 publication also lists the eminent British Orientalist, Sir Thomas
Walker Arnold, as a subscriber. He taught philosophy at Aligarh College between
1888 and 1898 and at the Government College of Lahore between 1898 and 1904.
Interested in promoting Anglo-Muslim cooperation, he published a sympathetic
reevaluation of Islam: *The Preaching of Islam* (1896; translated in Urdu in 1898), a
scholarly work that upholds this Abrahamic faith as a peaceful, tolerant, and egalitarian religion. Despite his loyalist politics, this work became influential among
Indo-Muslim pan-Islamists and national separatists. Shairani was Arnold's student during his enrolment in the Government College. Under his tutelage, he
studied Urdu language and literature, which Arnold introduced to the Aligarh
curriculum only to later become the nationalist language for Indo-Muslim rebels.[19] Indeed, Shairani praises *The Preaching of Islam* for its unbiased assessment
and syncretistic vision. He compares this "great mine of learning" to *The Rise and
Progress of Mahometanism*. As with Amir Ali's and Arnold's revisionist works,
Shairani's publication is a byproduct of the Aligarh social network, a student-led
Muslim movement that spawned the later development of communal Muslim
nationalism in the Indian subcontinent.[20]

This communal Muslim nationalism became pervasive after the Turco-Italian war of 1911, the year during which Aligarh College was transformed from a loyalist institution that favored British rule in India into the militant site for generating anti-imperial resentment against British disdain for the Muslim world. The Italian invasion of the Ottoman territory of Tripolitania catalyzed an unprecedented wave of pan-Islamic sentiments throughout the Muslim world and from within the Aligarh network. Pan-Islamists and empire loyalists perceived the British decision not to intervene in this military takeover—abandoning their long-term ally, the Ottomans—as an ominous sign: the empire has betrayed its Muslim subjects by secretly joining the united Western opposition to the true caliphate, an Islamic republic. Azim Ozcan points out that this distrust, as generated by Indo-Muslims, "led to the crumbling of the long-cherished idea that Britain was the protector of the interests of the Muslims in the world in general, as well as those of her subjects."[21] Like so many Indo-Muslims who opposed the Turco-Italian war and Western imperialism, Sayyid Amir Ali, a loyalist, funneled aid to the embattled Young Turks, rendering him a potentially seditious subject from the viewpoint of a paranoid British government.[22] After 1911, the pan-Islamic movement—involving Young Turks, Aligarh Indian nationalists, and Egyptian socialists—became associated with clandestine activities intent on undermining imperial interests.

Reinforcing this stigma, pro-Ottoman subscriptions rapidly increased during this year, resulting in a flood of anti-British propaganda that referenced Christian Europe's age-old aggression against Islam as proof of a joint Anglo-Italian conspiracy to seize Tripoli.[23] Made possible through these politically motivated subscriptions, Shairani's 1911 publication would have joined the anti-imperialist propaganda campaign, lending ideological coherence to various Muslim groups who stood united in their resentment toward British foreign policy. In this political context, Stubbe—the seventeenth-century republican who boldly (although privately) vindicated Mahometanism—embodies radical pan-Islamism's "good old cause." For Shairani, he is a role model for Indo-Muslim separatists; a defeated national hero who nonetheless "speaks the truth fully and fearlessly, without being deterred, as many are to our day, by religious and political considerations" (xvi).

With Shairani, Stubbe enters Carlyle's republican pantheon on the verge of World War I, on the cusp of the Indo-Muslim independence campaign, on the storm cloud of the Bolshevik Revolution, and on the eve of Ottoman collapse. Taking my cue from Dipesh Chakrabarty, I have shown how *The Rise and Progress of Mahometanism* provincializes British intellectual history, from the late seventeenth to early twentieth century, and also that Romantic views of the Islamic republic redefined British constitutional liberty, from the periphery to the metropole, from the Empire to the Nation, and back again. Islamic republicanism constitutes a resilient constitutional idiom that has survived Carlyle's celebratory epitaph on the Prophet-hero as well as Victorian stereotypes about backward Muslims; it has become, via Shairani, a voice of anti-Orientalist, anti-imperialist protest decades before Edward Said's work, only to be forgotten by postcolonial critics who trace the critique of empire exclusively to Western Europe's insular Enlightenment; and it has become the object of xenophobic contempt following Rowan Williams's controversial remarks on the partial compatibility between Shar'ia and English common Law. Stubbe's twentieth-century comeback reminds us that Islam has a positive constructive role to play in the story of Western modernity, then and now. There is much to learn from a prophetic tradition based on intercultural reconciliation rather than the "clash of civilizations," an exhausted paradigm that has stalled public debate in the post-9/11 era.

Nevertheless, Islamic republicanism is not a utopian solution free from oppressive ideological formations. The Pakistani opposition twice co-opted Shairani's publication when it was reprinted in Lahore in 1954 and 1975: in the former year, as a backlash against Governor General Ghulam Muhammad's decision to dissolve the Constitutional Assembly after it tried to limit his military power and, in the latter year, as a retaliation against Prime Minister Z. A. Bhutto's single-party dictatorship under the Pakistan People's Party.[24] *The Rise and Progress of Mahometanism* helped congeal Indo-Muslim solidarity. In its reprinted versions, this publication fueled the anti-imperialist/nationalist ideology that underpins Pakistan: a postcolonial state founded on regional conflict over Kashmir and on the genocidal displacement of non-Muslims and the Bengali-speaking people of East Pakistan, present-day Bangladesh. As such, Stubbe's twentieth-century comeback also involves a complicated story about postcolonial violence that this book does not wish to ignore or silence.

On a more cautionary note, this book addresses the urgent need voiced by Derrida, Rowan Williams, and others to deconstruct Eurocentric narratives of Enlightenment secularization. By casting Islam as a reactionary religion, these narratives continue to act as a stumbling block in initiating a productive dialogue with the Muslim world. Hence, documenting Islam's historical contributions to secular modernity is paramount. To quote Chakrabarty, "the project of provincializing 'Europe' refers to a history that does not yet exist."[25] This nonexistent history is "radically heterogeneous" in that it overwrites "the given and privileged narratives of citizenship" and defines human collectivities "neither by the rituals of citizenship nor the nightmare of 'tradition' that 'modernity' creates."[26] Ever mindful of the problems plaguing Islamic republics in today's Afro-Eurasia, I hope to have shown that a "radically heterogeneous" history has stirred political reform in the global eighteenth century and could potentially do the same in the present and the future.

Outline of "MOHAMMED"

1st Book

The Deathbed of Abu Taleb. herein we develope the character of Mohammed.
. . . After the Death of Abu Taleb the Tumult, & his escape by the heroism of Ali.

2nd Book

Mohamed & Abu[beker][1] in the Cavern [—] *Fatima & Ali.*—resolves . . .[2] by conquest[3]—3. Journey thro' the Desert—the Arab—an exposed Infant. +*Hagar & Ishmaël+* {Rough memoranda in R. Southey's handwriting. D. C.[4] Convent.[5] Mary—. 3rd ["3" altered to "4" apparently by Southey] Book

4 [altered to "5" apparently by Southey] Arrival at Medina. *Jews. intrigues to expel him. When a Son accuses his father. Mary.*

4th ["4" altered to "5" and then to "6" apparently by Southey] *Battle of Beder. at-tempt to assassinate him when sleeping*

This autograph outline, jointly prepared by Coleridge and Southey, comes from a manuscript found in the Mitchell library of Sydney. My transcription is based on Warren U. Ober's edited version of the outline: "'MOHAMMED': The Outline of a Proposed Poem by Coleridge and Southey," *Notes and Queries* 5 (1958): 448. The use of italics indicates the parts that appear to be in Southey's handwriting. For the sake of editorial accuracy, I am including Ober's footnotes and in(-)text bracketed notes.

1. In his footnote, Warren U. Ober writes "I have supplied the word 'hide'; Cole-ridge wrote what appears to be 'beher'" (448). However, I prefer A. R. Kidwa's editorial suggestions: Coleridge and Southey were probably referring to "Abubeker," the name of the Prophet's closest companion and the faithful follower who accompanied him in his journey from Mecca to Medina. "Abubekr" is named in Southey's incomplete poem, "Mohammed" (1799) and in his original plans for that poem (Kidwa 39; "Mohammed" 476; Southey, *The Common-Place Book* 19). See A. R. Kidwa, "The Outline of Coleridge's and Southey's 'Mohammed,'" *Notes and Queries.* 238.40 (1993): 38–9.
2. There is a deleted word here that is illegible
3. "Conquest" is supplied as a conjectural word.
4. This note was written by Derwent Coleridge. The "Plus" signs are presumably by him as well.
5. Ober cannot determine whether "convent" is in Coleridge's or Southey's handwriting.

5 [altered to "6" and then to "7" apparently by Southey] *Defeat of Mount Ohud— ~~conversion of Caled.~~*[6] *Hamza slain. Fatima.*

6 [altered to "7" and then to "8" apparently by Southey] ~~*Capture of Mecca. Exultation of the Koreish.*~~[7]

6. This line was most likely crossed out by Southey.
7. These two lines were apparently marked for deletion by Southey.

Southey's Sketch of "MOHAMMED"

P. 1. The death-bed of Abu Taleb. Elevation of Abu Sophian. Tumult of the Koreish. Danger of Mohammed, and his escape by the heroism of Ali. He looks back upon the crescent moon.

2. The Koreish pursue; they reach the cavern; at whose entrance the pigeon has laid her eggs and the spider drawn his web; and turn away, satisfied that no one can have entered. Fatima and Ali bring them food and tidings.

3. Journey through the desert. The pursuers overtake them, and Mohammed is at the mercy of an Arab. They find an exposed infant.

4. They halt at an islanded convent. Mary the Egyptian is among the nuns. Her love and devotional passion transferred to the prophet.

5. Arrival at Medina. Intrigues to expel him—chiefly among the Jews. This danger averted by a son accusing his father.

6. Battle of Beder. Attempt to assassinate him afterwards when sleeping. What hinders me from killing thee? This was Daathur, leader of the foes.

7. Defeat at Mount Ohud. Death of Kamza. Conversion of Caled in the very heat of victory.

This sketch outline is transcribed from Southey's *The Commonplace Book*, 4th Series, ed. John Wood Warter (London: Longman, Brown, Green, and Longmans, 1850), 19.

8. Siege of Medina by the nations. The winds and the rain and the hail compel them to retire.

9. The Nadhirites defeated, and the Jews of Kainoka, Koraidha, and Chaibar.

10. The prophet lays siege to Mecca. Truce on permission to visit the Caaba. Amron lays in wait for him there, and is overawed and converted. He tells them that the worm has eaten the words of their treaty, leaving only the name of God. Astonished by this, terrified by the irresistible number of his swelling army, the Koreish yield the city. He burns the idols, and Henda clings to her God, and is consumed with him.

Preface

1. On the need to provincialize conventional narrative accounts about the triumphal rise of the "secular West" over the "religious East," see Dispesh Chakrabarty, *Provincializing Europe: Postcolonial Thought and Historical Difference* (Princeton: Princeton UP, 2000).

2. Bernard Lewis, *From Babel to Dragomans: Interpreting the Middle East* (New York: Oxford UP, 2004), 330. "The Roots of Muslim Rage" comprises 319–31.

3. Samuel Huntington, "The Clash of Civilizations?" *Foreign Affairs* (Summer 1993), and *The Clash of Civilizations and the Remaking of World Order* (New York: Simon and Schuster, 1996).

4. See Lewis, *From Babel to Dragomans,* 370, 376–77, 379–80, and Ian Buruma, "Lost in Translation," *The New Yorker* (June 14, 2004).

5. Peter Waldman, "A Historian's Take on Islam Steers US in Terrorism Fight," *Wall Street Journal* (Feb. 4, 2004).

6. Edward W. Said, *Orientalism* (New York: Vintage Books, 1978), 316.

7. Rose Flemming, ed. "Muhammeds Ansigt." *Jyllands-Posten* (Sept. 3, 2005).

8. See "Danish Muhammed Cartoon Reprinted," *BBC News* (Feb. 13, 2008).

9. "Cartoon Wars, Part II," *South Park,* Comedy Central (Apr. 12, 2006).

10. "200," *South Park.* Comedy Central (Apr. 14, 2010), and "201," *South Park,* Comedy Central (Apr. 21, 2010).

11. The following newspaper articles, among many others not listed, popularize the "clash of civilization" thesis in their discussions of the Danish cartoon scandal: Ben Griffiths and Tim McEvoy, "The Right to Offend Belongs to All," *The Daily Illini* (Feb. 6, 2006); Salim Muwakkil, "Islam vs. the West: Clashing Sensibilities," *The Third Coast* (Mar. 6, 2006): 17; As'ad Abul Rahman, "Respect Each Other to Avoid a Clash of Civilizations," *Global News Wire* (Mar. 11, 2006); Sara Wajid, "Secular, Liberal, and Doggedly Fundamentalist," *The Times Higher Education Supplement* (Mar. 17, 2006): 18; Michael Slackman, "Bin Laden Says West Is Waging War Against Islam, and Urges Supporters to Go to Sudan," *New York Times* (Apr. 24, 2006): A1; Michael Slackman, "Bin Laden Reaffirms Role on World Stage," *International Herald Tribune* (Apr. 25,

2006): 4; "Beware Loose Talk about a Clash of Civilizations," *The Independent* (London) (Oct. 4, 2006): 26; and Richard C. Dujardin, "Religion, The Year in Review—Cultures in collision—2006 finds faiths at odds at home and abroad," *Providence* (RI) *Journal* (Dec. 30, 2006): D–01.

12. The following newspaper articles on the Danish cartoons record emphatic and persistent attempts, in the university setting, to defend secular, democratic values at the expense of Islamic religious views: "Ayn Rand Institute: NYU's Surrender Underscores Need to Display Danish Cartoons," *US Newswire* (Mar. 28, 2006); "Danish Cartoons Arrive (Almost) at N.Y.U.," *New York Observer* (Apr. 10, 2006): 2; and "Panel Discussion on Free Speech and the Danish Cartoons to Be Held at the University of Chicago; Cartoons Will Be on Display," *US Newswire* (Apr. 17, 2006).

13. For key examples of this polemical use of Voltaire's play, see Theodore Dalrymple, "Unenlightened—As Extremist Muslims React to the Danish Cartoons, the Enlightenment Doesn't Look So Bad, Huh?" *National Review* (Feb. 27, 2006), and Andrew Higgins, "Muslims Ask French to Cancel 1741 Play by Voltaire," *Wall Street Journal* (Mar. 6, 2006).

14. Published in Feb. 2006, "Manifesto: Together Facing the New Totalitarianism" was signed by Ayaan Hirsi Ali, Salman Rushdie, Chahla Chafiq, Caroline Fourest, Bernard-Henri Levy, Irshad Manji, Mehdi Mozaffari, Maryam Namazie, Taslima Nasreen, Ibn Warraq, Philippe Val, and Antoine Sfeir.

15. A provocative diagnosis of this liberal-secularist quandary is provided in Saba Mahmood's "Secularism, Hermeneutics, and Empire: The Politics of Islamic Reformation," *Public Culture* 18.2 (2006): 323–47.

16. These authors have received scholarly treatment on their interest in Islam. See G. M. Wickens, "*Lalla Rookh* and the Romantic Tradition of Islamic Literature in English," *Year Book of Comparative and General Literature* 20 (1971): 61–6; Bernard Blackstone, "Byron and Islam: The Triple Eros." *Journal of European Studies* 4 (1974): 63–81; and Humberto Garcia, "In the Name of the 'Incestuous Mother': Islam and Excremental Protestantism in De Quincey's *Infidel* Book," *Journal for Early Modern Cultural Studies* 7.2 (2007): 57–87.

17. The case for the Oriental tale's influence on eighteenth-century British literature and culture has been argued, most persuasively, in Ros Ballaster's *Fabulous Orients: Fictions of the East in England, 1662–1785* (Oxford: Oxford UP, 2005). Also see *The Arabian Nights in Historical Context: Between East and West*, ed. Saree Makdisi and Felicity Nussbaum (Oxford: Oxford UP, 2008).

Introduction • *Rethinking Islam in the Eighteenth Century*

Epigraph. Jacques Derrida, "Faith and Knowledge: The Two Sources of 'Religion' at the Limits of Reason Alone," in *Religion*, ed. Jacques Derrida and Gianni Vattimo (Stanford: Stanford UP, 1996), 5.

1. Gil Anidjar, *The Jew, The Arab: A History of the Enemy* (Stanford: Stanford UP, 2003), 59.

2. On the distinction between tyrannical Barbary enslavement and British consti-

tutional liberty, see Linda Colley, *Captives: Britain, Empire and the World, 1600–1850* (New York: Pantheon Books, 2002), 23–134. After the English ceded the garrison city of Tangier to Morocco in 1684, they recast the North African Moor as a threat to English national liberty; see Nabil Matar, *Britain and Barbary, 1589–1689* (Gainesville: UP of Florida, 2005), 133–66. However, some eighteenth-century Britons saw Muslim North Africa as a tolerant civilization preferable to Catholic Europe's intolerance; see Ann Thomson, *Barbary and Enlightenment: European Attitudes Towards the Maghreb in the Eighteenth Century* (Leiden: E. J. Brill, 1987). Robert Travers's seminal work has shown that positive English notions of the ancient Mughal constitution coexisted, often uneasily, with negative notions of Asiatic tyranny until the late eighteenth century. See his *Ideology and Empire in Eighteenth-Century India: The British in Bengal* (Cambridge: Cambridge UP, 2007).

3. Maxime Robinson, *Europe and the Mystique of Islam*, trans. Roger Venius (Seattle: U of Washington P, 1987), 48.

4. My approach to the radical Enlightenment needs to be distinguished from Jonathan Israel's definition in *Radical Enlightenment: Philosophy and the Making of Modernity 1650–1750* (Oxford: Oxford UP, 2001). Even though we both treat the radical Enlightenment as an underground international movement, my definition places more emphasis on the deist fascination with Islam and near eastern monotheisms in late-seventeenth-century England than on the influential works of Benedict de Spinoza on the Continent. As a corrective to Israel's definition, the following works focus on Islam's radical theological status during the Enlightenment: Matthew Birchwood, "Vindicating the Prophet: Universal Monarchy and Henry Stubbe's biography of Mohammed," *Prose Studies* 29.1 (2007): 59–72; John Marshall, *John Locke, Toleration and Early Enlightenment Culture* (New York: Cambridge UP 2006), 375, 391–95; Justin Champion, *The Pillars of Priestcraft Shaken: The Church of England and Its Enemies, 1660–1730* (Cambridge: Cambridge UP, 1992), 99–132; and László Kontler, "The Idea of Toleration and the Image of Islam in Early Enlightenment English Thought," in *Sous le signe des lumieres* (Budapest: ELTE, 1987), 6–26.

5. The following scholars have shown that Edward Said's monolithic Orientalism cannot account for the diverse intercultural relations between East and West in the seventeenth and eighteenth centuries: Ziad Elmarsafy, *The Enlightenment Qur'an: The Politics of Translation and the Construction of Islam* (Oxford: Oneworld, 2009); Matthew Birchwood, *Staging Islam in England: Drama and Culture* (Cambridge: D. S. Brewer, 2007); Bernadette Andrea, *Women and Islam in Early Modern English Literature* (Cambridge: Cambridge UP, 2007); Matthew Dimmock, *New Turkes: Islam and the Ottomans in Early Modern England* (Burlington, VT: Ashgate, 2005); and Nabil Matar, *Islam in Britain 1558–1685* (Cambridge: Cambridge UP, 1998).

6. On the problems with European diffusionism—the commonplace thesis that the non-European world did not originally have the unique "gifts" bestowed on them by Europe—see James Morris Blaut, *The Colonizer's Model of the World: Geographical Diffusionism and Eurocentric History* (New York: The Guilford Press, 1993). On Eurasian and global approaches to eighteenth-century history, see Christopher Alan Bayly, *The Birth of the Modern World 1780–1914* (Malden, MA: Blackwell, 2004); Victor

Lieberman, *Strange Parallels: Southeast Asia in a Global Context c. 800–1830* (Cambridge: Cambridge UP, 2003); and A. G. Hopkins, ed. *Globalization in World History* (New York: W. W. Norton, 2002). Also see Robert Markley, *The Far East and the English Imagination 1660–1730* (Cambridge: Cambridge UP, 2006); Srinivas Aravamudan, *Guru English: South Asian Religion in a Cosmopolitan Language* (Princeton, NJ: Princeton UP, 2006), and *Tropicopolitans: Colonialism and Agency, 1688–1804* (Durham: Duke UP, 1999); Kathleen Wilson, ed. *A New Imperial History: Culture, Identity, and Modernity in Britain and the Empire, 1660–1840* (Cambridge: Cambridge UP, 2004); and Felicity A. Nussbaum, ed. *The Global Eighteenth Century* (Baltimore: The Johns Hopkins UP, 2003).

7. J. G. A. Pocock, "Criticism of the Whig Order in the Age between the Revolutions," in *The Origins of Anglo-American Radicalism*, eds. Margaret Jacob and James C. Jacob (London: Allen and Unwin, 1984), 33.

8. James R. Jacob, *Henry Stubbe, Radical Protestantism and the Early Enlightenment* (Cambridge: Cambridge UP, 1983), 139–60.

9. *Mahomet the impostor. A Tragedy as it is acted at the theatre-Royal in Drury Lane* was reprinted in several English editions: 1745, 1755, 1766, 1782, 1790, and 1795 and "Of the Alcoran; and of Mahomet." *The Works of M de Voltaire. Translated from the French with notes, historical and critical* (London, 1762), 10:103–4, 107–10. Like most eighteenth-century thinkers, Voltaire deploys Islam negatively to launch a satiric attack on Catholicism and Christian practices. But in *Candide*, he uses a Turkish dervish as a spokesperson for enlightened wisdom. See his "Essai sur les moeurs," chap. 93 in *Oeuvres Complétes*, ed. Louis Moland, vol. 8 (Paris: Garnier Fréres, 1878).

10. Jacob, *Henry Stubbe, Radical Protestantism and the Early Enlightenment*, 72.

11. See John Toland, *Nazarenus: or, Jewish, Gentile, and Mahometan Christianity*, ed. Justin Champion (1718; Oxford: Voltaire Foundation, 1999).; Thomas Morgan, *The Moral Philosopher in a dialogue between Philalethes a Christian deist, and Theophanes a Christian Jew* (London, 1737), 167–68, 410–12; Matthew Tindal, *Christianity as Old as the Creation* (London, 1730), 178–79, 387; and Peter Annet, *Deism fairly stated, and fully vindicated from the gross imputations and groundless calumnies of modern believers* (London: W. Webb, 1746), 73–74; 81–82. In *Remarks upon a Late Discourse of Freethinking* 8th ed. (London, 1743), Richard Bentley describes deists as those who "ransack all impious books for objects against [true religion]; they are biased in their favour. . . . Pagans, Mahometans, Pavawers, and Talapoins are all good vouchers against Christianity" (45).

12. On deism and toleration, see Richard H. Popkin, "The Deist Challenge," in *From Persecution to Toleration*, eds. Ole Peter Grell, Jonathan I. Israel, and Nicholas Tacke (Oxford: Clarendon Press, 1991), 195–215. The following works define deism as a movement that sought to replace revealed religion and scriptural authority, the two "mysteries" of state priestcraft, with a system of natural religion and morality: James E. Force, "The Newtonians and Deism," in *Essays on the Context, Nature, and Influence of Isaac Newton's Theology*, eds. James E. Force and Richard H. Popkin (Dordrecht: Kluwer, 1990), 56; his "Introduction" to William Stephens, *An account of the Growth of*

Deism in England (1696; repr. Los Angeles: William Andrews Clark Memorial Library, 1990) iv; Peter Byrne, *Natural Religion and the Nature of Religion: The Legacy of Deism* (London: Routledge, 1989), xiii; and Peter Gay, *Deism: An Anthology* (Toronto: D. Van Nostrand Co, 1968), 9–13. On deism's elusiveness and the difficulty of defining this term, see Clement Walsh, "A Note on the Meaning of 'Deism,'" *Anglican Theological Review* 38 (1956): 160–65; Arthur R. Winnett, "Were the Deists 'Deists'?" *Church Quarterly Review* 161 (1960): 70–77; Robert E. Sullivan, *John Toland and the Deist Controversy* (Cambridge, MA: Harvard UP, 1982), 205–34; Chester Chapin, "Was William Wollaston (1660–1724) a Deist?" *A Quarterly Journal of Short Articles* 7.2 (1994): 72–76; James A. Herrick, *The Radical Rhetoric of the English Deists: The Discourse of Skepticism, 1680–1750* (Columbia: U of South Carolina P, 1997), 24; and Gerald R. McDermott, *Jonathan Edwards Confronts the Gods* (Oxford: Oxford UP, 2000), 21.

13. On deist historiography and comparative religious studies, see Peter Harrison, *'Religion' and Religions in the English Enlightenment* (Cambridge: Cambridge UP, 1990), 61–98; Frank E. Manuel, *The Eighteenth Century Confronts the Gods* (New York: Atheneum, 1967); Byrne, *Natural Religion and the Nature of Religion*, 79–110; and Albert J. Khun, "English Deism, and the Development of Romantic Mythological Syncretism," *PMLA* 71 (1956): 1094–1116. Taking my cue from Margaret C. Jacob's *The Radical Enlightenment*, I define *deism* as an underground movement that promoted theological heresy and political opposition.

14. Of course, deism did not originate with Henry Stubbe. I recognize that this term has a long and complex history that goes back to Lord Herbert of Cherbury in 1624, and possibly before him, and to its early development in Renaissance Europe. See Louis Bredvold, "Deism Before Lord Herbert," *Papers of the Michigan Academy of Science, Arts, and Letters* 4 (1924): 431–42, and C. J. Betts, *Early Deism in France* (Hague: Martinus Nijhoff, 1984). My main point is that deism, as articulated through Stubbe's defense of Islam, becomes inextricably intertwined with the problem of defining the scope of Anglican toleration in the Restoration and eighteenth century. On deism as an attitude rather than a creed, see Sullivan, *John Toland*, 205–34; Gerald R. Cragg, *Reason and Authority in the Eighteenth Century* (London: Cambridge UP, 1964), 63–64; and McDermott, *Jonathan Edwards Confronts the Gods*, 19–21.

15. On the "problem of particularity," see McDermott, *Jonathan Edwards Confronts the Gods*, 17–33, and Byrne, *Natural Religion and the Nature of Religion*, 52–78.

16. On the Protestant Reformation and comparative religion, see Harrison, *'Religion' and Religions in the English Enlightenment*, 9–10.

17. Henry Stubbe, *The Rise and Progress of Mahometanism* (1911; repr., Lahore: Orientalia, 1975), 43, 190–91. All subsequent citations refer to this edition.

18. William Hamilton Reid, *The Rise and Dissolution of the Infidel Societies in the Metropolis* (1800; repr. Plymouth: Woburn Press, 1971), 16, 69, 83–84. All subsequent citations refer to this edition.

19. Although Reid does not explicitly mention this, the Stubbean defense of the propagation of Islam would have been most clearly articulated in Thomas Chubb's *Posthumous Works*, which, according to Reid, was a well-read work since its first ap-

pearance in 1748–9 (86, 89). See Thomas Chubb, *The Posthumous Works of Mr. Thomas Chubb* (London: R. Baldwin, 1748), 2:30–40, 170–71.

20. On the tradition of the *prisca theologia*, see McDermott, *Jonathan Edwards Confronts the Gods*, 93–109, 132–33; Harrison, *'Religion' and Religions in the English Enlightenment*, 130–38; Daniel Pickering Walker, *The Ancient Theology: Studies in Christian Platonism from the Fifteenth to the Eighteenth Century* (Ithaca: Cornell UP, 1972); Arthur J. Droge, *Homer or Moses? Early Christian Interpretations of the History of Culture* (Tubingen: J. C. B. Mohr, 1989); Charles B. Schmitt, "Perennial Philosophy: From Agostino Steuco to Leibniz," *Journal of the History of Ideas* 27 (1966): 505–32; and Frances A. Yates, *Giordano Bruno and the Hermetic Tradition* (1964; Chicago: U of Chicago P, 1979).

21. Iain McCalman, "The Infidel as Prophet: William Reid and Blakean Radicalism," in *Historicizing Blake* eds. Steve Clarke and David Worrall (New York: St. Martin's Press, 1994), 24–42.

22. Jon Mee, *Dangerous Enthusiasm: William Blake and the Culture of Radicalism in the 1790s* (Oxford: Clarendon Press, 1992), 3.

23. The following scholars define English radicalism through its rhetorical eclecticism and internal inconsistencies: James A. Epstein, *Radical Expression: Political Language, Ritual, and Symbol in England, 1790–1850* (New York: Oxford UP, 1994), chap. 1, "The Constitutional Idiom," 3–28, and his *In Practice: Studies in the Language and Culture of Popular Politics in Modern Britain* (Stanford: Stanford UP, 2003); Daniel C. Fouke, *Philosophy and Theology in a Burlesque Mode: John Toland and "the Way of Paradox"* (New York: Humanity Books, 2007); "Introduction," *Radicalism in British Literary Culture, 1650–1830*, eds. Timothy Morton and Nigel Smith (Cambridge: Cambridge UP, 2002), 1–26; Mark Philip, "English Republicanism in the 1790s," *The Journal of Political Philosophy* 6.1 (1998) 1–28; Kevin Gilmartin, *Print Politics: the Press and Radical Opposition in Early Nineteenth-Century England* (Cambridge: Cambridge UP, 1996); Isabel Rivers, *Reason, Grace, and Sentiment: A Study of the Language of Religion and Ethics in England, 1660–1780*, vol. 2. (Cambridge: Cambridge UP, 1999–2000); David Worrall, *Radical Culture: Discourse, Resistance and Surveillance, 1790–1820* (Detroit: Wayne State UP, 1992); and Iain McCalman, *Radical Underworld: Prophets, Revolutionaries and Pornographers in London, 1795–1840* (Cambridge: Cambridge UP, 1988).

24. James A. Herrick, "The English Deists' Argument for Freedom of Expression," *Free Speech Yearbook* 34 (1996): 131–40, and David Berman, "Deism, Immortality, and the Art of Theological Lying," in *Deism, Masonry, and the Enlightenment*, ed. J. A. Leo Lemay (Newark: U of Delaware P, 1987), 61–78.

25. On the "ancient constitution" in seventeenth-century legal and political thought, see J. G. A. Pocock, *The Ancient Constitution and the Feudal Law . . . A Reissue with a Retrospect* (1957; Cambridge: Cambridge UP, 1987) and Glenn Burgess, *The Politics of the Ancient Constitution* (University Park: Pennsylvania State UP, 1992).

26. Charles Taylor, *Modern Social Imaginaries* (Durham: Duke UP, 2004), 23.

27. On reinvention and transmission in English revolutionary history, see the essays in *Radicalism and British Literary Culture, 1650–1830*, eds. Timothy Morton

and Nigel Smith; David Norbrook, *Writing the English Republic: Poetry, Rhetoric and Politics 1627–1660* (Cambridge: Cambridge UP, 1999); the special edition of *The Wordsworth Circle* 25.3 (1994), esp. Greg Kucich, "Inventing Revolutionary History: Romanticism and the Politics of Literary Tradition," 138–45. On seventeenth-century pamphlets, periodicals, and letters and the invention of American revolutionary history, see Bernard Bailyn, *Ideological Origins of the American Revolution* (Cambridge, MA: Belknap Press of Harvard UP, 1967), 1–54.

28. For an intriguing cultural history on how Islamic Orientalism transformed and redefined the American republican project, see Timothy Marr, *The Cultural Roots of American Islamicism* (Cambridge: Cambridge UP, 2006). According to Gerald R. McDermott, Jonathan Edward's defense of reformed doctrines against the deist threat, as coded in "Mahometanism," allowed him to reconstruct an "Enlightened" approach to religion more inclusive of non-Christian religions than previous forms of Protestant orthodoxy (166–75). As a result, "Edwards may have been the first American intellectual to give non-Christian religions positive significance in a Christian understanding of God and history" (7). Although lying beyond this book's scope, the early American Republic is worth examining in relation to a British- and Afro-Eurasian imported Islamic republicanism.

29. See Tala Asad, *Genealogies of Religion: Discipline and Reasons of Power in Christianity and Islam* (Baltimore: The Johns Hopkins UP, 1993); Richard King, *Orientalism and Religion: Postcolonial Theory, India and "the Mystic East"* (New York: Routledge, 1999); Daniel Boyarin, "Hybridity and Heresy: Apartheid Comparative Religion in Late Antiquity," *Postcolonial Studies and Beyond*, eds., Ania Loomba, Suvir Kaul, Matti Bunzl, Antoinette Burton, and Jed Esty (Durham: Duke UP, 2005), 339–58; and Tomoko Masuzawa, *The Invention of World Religions: Or, How European Universalism Was Preserved in the Language of Pluralism* (Chicago: U of Chicago P, 2005), esp. chap. 6, "Islam, a Semitic Religion," 179–206.

30. Edward Said, *Orientalism* (New York: Vintage Books, 1978), 70. All subsequent citations refer to this edition.

31. On the conceptual limitations of Romantic Orientalism, see Eitan Bar-Yosef, *The Holy Land in English Culture 1799–1917: Palestine and the Question of Orientalism* (Oxford: Clarendon Press, 2005); Deirdre Coleman, *Romantic Colonization and British Anti-Slavery* (Cambridge: Cambridge UP, 2005); Filiz Turhan, *The Other Empire: British Romantic Writings about the Ottoman Empire* (New York: Routledge, 2003); Tim Fulford and Peter J. Kitsan, eds. *Romanticism and Colonialism* (Cambridge: Cambridge UP, 1998); Sonia Hofkosh and Alan Richardson, eds. *Romanticism, Race, and Imperial Culture 1780–1834* (Bloomington: Indiana UP, 1996); Nigel Leask, *British Romantic Writers and the East: Anxieties of Empire* (Oxford: Oxford UP, 1992); Saree Makdisi, *Romantic Imperialism: Universal Empire and the Culture of Modernity* (Cambridge: Cambridge UP, 1991); Javed Majeed, *Ungoverned Imaginings: James Mill's the History of British India and Orientalism* (Oxford: Clarendon Press, 1992); and John Barrel, *The Infection of Thomas De Quincey: A Psychopathology of Imperialism* (New Haven: Yale UP, 1991).

32. See the essay collection in *Romantic Representations of British India*, ed. Mi-

chael J. Franklin (New York: Routledge, 2006), esp. Nigel Leask, "'Travelling the other way': *The Travels of Mirza Abu Taleb Khan* (1810) and Romantic Orientalism," 220–37; Michael Fisher, *Counterflows to Colonialism: Indian Travellers and Settlers in Britain 1600–1857* (Delhi: Permanent Black, 2004); and Gulfishan Khan, *Indian Muslim Perceptions of the West during the Eighteenth Century* (Karachi: Oxford UP, 1998).

33. Michel de Certeau, *The Writing of History*, trans. Tom Cowley (New York: Columbia UP, 1988), 135.

34. See Matthew Dimmock, "'Machomet dyd before as Luther doth nowe': Islam, the Ottomans and the English Reformations," *Reformation* 9 (2004): 99–130; and his book, *New Turkes*, 20–86. Also see Daniel E. White, *Early Romanticism and Religious Dissent* (Cambridge: Cambridge UP, 2006), 152–81, and Kenneth M. Setton, "Lutherism and the Turkish Peril," *Balken Studies* 3.1 (1962): 133–68.

35. A broader historical treatment on the British church-state alliance and the growth of an attendant Anglican imperialism is offered in Rowen Strong, *Anglicanism and the British Empire, c. 1700–1850* (Oxford: Oxford UP, 2007).

36. Herbert Butterfield, *The Whig Interpretation of History* (New York: W. W. Norton, 1965), 11–12. I have borrowed the term "Whig fallacy" from Butterfield to describe the faulty assumptions that govern liberal-progressivist historiography until today (23–24).

37. See Norman Daniel, *Islam, Europe, and Empire* (Edinburgh: Edinburgh UP, 1966), 9; Kenneth Parker, "Introduction," *Early Modern Tales of Orient: A Critical Anthology* (London: Routledge, 1999), 6; and Ros Ballaster, *Fabulous Orients: Fictions of the East in England 1662–1785* (Oxford: Oxford UP, 2005), 365.

38. As far as I am aware, only three critics have questioned this cultural divide by reading late eighteenth-century Orientalism as a site for covert political discourses: M. O. Grendy, "Orientalism and Propaganda: The Oriental Tale and Popular Politics in Late Eighteenth-century Britain," *The Eighteenth-Century Novel* 2 (2002): 215–37; Srinivas Aravamudan, "In the Wake of the Novel: The Oriental Tale as National Allegory," *Novel* 33 (1999): 5–31; and Arthur Weitzman, "The Oriental Tale in the Eighteenth Century: A Reconsideration," *Studies in Voltaire and the Eighteenth Century* 58 (1967): 1839–55.

39. On the prevalence of the Whig-secular narrative in the eighteenth century, see Alan Houston and Steve Pincus, "Introduction: Modernity and Later Seventeenth-Century England," *A Nation Transformed: England after the Restoration* (Cambridge: Cambridge UP, 2001), 1–19; Roy Porter, *The Creation of the Modern World: The Untold Story of the British Enlightenment* (New York: W. W. Norton, 2000); and Israel, *Radical Enlightenment.* The following notable works on dissenting religion in eighteenth-century Britain offer revisionist critiques of Whig historiography: Christopher Hill, *The World Turned Upside Down* (New York: Viking Press, 1972); James E. Bradley, *Religion, Revolution, and English Radicalism: Nonconformity in Eighteenth-Century Politics and Society* (Cambridge: Cambridge UP, 1990); J. A. I. Champion, *The Pillars of Priestcraft Shaken*; Knud Haakonssen, ed. *Enlightenment and Religion: Rational Dissent in Eighteenth Century Britain* (Cambridge: Cambridge UP, 1996); Robert Ryan,

The Romantic Reformation: Religious Politics and English Religion; Brian W. Young, *Religion and Enlightenment in Eighteenth-Century England: Theological Debate from Locke to Burke* (Oxford: Oxford UP, 1998); Timothy Morton and Nigel Smith, eds. *Radicalism in British Literary Culture*; Saree Makdisi, *William Blake and the Impossible History of the 1790s* (Chicago: U of Chicago P, 2003); William Gibson and Robert G. Ingram, eds. *Religious Identities in Britain, 1660–1832* (Aldershot, UK: Ashgate, 2005); and White, *Early Romanticism and Religious Dissent.*

40. M. H. Abrams, *Natural Supernaturalism: Tradition and Revolution in Romantic Literature* (New York: W. W. Norton, 1971), 12, 357.

41. On the critique of the natural supernaturalism model, see Kevin Gilmartin, "Romanticism and Religious Modernity: From Natural Supernaturalism to Literary Sectarianism," in *The Cambridge History of English Romantic Literature*, ed. James Chandler (Cambridge: Cambridge UP, 2009), 621–47; Colin Jager, *The Book of God: Secularization and Design in the Romantic Era* (Philadelphia: U of Pennsylvania P, 2007), 26–36; William R. McKelvy, *The English Cult of Literature: Devoted Readers, 1774–1880* (Charlottesville: U of Virginia P, 2007); Bar-Yoself, *The Holy Land in English Culture, 1799–1917*, 1–60; Mark Canuel, *Religion, Toleration, and British Writing, 1790–1830* (Cambridge: Cambridge UP, 2002); and Robert M. Ryan, *The Romantic Reformation: Religious Politics in English Literature, 1789–1824.*

42. Jose Casanova, *Public Religions in the Modern World* (Chicago: U of Chicago P, 1994), 19.

43. Jager, *The Book of God*, 19–20.

44. This critique of natural/supernatural secularization was first advanced in Hans Blumenberg's *The Legitimacy of the Modern Age*. Trans. Robert M. Wallace (Cambridge, MA: The MIT Press, 1983), 9–10, 93.

45. On Bonaparte and his Islamic republic in Egypt, see Juan Cole, *Napoleon's Egypt: Invading the Middle East* (New York: Palgrave Macmillan, 2007), 30–33, 123–42.

46. Baron Gourgaud, *Talks of Napoleon at St. Helena*, trans. Elizabeth Wormeley (1817; repr. Chicago: A. C. McClurg and Co., 1904), 274–75, 280.

47. On Euro-Muslim Creolization in French Egypt, see Juan Cole, "Playing Muslim: Bonaparte's Army of the Orient and Euro-Muslim Creolization," in *The Age of Revolutions in Global Context, c. 1760–1840*, eds. David Armitage and Sanjay Subrahmanyam (New York: Palgrave Macmillan, 2010), 125–43.

48. Talal Asad, *Formations of the Secular: Christianity, Islam, and Modernity* (Stanford: Stanford UP, 2003) and *Genealogies of Religion*, 200–36.

49. Masuzawa, *The Invention of World Religions*, 21.

50. Amartya Sen, "Passage to China," *New York Review of Books* 51.19 (2004): 61.

51. Norman O. Brown, "The Prophetic Tradition," *Studies in Romanticism* 21.3 (1982): 372. The ideas discussed in this essay were originally developed throughout a series of public lectures Brown delivered during the early 1980s; see Brown's *The Challenge of Islam: The Prophetic Tradition*, ed. Jerome Neu (Santa Cruz: New Pacific Press, 2009).

52. G. E. Bentley Jr. *Blake Books Supplement* (Oxford: Clarendon Press, 1995), xx–vii.

53. Ibid., 81–82.

54. On Blake's use of visual semiotics to invert racial and colonial typologies, see Srinivas Aravamudan's *Tropicopolitans*, 6–9. On the politics of Blake's deexoticizing of the East, see Saree Makdisi, *William Blake and the Impossible History of the 1790*, 252–27.

55. Brown, "The Prophetic Tradition," 369.

56. On the challenge that Hodgson's work poses to Said's model, see Edmund Burke, III, "Islamic History as World History: Marshall Hodgson, 'The Venture of Islam,'" *International Journal of Middle East Studies* 10.2 (1979): 241–64.

57. Brown, "The Prophetic Tradition," 368.

58. On prophecy as a mode of social and political protest, see Michael Adas, *Prophets of Rebellion: Millenarian Protest Movements against the European Colonial Order* (Cambridge: Cambridge UP, 1979); John Fletcher Clews. Harrison, *The Second Coming: Popular Millenarianism 1780–1850* (New Brunswick, NJ: Rutgers UP, 1979); W. H. Oliver, *Prophets and Millennialists: Thee Uses of Biblical Prophecy in England from the 1790s to the 1840s* (New Zealand: Auckland UP, 1978); and Clarke Garrett, *Respectable Folly: Millenarians and the French Revolution in France and England* (Baltimore: The Johns Hopkins UP, 1975).

59. Hodgson, *The Venture of Islam* (Chicago: U of Chicago P, 1974), 1:37.

60. Ahmed Gunny, Jonathan Israel, and Charles Taylor have treated Islam as the negative foil of eighteenth-century rationalism and the Western Enlightenment. See Charles Taylor, *A Secular Age* (Cambridge, MA: Harvard UP, 2007); Israel, *Radical Enlightenment*, 703; and Ahmed Gunny, *Images of Islam in Eighteenth-Century Writings* (London: Grey Seal, 1996), 84–105. In *Imperial Encounters: Religion and Modernity in India and Britain* (Princeton, NJ: Princeton UP, 2001), Peter Van der Veer resists these insular narratives by treating secularism as a product of Anglo-Indian interaction in a colonial context (7).

61. J. G. A. Pocock, *The Machiavellian Moment: Florentine Political Thought and the Atlantic Republican Tradition* (Princeton, NJ: Princeton UP, 1975).

62. Bayly, *The Birth of the Modern World*, 285–90.

63. Jager, *The Book of God*, 29.

64. Ibid., 31.

65. This argument is discussed in Colin Jager, "After the Secular: The Subject of Romanticism," *Public Culture* 18.2 (2006): 301–21.

66. Casanova, *Public Religions in the Modern World*, 239 n. 24.

67. The following works avoid the "decline-of-Islam" thesis or any attempt to posit Western influence prior to the nineteenth century: Muzaffar Alam, *The Languages of Political Islam, India 1200–1800* (Chicago: U of Chicago P, 2004); Bernard Haykel, *Revival and Reform in Islam: The Legacy of Muhammad al-Shawkânî* (Cambridge: Cambridge UP, 2003); John Obert Voll, "Foundations for Renewal and Reform: Islamic Movements in the Eighteenth and Nineteenth Centuries," *The Oxford History of Islam* ed. John Esposito (New York: Oxford UP, 1999), 509–48; Nehemiah Levtzian

and John O. Voll, eds. *Eighteenth-Century Renewal and Reform in Islam* (Syracuse, NY: Syracuse UP, 1987); John Obert Voll, "Renewal and Reform in Islamic History: *Tajdid and Islah*," *Voices of Resurgent Islam*, ed. John L. Esposito (New York: Oxford UP, 1983), 32–47; and Fazlur Rahman, "Revival and Reform in Islam," *The Cambridge History of Islam*, eds. Peter M. Holt, Ann K. S. Lambton, and Bernard Lewis (Cambridge: Cambridge UP, 1970), 2: 632–56.

68. See David Armitage and Sanjay Subrahmanyam, eds. *The Age of Revolutions in Global Context, c. 1760–1840* (New York: Palgrave Macmillan, 2010). This collection studies the long-lasting effects and cross-cultural relevance of the "Age of Revolutions" on a global scale that includes Afro-Eurasia.

69. Sanjay Subrahmanyam, "Connected Histories: Notes towards a Reconfiguration of Early Modern Eurasia." *Modern Asian Studies* 31.3 (1997): 750.

70. Ibid., 759.

71. Bayly, *The Birth of the Modern World*, 47.

72. This controversial term first appeared in two of Reinhard Schulze's articles, in which he argues that a distinct Enlightenment humanism and anthropocentrism developed in the eighteenth-century Muslim world: "Das islamische achtzehnte jahrhundert: Versuch einer historiographischen kritik," *Die Welt des Islams* 30 (1990), 140–49, and "Was ist die islamische Aufkärung?" *Die Welt des Islams* 36 (1996): 276–325. Peter Grand has also defended the "Islamic Enlightenment" thesis in *Islamic Roots of Capitalism* (Syracuse: Syracuse UP, 1998), 49–56. The application of this term outside a European frame of cultural reference has ignited much debate and has been severely criticized for its highly speculative nature. For a summary account of the Schulze controversy, see Haykel, *Revival and Reform in Islam*, 13.

73. On the ethical humanism implicit in iconoclastic monotheism, see Lenn Evan Goodman's *God of Abraham* (New York: Oxford UP, 1996). Also see his book, *Islamic Humanism* (Oxford: Oxford UP, 2003) for an engaging discussion on Islam's pivotal role in reviving the humanistic spirit of Abrahamic monotheism. He argues that Islamic humanism, throughout the medieval period, entailed a mode of secularity intrinsic to Muslim religiosity.

74. William Blake, "The Divine Image." *The Complete Poetry and Prose of William Blake*. Ed. David V. Erdman (Berkeley: U of California P, 2008), 13.

75. Bayly, *The Birth of the Modern World*, 77.

76. Mustapha Chérif, *Islam and the West: A Conversation with Jacques Derrida*, trans. Teresa Lavendar Fagan (Chicago: U of Chicago P, 2008), 100–101.

77. Ibid., 44.

Chapter 1 • *A True Protestant Mahometan*

Epigraph. Great news from Count Teckely, or, An Account of Some Passages 'twixt a True Protestant English Volunteer, and a Teckelytish MAHOMETAN in the Turkish Camp sent over by the Counts secretary to a brother in London (London, 1684), 2. All subsequent citations to this work are from this edition.

1. The following works treat English encounters with Islam and the Ottoman em-

pire as fundamental to the construction of Protestant national culture in the late seventeenth century: Matthew Birchwood, *Staging Islam in England: Drama and Culture, 1640–1685* (Woodbridge, UK: D. S. Brewer, 2007); Nabil Matar, *Britain and Barbary, 1589–1689* (Gainesville: UP of Florida, 2005); and *Islam in Britain, 1558–1685* (Cambridge: Cambridge UP, 1998).

2. Historical and textual evidence suggests that the manuscript had been circulating privately since its composition in 1671. Hafiz Mahmud Khan Shairani, the editor of the 1911 publication of Stubbe's manuscript, speculates that the work was composed sometime between 1671 and 1676 (vii). P. M. Holt follows very similar dates in *A Seventeenth-Century Defender of Islam: Henry Stubbe (1632–76) and His Book* (London: Friends of Dr. William's Library, 1976), 10. James R. Jacob confirms these dates based on evidence from Stubbe's other works, arguing that 1671 is closer to the date of composition. See James R. Jacob, *Henry Stubbe, Radical Protestantism and the Early Enlightenment* (Cambridge: Cambridge UP, 1983), 64–65. I discuss the historical and political significance of the 1911 publication in the epilogue.

3. Jacob, *Henry Stubbe, Radical Protestantism and the Early Enlightenment*, 139–160. Also see Caroline Robbins, *The Eighteenth-Century Commonwealthman* (Cambridge, MA: Harvard UP, 1961); Richard L. Greaves, *Enemies Under His Feet: Radicals and Nonconformists in Britain, 1664–1677* (Stanford: Stanford UP, 1990); Christopher Hill, *The Experience of Defeat: Milton and Some Contemporaries* (London: Faber and Faber, 1984), esp. chap. 8, 252–77; and Robert Zaller, "The Continuity of British Radicalism in the Seventeenth and Eighteenth Centuries." *Eighteenth-Century Life* 6.2–3 (1981): 17–38. Margaret C. Jacob sees the ideas of the deists and radical Whigs as an outgrowth of seventeenth-century republicanism. See *The Radical Enlightenment: Pantheists, Freemasons and Republicans* (London: George Allen & Unwin, 1981), 65–86, and *The Newtonians and the English Revolution, 1689–1720* (Ithaca: Cornell UP, 1976), 201–50.

4. Besides James R. Jacob's groundbreaking book, the following works argue for Henry Stubbe's centrality to national controversies on Islam's theological status during the early English Enlightenment: Matthew Birchwood, "Vindicating the Prophet," *Prose Studies* 29.1 (2007): 59–72; Justin Champion, *The Pillars of Priestcraft Shaken: The Church of England and Its Enemies, 1660–1730* (Cambridge: Cambridge UP, 1992), 99–132; and David A. Paulin, *Attitudes to Other Religions* (Manchester: Manchester UP, 1984), 81–104. On English antitrinitarianism and Islam, see Matar, *Islam in Britain, 1558–1685*, 48, 80; on Islam and the tolerationist cause in Restoration England, see John Marshall, *John Locke, Toleration and Early English Enlightenment Culture* (New York: Cambridge UP, 2006), 375, 391–95, and László Kontler, "The Idea of Toleration and the Image of Islam in Early Enlightenment English Thought," in *Sous le signe des lumieres* (Budapest: ELTE, 1987), 6–26.

5. On the crucial role of late Stuart and Augustan satire in rendering "secret" conspiracies public (rather than private) knowledge, see Melinda Alliker Rabb, *Satire and Secrecy in English Literature from 1650 to 1750* (New York: Palgrave Macmillan, 2007).

6. See N. H. Keeble, *The Restoration: England in the 1660s* (Oxford: Blackwell, 2002), 154–58, and John Spurr, *England in the 1670s: "This Masquerading Age"* (Malden, MA:

Blackwell, 2002), 241–98. The following two articles situate these national fears in relation to a resurgent counterreformation in central and Western Europe: Matthew Birchwood, "News from Vienna: Titus Oates and the True Protestant Turks," in *Cultural Encounters Between East and West*, eds. Matthew Birchwood and Mathew Dimmock (Newcastle: Cambridge Scholars Press, 2005), 64–76, and Jonathan Scott, "England's Troubles: Exhuming the Popish Plot," in *The Politics of Religion in Restoration England*, eds. Tim Harris, Paul Seaward, and Mark Goldie (Oxford: Basil Blackwell, 1990), 107–31.

7. Traditional histories of the 1683 siege of Vienna are spurious in casting this final "clash" as marking the decline of the Ottoman empire; see Simon Millar, *Vienna 1683: Christian Europe Repels the Ottomans* (Oxford: Osprey Publishing, 2008), and John Stoye, *Siege of Vienna: The Last Great Trial Between the Cross and Crescent* (New York: Pegasus Books, 2006).

8. See, for example, the following anonymous polemics: the English translation of Du Perron Jacques Davy's *Luthers Alcoran being a Treatise First Written in French by the learned Cardinall Person, of Famous Memory, against the Hugenots of France* (1642), an anti–French Huguenot work translated as royalist propaganda that is interested in linking Puritans to Mahometan Turks, and *Liberty of Conscience Confuted by reasons of Argument and Policie. Delivered in a Discourse betwixt a Turke and a Christian. Occasioned by a Letter written to a Peere of this Realme* (1648), in which the argument for "Liberty of Conscience" is directly compared with the "policy of the Ottoman Empire" (1). On the association between Protestant reformers and the Ottoman incursions of the 1520s, see John Tolan, "Looking East Before 1453: The Saracen in the Medieval European Imagination," *Cultural Encounters Between East and West*, eds. Matthew Birchwood and Mathew Dimmock (Newcastle: Cambridge Scholars Press, 2005), 13–28.

9. On Hungarian history in the late seventeenth century, see László Kontler, *A History of Hungary* (New York: Palgrave Macmillan, 2002), 137–190; Miklós Molnár, *A Concise History of Hungary* (Cambridge: Cambridge UP, 2001), 87–133; and Kenneth M. Setton, *Venice, Austria, and the Turks in the Seventeenth Century* (Philadelphia: American Philosophical Society, 1991), 244–270.

10. On Queen Elizabeth's letters to Sultan Murad III and the transmonotheistic language that characterized Anglo-Ottoman diplomatic dispatches in the late sixteenth century, see Bernadette Andrea, 12–29. Queen Elizabeth's original treaty with the Ottoman Porte was renewed by Charles II and Sultan Mehmed IV several times during the Restoration. See *The capitulations and articles of peace between the Majesty of the King of Great Britain, France, and Ireland, &c. and the Sultan of the Ottoman Empire as they have been augmented and altered in the times of several ambassadors, and particularly as they have been renewed, augmented, and amplified at the city of Adrianople in the month of January 1661/2, by Heneage, Earl of Winchelsea, Ambassador Extraordinary from His Majesty: and also as they have been since renewed in the month of September 1675 : with divers additional articles and privileges, by Sir John Finch, to Sultan Mahomet Han ,the most puissant Prince and Emperour of the Turks* (London, 1679).

11. See *The Intreigues of the French King at Constantinople to embroil Christendom discovered in several dispatches past betwixt him and the late Grand Seignior, Grand Vizier and Count Teckily: all of them found among that Count's papers seiz'd in December last: with some reflections upon them* (London, 1689) and *An Abstract of the procedure of France since the Pyrenaean Treaty under these heads* (London, 1684), 37–39. Note that *The Intreigues* was probably published as court propaganda after King James fled to France and William III and Mary ascended the English throne, securing a Protestant succession.

12. On Pocock's Arabic studies and his refutation of medieval fables on Islam, see P. M. Holt, *Studies in the History of the Near East* (London: Frank Cass, 1973), 11, 17; Kontler, "The Idea of Toleration," 21; and Bernard Lewis, *British Contributions to Arabic Studies* (Cambridge: Cambridge UP, 1937).

13. On Arabic-Islamic studies and the propagation of Protestant Christianity in the Levant, see Charles G. D. Littleton, "Ancient Languages and New Science: The Levant in the Intellectual Life of Robert Boyle," in *The Republic of Letters and the Levant*, eds. Alastair Hamilton, Maurits H. Van Den Boogart, and Bart Westerweel (Leiden: Brill, 2005), 151–71, and G. J. Toomer, *Eastern Wisdome and Learning: The Study of Arabic in Seventeenth-Century England* (Oxford: Clarendon Press, 1996), 216–18.

14. See Ezel Kural Shaw, "The Ottoman Aspects of *Pax Ottomanica*," in *Tolerance and Movements of Religious Dissent in Eastern Europe*, eds. Béla K. Király (New York : Columbia UP, 1975), 165–82.

15. Ibid., 181.

16. A significant body of scholarship on the early modern Mediterranean has focused on Christian (including English) captives who "turned Turk," forcefully and voluntarily. English conversions to Islam suggest the fluidity and vulnerability of national identity and religious differences among Catholics, Protestants, and other sects. See Jonathan Burton, *Traffic and Turning: Islam and English Drama, 1579–1624* (Newark: U of Delaware P, 2005); Matthew Dimmock, *New Turkes: Islam and the Ottomans in Early Modern England* (Burlington, VT: Ashgate, 2005); and Daniel Vitkus, *Turning Turk: English Theater and the Multicultural Mediterranean, 1570–1630* (New York: Palgrave Macmillan, 2003).

17. Jean Le Clerc, *Memoirs of Emeric Count Teckely. In four books* (London, 1693), xii.

18. Jacob, *Henry Stubbe, Radical Protestantism and the Early Enlightenment*, 132.

19. Ibid., 143.

20. This satiric tract includes the names of "Tytus" (Titus Oates), Whig "King-Killers & Assassinators," and "Proto-martyr" Exclusionists under its list of members belonging to the Hungarian "Association" (2).

21. John Dryden, *A true coppy of the Epilogue to Constantine the Great that which was first published being false and surreptitious* (London, 1684), 1. The epilogue is also included in the printed edition of Nathaniel Lee's *Constantine the Great, a Tragedy acted at the Theatre-Royal, by their majesties servants* (London, 1684).

22. See A. L. Cooke and Thomas B. Stroop, "The Political Implications in Lee's *Constantine the Great*," *Journal of English and German Philology* 49 (1950): 506–15.

23. See Oates's *True and Exact Narrative of the Horrid Plot and Conspiracy of the Popish Party against the Life of His Sacred Majesty, the Government and the Protestant Religion, etc. published by the Order of the Right Honorable the Lords Spiritual and Temporal in Parliament assembled* (London, 1679).

24. On the centrality of the Titus-Turk figure in the polemical debates of the Exclusion Crisis, see Matthew Birchwood, "News from Vienna," 64–67, quote from 73.

25. I am borrowing this term from Melinda Alliker Rabb, *Satire and Secrecy in English Literature from 1650 to 1750*, 93.

26. Alan Marshall, "Oates, Titus (1649–1705)," *Oxford Dictionary of National Biography* (Oxford: Oxford UP, 2004), online ed., Jan. 2008, www.oxforddnb.com.proxy .library.vanderbilt.edu/view/article/20437, accessed Apr. 6, 2011.

27. See the following Tory burlesques: *Dr. Oates last Farewell to England he went on ship-board Sunday last, with forescore bums to attend his sir-reverence to stom-bula, where he's a going to be mufty to the Grand Turk* (London, 1680); *The Character of an Ignoramus Doctor* (1681) compares the "Whiggish" Oates "to an Algerine [who] wear[s] *Christian colours*" (1); and *Dr. Oates last legacy's and his farewell sermon to being sent far to be the high priest to the Grand Turk* (London, 1683).

28. See John Northleigh, *A gentle reflection on the modest account, and a vindication of the loyal abhorrers from calumnies of a factious pen by the author of the Parallel* (London, 1682), 12.

29. Jacob, *Henry Stubbe, Radical Protestantism and the Early Enlightenment*, 117–18.

30. J. G. A. Pocock coined this term to describe reformers who adapted James Harrington's views on the ideal republican commonwealth as an ideological justification for the reformed monarchy under Shaftesbury's leadership. See his *Political Works of James Harrington* (Cambridge: Cambridge UP, 1977), 128–52. James R. Jacob revises Pocock's exclusive focus on Shaftesbury, arguing that "Stubbe's use in 1673 of Harringtonian language strongly suggests that there was already a revival of Harringtonian ideas at court . . . two years before the 'Country' neo-Harringtonianism appeared" (118).

31. Jacob, *Henry Stubbe, Radical Protestantism and the Early Enlightenment*, 126.

32. See Pocock, John G. A., *The Ancient Constitution and the Feudal Law . . . A Reissue with a Retrospect* (New York: Cambridge UP, 1987).

33. See Pocock, John G. A., *The Machiavellian Moment: Florentine Political Thought and the Atlantic Republican Tradition* (1975; repr. with a New Afterword, Princeton, NJ: Princeton University Press, 2003), 170–72.

34. Ibid., 180.

35. Ibid., 417.

36. See Thomas Hobbes, *Leviathan*, ed. C. B. Macpherson (New York, 1968), 611–12. For an analysis of the striking connections between Stubbe's defense of Islam and Hobbes's view of an Erastian religion, see Jacob *Henry Stubbe, Radical Protestantism and the Early Enlightenment*, 70–73.

37. Hobbes, *Leviathan*, 711.

38. See Holt, *Studies in the History of the Near East*, 51–52.

39. Charles Blount, *The Oracles of Reason* (London, 1693), 123–24, 125–27, 156. See Blount's letter to Rochester, dated December 1678, in *The Letters of John Wilmot, Earl of Rochester*, ed. J. Treglown (Oxford: Oxford UP, 1980), 206–16. Also see Blount's preface to *A Just Vindication of Learning* (London, 1680). In his *general Dictionary, historical and critical* (London, 1734–41), Pierre Bayle notes that Blount had undertaken to write an account of Mahomet's life in 1682.

40. Humphrey Prideaux, *The True Nature of Imposture Fully Displayed in the Life of Mahomet* (London, 1697), vii–viii.

41. On Stubbe's and Toland's views on Islam in the deist controversy, see Jacob, *Henry Stubbe, Radical Protestantism and the Early Enlightenment*, 153–60, and Justin Champion, *The Pillars of Priestcraft Shaken*, 120–32.

42. John Toland, *Nazarenus: or, Jewish, Gentile, and Mahometan Christianity*, ed. Justin Champion (Oxford: Voltaire Foundation, 1999). All citations refer to this edition.

43. The Copyright Act of 1710 made it difficult for deist freethinkers to publish subversive ideas, because the author, who legally "owned" the work, was now responsible for its contents and therefore vulnerable to government persecution. See Jody Greene, *The Trouble with Ownership: Literary Property and Authorial Liability in England, 1660–1730* (Philadelphia: U of Pennsylvania P, 2005), 1–24.

44. Thomas Mangey, *Remarks upon Nazarenus* (London, 1718), 43.

45. On Toland, deism, and the Jews, see Justin Champion, "Toleration and Citizenship in Enlightenment England: John Toland and the Naturalization of the Jews, 1714–1753," *Toleration in Enlightenment Europe*, ed. Ole Peter Grell and Roy Porter (Cambridge: Cambridge UP, 2000), 3–21, and Pierre Lurbe, "John Toland and the Naturalization of the Jews," *Eighteenth-Century Ireland* 14 (1999): 37–48.

46. Justin Champion, *Republican Learning: John Toland and the Crisis of Christian culture, 1696–1722* (Manchester: Manchester UP, 2003), 167–89.

47. On the differences between the limited scope of the Toleration Act and a radical model of toleration in which civic equality among free citizens entails the elimination of any reigning orthodoxy, making the ecclesiastical order a constituency of the secular state, see Jonathan Israel, "Spinoza, Locke and the Enlightenment Battle for Toleration," *Toleration in Enlightenment Europe*, eds. Ole Peter Grell and Roy Porter (Cambridge: Cambridge UP, 2000), 102–13, and Justin Champion, "Toleration and Citizenship."

48. The *English Short Title Catalogue* notes that "an Arabian physician is possibly a pseudonym of Anthony Collins." Given its anticlerical sentiments and its use of materialist arguments, the letter could have been written by Collins. However, scholars have traced the authorship and publication of this work to John Toland. See Margaret C. Jacob, *The Radical Enlightenment*, 162, 197, and Robert E. Sullivan, *John Toland and the Deist Controversy* (Cambridge, MA: Harvard UP, 1982), 337. My argument relies on the rhetorical techniques shared by this text and *Nazarenus* and not on the author function.

49. On Toland and the Whig opposition to the Toleration Act, see Daniel C. Fouke, *Philosophy and Theology in a Burlesque Mode: John Toland and "the Way of Paradox"*

(New York: Humanity Books, 2007), 43.

50. On Toland's connection to Robert Harley and the "old Country" Whigs, see ibid., 35–52.

51. Evans, Robert Rees, *Pantheisticon: The Career of John Toland* (New York: Peter Lang, 1991), 183–86.

52. On Toland's relationship to the Third Earl and the commonwealthean-republican tradition of the 1690s and 1700s, see Champion, *Republican Learning*, 32–23, 151–52. The reemergence of Stubbe's Mahometanism in Toland's republican writing is discussed in Jacob, *Stubbe, Radical Protestantism and the Early Enlightenment*, 153–60.

53. See *A Dialogue between Dr. Sherlock, the king of France, the Great Turk, and Dr. Oates* (London, 1691). In this satire, William Sherlock's "Jacobite" defense of the ex-king James is cast as another Oates-led conspiracy to further the "Teckelite" cause in England and abroad; after William III's Protestant settlement, the anonymous author draws a parallel between the defense of the Stuart line and the Catholic-French role in abetting an Ottoman invasion of central Europe. As such, Sherlock is cast as a seditious "Tory" who betrayed the settlement of 1688. Also see note 11 above.

54. I am alluding to the Quadruple Alliance formed among England, France, Holland, and Austria against Spain's infringement of the peace settlement protected under the 1713 Treaty of Utrecht. Nabil Matar offers an informed analysis on how positive perceptions of Islam were shaped by England's increasing dependence on the economic and military aid of Muslim North Africa during the Nine Years' War and the War of the Spanish Succession. See "Islam in Britain, 1689–1750," *Journal of British Studies* 47.2 (2008): 284–300, esp. 290–300.

55. On the ideological implications of Stubbe's anti-Catholic rhetoric for England's national and imperial identity, see Raymond D. Tumbleson, *Catholicism in the English Protestant Imagination* (Cambridge: Cambridge UP, 1998) 12, 89.

56. In *Philosophy and Theology in a Burlesque Mode*, Daniel C. Fouke convincingly argues that Toland and other freethinkers are "radical" in "the seditious implications of their arguments, and the effects produced by their rhetoric" (221). This definition of radicalism is too broad, because (as I have shown above) this subversive "burlesque mode" could potentially apply to Tory broadsides that lampooned Whig Mahometans. In my definition of *radical,* I emphasize how the burlesque mode is effectively combined with a subversive and heretical biblical hermeneutics.

57. See Mangey, *Remarks upon Nazarenus* 43; John Norris, *An Account of Reason and Faith: in Relation to the Mysteries of Christianity* (London, 1697) 329; and Des Maizeaux, "Some Memoirs of the life and writings of Mr. John Toland," *A Collection of Several Pieces of Mr. John Toland* (London, 1726), 1:xxvi.

58. John Toland, "English Extracts of *Nazarenus*." 1698. *Nazarenus: or, Jewish, Gentile, and Mahometan Christianity,* ed. Justin Champion (Oxford: Voltaire Foundation, 1999), 300.

59. Rabb, *Satire and Secrecy in English Literature from 1650 to 1750,* 5.

60. Jonathan Israel has questioned Locke's privileged status in liberal thought by arguing that his writings are not as central to the radical Enlightenment as scholars

Notes to Pages 59–61

have commonly believed. See, "John Locke and the Intellectual Legacy of the Early Enlightenment," *Eighteenth-Century Thought* 3 (2007): 37–55.

61. In *A Letter concerning Toleration* (1668; repr. New York: Bobs Merrill, 1955), Locke suggests that Islamic toleration of non-Muslims presents a just policy that England should adopt in favor of Muslims, Jews, and, implicitly, antitrinitarians (22, 56). According to Nabil Matar, he is the first seventeenth-century theorist to insist on extending toleration to non-Christians—Jews and Muslims—on moral grounds. See "John Locke and the 'Turbanned Nations,'" *Journal of Islamic Studies* 2 (1991): 67–77. On Locke's interest in the deist defense of Islamic toleration, see John Marshall, *John Locke*, 612–15.

Chapter 2 • Letters from a Female Deist

Epigraph. Qtd. in Norman Daniel, *Islam, Europe, and Empire* (Edinburgh: Edinburgh UP, 1966), 20.

1. The following works examine Montagu as progressive feminist in the context of Anglo-Ottoman cross-cultural relations, but do not consider the significance of her radical Protestant commitments in her letters: John C. Beynon, "Lady Mary Wortley Montagu's Sapphic Vision," in *Imperial Desire: Dissident Sexualities and Colonial Literature*, eds. Philip Holden and Richard R. Ruppel (Minneapolis: U of Minnesota P, 2003), 21–43; Teresa Heffernan, "Feminism against the East/West Divide: Lady Mary's *Turkish Embassy Letters*." *Eighteenth-Century Studies* 33.2 (2000): 201–15; Mary Jo Kietzman, "Montagu's *Turkish Embassy Letters* and Cultural Dislocation," *SEL* 38 (1998): 537–51; Srinivas Aravamudan, "Lady Mary Wortley Montagu in the *Hammam*: Masquerade, Womanliness, and Levantinization," *ELH* 62.1 (1995): 69–104; Elizabeth A. Bohls, *Woman Travel Writers and the Language of Aesthetics, 1716–1818* (Cambridge: Cambridge UP, 1995), 23–45; and Joseph W. Lew, "Lady Mary's Portable Seraglio," *Eighteenth-Century Studies* 24 (1991), 432–50. As Sharon Archinstein has shown, theology offers early modern women a critical language through which to envision "an agency that might properly be called 'feminist'" (22). See "Mary Astell, Religion, and Feminism: Texts in Motion," in *Mary Astell: Reason, Gender, Faith*, eds. William Kolbremer and Michal Michelson (Burlington, VT: Ashgate, 2007), 17–30. On Montagu's deist perspective on Muslim woman and Islam in relation to the early English Enlightenment (but not early modern English feminism), see Jane Shaw, "Gender and the 'Nature' of Religion: Lady Mary Wortley Montagu's Embassy Letters and Their Place in Enlightenment Philosophy of Religion," *Bulletin of the John Rylands University Library of Manchester* 80.3 (1998): 129–45.

2. I am borrowing the label "female deist" from Jane Shaw. She treats Montagu as an important figure in the English Enlightenment: "an early example of the *practice* of the comparative study of religion . . . by a woman" more receptive to the freedoms of elite Muslim women in the Ottoman empire than her armchair male counterparts, such as John Toland (144).

3. I define "libertinism" broadly as a literary and philosophical movement that loosely encompasses clandestine sexual literature, anticlerical dissent, and skeptical

and scientific materialism, in contrast to a narrower definition that circumscribes libertinism within the tradition of French courtly writing. On libertinism's broader definition, see the essays in Peter Cryle and Lisa O' Connell, eds. *Libertine Enlightenment: Sex, Liberty and License in the Eighteenth Century* (New York: Palgrave Macmillan, 2004), and James G. Turner, "The Properties of Libertinism," in ed. Robert Purks Maccubbin, '*Tis Nature's Fault: Unauthorized Sexuality during the Enlightenment* (Cambridge: Cambridge UP, 1985), 75–87. To learn more about libertine sexuality and radical politics in early modern London, see Turner's *Libertines and Radicals in Early Modern London: Sexuality, Politics, and Literary Culture* (Cambridge: Cambridge UP, 2002). For a detailed account on how enlightened libertinism entailed a double standard in which men are "enlightened" while women are "rakes," see Kathleen Wilson, "The Female Rake: Gender, Libertinism and Enlightenment," in *Libertine Enlightenment: Sex, Liberty and License in the Eighteenth Century*, eds. Peter Cryle and Lisa O' Connell (New York: Palgrave Macmillian, 2004), 93–111. In this regard, Pope's satiric letter primarily stigmatizes Montagu as a vulgar "rake" for practicing Oriental libertinism. On Pope's quarrel with her and his attempt to scandalize her name in public, see Isobel Grundy, *Lady Mary Wortley Montagu: Comet of the Enlightenment* (Oxford: Clarendon Press, 1999), 270–75, 77–78, 282, 285–86.

4. The term *feminotopia* was first formulated by Mary Louise Pratt, refined by many critics thereafter. See *Imperial Eyes: Travel Writing and Transculturation* (New York: Routledge, 1992), 155–71. In *Women, Space and Utopia: 1660–1800* (Aldershot, UK: Ashgate, 2006), Nicole Pohl defines the harem's feminotopia as a symbolic space for "the imaginative resistance to the existing social economy" (146). Taking my cue from Felicity A. Nussbaum's work, I will use the term *feminotopia* to include broader socioeconomic issues involving sexuality, citizenship, and empire in eighteenth-century England. See *Torrid Zones: Maternity, Sexuality, and Empire in Eighteenth-Century English Narratives* (Baltimore: The Johns Hopkins UP, 1995), 160–62.

5. Hilda L. Smith's *All Men and Both Sexes: Gender, Politics, and the False Universal in England, 1640–1832* (University Park: Pennsylvania State UP, 2002) calls attention to the uneasy application of democratic terms to women in the eighteenth century and in current scholarship, such as the problematic use of "freeborn Englishman" in David Underwood's *A Freeborn People: Politics and the Nation in Seventeenth-Century England* (Oxford: Clarendon Press, 1996).

6. Bernadette Andrea's *Women and Islam in Early Modern English Literature* (Cambridge: Cambridge UP, 2007) situates Montagu's feminism in relation to that of previous female writers responding to Islam and the Ottoman empire. However, this work does not examine Montagu's place in the English Enlightenment, nor does it consider how her choice of genre is informed by her Protestant heterodoxy.

7. A compelling postcolonial reading that qualifies Montagu's progressive feminism in relation to the Ottoman slave institution is provided in Adam R. Beach, "Lady Mary Wortley Montagu and Slavery in the Ottoman (and the British) Empire," *Philological Quarterly* 85.3 (2006): 293–314.

8. Nussbaum, *Torrid Zones*, 162. On the national and imperial significance of Englishwomen's sexuality, see Kathleen Wilson, *The Island Race: Englishness, Empire and*

Gender in the Eighteenth Century (London: Routledge, 2003). See Aravamudan, "Lady Mary Wortley Montagu in the *Hammam*," 89–93.

9. These writers were interested in revising "imposture" theories by recasting Mahomet in a positive, Greco-Roman republican mold—a wise "Arabian legislator": Henri Comte de Boulainvilliers, *The Life of Mahomet* (London, 1731); George Sale, "The Preliminary Discourse," in *The Koran; or Alcoran of Mohammed* (1734; London: Frederick Warne and Co., 1910), 1–132; and "A Letter from Mr. Leibnitz to the Author of the Reflections upon the Origin of Mahometanism," in *Four Treatises concerning the doctrine, discipline, and worship of the Mahometans* (London, 1712), 245–54. The anonymous *Reflections on Mahommedanism, and the Conduct of Mohammed. Occasioned by a late learned translation and exposition of the Koran* (London, 1735), a work occasioned by Sale's translation of the Qur'an, suggests that Islam anticipates the Protestant Reformation: Mahomet "laid the foundations of a general and thorough Reformation, Conversion, and Re-union in ages to come" (50). See Justin Champion, "Legislators, Impostors, and the Politic Origins of Religion: English Theories of 'Imposture' from Stubbe to Toland," in *Heterodoxy, Spinozism, and Free Thought in Early Eighteenth-Century Europe,* eds. Silvia Berti, Francois Charles-Daubert, and Richard H. Popkin (Dordrecht: Kluwer Academic Publishers, 1996), 333–56.

10. Cythnia Lowenthal, *Lady Mary Wortley Montagu and the Eighteenth-Century Familiar Letter* (Athens: U of Georgia P, 1994).

11. Leibniz, Gottfried Wilhelm. "A Letter from Mr. Leibnitz to the Author of the Reflections upon the Origin of Mahometanism." *Four Treatises concerning the doctrine, discipline, and worship of the Mahometans* (London, 1712), 245, 249.

12. A list of editions is included in *Letters Writ by a Turkish Spy, by Giovanni P. Marcana,* ed. Arthur J. Weitzman (London: Routledge, 1970), 232, and C. J. Betts, *Early Deism in France* (Hague: Martinus Nijhoff, 1984), chap. 7. On these letters' deist implications, especially as a precursor to Montesquieu's work, see Gustave Leopold Van Roosbroeck, *Persian Letters Before Montesquieu* (New York: Publications of the Institute of French Studies, 1932). Also see Richard H. Popkin, "Polytheism, Deism, and Newton," in *Essays on the Context, Nature, and Influence of Isaac Newton's Theology,* eds. James E. Force and Richard H. Popkin (Dordrecht: Kluwer, 1990), 33–34.

13. All citations are based on the original English translations of Giovanni Paolo Marana's *Letters Writ by a Turkish Spy,* 8 vols. (London, 1702–3).

14. All subsequent citations to Montagu's letters are from *The Turkish Embassy Letters.* ed. Malcolm Jack (London: Virago, 1994).

15. See Richard Knolles, *The Turkish history from the original of that nation . . . whereunto is added, the present state of the Ottoman Empire by Sir Paul Pycaut* (London, 1687), 65.

16. Radical Enlightenment thinkers such as Pierre Bayle and Bernard Mandeville were interested in tracing the legacy of freethinking skepticism to the early Islamic engagement with Greek philosophy. Jonathan Israel, *Enlightenment Contested: Philosophy, Modernity and the Enlightenment of Man, 1670–1752* (Oxford: Oxford UP, 2006), offers plausible historical inferences suggesting that this extended genealogy may not be as improbable as it may initially appear (630–39).

17. Grundy, *Lady Mary Wortley Montagu*, 88.

18. Newton's clandestine investigations into scripture led him into a closet Arianism, whereas his pupil, William Whiston, openly professed his opposition to the Trinity and faced persecution as a result. See James E. Force, *William Whiston: Honest Newtonian* (Cambridge: Cambridge UP, 1985); Frank E. Manuel, *The Religion of Isaac Newton* (Oxford: Clarendon Press, 1974); Richard S. Westfall, *Never at Rest* (Cambridge: Cambridge UP, 1980), 312–19, 321, 344–45, 355–56; and Richard H. Popkin, "Newton as a Bible Scholar," in *Essays on the Context, Nature, and Influence of Isaac Newton's Theology*, eds. James E. Force and Richard H. Popkin (Dordrecht: Kluwer, 1990), 103–8.

Newton relied on Joseph Mede's treatises on ancient Indian and Arabic dream-books as a hermeneutic tool for deciphering the complex symbolism of prophetic texts. Newton was convinced that the Near East contained a common prophetic language. As such, the works of a learned Arabian scholar, Achmet (similar to Montagu's "Achmed"), who discloses the interpretation of the dream symbols as recorded on ancient Egyptian, Persian, and Indian monuments, unlocks the full eschatological significance of biblical prophetic history (Manuel, *The Religion of Isaac Newton*, 90–91; Westfall, *Never at Rest*, 327).

19. Simon Ockley, "Preface," *The history of the Saracens*, 2nd ed. (London, 1718).

20. Thomas Hearne, *Remarks and Collections*. ed. Charles Edward Doble (Oxford: Clarendon Press, 1875), 3:57, 485.

21. For a contemporary attack on Whiston's heretical interest in Arabic manuscript accounts of the Apostles, as discussed in Joannes Ernestus Grabe's *An Essay upon Two Arabick manuscripts of the Bodlejan Library* (London, 1711), see Richard Smalbroke, *The New Arian reprov'd: or, a Vindication of some Reflections on the conduct of Mr. Whiston, in his revival of the Arian heresy* (London: Timothy Childe, 1711), 13, 17–18, 52–54. Newton and Whiston were identified as deists in their time, although they fiercely denounced deist presumptions and ideas. On the intersections between Newtonianism and deism, see Gerald R. Cragg, *Reason and Authority in the Eighteenth Century* (Cambridge: Cambridge UP, 1964), 13; John Redwood, *Reason, Ridicule and Religion* (London: Thames and Hudson, 1976), 169; Richard S. Westfall, "Isaac Newton's *Theolofiae Gentilis Origines Philosophicae*," in *The Secular Mind: Essays Presented to Franklin L. Baumer*, ed. Warren Wagar (New York: Holmes and Meier Publishers, 1982), 15–34; Popkin, "Polytheism, Deism, and Newton," 27–42; and James E. Force, "The Newtonians and Deism," in *Essays on the Context, Nature, and Influence of Isaac Newton's Theology*, 43–74. On the popularity of Arabic manuscripts among natural philosophers and alchemists such as Robert Boyle and Newton, see *The "Arabick" Interest of the Natural Philosophers in Seventeenth-Century England*. ed. G. A. Russell (Leiden: Brill, 1994), particularly M. B. Hall's "Arabic Learning in the Correspondence of the Royal Society 1660–1677," 147–57.

22. In the early eighteenth century, entering into any controversial topic that reflected on government, the Crown, the church, the Parliament, or prominent people could make both the author and the publisher vulnerable to libel persecution. For an overview of seditious libel prosecutions in the late seventeenth and early eighteenth

century, see Donald Thomas, *A Long Time Burning: The History of Literary Censorship in England* (New York: Routledge & Kegan Paul, 1969), 34–74, and Laurence Hanson, *The Government and the Press, 1695–1763* (Oxford: Clarendon Press, 1936).

23. Grundy, *Lady Mary Wortley Montagu*, 197, 89; Robert Halsband, *Life of Lady Mary Wortley Montagu* (Oxford: Clarendon Press, 1936), 100.

24. See n. 48 in chap. 1.

25. Jane Shaw, "Gender and the 'Nature' of Religion," 136. On deism's two-tiered approach to religion, see Frank Manuel, *The Eighteenth Century Confronts the Gods* (New York: Atheneum, 1967), 66.

26. "Mary Astell's Preface to the *Embassy Letters; the Travels of an English Lady in Europe, Asia and Africa*, by Lady Mary Wortley Montagu 1724 & 1725," in *The First Feminist: Reflections upon Marriage and other Writings by Mary Astell*, ed. Bridget Hill (New York: St. Martin's Press, 1986), 233–35. Toward the end of this chapter, I discuss the theological-political significance of this preface in the context of Montagu's deist-inspired feminism.

27. William Warburton, *The Divine Legation of Moses demonstrated, on the principles of a religious deist* (London: Mr. Fletcher Gyles, 1742–58), 1:xxxv.

28. Mohja Kahf, *Western Representations of the Muslim Woman* (Austin: U of Texas P, 1999), 135–36, and Billie Melman, *Women's Orients: English Women and the Middle East, 1718–1918* (Houndmills, UK: Macmillan, 1992), 17.

29. In *Britons in the Ottoman Empire, 1642–1660* (Seattle: U of Washington P, 1998), Daniel Goffman documents the journeys of female family members who accompanied English diplomats and merchants in the Ottoman empire as early as the mid-seventeenth century (27, 46, 226 n. 25).

30. Glasse, Cyril, ed. *The Concise Encyclopedia of Islam* (San Francisco: Harper and Row, 1989), 420.

31. Barbara Freyer Stowasser argues that the Qur'anic concept of equality should not be equated with eighteenth-century democratic notions, which ideally seek to eliminate economic and social inequality. Instead, Qur'anic equality reflects a morality that serves the collective well-being of the citizens of a given community (without eliminating class and gender hierarchies), a task that falls with *equal* measure on both men and women (33–34). See "Women and Citizenship in the Qur'an," *Women, the Family, and Divorce Laws in Islamic History*, ed. Amira El Azhary Sonbul (Syracuse, NY: Syracuse UP, 1996), 23–38.

32. See Roy Porter, "Mixed Feelings: The Enlightenment and Sexuality in Eighteenth-Century Britain," in *Sexuality in Eighteenth-Century Britain*, ed. Paul-Gabriel Boucé (Totowa, NY: Barnes & Noble Books, 1982), 1–27, esp.4, 7, 11. In *The Rise and Progress of Mahometanism* (1911; Lahore: Orientalia, 1975), Stubbe argues that the Christian doctrine of monogamous marriage is "a Paganical tenant derived from Roman Constitutions, and complied with by the degenerate Christians" (173–74). He may have derived his arguments from earlier Christians who argued that the church patriarchs were polygynists and that monogamy is a corrupt Catholic doctrine. See John Cairncross, *After Polygamy Was Made Sin, the Social History of Christian Polygamy* (London: Routledge & Kegan Paul, 1974).

33. See Porter, "Mixed Feelings," 15, and Melman, *Women's Orients*, 95. Radical Protestant views of sexuality entail a double standard in which lack of chastity, before and outside marriage, is permissible for men but a grave offense for women. See Keith Thomas, "The Double Standard," *Journal of the History of Ideas* 20 (1959): 195–216, and Kathleen Wilson, "The Female Rake." For more information on how English Enlightenment "reason" represses women's sexuality, see Patricia Meyer Spacks, "'Ev'ry Woman Is at Heart a Rake,'" *Eighteenth-Century Studies* 8.1 (1974–5): 27–46. Spacks argues that Christian chastity casts unmarried women and virgin girls as valuable property in the English marriage market (209–11).

34. Gayle Rubin, "The Traffic in Women: Notes on the Political Economy of Sex," *Toward an Anthropology of Women* (New York: Monthly Review Press, 1975), 157–210, esp. 177.

35. See Adrian Wilson, *The Making of Man-Midwifery: Childbirth in England 1660–1700* (London: UCL Press, 1995), 29.

36. Qtd. in Grundy, *Lady Mary Wortley Montagu*, 160.

37. Carol Pateman, *The Sexual Contract* (Stanford: Stanford UP, 1988), 88.

38. See Amy Louise Erickson, *Women and Property in Early Modern England* (London: Routledge, 1993), 1–20, 29, 230.

39. For more information on English women and property law in the nineteenth century, see Lee Holcombe, *Wives and Property: Reform of the Married Women's Property Law in Nineteenth-Century England* (Toronto: U of Toronto P, 1983). An introductory summary to these historical developments is provided in Tim Stretton, "Women, Property and Law," in *A Companion to Early Modern Women's Writing*, ed. Anita Pacheco (London: Blackwell, 2002), 40–57.

40. Weibke Walther, *Women in Islam* (Princeton, NJ: Markus Wiener, 1981), 7–8, 54, 59, 65–66. In *Subjects of the Sultan: Culture and Daily Life in the Ottoman Empire* (London: I. B. Tauris, 2000), Suraiya Faroqhi points out that Ottoman Muslim women, in addition to their entitlement to property and wealth, "were subjects of the empire in their own right as soon as they reached puberty" (101).

41. Amira El Azhary Sonbul, *Women, the Family, and Divorce Laws in Islamic History*, ed. Amira El Azhary Sonbul (Syracuse, NY: Syracuse UP, 1996), 7. See Lelia Ahmed's *Women and Gender in Islam: Historical Roots of a Modern Debate* (New Haven: Yale UP, 1992) for a historical account of Muslim women's property rights under the Ottoman empire (110–12). For a concise study of Muslim women and eighteenth-century property rights in the Ottoman empire, see Mary Ann Fay, "Women and *Waqf*: Property, Power, and the Domain of Gender in Eighteenth-Century Egypt," in *Women in the Ottoman Empire: Middle Eastern Women in the Early Modern Era*, ed. Madeline C. Zilfi (Leiden: Brill, 1997), 28–47.

42. See John Milton's *Paradise Lost*, 4.1.492, for a description of Eve and her unsinful, sensual pleasures.

43. Throughout her life, Montagu was extremely conscious of herself as a woman without socioeconomic independence. Under the common law of coverture, she was forced to surrender her wealth and inheritances to her husband, Edward Wortley. Isobel Grundy discusses Montagu's unhappy marriage life in the fourth chapter of

her *Lady Mary Wortley Montagu*: "February-August 1712: Elopement: 'ran away with, without fortunes'" (45–56).

44. On deism's cultural location in London's coffeehouses, see Stephen H. Daniel, *John Toland: His Methods, Manners and Mind* (Kingston: McGill-Queen's UP, 1984), 145–46. Markman Ellis provides a rich cultural history of the coffeehouse as an Islamic practice of consumption that was transformed, by the mid-seventeenth century, into the locus for urban forms of Western publicity. See *The Coffee House: A Cultural History* (London: Weidenfeld & Nicolson, 2004).

45. The segregation of imperial Ottoman women in the harem did not prevent them from assuming a political role; on the contrary, they directly trained their sons as future successors, arranged political marriages, negotiated with foreign ambassadors, and generated public scandals. See Leslie P. Peirce, *The Imperial Harem: Women and Sovereignty in the Ottoman Empire* (New: Oxford UP, 1993). For a more focused study on how political decisions and actions centered on the elite Muslim women of the Ottoman household, see Dina Rizk Khoury, "Slippers at the Entrance or Behind Closed Doors: Domestic and Public Spaces for Mosuli Women," in *Women in the Ottoman Empire*, ed. Madeline C. Zilfi (Leiden: Brill, 1997), 107–8, 123, 126–27.

46. Robert Halsband, ed. *The Complete Letters of Lady Mary Wortley Montagu* (Oxford: Clarendon, 1965), 1:415–27.

47. See Beach, "Lady Mary Wortley Montagu and Slavery in the Ottoman (and the British) Empire," 300–302.

48. Despite its conservative and royalist tendencies, Toryism enabled a mode of early modern feminism that sought to avoid the gender-exclusive language of republican "liberty." See Patricia Springborg, ed. *Mary Astell: Theorist of Freedom from Domination* (Cambridge: Cambridge UP, 2005), esp. Hilda L. Smith, "'Cry up Liberty': The Political Context for Mary Astell's Feminism," in *Mary Astell: Reason, Gender, Faith*, eds. William Kolbrener and Michal Michelson (Burlington, VT: Ashgate, 2007), 193–204; and Catherine Gallagher, "Embracing the Absolute: The Politics of the Female Subject in Seventeenth-Century England," *Genders* 1 (1988): 24–39.

49. See Gallagher, "Embracing the Absolute: The Politics of the Female Subject in Seventeenth Century England," 38.

50. See Bridget Hill, *The First English Feminist: "Reflections upon Marriage" and Other Writings by Mary Astell* (Aldershot, UK: Gower Publishing, 1986).

51. On Tory authors' contribution to the broader history of English freethinking, in which unbelief is compatible with orthodox adherence to the Anglican church, see Sarah Ellenzweig, *The Fringes of Belief: English Literature, Ancient Heresy, and the Politics of Freethinking, 1660–1760* (Stanford: Stanford UP, 2008), esp., chap. 2, 53–79.

52. On the domestication of tea and the tea table as crucial to the cultural formation of eighteenth-century White upper-class female subjectivity, see Elizabeth Kowaleski-Wallace, *Consuming Subjects: Women, Shopping, and Business in the Eighteenth Century* (New York: Columbia UP, 1997), 19–69; on the differences between the tea table and the coffeehouse, see 23–24.

53. See Lady Mary Wortley Montagu's letter to the Countess of Bute in *The Let-*

ters and Works of Lady Mary Wortley Montagu, ed. Lord Wharncliffe (London, 1837), 4:184.

54. On Mary Astell and the tradition of radical Tory feminism, see Patricia Springborg, *Mary Astell*, and Hilda Smith, "'Cry up Liberty,'" 204.

55. All citations to "Reflections upon Marriage" are from *Astell: Political Writings*, ed. Patricia Springborg (Cambridge: Cambridge UP, 1996), 1–80. The quotation from Hobbes is taken from the editor's n. 5 (11). In n. 6 (11) Springborg includes a quotation from Whiston's *A New Theory of the Earth, From its Original, to the Consummation of all Things* (1696), 4.2.25, that Astell references: "[T]he Female [of the antediluvian period] was then very different from what she is now; particularly she was in a state of greater Equality with the Male."

56. On seventeenth-century Englishwomen's pious use of an alternative exegesis of Christian scripture in their arguments against patriarchy, see Patricia Crawford, *Women and Religion in England, 1500–1720* (London: Routledge, 1993), 73–97, esp. 94.

57. The differences between the Qur'anic and Pauline traditions of veiling is discussed in Bernadette Andrea, "Women and Their Rights: Gülen's Gloss on Lady Montagu's 'Embassy' to the Ottoman Empire," in *Muslim Citizens of the Globalized World*, ed. Robert A. Hunt and Yüksel A. Aslandoğan (Somerset, NJ: The Light, 2007), 161–82, esp. 170–71.

58. On the early-seventeenth-century response to the querelle des femmes, prompted by the publication of John Swetnam's misogynist pamphlet *The Arraignment of Women* (1615), see Rachel Speght's *A Mouzell for Melastomus* (1617), the earliest response to Swetnam that reinterprets the Genesis creation story and the Pauline injunctions for women's submission to men from a feminist perspective. Margaret Askew Fell Fox's *Womens Speaking Justified, Proved and Allowed of by the Scriptures* (1667) could be seen as the culmination of the querelle des femmes. In this feminist polemic, Fox protests women's exclusion from church involvement by reinterpreting the Pauline injunctions against women's public preaching.

59. On Astell's occasional skepticism and radical Protestant attitude toward "corrupt" Anglican clergymen, priestly confessors, and spiritual guides, see Sarah Apetrei, "Call No Man Master Upon Earth": Mary Astell's Tory Feminism and an Unknown Correspondence," *Eighteenth-Century Studies* 41.4 (2008): 507–23. On Astell's unintentional appropriation of heterodox ideas—particularly from Spinoza—see Sarah Ellenzweig, "The Love of God and the Radical Enlightenment: Mary Astell's Brush with Spinoza," *Journal of the History of Ideas* 64.3 (2003): 379–97.

60. Late-seventeenth-century feminists adopted a rationalist, Cartesian rhetoric that become increasingly unpopular by the early eighteenth century, a period that witnessed "feminine" sentimental writings that displaced an older "rationalist" feminism. This emerging sentimental tradition resulted in a political compromise for women writers: "feminine" genres such as the novel may have established the worth of female perceptions and emotions, but it also confined women to an "inferior" genre not taken seriously by men. Thus, women's views became frivolous compared

to "manly" genres of rational and political importance. See Hilda Smith, *Reason's Disciples: Seventeenth-Century English Feminists* (Urbana: U of Illinois P, 1982), 16, 201–3, 206, and Katharine M. Rogers, *Feminism in Eighteenth-Century England* (Urbana: U of Illinois P, 1982), 22–23, 103, 119–47, 171.

61. Fidelis Morgan, *A Woman of No Character: An Autobiography of Mrs. Manley* (London: Faber and Faber, 1986), 144.

62. According to Manley's account, Sir Roger Manley authored the first two volumes of the English translation of Giovanni Paolo Marana's *Letters Writ by a Turkish Spy*. She may have confused her father's continuation of *The Turkish History* (1687), written by Richard Knolles and Sir Paul Rycant, with Marana's *The Turkish Spy*. See Morgan, *A Woman of No Character,* 29, 37. In *Persian Letters Before Montesquieu,* Gustave Leopold Van Roosbroeck entertains the possibility that Roger Manley could have been one among three authors who wrote *The Turkish Spy* and refined the genre of the Persian letter (45). Also see Roger Manley, "The History of the Turkish Empire Continued," in *Turkish History,* 6th ed. Richard Knolles (London, 1687), 277–338.

63. A revisionist account of Manley's political career is provided in Rachel Carnell, *A Political Biography of Delarivier Manley* (London: Pickering & Chatto, 2008). On *Almyna,* see 152.

64. On *The Arabian Nights Entertainment* as a crucial context for *Almyna,* see Bernadette Andrea, *Women and Islam in Early Modern English Literature,* 91–104; Ros Ballaster's *Fabulous Orients: Fictions of the East in England, 1662–1785* (Oxford: Oxford UP, 2005), 85; and Bridget Orr, *Empire and the English Stage, 1660–1714* (Cambridge: Cambridge UP, 2001), 131–34.

65. For example, Bernadette Andrea forcefully argues that "Almyna/Manley may be termed the inaugural English(ed) Scheherazade." See *Women and Islam in Early Modern English Literature,* 101. Indeed, Manley suggests this connection in her preface to the play: "The Fable is taken from the Life of that great Monarch, *Caliph Valid Almanzor,* who Conquer'd *Spain,* with something of a Hint from the *Arabian* Nights Entertainments" (97).

66. All citations from *Almyna* are from Ruth Herman's edition, *The Selected Works of Delarivier Manley* (London: Pickering & Chatto, 2005), 5:93–168.

67. Andrea, *Women and Islam in Early Modern English Literature,* 103.

68. Ballaster, *Fabulous Orients,* 87.

69. The Qur'an states that men and women are spiritually equal because they are physically "created of a single soul." See 4:1 and 39:6 in the Qur'an and Glasse, *The Concise Encyclopedia of Islam,* 420.

70. Ruth Herman. *The Business of a Woman: The Political Writings of Delarivier Manley* (Delaware: U of Delaware P, 2003), 182, 198.

71. John Dennis, "An Essay on the Opera's After the Italian Manner, which are about to be Establish'd on the English Stage: with some Reflections on the Damage which they may bring to the Publick," in *The Critical Works of John Dennis,* ed. Edward Niles Hooker (Baltimore: The Johns Hopkins UP, 1939), 1:389–90.

72. See *The London Stage: 1660–1800,* ed. Charles Beecher Hogan (Carbondale: Southern Illinois UP, 1960–68), 1:clvii, 135.

73. On Giovanni's *Camilla*, see Donald Jay Grout and Hermine Weigel Williams, *A Short History of the Opera* (New York: Columbia UP, 2003), 232–33.

74. On Elizabeth Barry's professional career in the theater, see Philip H. Highfill Jr., Kalman A. Burnim, and Edward A. Langhans, *A Biographical Dictionary of Actors, Actresses, Musicians, Dancers, Managers, and Other Stage Personal in London: 1600–1800* (Carbondale: Southern Illinois UP, 1973), 1:318, and Paula R. Backscheider, "Barry, Elizabeth (1656/8–1773)," *Oxford Dictionary of National Biography* (2004), http://www.oxforddnb.com.proxy.library.vanderbilt.edu/view/article/1557, accessed Apr. 8 2011.

75. See Highfill et al., *A Biographical Dictionary*, 271–75.

76. See Felicity Nussbaum, *Rival Queens: Actresses, Performances, and the Eighteenth-Century British Theater* (Philadelphia: U of Pennsylvania P, 2010), 17.

77. On actress's bodies as proxies for competing versions of classical republican virtue, see ibid., 92–121. A detailed account of Barry's sexual promiscuity, frequently satirized in print as an example of her status as a prostitute and unorthodox libertine, is discussed in Highfill et al., *A Biographical Dictionary*, 318–20.

78. On Barry's relationship with Rochester and its effect on her acting career, see. Highfill et al., *A Biographical Dictionary*, 313–15.

79. See Carnell, *A Political Biography of Delarivier Manley*, 152. A biography of Elizabeth Montagu is included in Mary L. Boyle, *Biographical Notices of the Portraits at Hinchingbrook* (London: Victoria Press, 1876), 99–107.

80. See Charles Blount's letter to Rochester dated December 1678 in *The Letters of John Wilmot, Earl of Rochester*, ed. J. Treglown (Oxford: Oxford UP, 1980), 206–16. Also see Blount's preface to *A Just Vindication of Learning* (London, 1680). Christopher Hill coins the term *radical royalists* to describe late-seventeenth-century royalist supporters—such as Rochester—attracted to an interregnum radical tradition as emblematized in Stubbe's writings. See *The Collected Essays of Christopher Hill* (Amherst: U of Massachusetts P, 1985), 1:275–316. On the Rochester's place in the broader history of Tory freethinking, see Sarah Ellenzweig, *The Fringes of Belief*, 31–51.

81. Hilda Smith and Catherine Gallagher presume that Toryism was a hermetically sealed ideology that avoids heterodox thought, and thus, their explanatory accounts of Tory feminism marginalize the importance of radical theologies, scientific materialism, and libertine skepticism in Tory women's writings. See Hilda L. Smith, *Reason's Disciples, Reason's Disciples: Seventeenth-Century English Feminists* (Urbana: U of Illinois P, 1982), chap. 1, and Gallagher, "Embracing the Absolute." On the difficulty of sorting Whig-deist writings from Tory Anglican writings, see Roger D. Lund, "Introduction," *The Margins of Orthodoxy: Heterodox Writing and Cultural Response, 1660–1750*, ed. Roger D. Lund (Cambridge: Cambridge UP, 1995), 1–29.

82. On Tory radicalism, see Eveline Cruickshanks, *Political Untouchables: The Tories and the '45* (London, 1979); Linda Colley, *In Defense of Oligarchy: The Tory Party, 1714–60* (Cambridge: Cambridge UP, 1982); her "Eighteenth-Century English Radicalism before Wilkes," *Transactions of the Royal Historical Society*, 5th series, 31 (1981): 1–20; and Jonathan Clark, *The Dynamics of Change: the Crisis of the 1750s and English Party* (Cambridge: Cambridge UP, 1982).

On Tory radicalism and the Whig interpretation of history, see J. G. A. Pocock, "The Varieties of Whiggism," in *Virtue, Commerce, and History* (Cambridge: Cambridge UP, 1985), 215–310; Robert M. Zaller, "The Continuity of British Radicalism in the Seventeenth and Eighteenth Centuries," *Eighteenth-Century Life* 6. 2–3 (1981): 17–38; and Christine Gerrard, *The Patriot Opposition to Walpole: Politics, Poetry, and National Myth, 1725–1742* (Oxford: Clarendon Press, 1994), 20–27. On the literary culture of Tory freethinking, see Sarah Ellenzweig, *The Fringes of Belief.*

83. The period 1660–1714 was successful for England's Levant Company in its tighter control of the Mediterranean, Austrian, and Ottoman markets in the eighteenth century. See Paul Cernovodeanu, *England's Trade Policy in the Levant and Her Exchange of Goods with the Romanian Countries under the latter Stuarts* (Bucharest: Academy of the Socialist Republic of Romania, 1972), 125–26. For further information, see *The Oxford History of the British Empire*, gen. ed. William Roger Lewis; vol. 2, *The Eighteenth Century*, ed. P. J. Marshall (Oxford: Oxford UP, 1998–99).

84. On Montagu's travels as a symbolic form of national inoculation against the East, parallel to Montagu's introduction of Turkish small pox inoculation in eighteenth-century Britain, see Srinivas Aravamudan, "Lady Mary Wortley Montagu in the *Hammam*," 90–91.

85. On British interests in the Treaty of Passarowitz, see Alfred Cecil Wood, *A History of the Levant Company* (New York: Barnes & Noble, 1964), 132, 174.

Chapter 3 • In Defense of the Ancient Mughal Constitution

Epigraph. "Speech on the Opening of Impeachment 15 February 1788," *The Writings and Speeches of Edmund Burke*, gen. ed. Paul Longford, vol. 6, ed. P. J. Marshall (Oxford: Clarendon Press, 1991), 353. Unless otherwise noted, all citations from Burke's speeches refer to this edition.

1. In *Ideology and Empire in Eighteenth-Century India: The British in Bengal* (Cambridge: Cambridge University Press, 2007), Robert Travers argues that, c. 1760, the colonial discourse of British India sought political legitimacy by presenting England as defending the declining Mughal empire's "ancient constitution." According to Travers, this discourse challenged entrenched stereotypes about "Oriental despotism" but eventually lost momentum in the 1780s and '90s.

2. On recent scholarship that challenges the commonplace view that Burke founded modern conservatism, see the collected essays in *An Imaginative Whig: Reassessing the Life and Thought of Edmund Burke*, ed. Ian Crowe (Columbia: U of Missouri P, 2005), esp. Frederick G. Whelan's essay: "Burke, India, and Orientalism," 127–57.

For a broader treatment of Burke's political philosophy in dynamic relationship to his engagement with Indian affairs, see Frederick Whelan, *Edmund Burke and India* (Pittsburgh: U of Pittsburgh P, 1996).

3. The following works examine how the impeachment scandal served as a public forum to stage, interrogate, and consolidate British imperial rule and theories of national sovereignty: Nicholas B. Dirks, *The Scandal of Empire: India and the Creation of*

Imperial Britain (Cambridge, MA: Harvard UP, 2006); Daniel O'Quinn, *Staging Governance: Theatrical Imperialism in London, 1770–1800* (Baltimore: The Johns Hopkins UP, 2005), 164–221; Anna Clark, *Scandal: The Sexual Politics of the British Constitution* (Princeton, NJ: Princeton UP, 2004), 84–112; and Sara Suleri, *The Rhetoric of English India* (Chicago: U of Chicago P, 1992), 24–74.

4. Antoinette M. Burton, "Introduction: On the Inadequacy and Indispensability of the Nation," in *After the Imperial Turn: Thinking with and through the Nation*, ed. Antoinette Burton (Durham, NC: Duke UP, 2003) 1–23, qtd. 2–3.

5. On the dynamic interrelationship between English metropole and Indian periphery, nation and empire, see H. V. Bowen, *The Business of Empire: The East India Company, 1756–1833* (Cambridge: Cambridge UP, 2006); Sudipta Sen, *Distant Sovereignty: National Imperialism and the Origins of British India* (New York: Routledge, 2002); Seema Alavi, "Introduction," *The Eighteenth Century in India*, ed. Seema Alavi (Oxford: Oxford UP, 2002), 1–56; and Peter J. Marshall, "Britain and the World in the Eighteenth Century: IV The Turning Outwards of Britain," *Transactions of the Royal Historical Society*, 6th ser., 11 (2001): 1–15.

6. On the formation of an Eastern empire based on cross-cultural, cross-religious alliances in response to the loss of an Atlantic empire, see Peter J. Marshall, *The Making and Unmaking of Empire: Britain, India, and America c. 1750–1783* (Oxford: Oxford UP, 2005).

7. Works that notably document crucial instances of Indo-Islamic cosmopolitanism among EIC officials living in eighteenth-century British India, focusing on moments of cross-cultural, cross-religious exchange rather than racial antagonism, include William Dalrymple, *White Mughals: Love and Betrayal in Eighteenth-Century India* (New York: Viking, 2002) and Maya Jasanoff, *Edge of Empire: Lives, Cultures, and Conquest in the East, 1750–1850* (New York: Knopf, 2005), 17–44. Robert Travers (*Ideology and Empire in Eighteenth-Century India*) notes that Indo-Islamic cosmopolitanism coexists alongside moments of colonial racism: "Languages of cross-cultural reconciliation always coexisted with fierce denunciations of the inherent corruption of Asiatic peoples. And the search for points of connection with Indian tradition was cut across by the need to draw clear distinctions between colonizer and colonized" (28). For a more balanced perspective on the role of a cosmopolitan deism in the formation of a British imperial "rhetoric of benevolence," see Christopher A. Bayly, "Van Leur and the Indian Eighteenth Century," in *On the Eighteenth Century as a Category of Asian History*, eds. Leonard Blusse and F. S. Gaastra (Brookfield, VT: Ashgate, 1998), 289–302; "The First Age of Global Imperialism, 1760–1830," *Journal of Imperial and Commonwealth History* 26.2 (1998): 28–47, esp. 39–40; and *Empire and Information: Intelligence Gathering and Social Communication in India, 1780–1870* (Cambridge: Cambridge UP, 1996). For a more tempered view of Burke as a periodic defender of empire in spite of his cosmopolitan and multicultural ethos, see Margaret Kohn and Daniel I. O'Neill, "A Tale of Two Indias: Burke and Mill on Empire and Slavery in the West Indies and America," *Political Theory* 34.2 (2006), 192–228.

8. Travers, *Ideology and Empire in Eighteenth-Century India*, 19.

9. The Hastings trial was a gigantic public spectacle that attracted huge crowds. For example, *The World* (Feb. 18, 1788) praised his speech as "the work of a Master . . . a MAP, as it were, of the MORAL World," and describes his argument against arbitrary power as "glorious indeed!—he called together all the forces of Truth and Equity." Qtd. in F. P. Lock, ed., *Edmund Burke: Volume II, 1784–1797* (Oxford: Clarendon Press, 2006), 156.

10. On the development of Burke's political concepts and arguments from an earlier English Common Law tradition, see J. G. A. Pocock, "Burke and the Ancient Constitution—A Problem in the History of Ideas," *Historical Journal* 3.2 (1960): 125–43.

11. On the widespread uses of legal histories of the ancient constitution in creating and defining Anglo-American conceptions of liberty, see John Phillip Reid, *The Ancient Constitution and the Origins of Anglo-American Liberty* (Dekalb: Northern Illinois UP, 2005).

12. British officials heavily relied on extensive networks of indigenous knowledge to secure their political position throughout most of the Indian subcontinent under the legitimacy of former Mughal and pre-Mughal rulers. See Bayly, *Empire and Information*, 52–53, and Travers, *Ideology and Empire in Eighteenth-Century India*, 1–66. On British Orientalist and Bengal Supreme Court judge Sir William Jones and his role in refining Anglo-Indian comparative law for the purpose of facilitating British rule in Bengal, see David Ibbetson, "Sir William Jones as Comparative Lawyer," in *Sir William Jones 1746–1794: A Commemoration*, ed. Alexander Murray (Oxford: Oxford UP, 1998), 19–42.

13. Warren Hastings, *The Defence of Warren Hastings* (London, 1786), 106.

14. Warren Hastings, *Memoirs relative to the state of India. A new edition, with additions* (London, 1786), 158. For more information on Hastings's position on the need for arbitrary governance in India as distinct from the application of common law in Britain, see 158–60.

15. Charles-Louis de Secondat Montesquieu. *The Spirit of the Laws,* trans. and eds. Anne M. Cohler, Basia Carolyn Miller, and Harold Samuel Stone (Cambridge: Cambridge UP, 1989), 61–62, 224, 255, 461, 466–68.

16. Burke occasionally subscribes to the Oriental despotism thesis when speaking about India, Turkey, or other Muslim nations: see his "Speech on Moving Resolutions for Conciliation with America" (1775) 2. 126 and "Speech on Bengal Judicature Bill" (1781) 5:140–41; these two speeches were written before Burke undertook a more careful study of India. In the *Reflections,* Burke refers to "the barbarous anarchic despotism of Turkey" and Asiatic "backwardness" (295, 299, 239), and in "Thoughts on French Affairs" he describes "The Republic of Algiers" and "the Republic of the Mammalukes in Egypt" as "a nuisance on the earth for several hundred years" (239). On Burke's use of Oriental despotism, see Whelan, *Edmund Burke and India*, 230–42; his "Burke, India, and Orientalism," 127–57; and Cecil P. Courtney, *Montesquieu and Burke* (Oxford: Basil Blackwell, 1963), 139.

17. See Frederick G. Whelan, "Oriental Despotism: Anquetil-Duperron's Responses to Montesquieu," *History of Political Thought* 22 (2001): 619–47; Peter J. Marshall, *The*

Great Map of *Mankind* (Cambridge, MA: Harvard UP, 1982), 140; and Franco Venturi, "Oriental Depotism," *Journal of the History of Ideas* 24 (1963): 133–42.

18. On the uses and abuses of forensic or legal history in the defense of ancient constitutionalism, see Reid, *The Ancient Constitution and the Origins of Anglo-American Liberty*, 8–16.

19. Great Britain House of Commons, *The minutes of what was offered by Warren Hastings . . . at the bar of the House of Commons* (London, 1786), 38.

20. On this commonplace imperial interpretation of Anglo-Indian history, see Nigel Leask, *British Romantic Writers and the East: Anxieties of Empire* (Cambridge: Cambridge UP, 1992), 100–101.

21. On Burke's creative adoption of anti-Islamic imperialist narratives for the purpose of criticizing the EIC, see Whelan, *Edmund Burke and India*, 249–50.

22. On conquest theories and their legal application to the 1688 revolutionary settlement, see Reid, *The Ancient Constitution and the Origins of Anglo-American Liberty*, 88–103, esp. 91–95.

23. Quoted in Pocock, "Burke and the Ancient Constitution," 138.

24. On Burke's relationship to the cosmopolitan historiography of Edward Gibbon and William Robertson, see Karen O' Brien, *Narratives of Enlightenment: Cosmopolitan History from Voltaire to Gibbon* (New York: Cambridge UP, 1997), 18–19; and Pocock, "Burke and the Ancient Constitution," 139.

25. As a subtle response to Burke and the Hastings trial, William Robertson's *An Historical Disquisition concerning the Knowledge which the ancients had of India* (1791) argues for the sophistication and antiquity of India—including the Arab Muslim conquerors of India—to encourage the benevolent and tolerant rule of the EIC in India. Karen O'Brien (*Narratives of Enlightenment*) treats this works as evidence of Burke's and Robertson's shared cosmopolitan sensibilities (163–64).

26. Richard Bourke argues that Burke's continuous preoccupation with conquest theory became the overarching intellectual framework through which he examined eighteenth-century British domestic and imperial politics throughout his career: "Edmund Burke and the Politics of Conquest," *Modern Intellectual History* 4.3 (2007): 403–32.

27. On George Sale's English translation of the Qur'an as a highly central and influential text in Enlightenment debates about Islam, see Ziad Elmarsafy, *The Enlightenment Qur'an: The Politics of Translation and the Construction of Islam* (Oxford: Oneworld, 2009), esp. 31–32, 37–63, and 80. Sale's authoritative translation was most likely the text Burke alluded to during the trial.

28. On Burke's reliance on revisionist accounts of Tamerlane during the Hastings trial, see Whelan, *Edmund Burke and India*, 247–48.

29. William Davy and Joseph White. "Preface." *Institutes Political and Military . . . by the Great Timour*, trans. William Davy and Joseph White (Oxford: Clarendon Press, 1783), vii.

30. Most Europeans were impressed by the scope of Tamerlane's conquest and admired his institution of virtuous laws, even as they considered him cruel and barba-

rous. One of the earliest sympathetic accounts of Tamerlane as a defender of religious toleration can be found in Albertus Warren's *An Apology for the Discourse of Human reason written by Martin Clifford* (London, 1680), 23. Ignoring most of the earlier historical records on Timur Khan, Nicolas Rowe's *Tamerlane, a Tragedy* (1702) marks a turning point in eighteenth-century representations of Timur Khan: he is depicted as a virtuous leader cast in the mold of William III. This "Whiggish" Tamerlane has "a zeal for religion, moderated by reason, without the rage and fire of persecution" ("Epistle Dedicatory"). John Darby's English translation of Ali Yazdi Sharaf al-Din's *The History of Timur-Bec, known by the name Tamerlain the Great,* trans. John Darby, 2 vols. (London, 1723), indicates Tamerlane's "Enlightened" government, which, according to the Persian author, is based on the egalitarian justice of Islamic law. In *The History of the Life of Tamerlane the Great* (London, 1753), Jean Du Bec depicts the wise Tarter as a republican who promotes "liberty of conscience" against the corruptions of state priestcraft (103). On the Italian humanist image of Tamerlane as a savior-figure who rescued Europe from the Turks, see Eric Voegelin, "Machiavelli's Prince: Background and Formation," *Review of Politics* 12 (1951), 155–64. In *Edmund Burke and India,* Frederick G. Whelan notes that Burke's revisionist portrayal of Timur Khan was usually featured in synchronized English accounts of Tartar-Gothic liberty (248).

31. On the centuries-long impact of the *Artháshastra* on Indian political culture and its subsequent incorporation within Indo-Islamic empires, see Stanley Wolpert, *A New History of India,* 8th ed. (New York: Oxford UP, 2009), 55–61, 115.

32. On the Mughal-Timurid imperial legacy, see Muzaffar Alam, *The Languages of Political Islam: India 1200–1800* (Chicago: U of Chicago P, 2004), 51–54, 81.

33. On the political and legal reinterpretation of Persian historical records for the effective rule of the EIC in Eastern India, post-1757, see Kumkum Chatterjee, "History as Self-Representation: The Recasting of a Political Tradition in Late Eighteenth-Century Eastern India," *Modern Asian Studies* 32.4 (1998): 913–48.

34. "Translator's Dedication," in Henri comte de Boulainvilliers, *The Life of Mahomet* (London, 1731).

35. Elmarsafy, *The Enlightenment Qur'an,* 58.

36. George Sale, "The Preliminary Discourse," in *The Koran: or, Alcoran of Mohammed* (1734; London: Frederick Warne and Co., 1910), xvii–xix. All subsequent citations refer to this edition.

37. Richard Alfred Davenport, "A Sketch of the Life of George Sale," in *The Koran: or, Alcoran of Mohammed,* xv–xvii. On the radical freethinking fascination with Sale's translation, see *Reflections on Mahommedanism, and the Conduct of Mohammed. Occasioned by a late learned translation and exposition of the Koran* (London, 1735), in which the anonymous freethinking author uses Sale's new translation of the Qur'an to argue that Mahomet is a "true and legitimate prophet" who acted under divine providence in overthrowing Christian priestcraft (22). In accordance with God's scheme, Islam anticipates the fulfillment of Protestant history: Mahomet "laid the foundations of a general and thorough Reformation, Conversion, and Re-union in ages to come" (50).

38. See Travers, *Ideology and Empire in Eighteenth-Century India,* 143. On Philip Francis' role in the formulation of a "country" interpretation of the ancient Mughal constitution, see 141–180.

39. For a more detailed account of how Indian affairs gradually assumed centrality in British politics during the reign of King George III, see Peter D. G. Thomas, *George III: King and Politicians, 1760–1770* (Manchester: Manchester UP, 2002), 36, 163–68, 183–84; W. M. Elofson, *The Rockingham Connection and the Second Founding of the Whig Party, 1768–1773* (Montreal: McGill-Queens UP, 1996), 145–58; and H. V. Bowen, *Revenue and Reform: The Indian Problem in British Politics, 1757–1773* (Cambridge: Cambridge UP, 1991).

40. On the Rockinghamite Whigs' search for ideological definition following the new political climate of George III's court, see John Brewer, *Party Ideology and Popular Politics at the Accession of George III* (Cambridge: Cambridge UP, 1976), 77–95.

41. On Philip Francis, oppositional Whiggism, and Wilkite radicalism, see Travers, *Ideology and Empire in Eighteenth-Century India,* 147–49.

42. In 1768, Burke and the Rockinghamite Whigs exploited the radical popularity of the Wilkite cause in order to garner public support, even though they firmly distinguished their position from the extra-parliamentary politics of the radical reform movement. See John Brewer, *Party Ideology and Popular Politics at the Accession of George III,* 257, 263–64. Philip Francis anonymously wrote for the Wilkite cause, popular radicalism, and freedom of the Press.

43. For a detailed account of the North-Fox coalition as a repetition of 1688, see John Aston Cannon, *The Fox-North Coalition: Crisis of the Constitution, 1782–4* (Cambridge: Cambridge UP, 1969), esp. 106–144; On Burke's paranoid reflections on this new "crisis," see 234.

44. On Burke's anticolonialism as culturally rooted in his views on Ireland, see Luke Gibbons, *Edmund Burke and Ireland: Aesthetics, Politics, and the Colonial Sublime* (Cambridge: Cambridge UP, 2003).

45. On the importance of the Begum charges for constitutional theories of British rule in India, see Daniel O'Quinn, *Staging Governance,* 200–21; Anna Clark, *Scandal,* 84–112; Jenny Sharp, *Allegories of Empire: The Figure of Women in the Colonial Text* (Minneapolis: U of Minnesota P, 1993), 67; and Suleri, *Rhetoric of English India,* 24–74.

46. The phrase "sexual metaphorics" is borrowed from Suleri, 61, 70.

47. For a detailed summary of the Begum charges, see Frederick G. Whelan, *Edmund Burke in India,* 177–87 and Peter J. Marshall, *The Impeachment of Warren Hastings* (London: Oxford UP, 1965), 109–110, 116, 122, and 127–8.

48. On the constitutionalist reevaluation of feudal law in eighteenth-century England, see Reid, *The Ancient Constitution and the Origins of Anglo-American Liberty,* 95–99. On the seventeenth-century discovery of the *feudum* as hereditary landed tenures, see J. G. A. Pocock, *The Ancient Constitution and the Feudal Law . . . A Reissue with a Retrospect* (1957; Cambridge: Cambridge UP, 1987), 91–123.

49. On Burke's and Francis's defense of the constitutional rights of female *zemindars,* see Anna Clark, *Scandal,* 263, n. 136.

50. On radical usages of sexual scandals for addressing British constitutional problems, see ibid., 4–6, 15.

51. For a historical overview of the Begums of Oudh as tactful politicians and imperial custodians of civic Islamic virtues, see Richard B. Barnett, "Embattled Begums: Women as Power Brokers in Early Modern India," in *Women in the Medieval Islamic World: Power, Patronage, and Piety*, ed. Gavin R. G. Hambly (New York: St. Martin's Press, 1998), 521–36, and Gregory C. Kozlowski, "Private Lives and Public Piety: Women and the Practice of Islam in Mughal India," in *Women in the Medieval Islamic World*, 469–88.

52. See Burke's letter to Philip Francis, dated Jan. 2, 1787, in *The Correspondence of Edmund Burke*, ed. Holden Furber (London: Cambridge UP, 1965), 5:304–5.

53. *The Speeches of the Late Right Honourable Richard Brinsley Sheridan* (London, 1816), 1:64. All references to Sheridan's Jun. 13, 1788, speech are from this work.

54. On Hastings defense against the Begum charges, see Whelan, *Edmund Burke*, 182.

55. To learn more about the Begums' deviation from orthodox Qur'anic law and Indo-Islamic polity, see Barnett, 532.

56. On the civic, military, and administrative role of the zenana, see Gavin R. G. Hambly, "Armed Women retainers in the Zenanas of Indo-Muslim Rulers: the Case of Bibi Fatima," in *Women in the Medieval Islamic World*, 429–67, esp. 433.

57. The Managers speeches on the sexual politics of the zenana created a political backlash among many Englishwomen who were deeply suspicious of Burke's and Sheridan's patriarchal Whig assumptions. See Daniel O'Quinn, 212–13, and Anna Clark, *Scandal*, 107. Although the Begums were astonished by the course of the trial, they were not moved by Sheridan's speech when Hastings's agent, Major Scott, read them a partial translation. See Linda Kelley, *Richard Brinsley Sheridan: A Life* (London: Sinclair-Stevenson, 1997), 143.

58. On the negative reception of Burke's and Sheridan's trope of female victimization, see Anna Clark, *Scandal*, 103–12, and Daniel O'Quinn, 211–20.

59. Broome, 142.

60. Ibid., 83.

61. Ibid., 84.

62. In contrast to the Ottoman concept of *valide sultan*, Mughal imperial women frequently adopted the sacred title of mothers, such as "Mary" the mother of Jesus, to consolidate "a common, international, Perso-Islamicate political discourse." The Ottoman hierarchal distinction between the *valide sultan*, which has greater political significance, and *haseki*, or favorite female concubine, has no analogue in the sacred titles adopted by Mughal imperial women. See Gregory C. Kozlowski, 471–75.

63. Demestrius Cantemir, *The History of the Growth and Decay of the Ottoman Empire*, trans. Nicholas Tindal (London, 1756), 296.

64. *The Trial of Warren Hastings, Esq.* (London, 1794) 1:71–72.

65. For a detailed summary of Hastings's appointment of Munny Begum and the charges of "presents," see Marshall, *The Impeachment of Warren Hastings*, 138–40.

66. In *A Letter to the Right Honourable Charles James Fox, on the extraneous matter contained in Mr. Burke's Speeches* (London, 1789), Major John Scott contrasts Burke's positive portrayal of Munny Begum in the "Eleventh Report" with his negative views of her in his Apr. and May 1789 impeachment speeches (129–131).

67. On the sexual politics of Queen Charlotte and the regency crisis, see Clark, *Scandal,* 114; L. G. Mitchell, *Charles James Fox and the Disintegration of the Whig Party 1782–1794* (Oxford: Oxford UP, 1971), 134; and *The Prospect before Us. Being a Series of Papers upon the Great Question which now Agitates the Public Mind* (London, 1788), 19.

68. On the inconsistencies that plagued Burke's defense of hereditary royal rights during the regency crisis, see Lock, ed., *Edmund Burke: Volume II, 1784–1797,* 210, and Stanley Ayling, *Edmund Burke: His Life and Opinions* (New York: St. Martin's Press, 1998), 182–92.

69. Qtd. in Lock, ed., *Edmund Burke: Volume II, 1784–1797,* 210, 211. On Burke's December speech on the regency crisis, see 211–12.

70. Burke's alleged involvement in the prince's sexual scandal is briefly discussed in ibid., 206.

71. For a more thorough discussion on Burke's role in the political disintegration of the Foxite Whig party by the end of the regency crisis, see John W. Derry, *The Regency Crisis and the Whigs, 1788–9* (Cambridge: Cambridge UP, 1963), 154–72. Burke's rhetorically excessive defense of the king's hereditary rights in his Feb. 1789 speech alienated members within his party and anticipates his later break with Fox and Sheridan over their defense of the French Revolution. By the time he gave his speech on Munny Begum, he was known as a crypto-royalist among enemies and friends. According to P. J. Marshall and F. P. Lock, the Whig opposition's morale was at an all-time low due to their mishandling of the regency crisis, which prompted serious doubts among the Managers and the public at large about the need to continue with the impeachment proceedings. See Marshall, *The Impeachment of Warren Hastings,* 78 and Lock, ed., *Edmund Burke: Volume II, 1784–1797,* 223.

72. See Travers, *Ideology and Empire in Eighteenth-Century India,* 223, 221.

73. The antideist theology of Burke's *Reflections* is a product of his earlier views in the 1740s. See Burke's "An Extempore commonplace on the Sermon of Our Saviour on the Mount," an antideist polemic that justifies the superiority of Christian revelation and scripture over the heathen pagan religions (3); "A Vindication of Natural Society," 4–57; and "Religion," in *Pre-Revolutionary Writings,* ed. Ian Harris (Cambridge: Cambridge UP, 1993), 78–87. Also see Burke's *Speech on the Toleration Bill* 17th March, 1773, 2:387–89.

74. Burke's engagement with India furnished him with the key political concepts through which he came to condemn similar patterns in the French Revolution. See Regina Janes, "Edmund Burke's Flying Leap from India to France," *History of European Ideas* 7 (1986): 509–27.

75. Militarily assisted by revolutionary France, the sultanate of Mysore, which had fought regional wars with the EIC in 1790–92 and 1799, was frequently depicted in

England as Oriental despotism, or the Jacobin terrorist of the East. See Jasanoff, *Edge of Empire,* 149–76.

Chapter 4 • *Ali Bonaparte in Hermetic Egypt*

Epigraphs. William Hamilton Reid, *The Rise and Dissolution of the Infidel Societies in the Metropolis* (1800; repr. Plymouth: Woburn Press, 1971), 2; and William Paley, *The Principles of moral and political philosophy,* 3rd ed. (London, 1786), 395.

1. Walter Savage Landor, "Gebir," *The Complete Works of Walter Savage Landor,* ed. Stephen Wheeler (London: Chapman and Hall, 1927), 13:44, line 193. All subsequent citations of *Gebir* refer to this edition.

2. For an interesting reading of Napoleon's messianic role in *Gebir,* see Simon Bainbridge, *Napoleon and English Romanticism* (Cambridge: Cambridge UP, 1995), 45.

3. *Copies of Original Letters from the Army of General Bonaparte in Egypt, intercepted by the Fleet under the command of Admiral Nelson,* 2nd ed. (London, 1798), 245. All subsequent citations refer to this edition. Published anonymously by the British government as anti-opposition, antiradical propaganda, this popular collection of intercepted French letters—reprinted in eight editions—shames English "opposition writers" for their admiration of Bonaparte's policies in Egypt and elsewhere. As such, the July proclamation was meant to be read as incriminating evidence of a radical Jacobin-Muslim alliance.

4. On Bonaparte's Egyptian proclamations and his ties to radical Enlightenment and deist debates about Islam, see Ziad Elmarsafy, *The Enlightenment Qur'an: The Politics of Translation and the Construction of Islam* (Oxford: Oneworld Publications, 2009), 143–157, and Juan Cole, *Napoleon's Egypt: Invading the Middle East* (New York: Palgrave Macmillan, 2007), 30–33, 217.

5. Simon Bainbridge points out that Landor could not have incorporated knowledge about Napoleon's Egyptian Campaign by the time he published *Gebir,* since, in June, Bonaparte's whereabouts still remained a mystery. Based on this information, however, one cannot conclude that the French occupation of Egypt does not serve as a significant cultural and political context for the reception of this poem in late 1798–99. See Bainbridge, *Napoleon and English Romanticism,* 32.

6. The original Arabic manuscript cannot be located. On the authenticity of this book, see Bernard Lewis and Stanley Burstein, eds., introduction, *Land of Enchanters: Egyptian Short Stories from the Earliest Times to the Present Day* (Princeton, NJ: Markus Wiener, 2001), 122, and Fatma Moussa Mahmoud, "The Arabic Original of Landor's *Gebir,*" *Cairo Studies in English* (1960): 69–86.

7. On the humanistic and syncretic aspects of medieval Islamic histories, see Lenn E. Goodman, *Islamic Humanism* (Oxford: Oxford UP, 2003), 1–29, specifically chap. 4, "The Rise of Universal Historiography," 161–211.

8. M. O. Grendy, "Orientalism and Propaganda: The Oriental Tale and Popular Politics in Late Eighteenth-Century Britain," *The Eighteenth-century Novel* 2 (2002): 215–37; Srinivas Aravamudan, "In the Wake of the Novel: The Oriental Tale as Na-

tional Allegory," *Novel: A Forum on Fiction* 33.1 (1999): 5–31; and Arthur J. Weitzman, "The Oriental Tale in the Eighteenth Century: A Reconsideration," *Studies in Voltaire and the Eighteenth Century* 58 (1967): 1839–55.

9. On Landor's inability to produce a sustained anticolonial rhetoric in *Gebir*, see Nigel Leask, *British Romantic Writers and the East: Anxieties of Empire* (Cambridge: Cambridge UP, 1992), 25–26, and Alan Richardson, "Epic Ambivalence: Imperial Politics and Romantic Deflections in William's *Peru* and Landor's *Gebir*," *Romanticism, Race, and Imperial Culture, 1780–1834*, eds. Alan Richardson and Sonia Hofkosh (Bloomington: Indiana UP, 1996), 265–82.

10. On the formation of Anglican imperialism in the 1790s, see Rowan Strong, *Anglicanism and the British Empire, c. 1700–1850* (Oxford: Oxford UP, 2007), 118.

11. On the widespread cultural and literary significance of alchemical-hermetic philosophies for eighteenth-century literature and British Romantic poetry, see Jennifer N. Wunder, *Keats, Hermeticism, and the Secret Societies* (Aldershot, UK: Ashgate, 2008), esp. chap. 2, "The Secret Societies and the Romantic Cultural Context," 47–67; and Marie Roberts, *British Poets and Secret Societies* (London: Croom Helm, 1986), 88–101.

12. John Davies, dedication, *The Egyptian History, treating of the Pyramids, the Inundation of the Nile, and other Prodigies of Egypt*, by Murtada Ibn al-Khafif (London, 1672), 2–3.

13. Anthony Wood, *Athenae Oxonienis*, new ed. 4 vols. (London, 1813–20), 904.

14. A. Chalmers, *The General Biographical Dictionary*, new ed. (London: J. Nichols and Son, 1812–17).

15. Christopher Hill, *The Century of Revolution, 1603–1714* (1961; London: Sphere Books, 1969), 124–26.

16. H. J. Rose, *A New General Biographical Dictionary* (1853).

17. Wood, *Athenae, Athenae Oxonienis*, 905.

18. Francis Yates, *The Rosicrucian Enlightenment* (London: Routledge, 1972), 194.

19. Qtd. in G. H. Turnbull, "Johann Valentin Andreae's Societas Christiana," *Zeitschrift Fur Deutsche Philologie* 74 (1955): 161, 164–65.

20. Charles Webster, *The Great Instauration: Science, Medicine and Reform, 1626–1660* (New York: Holmes and Meier, 1975), 42–43, 50.

21. Ibid., 69–70.

22. G. H. Turnbull, "John Hall's Letters to Samuel Hartlib," *The Review of English Studies*, n.s., 4.15 (1953): 222–24. In his letters, Boyle also approved Hall's proposal to translate the whole of Andreae's *Reipublicae Christianopolitanae*—a project that never materialized. Hall's *Leucenia*, a literary romance that depicts the Protestant Commonwealth and the establishment of a secret college, was a work much appraised by Boyle.

23. Webster, *The Great Instauration*, 58, 99, and Betty Jo Teeter Dobbs, *The Foundations of Newton's Alchemy, or the Hunting of the Greene Lyon* (Cambridge: Cambridge UP, 1975), 80.

24. Christopher Hill, *The World Turned Upside Down* (New York: The Viking Press, 1972), 240.

25. Christopher Hill, *Intellectual Origins of the English Revolution* (Oxford: Clarendon, 1965), 123, 174.

26. Turnbull, "John Hall's Letters," 226–27. He claims that in John Davies's biography it is stated that Hall was "intimately acquainted" with More at Cambridge. As a way of interesting More in joining the "Office of Address," Hall introduced Hartlib to More as early as Oct. 1647. More's first letter to Hartlib is dated Nov. 1648.

27. Dobbs, *The Foundations of Newton's Alchemy*, 105–10, 118–19.

28. Webster, *The Great Instauration*, 152. Interested in promoting Oriental studies, the Parliament provided Hartlib with five hundred pounds to purchase a collection of Oriental books as well as an additional forty or fifty pounds for the printing of Arabic books. On the links between Hartlib's collection of hermetic books and the utopian politics of the English Commonwealth, see Stephen Clvcas, "Samuel Hartlib's Ephemerides, 1635–59, and the Pursuit of Scientific and Philosophical Manuscripts: The Religious Ethos of an Intelligencer," *Seventeenth Century* 6.1 (1991): 33–55.

29. For a thorough discussion on the legacy of Arabic Islam in late seventeenth-century Britain, see Nabil Matar, *Islam in Britain, 1558–1685* (Cambridge: Cambridge UP, 1998), 73–119, Justin Champion, *The Pillars of Priestcraft Shaken: The Church of England and Its Enemies, 1660–1730* (Cambridge: Cambridge UP, 1992), 99–169, and David A. Pauline, *Attitudes to Other Religions* (Manchester: Manchester UP, 1984), 81–104, 121–36. On English and European radicals interested in using Ibn Tufayl's work as evidence for a freethinking tradition grounded in the Greco-Arabia philosophical legacy, see Jonathan Israel, *Enlightenment Contested: Philosophy, Modernity, and the Emancipation of Man, 1670–1752* (Oxford: Oxford UP, 2006), 628–31.

30. On the Quaker fascination with Ibn Tufayl's book, see Nawal Muhammad Hassan, *Hayy Bin Yaqzan and Robinson Crusoe: A Study of an Early Arabic Impact on English Literature* (Baghdad: Al-Rashid House, 1980), 5–6. In *The True Christian Divinity* (1678), the Quaker apologist Robert Barclay identifies the views expressed in *Hayy ibn Yaqzan* with the Quaker teachings of the "inner light."

31. On the connection between Quakerism and Mahometanism, seen as two heresies that share the same republican spirit, see Francis Bugg, *Hidden things brought to light, whereby the Fox is unkennell'd: and the bowells of Quakerism ript up, laid open, and expos'd to publick view* (London, 1707), 175, 202, and *Life and Actions of Mahomet in Four Treatises concerning Mahometanism* (London, 1712), 29. A discussion on Islam and Quakerism in seventeenth-century England is provided in Nabil Matar, "Some Notes on George Fox and Islam," *The Journal of the Friends' Historical Society* 55 (1989): 271–76.

32. Webster, *The Great Instauration*, 86, 93–7.

33. Hill, *Intellectual Origins of the English Revolution*, 127, and *Change and Continuity in Seventeenth-Century England* (Cambridge, MA: Harvard UP, 1975), 175.

34. Murtada, *The Egyptian History*, 4, 63.

35. Lewis, Bernard and Stanley Burstein, eds. *Land of Enchanters: Egyptian Short Stories from the Earliest Times to the Present Day* (Princeton, NJ: Markus Wiener, 2001), 8–11, 122.

36. Landor, "The Birth of Poesy," *The Complete Works of Walter Savage Landor*, ed.

Stephen Wheeler (London: Chapman and Hall, 1927), 16:239, lines 458–60. All subsequent citations refer to this edition.

37. Murtada, *The Egyptian History*, 137, 239.

38. Malcolm Elwin, *Landor: A Replevin* (London: Macdonald, 1958), 82.

39. Landor, "Extract from the French Preface," *The Complete Works of Walter Savage Landor*, ed. Stephen Wheeler (London: Chapman and Hall, 1927), 15:434.

40. See Frances A. Yates, *Giordano Bruno and the Hermetic Tradition* (1964; repr. Chicago: U of Chicago P, 1979), 367–73, and Martin Bernal, *Black Athena: The Afroasiatic Roots of Classical Civilization* (London: Free Association Books, 1987), 1: 146,176, 184.

41. For an illuminating discussion on Bonaparte's propagandistic use of Islam and Ottoman political rhetoric during his occupation of Egypt, see Cole, *Napoleon's Egypt*, 73–75, 123–26, 131.

42. Ibid., 134–35, 140.

43. The following works provide a helpful brief survey of the key concepts and doctrines of Mahdism in Islamic messianic thought: Heinz Halam, *The Shi'ites: A Short History*, trans. Allison Brown (Princeton, NJ: Markus Wiener, 2007), 34–37; John L. Esposito, *Islam: The Straight Path* (New York: Oxford UP, 1991), 46–48, 120; and Abdulaziz Abdulhussein Sachedina, *Islamic Messianism: The Idea of the Mahdi in Twelver Shi'ism* (Albany: State U of New York P, 1981), 1–14.

44. Qtd. in Cole, *Napoleon's Egypt*, 130.

45. Ibid., 141–42.

46. On the cross-cultural dimensions to Franco-Egyptian republicanism during the Festival of the Nile, see Maya Jasanoff, *Edge of Empire: Lives, Cultures, and Conquest in the East, 1750–1850* (New York: Knopf, 2005), 138–48.

47. Cole, *Napoleon's Egypt*, 130.

48. *Copies of Original Letters from the Army of General Bonaparte in Egypt*, xi.

49. Ibid., 20, 31.

50. *The Life of Mahomet*, 187.

51. Ibid., 182.

52. Ibid., 196.

53. Qtd. in Elwin, *Landor*, 70.

54. Ibid., 289–93.

55. Ibid., 47–48.

56. Margaret Jacob, *Living the Enlightenment: Freemasonry and Politics in Eighteenth-Century Europe* (New York: Oxford UP, 1991), 56–58.

57. Qtd. in ibid., 174.

58. William Warburton, *The Divine Legation of Moses demonstrated, on the principles of a religious deist* (London, 1742), 2:155–56, 200–201. All subsequent citations refer to this edition.

59. Robert M. Ryley, *William Warburton* (Boston: Twayne, 1984), 31, and Paolo Rossi, *The Dark Abyss of Time: The History of the Earth and the History of Nations from Hooke to Vico*, trans. Lydia G. Cochrane (Chicago: U of Chicago P, 1984), 243–44.

60. On the significance of speculative mythologies among Freemason Whigs and

deists, see Margaret C. Jacob, *The Radical Enlightenment: Pantheists, Freemasons and Republicans* (London: George Allen & Unwin, 1981), 142–81.

61. George Sale, ed. and trans., *The Koran commonly called Al Koran of Mohammed 1734* (London: Frederick Warne and Co., 1910), 345, 489.

62. Ibid., 488–89.

63. Mohammed Sharafuddin, *Islam and Romantic Orientalism* (London: I. B. Tauris, 1994), 12–14.

64. Qtd. in Elwin, *Landor*, 66–68.

65. Thomas Paine, *The Age of Reason* (Secaucus: Carol Publishing Group, 1998), 50–51. Paine makes the following point after discussing Trinitarian Christianity: "It has been the scheme of the Christian Church, and of all the other invented systems of religion, to hold man in ignorance of the Creator, as it is of Governments to hold man in ignorance of his rights. The system of the one are as false as those of the other, and are calculated for mutual support" (187).

66. Paine, *The Age of Reason*, 5.

67. Elwin, *Landor*, 77.

68. Qtd. in John Forster, *Walter Savage Landor: A Biography*, 2 vols. (London: Chapman and Hall, 1869), 1:166.

69. Ibid.,123.

70. Ibid., 158.

71. Paine, *Rights of Man* (Mineola: Dover Publications, 1999), 158.

72. Thomas Paine, "Origin of Freemasonry," *The Life and Works of Thomas Paine*, 10 vols., ed. William M. Van der Weyde (New Rochelle: Thomas Paine National Historical Association, 1925), 5:9: 171–72, 185.

73. Paine, *The Age of Reason*, 60.

74. On Paine's possible affiliation with radical Whig politics and freemasonry, see Jacob, *The Radical Enlightenment*, 154.

75. Paine, *The Age of Reason*, 80.

76. Paine, *Rights of Man*, 28–30.

77. In his essay titled "Notes on Walter Savage Landor (part II)," De Quincey makes the following remarks about the theological views that appear in Landor's "Melanchthon and Calvin," a subsection of the *Imaginary Conversations*: "if [Melanchthon's] view of idolatry (as reported by L.) be sound, the Bible must have been at the root of the worst mischief ever yet produced by idolatry. He begins by describing idolatry as *Jewish*, insinuating that it was an irregularity chiefly besetting the Jews." *The Works of Thomas De Quincey*, ed. Robert Morrison (London: Pickering & Chatto, 2003), 16:18–19,

78. Qtd. in Elwin, *Landor*, 64.

79. Leask, *British Romantic Writers and the East*, 26–27, 93–94.

80. Richardson, "Epic Ambivalence," 275–76.

Chapter 5 · *The Flight and Return of Mohammed*

Epigraph. Review of *Helga; A Poem. In Seven Cantos,* by William Herbert. *The Edinburgh Review, or the Critical Journal* 25 (1815): 151.

1. "Mahomet" was first published as a minor "juvenile" poem in his *Poetical Works* (1834). Southey's contribution did not even appear in his self-collected volumes, *Poetical Works* (1837–8); it was first published posthumously in his uncle's (H. Hill) collection of Southey's poems: Robert Southey and Herbert Hill, *Oliver Newman: a New-England tale (unfinished): with other Poetical Remains* (London: Longman, Brown, Green, & Longmans, 1845).

2. On Unitarian politics in England, see George S. Erving, "Coleridge, Priestley, and the Culture of Unitarian Dissent," Ph.D. thesis (U of Washington, 2005), and John Seed, "The Role of Unitarianism in the Formation of Liberal Culture 1775–1851: A Social History," Ph.D. thesis (U of Hull, 1981).

3. I use these terms interchangeably. Both Unitarians and Socinians believe in the necessity of reason and revelation, the rational appeal of the scriptures, the unipersonality of God, Christ's humanity, and the falsity of the Trinity. Earl Morse Wilbur proposes that the term "Socinian" was deployed by orthodox Anglicans as a term of reproach leveled against Unitarian thinkers. See Earl Morse Wilbur, *A History of Unitarianism* (Cambridge, MA: Harvard UP, 1952), 2:222.

4. "An Epistle Dedicatory, to His Illustrious Excellency *Ameth Ben Ameth* Embassador of the Mighty Emperor of *Fez* and *Morrocco,* to *Charles* the 2d, King of *Great Britain,*" in Charles Leslie, *The Socinian Controversy Discuss'd* (London, 1708), iii–xiii. All subsequent citations refer to this edition.

5. According to Alexander Gordon, the term *Unitarian* was first deployed in the 1682 Epistle to the Moroccan ambassador. In that case, the definition of this term was determined by the mode of address to the followers of Muhammad. The first appearance of the term in English print (unlike the Epistle, which was printed many years later) is in Stephen Nye's *Brief History of the Unitarians, called also Socinians in Four Letters, written to a friend* (1687), a Unitarian work in which the term is broadly defined to include all religions that acknowledge the unipersonality of God. See Alexander Gordon, *Heads of English Unitarian History* (1895; repr. Trowbridge: Redwood Press, 1970), 22–24. However, the earliest use of the term dates to Henry Hedworth's *Controversy Ended* (London, 1672–3), in which it describes all Christian heresies. See Wilbur, *A History of Unitarianism,* 199. This earlier occurrence suggests that the term was used before it was redefined by the Unitarian Epistle and Nye's work. At any rate, from the late seventeenth century onward, the term "Unitarian" also referred to Muslims. See "Unitarian" (n. and adj.), *The Oxford English Dictionary.* 2nd ed. 1989; online ed. Mar. 2011, http://www.oed.com.proxy.library.vanderbilt.edu/Entry/214751, accessed Apr. 11, 2011. In "Historical and Critical Reflections on Mahometanism and Socinianism," *Four Treatises concerning the doctrine, discipline, and worship of the Mahometans* (London: J. Darby, 1712), 161–244, Muslims and Socinians are described as "two sects [that] are proud to be call'd *Unitarians*; a name that signifies the same

thing with both parties" (182). By 1794, some Unitarians identified themselves with Islam: "The Mahometans in Europe, and all over the east, are *Unitarians*, believers in, and worshipers of the one only true God." See *Tracts Printed and Published by the Unitarian Society for promoting Christian Knowledge and the Practice of Virtue* (London, 1794), 6:vii–viii. On Islam's crucial role in the Unitarian controversy, see Justin Champion, *The Pillars of Priestcraft Shaken: The Church of England and Its Enemies* (Cambridge: Cambridge UP, 1992), 99–120, and David A. Pailin, *Attitudes to Other Religions: Comparative Religion in Seventeenth- and Eighteenth-Century Britain* (Manchester: Manchester UP, 1984), 99, 129–32, 269–70. Martin Mulsow argues that the Epistle reshaped the social identity of the "New Socinians" in the late seventeenth century, rendering Unitarianism with "an integrative, connective potential, which . . . was able to connect cultures" (60–61). See his "The 'New Socinians': Intertextuality and Cultural Exchange in Late Socinianism," *Socinianism and Arminianism: Antitrinitarians, Calvinists and Cultural Exchange in Seventeenth-Century Europe*, eds. Martin Mulsow and Jan Rohls (Leiden: Brill, 2005), 49–80.

6. The original copy of the tract is found in the Mclachlan library of the Unitarian College in Manchester and contains an inscription by Archbishop Tenison: "These are the Originall papers which a Cabal of Socinians in London offered to present to the Embassadour of ye King of Fez and Morocco, when he was taking leave of England." He further claims that "the Agents of the Socinians" was a "Monsieur de Verzé." "Monsieur de Verzé" may have been Noel Aubert, sieur de Versé (1650–1714), a former Roman Catholic physician and a friend of the English Socinian Christopher Sand. See John McLachlan, *Socinianism in Seventeenth-Century England* (Oxford: Oxford UP, 1951), 319. The above quote is from this work.

7. For an example of the conflation of Unitarianism with Islam, see Francis Cheynell, *The Divine Trinunity of the Father, Son, and Holy Spirit* (London, 1650), 422.

8. See Richard Baxter, *The cure of church-divisions, or, Directions for weak Christians to keep them from being dividers or troublers of the church with some directions to the pastors how to deal with such Christians* (London, 1670), 49.

9. Both Catholic and Protestant polemics against the teachings of Michael Servetus (1511–1532) speculated that he had formed a political alliance with the Turks to overthrow Christendom and facilitate the growth of the Ottoman empire, which was a real political threat at the time. They also believed that Servetus traveled to Africa to learn Arabic among the Moors before writing his first antitrinitarian book, a quasi-Islamic work based on the Qur'an. See Wilbur, *A History of Unitarianism*, 52–54, 71. This theory is also echoed in John Edwards's *The Socinian Creed, or a brief account of the professed tenets and doctrines of the foreign and english socinians* (London, 1697), 22. Faustus Socinus appeared in a very similar light, even during his lifetime. Many anti-Unitarian writers were eager to exploit the fact that Socinus consulted the Qur'an to score polemical points against his opponents. See Francis Cheynell, *The rise, growth, and danger of Socinianisme together with a plaine discovery of a desperate designe of corrupting the Protestant religion* (London, 1643), 31; his *Divine Trinunity of the Father,*

Son, and Holy Spirit, 425; and *Historical and Critical Reflections,* 195. In the case of Paul Alciat, Protestant theologians widely believed that sometime between his trip from Monrovia to Constantinople and back he renounced the Bible and embraced the Qur'an, the text from which he supposedly derived his arguments against the Trinity. See Benedictus Aretius, *A Short History of Valentinus Gentilis* (London, 1696), 20, and Cheynell, *The rise, growth, and danger of Socinianisme,* 11–12.

10. William Freke, *Vindication of the Unitarians, against the late reverend author on the Trinity in a letter* (London, 1690), 29.

11. See Arthur Bury, Preface, *Naked Gospel* (London, 1690).

12. On the persecution of Freke and Bury, see Champion, *The Pillars of Priestcraft Shaken,* 107, 109, and Wilbur, *A History of Unitarianism,* 231.

13. On the Aikenhead trial, see Champion, *The Pillars of Priestcraft Shaken,* 107; Michael M. Hunter, "Aikenhead the Atheist: the Context and Consequences of Articulate Irreligion in the Late Seventeenth Century," in *Atheism from the Reformation to the Enlightenment* (Oxford: Clarendon Press, 1992), 221–54; Leonard W. Levy, *Treason against God: A History of the Offense of Blasphemy* (New York: Schocken Books, 1981), 325–27; and Wilbur, *A History of Unitarianism,* 231–32. In the published proceedings of the trial, Aikenhead was accused of preferring Islam over Christianity and that he publicly claimed that Western Christendom will eventually be extinguished by Mohammedanism. On these recoded comments, see William Cobbett, *A Complete Collection of State Trials,* ed. Thomas Bayly Howell (London: T. C. Hansard, 1812), 13:919.

14. Stephen Nye, *A Letter of Resolution concerning the doctrines of the Trinity and the Incarnation* (London, 1691?), 16–18.

15. Ibid., 18.

16. This orthodox Anglican reading of *A Letter,* in the context of the above passage, is found in two popular anti-Unitarian tracts: John Edward's *The Socinian Creed,* 228, and Edward Stillingfleet's preface to *A Discourse in Vindication of the Doctrine of the Trinity* (London, 1697), lix–lxi. In *Socinian Controversy Discussed* (1708), Leslie is convinced that Nye's views on Islam offer indisputable evidence of a secret conspiracy: the Unitarians seek to "vilifie Christianity" and replace it with Mahometanism (xxviii).

17. Stephen Nye, *A Brief History of the Unitarians, called also Socinians in Four Letters, written to a friend* (London, 1687), 26–29.

18. Ibid., 26–30.

19. See Stillingfleet, lxii; Edwards, *The Socinian Creed,* 14–15, 220; and William Sherlock, *A Vindication of the doctrine of the Holy and ever blessed Trinity and the Incarnation of the Son of God* (London, 1691), 257.

20. Nabil Matar, *Britain and Barbary, 1589–1689* (Gainesville: UP of Florida, 2005), 158.

21. Ibid., 164–65.

22. The following tracts anxiously insist on classifying the Socinians and Muslims in the same heretical camp: Joshua Toulmin, *A Free and Serious Address to the Chris-

tian Laity (London, 1781), 72, 81–2; George Berkeley, *A Caution Against Socinianism* (Canterbury, 1787), 6–7; and *A Testimony and Warning against Socinian and Unitarian Errors* (Glasgow, 1793), 17.

23. Gordon, *Heads of English Unitarian History*, 104.

24. Priestley's part in the controversy is found in his *The Theological and Miscellaneous Works*, vol. 18; for a partisan look at the controversy from both sides, see the two opposed collections: Priestley, *Letters to Dr. Horsley* (Birmingham, 1783–6), and Horsley, *Tracts in Controversy with Dr. Priestley* (Glocester, 1789). On this theological controversy, see Robert E. Schofield, *The Enlightened Joseph Priestley: A Study of His Life and Work from 1773 to 1804* (University Park: Pennsylvania State UP, 2004), 225–29; Wilbur, *A History of Unitarianism*, 303–5; and Gordon, *Heads of English Unitarian History*, 115–17.

25. Samuel Horsley, *Letters from the Archdeacon of Saint Albans, in reply to Dr. Priestley* (London, 1784), 151.

26. Ibid., 152.

27. Joseph Priestley, *Defences of the History of the Corruptions of Christianity* (London, 1786), 161–62.

28. Ibid., 163.

29. Ibid., 163–164. Thomas Emlyn (1663–1741), *The Works of Mr. Thomas Emlyn* (London, 1746), 2:93.

30. Priestley, *Defences of the History of the Corruptions of Christianity*, 162.

31. See note 6.

32. See *Disquistions relating to matter and spirit*, 2nd ed. (Birmingham, 1782), 1:378–79; *Discourses on Various Subjects* (Birmingham, 1787), 191–92, 457–58; *Discourses on the Evidence of Revealed Religions* (London, 1794), 340–41; and *Discourses relating to the Evidence of Revealed Religion* (London, 1796), 330, 336, 343.

33. See David L. Wykes, "Elwall, Edward (*bap.* 1676, *d.* 1744)," *Oxford Dictionary of National Biography* (Oxford University Press, 2004), http://www.oxforddnb.com.proxy.library.vanderbilt.edu/view/article/8775, accessed Apr. 12, 2011. As evidence for the unity of God, Elwall quotes antitrinitarian passages in the Qur'an. He argues that Mahomet disapproves of the Trinity because he "detests and abominates those who make God to have an Equal." See Edward Elwall, *A Declaration against all the kings and temporal powers under heaven* (London, 1741), 102. Also see his *Idolatry discovered and detested* (London, 1744), 30.

34. Edward Elwall, *The Triumph of Truth: being an account of the trial of Mr. E. Elwall, for heresy and blasphemy. An Appeal to the Serious and Candid Professors of Christianity* (Leeds, 1771), 19.

35. See Priestley, *Defences of Unitarianism for the year 1787* (Birmingham, 1788), 72. He may be referring to Thomas Howes's *Critical Observations on books, ancient and modern*, vol. 4 (London: W. Richardson, 1776–), but the quoted passage cannot be located there or in any of the work's other three volumes or elsewhere in Howes's writings.

36. James Barnard, *The Divinity of our Lord Jesus Christ Demonstrated* (London: J. C. Coghlan, 1789), 287.

37. This argument was first proposed in John Macgowan's attack on Priestley in *Socinianism Brought to the Test* (London, 1773), as evident in the subtitle to this work: *that if Jesus Christ is not a Divine Person, the Mohammedan is, in all Respects, preferable to the Christian Religion, and the Koran is a better Book than the Bible.* Also see John Parkhurt, *The divinity and pre-existence of our Lord and Saviour Jesus Christ* (London, 1787), vi–vii; and Andrew Fuller, *The Calvinistic and Socinian Systems examined and compared* (Market-Harborough, UK: Button, Thomas, Matthews, and Gardiner, 1793), 185.

38. Alexander Pirie, *An Attempt to Expose the weakness, fallacy, and absurdity, of the Unitarian or Socinian arguments* (Perth, 1792), 32.

39. Priestley, *Letters to the Rev. Edward Burn* (Birmingham, 1790), v.

40. See George S. Erving, "Coleridge, Priestley, and the Culture of Unitarian Dissent," Ph.D diss. (U of Washington, 2005). Ian Wylie, *Young Coleridge and the Philosophers of Nature* (Oxford: Clarendon Press, 1989); Robert Schofield, "Joseph Priestley, Eighteenth-century British Neoplatonism, and S. T. Coleridge," in *Transformation and Tradition in the Sciences*, ed. Everett Mandelsohn (Cambridge: Cambridge UP, 1984), 237–54; Thomas Mcfarland, *Coleridge and the Pantheist Tradition* (Oxford: Clarendon Press, 1969); Herbert Walter Piper, *The Active Universe: Pantheism and the Concept of Imagination in English Romantic Poets* (London: The Athlone Press, 1962), 29–59; and Piper, "Coleridge and the Unitarian Consensus," *The Coleridge Connection*, ed. Richard Gravil and Molly Lefebure (New York: St. Martin's Press, 1990), 273–90. On the impact of Priestleyan speculation on Coleridge's use of rhetoric and poetics, see Jane Stabler, "Space for Speculation: Coleridge, Barbauld, and the Poetics of Priestley," in *Samuel Taylor Coleridge and the Sciences of Life*, ed. Nicholas Roe (Oxford: Oxford UP, 2001), 175–206.

41. On the Priestley-Horsley controversy, see *The Collected Letters of Samuel Taylor Coleridge*, ed. Earl Leslie Griggs (Oxford: Clarendon Press, 1956), 2:821, 829. In his "Lectures on Revealed Religion" and in a canceled footnote to the "Religious Musings," Coleridge attacks the bigotry that he finds in Bishop Horsley's controversial circular letter of May 1793, a tract in which Protestant dissenters are compared to Mahometans. See "Lectures on Revealed Religion, Its Corruptions, and Its Political Views," *The Collected Works of Samuel Taylor Coleridge*, gen. ed. Kathleen Coburn, vol. 1, *Lectures 1795 on Politics and Religion*, eds. Lewis Patton and Peter Mann (Princeton, NJ: Princeton UP, 1971), 210, and "Religious Musings," *Collected Works* (Princeton, NJ: Princeton UP), 1:187.

42. See Coleridge, *The Notebooks of Samuel Taylor Coleridge*, ed. Kathleen Coburn (London: Routledge & Kegan Paul, 1957), 1:94–396, and "The Power of Turkey," from *The Courier*, Aug. 30, 1811, *Collected Works*, vol. 3, *Essays on His Times*, ed. David V. Erdman (Princeton, NJ: Princeton UP, 1978), 60. All subsequent citations refer to this edition.

43. Elinor S. Shaffer, *"Kubla Khan" and the Fall of Jerusalem: the Mythological School in Biblical Criticism and Secular Literature 1770–1880* (Cambridge: Cambridge UP, 1975), 14, 105.

44. On the significant effects that Priestleyan Unitarianism had on biblical criti-

cism before the advent of German higher criticism, see Robert Schofield, *The Enlight-ened Joseph Priestley*, 235.

45. Coleridge, "Lectures on Revealed Religion," 202, 207–9, 212. According to Lewis Patton and Peter Mann, editors of vol. 1 of *The Collected Works*, these lectures mostly summarize Priestley's two works on the history of early Christianity (lxi–lxii). Coleridge borrowed the two volumes of *An History of the Corruptions of Christian-ity* from the Bristol library in 1795, the period during which he was preparing notes for his lectures. See George Whalley, *The Bristol Library Borrowings of Southey and Coleridge, 1793–8* (London: The Bibliographical Society, 1949), 119.

46. Coleridge, "Lectures on Revealed Religion," 160–61, 218.

47. Ibid., 226.

48. Ibid., 125–28.

49. See Coleridge, "Religious Musings," 31–32.

50. Coleridge, "On the Present War," in *Collected Works* (Princeton, NJ: Princeton UP, 1971), 1:68.

51. Coleridge, "Introductory Address," in *Conciones ad Populum or Addresses to the People*, 35.

52. Morton D. Paley, *Apocalypse and Millennium in English Romantic Poetry* (Ox-ford: Clarendon Press, 1999), 139–40.

53. See Daniel White, *Early Romanticism and Religious Dissent* (Cambridge: Cam-bridge UP, 2006), chap. 6, "'A Saracenic Mosque, Not a Quaker Meeting-house': Southey's *Thalaba*, Islam, and Religious Nonconformity," 152–81. The above quote is from White, 227. On Nigel Leask's comments on *Thalaba*, see his *British Romantic Writers and the East: Anxieties of Empire* (Cambridge: Cambridge UP, 1992), 26.

54. The following scholars are unduly focused on Southey's religious belief, over-looking important sociopolitical and historical factors. According to Ernest Bern-hardt-Kabisch, Southey's Islamic epic "was bound to fail . . . because he could not suspend his disbelief sufficiently to create Mohammed as the hero of a serious work." Hence, he looked for other epic heroes as replacements: Ali and Thalaba. See *Robert Southey* (Boston: Twayne Publishers, 1977), 84. Following Kabisch's suggestion, Carol Bolton argues that Southey abandoned his Islamic project because he could not sus-pend his disbelief in Islam. See Carol Bolton, *Writing the Empire: Robert Southey and Romantic Colonialism* (London: Pickering and Chatto, 2007), 173–174. Tim Fulford also assumes that he abandoned the Islamic epic because of his inability to believe in the prophet's divine mission. See "Introduction," *Robert Southey: Poetical Works 1793–1810*, eds. Lynda Pratt and Tim Fulford (London: Pickering and Chatto, 2004), 3:xiii. Of course, Southey was not a proponent of Islam: he disparaged the Qur'an and called the prophet an "impostor." See his *Selections from the Letters of Robert Southey*, ed. John Wood Warter (London: Longman, Brown, Green, and Longmans, 1856), 1:77; William Taylor, *A Memoir of the Life and Writings of the Late William Taylor* (London: John Murray, 1843), 2:227; Mark Storey, *Robert Southey: A Life* (Oxford : Oxford UP, 1997), 130; and William W. Haller, *The Early Life of Robert Southey 1774–1803* (New York: Columbia UP, 1917), 259. Nevertheless, Southey was undeniably attracted to the Prophet's enthusiastic mission: "My Mohammed will be, what I believe the Arabian

was in the beginning of his career, sincere in enthusiasm." See Taylor, *A Memoir of the Life and Writings of the Late William Taylor,* 1:325.

55. Taylor, *A Memoir of the Life and Writings of the Late William Taylor,* 1:227, 301.

56. Southey, "Mohammed. Book 2." *Robert Southey: Poetical Works 1793–1810,* 5:478.

57. The sections under "Orientalia" and "Ideas and Studies for literary compositions" in Southey's *The Commonplace Book* cite many works on Islamic culture and religion; excerpts from Edward Gibbon's account of Mohammed's flight from Mecca are contained therein. Southey, *The Commonplace Book,* ed. John Wood Warter (London: Longman, Brown, Green, and Longmans, 1850), 4:177–79; 224–25. Southey's library catalogue also includes Boulainvillers' *Vie de Mahomed* (1730) and Toland's *Collection of several pieces of Mr. John Toland* (1726). See Roy Park, ed., *Sales Catalogues of Libraries of Eminent Persons: Poets and Men of Letters* (London: Scholar Press, 1974), 9:20, 115, 141.

58. Southey, "The Curse of Kehama," *Robert Southey: Poetical Works 1793–1810,* 4:4.

59. Southey, "Thalaba the Destroyer," *Robert Southey: Poetical Works 1793–1810,* 3:277, 246–47. All subsequent citations refer to this edition.

60. Southey, *Selections from the Letters of Robert Southey,* 78.

61. Southey, *The Life and Correspondence of the Late Robert Southey,* ed. Charles C. Southey (London: Longman, Brown, Green & Longmans, 1850), 2:8.

62. Before the massacre of Ali's second son, al-Husayn, in 680, "the Party of Ali" was an oppositional political movement that had not yet acquired its spiritual and sectarian character. See Heinz Halm, *The Shi'ites: A Short History,* 2nd ed., trans. Allison Brown (Princeton, NJ: Markus Wiener Publishers, 2007), 16.

63. White, *Early Romanticism and Religious Dissent,* 155, and Taylor, *A Memoir of the Life and Writings of the Late William Taylor,* 1: 272.

64. Southey, *The Commonplace Book,* 4.

65. Southey, *The Letters of Robert Southey to John May, 1797 to 1838,* ed. Charles Ramos (Austin, TX: Jenkins Publishing, 1976), 26.

66. Ibid., 73–74, 76.

67. Geoffrey Carnall, *Robert Southey and His Age: The Development of a Conservative Mind* (Oxford: Clarendon Press, 1960), 24–25.

68. Taylor, *A Memoir of the Life and Writings of the Late William Taylor,* 1:294.

69. John Davy, *Fragmentary Remains, literary and scientific, of Sir Humphry Davy* (London: J. Churchill, 1858), 35–36.

70. Jean-Honoré Horace Say, Bonaparte's captain, noted in his memoir that during the Festival of the Nile his commander-in-chief "dressed in oriental costume and declared himself protector of all the religions. The enthusiasm was universal, and he was unanimously given the name of the son-in-law of the Prophet. Everyone called him Ali Bonaparte." Qtd. in Juan Cole, *Napoleon's Egypt: Invading the Middle East* (New York: Palgrave Macmillan, 2007), 126.

71. In the Introduction to *Copies of Original Letters from the Army of General Bonaparte in Egypt, intercepted by the Fleet under the command of Admiral Nelson,*

2nd ed. (1798), the loyalist author mocks "Ali Bonaparte's" Islamic pretensions to shame and ridicule English "opposition writers" who support his Egyptian campaign (xviii).

72. Taylor, *A Memoir of the Life and Writings of the Late William Taylor,* 1:224. In another letter to Taylor, Southey claims that he will write "Mohammed" after completing *Thalaba* (1:53).

73. On Southey's republicanism, see Bernhardt-Kabisch, *Robert Southey,* 50, and Carnall, *Robert Southey and His Age,* 101–20.

74. Ibid., 54–55.

75. Fulford, "Introduction," *Robert Southey: Poetical Works 1793–1810,* xiii.

76. Southey, *The Commonplace Book,* 182–83.

77. Ibid., 188.

78. Bernhardt-Kabisch, *Robert Southey,* 94, and Bolton, *Writing the Empire,* 206.

79. Nigel Leask, *The Politics of Imagination in Coleridge's Critical Thought* (Houndmills, UK: The Macmillan Press, 1988), 9–33.

80. Coleridge, *The Collected Letters,* 2:759–760. Between Sept. and Nov. of 1799, Coleridge displayed enthusiasm for *Thalaba* and offered editorial suggestions for revising rough drafts of the poem. See *The Collected Letters,* 1:533, 546; 2:745. The scenes included in his review are based on book 3:229–73 and 323–70; 8:287–390; and 9:49–83.

81. Edmund Burke, "Speech on the Petition of the Unitarian Society," 1792. *Edmund Burke: Selected Writings and Speeches,* ed. Peter J. Stanlis (Garden City, NY: Anchor Books, 1963), 313–17. On negative representations of Unitarians after their petition failed to pass, see Erving, "Coleridge, Priestley, and the Culture of Unitarian Dissent," 47.

82. Charles Leslie, *The Truths of Christianity Demonstrated in a dialogue betwixt a Christian and a Deist* (1711; repr. London, 1799), 120.

83. Since John Livingston Lowes's *The Road to Xanadu* (1929), scholars have typically located sources for "Kubla Khan" only in seventeenth- and eighteenth-century English travelogues and Western literary works. Most recently, this scholarly bias has been reinforced in Robert F. Fleissner's *Sources, Meaning, and Influences of Coleridge's Kubla Khan: Xanadu Re-Routed* (Lewiston, UK: The Edwin Mellen Press, 2000). The following works have paid more attention to Coleridge's Oriental sources: chap. 5 of Munir Ahmad's "Oriental Influences in Romantic Poetry with Special Reference to Coleridge and Southey." Ph. D. thesis (U of Birmingham, 1959), 146–86; E. S. Shaffer's *"Kubla Khan" and the Fall of Jerusalem: The Mythological School in Biblical Criticism and Secular Literature 1770–1880* (Cambridge: Cambridge UP, 1975); and John Drew, "'Kubla Khan' and Orientalism," *Coleridge's Visionary Language: Essays in Honor of J. B. Beer,* eds. Tim Fulford, Morton D. Paley (Cambridge: D. S. Brewer, 1993), 41–47.

84. On the dating of "Kubla Khan," see Elisabeth Schneider, *Coleridge, Opium and "Kubla Khan"* (1953; repr. New York: Octagon Books, 1968), 235, and Warren U. Ober, "Southey, Coleridge, and "Kubla Khan," *Journal of English and Germanic Philology* (1959): 414–22. According to Tim Fulford, the extracts made available to Coleridge from Southey's *The Commonplace Book* and the early books of *Thalaba* made it pos-

sible to write "Kubla Khan." See his Introduction, xviii–iv. Coleridge was invested in the editing, publication, and review of *Thalaba*. See note 80 above.

85. Southey, *The Life and Correspondence of the Late Robert Southey*, 2:24; Taylor, *A Memoir of the Life and Writings of the Late William Taylor*, 1:299, 310; and Joseph Cottle, *Reminiscences of Samuel Taylor Coleridge and Robert Southey*, 2nd ed. (London: Houlston and Stoneman, 1848), 219.

86. Southey, Review of *Gebir*, by Walter Savage Landor, *Critical Review* 27 (1799): 29–39. On his reflections on the "Gaditte" excavation, see 32–33.

87. See Southey, *The Life and Correspondence of the Late Robert Southey*, 2:56, and Taylor, *A Memoir of the Life and Writings of the Late William Taylor*, 1:352.

88. Southey, *The Life and Correspondence of the Late Robert Southey*, 1:346, and Taylor, *A Memoir of the Life and Writings of the Late William Taylor*, 1:247.

89. On the general crisis of the seventeenth century, see Jack Goldstone's *Revolution and Rebellion in the Early Modern World* (Berkeley: U of California P, 1991). A historicized reading of early modern universal histories is provided in Robert Markley, "Newton, Corruption, and the Tradition of Universal History," in *Newton and Religion*, eds. James E. Force and Richard H. Popkin (Dordrecht: Kluwer, 1999), 121–43, and Kenneth Knoespel, "Newton in the School of Time: The Chronology of the Ancient Kingdoms Amended and the Crisis of Seventeenth-Century Historiography," *The Eighteenth Century: Theory and Interpretation* 30.3 (1989): 19–41. On Noah as cultural myth, see Don Cameron Allen, *The Legend of Noah: Renaissance Rationalism in Art, Science, and Letters* (Urbana: U of Illinois P, 1949).

90. *An Universal History, from the earliest account of time to the present* (Dublin: Edward Bate, 1746), 17:564–58, 597–98.

91. Southey, *The Commonplace Book*, 3.

92. *The Correspondence of Robert Southey with Caroline Bowles*, ed. E. Dowden (Dublin: Hodges and Friggs; London: Longmans and Green, 1881), 52.

93. Southey, *The Commonplace Book*, 2–3.

94. Southey, *The Life and Correspondence of the Late Robert Southey*, 2:16

95. Coleridge, "Kubla Khan; or, A Vision in a Dream," *Collected Works*, vol. 16, bk. 1, *Poetical Works*, ed. J. C. C. May, 509–14. All subsequent citations refer to this edition.

96. Coleridge, *The Notebooks of Samuel Taylor Coleridge*, 1:8.

97. The link between Wordsworth's "Dream of the Arab" and Southey's imaginative projects between 1799 and 1801 is convincingly proposed in David Chandler's "Robert Southey and the Prelude's "Arab Dream." *Review of English Studies* 52. 214 (2003): 203–19. Coleridge and Wordsworth, two aged and conservative poets, were eager to disassociate their earlier Oriental writings from *Thalaba*. Although I explore the larger political implications behind this disavowal, a thorough analysis of "The Dream of the Arab" lies beyond this book's scope.

98. Marilyn Butler, "Plotting the Revolution: The Political Narratives of Romantic Poetry and Criticism," *Romantic Revolutions: Criticism and Theory*, eds. Kenneth R. Johnston, Gilbert Chaitin, Karen Hansen, and Herbert Marks (Bloomington: Indiana UP, 1990), 147, 149.

99. Ibid., 153.

100. Because Islamism and Socinianism deny the Trinity, Coleridge maintains that they are actually a form of deism (atheism in disguise) rather than a radical sect within Christianity; in this case, these two movements do not deserve to be called "religions." According to him, "Mohammedanism could not but pass into Deism, and Deism never did, never can, establish itself as a religion." See Coleridge, *Anima Poetae*, ed. Ernest Hartley Coleridge (London: William Heinemann, 1895), 288. As non-Christians, the Unitarians and the Muslims have no hope for salvation or the mercy of God. Therefore, "Socinianism is not only not Christianity, it is not even *Religion*," and because it is not based on the New Testament, it "scarcely deserve[s] the name of a religion in any sense." See *The Collected Letters*, 3:479; 2:1189, and "Lay Sermons," *Collected Works*, vol. 6, ed. Reginald James White (Princeton, NJ: Princeton UP, 1972), 181–84.

101. Coleridge, *Anima Poetae*, 288.

102. On Coleridge's *Diadesté*, as a Thalaba-inspired Unitarian play, see Erving, "Coleridge, Priestley, and the Culture of Unitarian Dissent," 169. One of Coleridge's 1804 notebook entries includes some verses titled "Nonsense," which strongly resemble the meter and theme of "Mahomet." See *Collected Works*, 16:1, 590.

In the stage directions to *Diadesté*, he refers to book 1 and 3 of *Thalaba* for information on the Arabian setting: "Arabian landscape (for which in consult Thalaba & the notes to it)." Qtd. in Earl Leslie Griggs, "Diadesté, a Fragment of an Unpublished play by Samuel Taylor Coleridge," *Modern Philology* 34.4 (1937): 377.

103. Erving, "Coleridge, Priestley, and the Culture of Unitarian Dissent," 51.

104. Francis Jeffrey, Review of *Thalaba the Destroyer*, by Robert Southey, *Edinburgh Review, or Critical Journal* 1 (1802): 63.

105. Qtd. in Haller, *The Early Life of Robert Southey 1774–1803*, 232.

106. Jeffrey, Review of *Thalaba the Destroyer*, by Robert Southey, 64.

107. Robert Ryan, *The Romantic Reformation: Religious Politics and English Religion* (Cambridge: Cambridge UP, 1997), 32, and White, *Early Romanticism and Religious Dissent*, 360.

108. Review of *Helga; A Poem. In Seven Cantos*, by William Herbert., 151.

109. On Southey's cautious approach toward popular enthusiasm and "Jacobin" Orientalism in the context of *The Curse of Kehama*, see Tim Fulford, "Pagodas and Pregnant Throes: Orientalism, Millenarianism and Robert Southey," in *Romanticism and Millenarianism*, ed. Tim Fulford (New York: Palgrave, 2002), 121–38. As in Coleridge's conservative publication of "Kubla Khan," Southey's strong dislike of the Oriental enthusiasm embedded in the Islamic and Hindu religions may explain why the 1838 editorial revisions to *Thalaba* removed many explicit references to "Allah" and the "Koran," creating an ironic self-distance between the author and his "scholarly" Western work. According to Tim Fulford, "the 1838 Thalaba was a hero of his conservative years, one who spoke, like a good iconoclastic Protestant, of 'the Lord' rather than a fervent believer in Mohammed. Southey no longer wished to disturb traditional loyalties to church and state." See Fulford, "Introduction," xxviii.

Chapter 6 • *A Last Woman's Eschatology*

Epigraph. *The Koran: or, Alcoran of Mohammed*, ed. and trans. George Sale (1734; repr. London: Frederick Warne and Co., 1910).

1. *The Assassins* was composed between Aug. 25 and Sept. 19, 1814, the period during which the Shelleys, along with Jane Clairmont, were traveling in Switzerland. In her 1840 edition of a *History of a Six Week's Tour*, Mary clarifies her important role in the composition of the romance: while in Brumen, Switzerland, their "amusement . . . was writing. S*** commenced a romance on the subject of the Assassins, and I wrote to his dictation." On Mary Shelley's collaboration, specifically the editorial changes she is responsible for, see E. B. Murray, "The Dating and Composition of Shelley's *The Assassins*," *Keats-Shelley Journal* 35 (1985): 14–17. All subsequent citations to the Shelleys' work come from the following edition: "The Assassins: A Fragment of a Romance," *The Prose Works of Percy Bysshe Shelley*, ed. E. B. Murray (Oxford: Clarendon Press, 1993), 1:124–39.

2. Mary Shelley, *Frankenstein*, ed. J. Paul Hunter (New York: Norton, 1996), 78; all subsequent citations refer to this edition. For a discussion on how Mary Shelley's views on Muslim women is framed by the discourse of liberal feminist Orientalism, see Joyce Zonana, "'They will prove the truth of my tale': Safie's Letters as the Feminist Core of Mary Shelley's *Frankenstein*," *Journal of Narrative Technique* 21.2 (1991): 170–84, and "The Sultan and the Slave: Feminist Orientalism and the Structure of *Jane Eyre*," *Signs: The Journal of Woman in Culture and Society* 18.3 (1993): 592–617. On Mary Shelley's subversive use of feminist Orientalism in *Frankenstein*, see Joseph W. Lee, "The Deceptive Other: Mary Shelley's Critique of Orientalism in 'Frankenstein,'" *Studies in Romanticism* 30 (1991): 255–83, and Mohja Kahf, *Western Representations of the Muslim Woman* (Austin: U of Texas P, 1999), 165–68.

3. See *The Other Mary Shelley: Beyond Frankenstein*, eds. Audrey A. Fisch, Anne K. Mellor, and Esther H. Schor (New York: Oxford UP, 1993). Thanks in part to this groundbreaking collection of essays, Mary Shelley's writings are being read as a unique literary response that stands apart from, and even criticizes, the political ideals of Percy Shelley and the Godwin circle. On *The Last Man*, see Lynn Wells, "The Triumph of Death: Reading the Narrative in Mary Shelley's *The Last Man*," 212–34; Paul A. Cantor, "The Apocalypse of Empire: Mary Shelley's *The Last Man*," in *Iconoclastic Departures: Mary Shelley After Frankenstein*, eds. Syndy M. Conger, Frederick S. Frank, and Gregory O'Dea (London: Associated UP, 1997), 193–211; and Joseph W. Lew, "The Plague of Imperial Desire: Montesquieu, Gibbon, Brougham, and Mary Shelley's *The Last Man*," in *Romanticism and Colonialism: Writing and Empire, 1780–1830*, eds. Tim Fulford and Peter J. Kitson (Cambridge: Cambridge UP, 1998), 261–78.

4. Shelley's novel adopts "the Last Man" theme featured in several literary works written during her time: Thomas Campbell and Thomas Hood both wrote "last man" poems. There is also a fragment of a play by Thomas Lovell Beddoes with that same title. Cousin de Granille wrote a novel titled, *The Last Man; or Onegarius*. But perhaps the greatest influence was Lord Byron's poem, "Darkness" (1816). For a survey of "Last Man" themes, see A. J. Sambrook, "A Romantic Theme: The Last Man," *Forum for*

Modern Language Studies 2 (1966): 25–33. As for the tendency to reduce Shelley's novel to personal allegory, a note of caution is necessary: early misogynist reviews of the novel promoted such a reading to devalue her literary merits, equating the sufferings of "the Last Man" (Lionel Verney) to the pathetic laments of "The Last woman." See the *Literary Gazette* (1826) in William H. Lyles, *Mary Shelley: An Annotated Bibliography* (New York: Garland Publishing, 1975), 175.

5. Mary Shelley, *Mary Shelley's Journal*, ed. Frederick L. Jones (Norman: U of Oklahoma P, 1947), 204.

6. Mary Poovey, *The Proper Lady and the Woman Writer* (Chicago: U of Chicago P, 1984), 115; Anne K. Mellor, *Mary Shelley: Her Life, Her Fiction, Her Monsters* (New York: Routledge, 1988), 217; and Jane Aaron, "The Return of the Repressed: Reading Mary Shelley's *The Last Man*," in *Feminist Criticism: Theory and Practice*, ed. Susan Sellers (New York: Harvester Wheatsheaf, 1991), 9–10.

7. Eamon Wright, *British Women Writers and Race, 1788–1818* (New York: Palgrave Macmillan, 2005), 101–5.

8. Morton D. Paley, *Apocalypse and Millennium in English Romantic Poetry* (Oxford: Clarendon Press, 1999), and Steven Goldsmith, *Unbuilding Jerusalem: Apocalypse and Romantic Representation* (Ithaca, NY: Cornell UP, 1993).

9. Mary Shelley, "The Last Man," *The Novels and Selected Works of Mary Shelley*, eds. Jane Blumberg and Nora Crook, vol. 4 (London: William Pickering, 1996). All subsequent citations refer to this edition.

10. John Lempriere, *Lempriere's Classical Dictionary of Proper Names in Ancient Authors*, ed. Fredrick Adam Wright (London: Routledge & Kegan Paul, 1958), 581.

11. See David S. Katz, "Vossius and the English Biblical Critics," in *Scepticism and Irreligion in the Seventeenth and Eighteenth Centuries*, eds. Richard H. Popkin and Arjo Vanderjagt (Leiden: Brill, 1993), 161–71. Since the late seventeenth century, questions over the authenticity of the Sibylline prophecies was part of a general rethinking of biblical chronology; these prophecies were seen as the missing link between the Old and New Testaments, between classical, eastern civilizations and the Judeo-Christian world. According to Katz, Sir Isaac Vossius's work on the Sibyls initiated a skeptical biblical criticism: in trying to anchor the sibylline prophecies within the accepted trajectory of biblical history, from the Jews to the Christians, Vossius's work was read as a skeptical attack on the foundations of Christian revelation and English Protestantism, even though his intended goal was to bring pre-Christian revelation within the Hebrew religious fold to reconfirm orthodox Christian chronology (159–61, 165). See Vossius's *De Sibyllinis aliisque quae Christi natalem praecessere oraculis accedit ejusdem responsio ad objectiones nuperae criticae sacra* (Oxoniae: E Theatro Sheldoniano, 1679). In the early eighteenth century, Vossius's work inspired unorthodox speculations on the Sibyls that maintain (contra Vossius) the independent authenticity and superiority of the Sibylline prophecies. See Sir John Floyer, *The Sibylline Oracles, Translated from the Best Greek Copies, and Compared with the Sacred Prophecies, Especially with Daniel and the Revelations* (London, 1713), and William Whiston, *A Vindication of the Sibylline Oracles* (London, 1715).

12. Review of Mackey's "Theory of the Earth," *Notes and Queries* 8.1 (1853): 565–66,

and 9.1 (1854): 179; see William Winks Edward, *Lives of Illustrious Shoemakers* (London: Sampson, Low, Marston, Searle and Rivington, 1883), 225. Mackey had to defend his speculations against the attacks of orthodox Christians disturbed by his passionate vindication of Asiatic and Hindu chronology. See Mackey, *A Reply, intended to be made to the various disputants, on an Essay on Chronology, which was read at the Philosophical Society of Norwich* (Norwich: R. Walker, 1825).

13. Sampson Arnold Mackey, *The Mythological Astronomy of the Ancients Demonstrated by Restoring to their Fables and Symbols their Original Meaning* (1822–23; Minneapolis: Wizards Bookshelf, 1973), iii–vii, x, 23–24, 138–39, 146–48.

14. Marilyn Butler, "Myth and Mythmaking in the Shelley Circle," *Journal of English Literary History* 49.1 (1982): 7. Also see her "Druids, Bards and Twice-Born Bacchus: Peacock's Engagement with Primitive Mythology," *Keats-Shelley Review* 36 (1985), 57–76, and "Romantic Manichaeism: Shelley's 'On the Devil and Devils' and Byron's Mythological Dramas," in *The Sun Is God: Painting, Literature and Mythology in the Nineteenth Century*, ed. J. B. Bullen (Oxford: Clarendon Press, 1989), 13–37; and Donald Reiman, *Intervals of Inspiration: The Skeptical Tradition and the Psychology of Romanticism* (Greenwood, FL: Penkevill, 1988), 213–61. The poetics of Shelleyean syncretism is discussed in Stuart Curran, *Shelley's Annus Mirabilis: The Maturing of an Epic Vision* (San Marino, CA: Huntington Library, 1975). On the sectarian and nonsectarian uses of infidel syncretism, see Daniel E. White, "'Mysterious Sanctity': Sectarianism and Syncretism from Volney to Hemans," *European Romantic Review* 15.2 (2004): 269–76. A general overview on English mythological syncretisms, from the late seventeenth to the late eighteenth century, is provided in Albert J. Kuhn, "English Deism and the Development of Romantic Mythological Syncretism," *PMLA* 71 (1956): 1094–1116.

15. Mary Shelley, preface, *Essays, Letters from Abroad, Translations and Fragments. By Percy Bysshe Shelley* (London: Edward Moxon, 1840), 1:x–xi.

16. On Western misconceptions of the historical Assassins, see Farhad Daftary, *A Short History of the Ismailis: Traditions of a Muslim Community* (Princeton, NJ: Markus Wiener, 1998), 13–16.

17. Mary Shelley, preface, *Essays, Letters from Abroad*, xi.

18. Iain McCalman, "New Jerusalems: Prophecy, Dissent and Radical Culture in England, 1786–1830," in *Enlightenment and Religion: Rational Dissent in Eighteenth-Century Britain*, ed. Knud Kaakonssen (Cambridge: Cambridge UP, 1996), 318.

19. Bryan Shelley, *Shelley and Scripture: The Interpreting Angel* (Oxford: Clarendon Press, 1994), 1–6.

20. Percy Shelley, "On Christianity," ed. E. B. Murray. *The Prose Works*, 1:260.

21. Bernard Lewis, *The Assassins: A Radical Sect in Islam* (New York: Basic Books, 1968), 28.

22. Ibid., 27–28, and Marshall G. S. Hodgson, *The Secret Order of the Assassins* (1955; Philadelphia: U of Pennsylvania P, 2005), 291. On the prevalence of Gnostic freethinking in extremist and radical forms of Shiism, see Farhad Daftary, *A Short History of the Ismailis*, 53, 55, 168; Sarah Stroumsa, *Freethinkers of Medieval Islam: Ibn Al-Rawandi, Abu Bakr Al-Razi and Their Impact on Islamic Thought* (Leiden: Brill, 1999), 142; Heinz

Halm, *Shiism* (Edinburg: Edinburg UP, 1991), 166–67, 169–70. Radical Shi'ite movements represent later Gnostic trends, suggesting that Islam is an integral part of Christian Gnostic history. See *The Gnostic Bible*, eds. Willis Barnstone and Marvin Meyer (Boston: Shambhala, 2003), 662–63.

23. Hodgson, *The Secret Order of the Assassins*, 17–19.

24. Bryan Shelley, *Shelley and Scripture*, 1.

25. Johann Lorenz Mosheim, *An Ecclesiastical History, Ancient and Modern* (London, 1765), 1:64–66.

26. Ibid., 63.

27. On Apr. 8, 1815, Mary wrote, "The Assassins—Gibbon Chap. LXIV—all that can be known of the assassins is to be found in Memoires of the Acad[e]my of Inscriptions tom. xvii p 127–170," a reference to Falconet's research on the Ismailis of Syria and Persia in his two *Memoires*, read before the Academy of Inscriptions as cited in n. 24, chap. 64 of Edward Gibbon's *History of the Decline and Fall of the Roman Empire.* Gibbon's work is also included in Mary Shelley's reading list. See Mary Shelley, *Mary Shelley's Journal*, 43, 221.

28. Edward Gibbon, *The History of the Decline and Fall of the Roman Empire* (London, 1788), 5:207.

29. On the Gnostic Shi'ite influence on the history of freethinking, see Jonathan Israel, *Enlightenment Contested: Philosophy, Modernity and the Enlightenment of Man, 1670–1752* (Oxford: Oxford UP, 2006), 635–639.

30. Mary Shelley, *Mary Shelley's Journal*, 11.

31. Ibid., 11, 19.

32. Abbe Barruel, *Memoirs, illustrating the History of Jacobinism*, trans. Robert Clifford (London: E. Booker, 1798), 142.

33. Ibid., 141–42.

34. Ibid., 142.

35. Bernard Lewis, *The Assassins*, 13.

36. Norman O. Brown, "The Prophetic Tradition," *Studies in Romanticism* 21.3 (1982): 370–71, 373–74. For a comparative analysis of theosophical mysticism, Swedenborg's prophecies, and Islam, see Henry Corbin and Leonard Fox, *Swedenborg and Esoteric Islam* (West Chester, PA: Swedenborg Foundation, 1995). Brown's thesis is indebted to the theological works of Hans Joachim Schreps's *Jewish Christianity* (Philadelphia: Fortress Press, 1969), Henry Corbin's "Divine Epiphany and Spiritual Birth in Ismailian Gnosis," *Man and Transformation: Papers from the Eranos Yearbooks.* Vol. 5, trans. Ralph Maneheim, Joseph Campbell (Princeton, NJ: Princeton UP, 1964); "Man and Transformation," 69–160, and Hodgson's *The Secret Order of the Assassins.* Unlike Bernard Lewis, who labels the Assassins "the first terrorists" in history (129–30), Brown and company attempt to restore Ismailian Islam to its Semitic-revolutionary-prophetic roots.

37. Gil Anidjar, *The Jew, The Arab: A History of the Enemy* (Stanford: Stanford UP, 2003), 60.

38. Percy Shelley, *The Letters of Percy Bysshe Shelley*, ed. Roger Ingpen (London: Sir Isaac Pitman & Sons, 1909), 2:559.

39. Filiz Turhan makes this argument in *The Other Empire: British Romantic Writings about the Ottoman Empire* (New York: Routledge, 2003), 78, 84–86, 91.

40. Shelley could have requested that his publisher, Ollier, replace the first title with "The Revolt of Islam" during the time other editorial changes were being made on Dec. 15, 1817, or not long afterward. In any case, Ollier probably insisted on the title change to moderate the radical political implications of the poem. See "Laon and Cythna; or the Revolution of the Golden City: A Vision of the Nineteenth Century," *The Poems of Shelley*, eds. Kelvin Everest and Geoffrey Matthews (Essex: Pearson Education Limited, 2000), 2:31, n. 143. All subsequent citations refer to this edition.

41. In *The Ruins, or the Meditations on the Revolution of Empires* (1792; repr. New York: Peter Eckler, 1890), Volney claims that the self-consumed snake is an ancient emblem of a pantheistic worldview in which nature is eternal and self-generating: "a great round serpent . . . devouring his tail—that is, folding and unfolding himself eternally, like the revolutions of the spheres" (142). Drummond's *Oedipus Judaicus* (London, 1811) provides a plate illustration of a serpent swallowing its tale and explains that "the tail of the serpent is placed in his mouth to show, that time is still resolved into time" (356). For Shelley's poetic use of the Ouroborus symbol in relation to the astrological speculations of Volney and Drummond, see Robert Hartley, "The Uroboros in Shelley's Poetry," *Journal of English and Germanic Philology* 73 (1974), 536–59, and Bryan Shelley, *Shelley and Scripture,* 65. Citations to Volney's *The Ruins* refer to the edition cited above.

42. Turham, *The Other Empire,* 3–28, 77–106. On the steady decline of the Ottoman Empire in the late eighteenth and early nineteenth centuries, see Donald Quataert, *The Ottoman Empire, 1700–1922* (Cambridge: Cambridge UP, 2000), 37–51, 55–56.

43. Percy Shelley, "Ozymandias," *The Poems of Shelley*, eds. Kelvin Everest and Geoffrey Matthews (Essex: Pearson Education Limited, 2000), 2:307–10.

44. Ibid., 307 n. 145.

45. Volney, *Travels Through Syria and Egypt* (London, 1787), 2:397.

46. Edward Said, *Orientalism* (New York: Vintage Books, 1978), 81.

47. Percy Shelley, "A Philosophical View of Reform," *Shelley's Revolutionary Year* (London: Redwords, 1990), 45.

48. On the politics of Anglo-Ottoman relations and 1815 Vienna settlement, see Allan Cunningham, *Anglo-Ottoman Encounters in the Age of Revolution: Collected Essays,* ed. Edward Ingram (Portland, OR: Frank Cass, 1993), 1:104, 156–57, 235, 257.

49. Marilyn Butler, "Shelley and the Empire in the East," in *Shelley: Poet and Legislator of the World*, eds. Betty T. Bennett and Stuart Curran (Baltimore: The Johns Hopkins UP, 1996), 158.

50. E. Douka Kabitoglou, "Shelley's (Feminist) Discourse on the Female: *The Revolt of Islam*," *AAA: Arbeiten Aus Anglistik und Amerikanistik* 15.2 (1990): 141.

51. Nathaniel Brown, *Sexuality and Feminism in Shelley* (Cambridge, MA: Harvard UP, 1979), 181.

52. Mary Wollstonecraft, *A Critical Edition of Mary Wollstonecraft's 'A Vindication of the Rights of Woman: with Strictures on Political and Moral Subjects,'* ed. Ulrich H. Hardt (Troy, NY: Whitston, 1982), 36.

53. Ibid., 197.

54. Ibid., 55.

55. Catherine MacCaulay, *Letters on Education. With Observations on religious and metaphysical subjects* (London, 1790), 213, 220, and Mary Robinson, *Thoughts on the Condition of Women, and on the Injustice of Mental Subordination*, 2nd ed. (London, 1799), 16.

56. Zonana, "The Sultan and the Slave," 593–94.

57. Turhan, *The Other Empire*, 89.

58. According to Asma Barlas, "Women's testimony also has been crucial to the correct reading of the Qur'an, especially the testimony of 'Ayesha, the Prophet's wife, who is said to have contributed more *Ahadith* than his cousin and son-in-law, Ali, the fourth Caliph." See Asma Barlas, *"Believing Women" in Islam: Unreading Patriarchal Interpretations of the Qur'an* (Austin: U of Texas P, 2002), 45–46. Mernissi contends that 'Ayesha's *Ahadith* constitutes "15 percent of the bases of the Sharia." See Fatima Mernissi, *Women's Rebellion and Islamic Memory* (London: Zed, 1996), 96. Moreover, Islam is the only major religion to incorporate women's accounts within its canonical religious texts. See Lelia Ahmed, *Women and Gender in Islam: Historical Roots of a Modern Debate* (New Haven: Yale UP, 1992), 73. Shelley may indirectly be acknowledging the centrality of Ayesha to Qur'anic revelation when composing his "feminist" world epic.

59. Percy Shelley, "Laon and Cythna," preface, 33; 2:2059–61.

60. Mary Wollstoncraft, *Historical and Moral View of the Origin and Progress of the French Revolution* (London, 1794), vi, 6.

61. Mary read *Laon and Cythna* on Dec. 9 and 13 of 1817, and read it once more as *The Revolt of Islam* between July 28 and Aug. 3 of 1818. See Mary Shelley, *Mary Shelley's Journal*, 87, 102, 103. She may have been directly involved in editing the "offensive" passages of his poem: on Dec. 15, 1817, the day that Percy was discussing the editorial details of his poem with his publisher, Ollier, and his close friend, Peacock, Mary was reading the "alterations for Cythna" (87).

62. In May 1824, the time during which Mary Shelley began working on her novel, she writes about her own despair and loneliness: "The Last Man! Yes I may well describe that solitary being's feelings, feeling myself as the last relic of a beloved race, my companions, extinct before me—." Mary Shelley, *Mary Shelley's Journal*, 476–77.

63. Sandra Gilbert and Susan Gubar, *The Madwoman in the Attic* (New Haven: Yale UP, 1979), 96–97.

64. Goldsmith, 279.

65. On *The Revolt of Islam*'s colonial discourse and its reliance on Mary Wollstonecraft's feminism, see Nigel Leask, *British Romantic Writers and the East: Anxieties of Empire* (Cambridge: Cambridge UP, 1992), 131.

66. Raymond is a leading crusader and skilled debater of the medieval Christian era, whose life Mary may have read about in Torquato Tasso's *Jerusalem Delivered* (1580) (*Last Man*, 34, n. a). This Italian epic poem records Raymond's victorious conquest of Egypt and Syria, and the downfall of the caliphate.

67. Sultana Valide is usually depicted as a devouring empress or queen mother, a

negative foil of the virgin Mary. In William Beckford's gothic novel *Vathek*, she appears as Vathek's cynical and manipulative mother. Montesquieu also makes use of her character in his writings. According to Joseph W. Lee, Frankenstein's monster is modeled after the Sultana Valide (259). To learn more about western literary representations of this female figure, see Alain Groscrichard, *The Sultan's Court: European Fantasies of the East,* trans. Liz Heron (London: Verso, 1998).

68. Turhan, *The Other Empire,* 50, 51–53, 132–34.

69. Martin Bernal, *Black Athena: The Afroasiatic Roots of Classical Civilization* (New Brunswick, NJ: Rutgers UP, 1985), 1:189–246.

70. On cyclical temporality and women's time, see Anne K. Mellor, "Blake, the Apocalypse and Romantic Women Writers," in *Romanticism and Millenarianism,* ed. Tim Fulford (New York: Palgrave, 2002), 140, and Eve Tavor Bannet, "The 'Abyss of the Present' and Women's Time in Mary Shelley's *The Last Man*," *The Eighteenth-Century Novel* 2 (2002): 354–57.

71. Mellor's and Bannet's analysis stems from a branch of feminist scholarship that interprets women's writings as displaying a strong mistrust of a progressive linear time frame, a masculinist mode of thinking. See the collection of essays in *Taking Our Time: Feminist Perspectives on Temporality,* eds. Frieda Johles Forman and Caoran Sowton (Oxford: Pergamon Press, 1989). However, I am arguing only for the intimate relationship between cyclical temporality and Ismaili gnosis. See Henry Corbin, *Cyclical Time and Ismaili Gnosis* (London: Kegan Paul International, Islamic Publications, 1983).

72. See Nabil Matar's *Islam in Britain, 1558–1685* (Cambridge: Cambridge UP, 1998), 153–83. On sixteenth- and seventeenth-century eschatological views on Islam, see Bryan W. Ball, *A Great Expectation: Eschatological Thought in English Protestantism to 1660* (Leiden: Brill, 1975), 102, 130–31, 141–46, and Paul Christianson, *Reformers and Babylon: English Apocalyptic Visions from the Reformation to the Eve of the Civil War* (Toronto: U of Toronto P, 1978), 64, 104–5, 126. On early-nineteenth-century English prophecy and the decline of the Muslims, see Le Roy Edwin Froom, *The Prophetic Faith of Our Fathers* (Washington, DC: Review and Herald, 1948), 3:284–85, 294–96.

73. On the depoliticizing involved in the writing and marketing of English women's novels in eighteenth and nineteenth-century England, see Paula McDowell, *The Women of Grub Street: Press, Politics, and Gender in the London Literary Marketplace, 1678–1730* (Oxford: Clarendon Press, 1998), 293; Catherine Gallagher, *Nobody's Story: The Vanishing Acts of Women Writers in the Marketplace, 1670–1820* (Berkeley: U of California P, 1994); Janet Todd, *The Sign of Angellica: Women, Writing and Fiction, 1660–1800* (New York: Columbia UP, 1989); and Jane Spencer, *The Rise of the Woman Novelist* (Oxford: Basil Blackwell, 1986). Anne Mellor argues that, despite the economic and political restrictions placed on the eighteenth-century female novel, Romantic women writers used this genre as "the site of a powerful struggle over the very construction of gender." See *Romanticism and Gender* (New York: Routledge, 1993), 10, and Eve Tavor Bannet, *The Domestic Revolution: Enlightenment Feminisms and the Novel* (Baltimore: The Johns Hopkins UP, 2000).

74. In the preface to his epic drama *Hellas* (1822), Percy Shelley declares, "We are all Greeks. Our laws, our literature, our religion, our arts, have their root in Greece." By this point in his life (as evident in *The Revolt of Islam*), Shelley had turned his back on his earlier interests in "Gnostic" Islam. With the Greek War of Independence underway, Shelley instead posits a dichotomy between a progressive "Western" Greece and a "backward" Muslim world. See "Hellas," *Shelley's Poetry and Prose*, eds. Donald H. Reiman and Sharon B. Powers (New York: W. W. Norton, 1977), 409.

Epilogue • Postcolonial Reflections

Epigraphs. Thomas Carlyle, *On Heroes, Hero-Worship, & the Heroic in History*, eds. Michael K. Goldberg, Joel J. Brattin, and Mark Engel (Berkeley: U of California P, 1993), 38–39. All subsequent citations refer to this edition. Rowan Williams, "Archbishop's Lecture-Civil and Religious Law in England: A Religious Perspective," *The Archbishop of Canterbury*, Feb. 7, 2008, http://www.archbishopofcanterbury.org/1575, accessed Sept. 2, 2010.

1. Qtd. in Ruth Glendhill and Philip Webster, "Archbishop of Canterbury argues for Islamic Law in Britain," *The Times*, Feb. 8, 2008, www.timesonline.co.uk/tol/comment/faith/article3328024.ece, accessed Sept. 2, 2010.

2. On the dynamic interaction, and often confliction, between nineteenth-century European expansion and diverse modes of Islamic universalism, see Amira K. Bennison, "Muslim Universalism and Western Globalization," in A. G. Hopkins, ed., *Globalization in World History* (London: Pimlico, 2002), 74–97. Tim Harper has argued that a large segment of the nineteenth-century colonial world existed as a "Euro-Islamic condominium," in which positive appeals to the Ottoman sultanate were pervasive across South and Southeastern Asia. See Tim Harper, "Empire, Disapora and the Languages of Globalism, 1850–1914," in Hopkins, ed., *Globalization in World History*, 145.

3. On Carlyle's Arab-Islamic primitivism as conducive to British empire-building in the mid Victorian period, see Muhammed A. Al-Da'mi, *Arabian Mirrors and Western Soothsayers: Nineteenth-Century Literary Approaches to Arab-Islamic History* (New York: Peter Lang, 2002), chap. 3, 65–98.

4. On the Indian Mutiny's global significance, see Christopher Alan Bayly, *The Birth of the Modern World 1780–1914: Global Connections and Comparisons* (Malden, MA: Blackwell, 2004), 153–54.

5. See Sugata Bose, *A Hundred Horizons: The Indian Ocean in the Age of Global Empire* (Cambridge, MA: Harvard UP, 2006), 65.

6. For a thorough discussion on copies of Stubbe's manuscript possessed by Unitarian library collectors, from the eighteenth to the early nineteenth century, see James R. Jacob, *Henry Stubbe, Radical Protestantism and the Early Enlightenment* (Cambridge: Cambridge UP, 1983), 161–62. How Shairani obtained Stubbe's manuscript remains a mystery.

7. Hafiz Mahmud Khan Shairani, "Preface and Introduction," *The Rise and Progress of Mahometanism* (1911; Lahore: Orientalia, 1975), v–xvi. All citations to these texts, including the appendix and list of subscribers, refer to this edition.

8. Qtd. in Humayun Ansari, *"The Infidel Within": The History of Muslims in Britain, 1800 to the Present* (London: Hurst & Co., 2004), 85.

9. Ibid., 61, 80–82.

10. On late-nineteenth-century Muslim reformist movements that stressed the compatibility between modern European thought and culture and Islamic principles, see Albert Hourani, *Arabic Thought in the Liberal Age, 1798–1939* (1962; Cambridge: Cambridge UP, 1983).

11. For more information on these Indo-Muslim activists, see David Lelyveld, *Aligarh's First Generation: Muslim Solidarity in British India* (Princeton, NJ: Princeton UP, 1978), esp. 93, 110–11, 130-4, 202–3, 249–51, 272, and 306–7. Also see Ansari, *"The Infidel Within,"* 85, and Shampa Lahir, *Indians in Britain: Anglo-Indian Encounters, Race and Identity, 1880–1939* (London: Frank Cass, 2000), 176–80.

12. On Kidwai's role in Indian national politics and the pan-Islamic movement, see Azim Ozcan, *Pan-Islamism: Indian Muslims, the Ottomans and Britain (1877–1924)* (Leiden: Brill, 1997), chap.4, 127–45, esp. 135–36, 127.

13. This quote is from Ozcan, *Pan-Islamism,* 172.

14. On Halil Halid's anti-imperial political legacy and his early critique of Orientalism, see Syed Tanvir Wasti, "Halil Halid: Anti-imperialist Muslim Intellectual," *Middle Eastern Studies* 29.3 (1993): 559–79.

15. On the Turkish press's increasingly influential role, see Ozcan, *Pan-Islamism,* 115–26, and Ami Ayalan, *The Press in the Arab Middle East: A History* (New York: Oxford UP, 1995), 66–69, 71, and 83.

16. See Humayun Ansari, "Making Transnational Connections: Muslim Networks in early Twentieth Century Britain," in *Islam in Inter-War Europe,* eds. Nathalie Clayer and Eric Germain (New York: Columbia UP, 2008), 31–63, esp. 62.

17. Qtd. from Ozcan, *Pan-Islamism,* 144.

18. On Sayyid Amir Ali's political career and works, see Ozcan, *Pan-Islamism,* 128–29, and Lelyveld, *Aligarh's First Generation,* 306–7. Echoing the central themes of Stubbe's work, Amir Ali published two Muslim reformist books on Islam as a civic religion compatible with enlightened western ideas: *A Critical Examination of the Life and Teachings of Mohammed* (1873) and *Spirit of Islam* (1891).

19. The following works focus on Thomas Arnold's groundbreaking contribution to Islamic studies and Urdu language and literature, rather than English, as the intellectual medium for Indian education: Katherine Watt, "Thomas Walker Arnold and the Re-Evaluation of Islam, 1864-1930," *Modern Asian Studies* 36.1 (2002): 1–98, esp. 53 and 69–70, and Lelyveld, *Aligarh's First Generation,* 245–46. As Arnold's former student and as an Urdu lecturer in Islamia College at Lahore, Shairani wrote a controversial linguistic work, *Punjab Mein Urdu* (1903), which traces the origins of Urdu to the Punjab region, a province of present-day Pakistan, proving that this language has native roots in the region. Against Hindi, the rival Indian language, this thesis consolidated Urdu as a symbol for Indo-Muslim national solidarity, indirectly promoting Muslim separatism in British India. With Pakistan's founding, Urdu has remained the official language of this Muslim-dominated state. On Arnold's influence on Shairani, see Simon Digby's review of *Politics and Society during the Early Medieval*

Period. Collected Works, vol. 1, by Mohammad Habibi and K. A. Nizami, in *Bulletin of the School of Oriental and African Studies, University of London* 39.2 (1976): 453–58. On Urdu's nationalist significance in the twentieth century, see Tariq Rahman, "The Urdu-English Controversy in Pakistan," *Modern Asian Studies* 31.1 (1997): 177–207.

20. In historical retrospect, the Aligarh movement's progressive ethos lent momentum to the separatist cause for Muslim national solidarity in India, although the connection between this movement and later offshoots of Muslim nationalism is more complex. Arnold's work on Islam was used to further Muslim national independence, even as he remained an unwavering loyalist throughout his life. For a more detailed discussion, see Watt, "Thomas Walker Arnold and the Re-Evaluation of Islam, 1864–1930," 48–49, 93.

21. See Ozcan, *Pan-Islamism,* 143. On the 1911–12 Turco-Italian War and Muslim perceptions of imperial Britain and the West, also see Ansari, *"The Infidel Within,"* 87–89.

22. Ibid., 87.

23. Ozcan, *Pan-Islamism,* 137–38, 141.

24. On 1975 as a momentous year for Pakistan that involved intense domestic opposition to Prime Minister Bhutto and PPP state rule, see Richard S. Wheeler, "Pakistan in 1975: The Hydra of Opposition," *Asian Survey* 16.2 (1976): 111–18.

25. Dipesh Chakrabarty, *Provincializing Europe: Postcolonial Thought and Historical Difference* (Princeton, NJ: Princeton UP, 2000), 42.

26. Ibid., 46.

Primary Sources

Al-Khafif, Murtada ibn. *The Egyptian History, treating of the Pyramids, the Inundation of the Nile, and other Prodigies of Egypt.* Trans. John Davies. London, 1672.
Ali, Ayaan Hirsi and Salman Rushdie. "Manifesto: Together Facing the New Totalitarianism." *Jyllands-Posten.* Feb. 28, 2006.
Ali, Sharaf al-Din, Yazdi. *The History of Timur-Bec, known by the name Tamerlain the Great.* Trans. John Darby. 2 vols. London, 1723.
Ali, Syed Amir. *A Critical Examination of the Life and Teachings of Mohammed.* London: Williams and Norgate, 1873.
An Abstract of the procedure of France since the Pyrenaean Treaty under these heads. London, 1684.
Annet, Peter. *Deism fairly stated, and fully vindicated from the gross imputations and groundless calumnies of modern believers.* London: W. Webb, 1746.
Aretius, Benedictus. *A Short History of Valentinus Gentilis.* London, 1696.
Astell, Mary. "Mary Astell's Preface to the *Embassy Letters; the Travels of an English Lady in Europe, Asia and Africa*, by Lady Mary Wortley Montagu 1724 & 1725." *The First Feminist: Reflections upon Marriage and other Writings by Mary Astell.* Ed. Bridget Hill. New York: St. Martin's Press, 1986.
———. "Reflections upon Marriage." *Astell: Political Writings.* Ed. Patricia Springborg. Cambridge: Cambridge UP, 1996.
"Ayn Rand Institute: NYU's Surrender Underscores Need to Display Danish Cartoons." *US Newswire*, Mar. 28, 2006.
Baker, E. *Eslam or the countries which have professed the faith of Mahomet.* Map. London: R. Wilkinson, 1817.
Barclay, Robert. *The True Christian Divinity.* London, 1678.
Barnard, James. *The Divinity of our Lord Jesus Christ Demonstrated.* London: J. C. Coghlan, 1789.
Barruel, Abbe. *Memoirs, illustrating the History of Jacobinism.* Trans. Robert Clifford. London: E. Booker, 1798.

Baxter, Richard. *The cure of church-divisions, or, Directions for weak Christians to keep them from being dividers or troublers of the church with some directions to the pastors how to deal with such Christians.* London, 1670.

Bayle, Pierre. "Charles Blount." *A general Dictionary, historical and critical.* London: James Bettenham, 1734–41.

Bentley, Richard. *Remarks upon a Late Discourse of Freethinking.* 8th ed. London, 1743.

Berkeley, George. *A Caution Against Socinianism.* Canterbury, 1787.

"Beware loose talk about a clash of civilizations." *The Independent* (London), Oct. 4, 2006: 26.

Blake, William. "The Divine Image." *The Complete Poetry and Prose of William Blake.* Ed. David V. Erdman. Berkeley: U of C Press, 2008.

Blount, Charles. *The Oracles of Reason.* London, 1693.

———. "Preface." *A Just Vindication of Learning.* London, 1680.

Boulainvilliers, Henri Comte de. *The Life of Mahomet.* London, 1731.

Broome, Ralph. *An Elucidation on the articles of Impeachment preferred by the last Parliament against Warren Hastings.* London, 1790.

———. *Letters from Simpkin the Second, to his dear brother in Wales; containing a humble description of the trial of Warren Hastings.* London, 1789.

Bugg, Francis. *Hidden things brought to light, whereby the Fox is unkennell'd: and the bowells of Quakerism ript up, laid open, and expos'd to publick view.* London, 1707.

Burke, Edmund. *The Correspondence of Edmund Burke.* Ed. Holden Furber. Vol. 5. London: Cambridge UP, 1965.

———. "Eleventh Report of Select Committee." *The Writings and Speeches of Edmund Burke.* Gen. ed. Paul Longford. Vol. 5, ed. P. J. Marshall. Oxford: Clarendon Press, 1991.

———. "Evidence on Begams of Oudh 22 April 1788." *The Writings and Speeches of Edmund Burke.* Gen. ed. Paul Longford. Vol. 6, ed. P. J. Marshall. Oxford: Clarendon Press, 1991.

———. "An Extempore Commonplace on the Sermon of Our Saviour on the Mount." *Pre-Revolutionary Writings.* Ed. Ian Harris. Cambridge: Cambridge UP, 1993.

———. "Opening of Impeachment 16 February 1788: Appendix." *The Writings and Speeches of Edmund Burke.* Gen. ed. Paul Longford. Vol. 6, ed. P. J. Marshall. Oxford: Clarendon Press, 1991.

———. "Policy of Making Conquests for the Mahometans." *The Writings and Speeches of Edmund Burke.* Gen. ed. Paul Longford. Vol. 5, ed. P. J. Marshall. Oxford: Clarendon Press, 1991.

———. *Reflections on the Revolution in France.* Ed. J. C. D. Clarke. Stanford: Stanford UP, 2001.

———. "Religion." *Pre-Revolutionary Writings.* Ed. Ian Harris. Cambridge: Cambridge UP, 1993.

———. "Speech on Almas Ali Khan." *The Writings and Speeches of Edmund Burke.* Gen. ed. Paul Longford. Vol. 5, ed. P. J. Marshall. Oxford: Clarendon Press, 1991.

———. "Speech on Fox's India Bill 1 December 1783." *The Writings and Speeches of Edmund Burke.* Gen. ed. Paul Longford. Vol. 5, ed. P. J. Marshall. Oxford: Clarendon Press, 1991.

———. "Speech on Method of Proceeding against Hastings 3 April 1786." *The Writings and Speeches of Edmund Burke.* Gen. ed. Paul Longford. Vol. 6, ed. P. J. Marshall. Oxford: Clarendon Press, 1991.

———. "Speech on the Opening of Impeachment 15 February 1788." *The Writings and Speeches of Edmund Burke.* Gen. ed. Paul Longford. Vol. 6, ed. P. J. Marshall. Oxford: Clarendon Press, 1991.

———. "Speech on the Opening of Impeachment 16 February 1788." *The Writings and Speeches of Edmund Burke.* Gen. ed. Paul Longford. Vol. 6, ed. P. J. Marshall. Oxford: Clarendon Press, 1991.

———. "Speech on the Opening of Impeachment 18 February 1788." *The Writings and Speeches of Edmund Burke.* Gen. ed. Paul Longford. Vol. 6, ed. P. J. Marshall. Oxford: Clarendon Press, 1991.

———. "Speech on the Opening of Impeachment 19 February 1788." *The Writings and Speeches of Edmund Burke.* Gen. ed. Paul Longford. Vol. 6, ed. P. J. Marshall. Oxford: Clarendon Press, 1991.

———. "Speech on the Petition of the Unitarian Society." 1792. *Edmund Burke: Selected Writings and Speeches.* Ed. Peter J. Stanlis. Garden City, NY: Anchor Books, 1963.

———. "Speech in Reply 28 May 1794." *The Writings and Speeches of Edmund Burke.* Gen. ed. Paul Longford. Vol. 7, ed. P. J. Marshall. Oxford: Clarendon Press, 1991.

———. "Speech in Reply 30 May 1794." *The Writings and Speeches of Edmund Burke.* Gen. ed. Paul Longford. Vol. 7, ed. P. J. Marshall. Oxford: Clarendon Press, 1991.

———. "Speech on the Sixth Article: Presents 21 April, 7 May 1789." *The Writings and Speeches of Edmund Burke.* Gen. ed. Paul Longford. Vol. 7, ed. P. J. Marshall. Oxford: Clarendon Press, 1991.

———. "Speech on the Toleration Bill 17th March, 1773." *The Writings and Speeches of Edmund Burke.* Gen. ed. Paul Longford. Vol. 2, ed. P. J. Marshall. Oxford: Clarendon Press, 1991.

———. "Thoughts on French Affairs." 1791. *Further Reflections on the Revolution in France.* Ed. Daniel E. Ritchie. Indianapolis: Liberty Fund, 1992.

———. "A Vindication of Natural Society." *Pre-Revolutionary Writings.* Ed. Ian Harris. Cambridge: Cambridge UP, 1993.

Bury, Arthur. *Naked Gospel.* London, 1690.

Buruma, Ian. "Lost in Translation." *The New Yorker.* June 14, 2004.

Cantemir, Demestrius. *The History of the Growth and Decay of the Ottoman Empire.* Trans. Nicholas Tindal. London, 1756.

The capitulations and articles of peace between the Majesty of the King of Great Britain, France, and Ireland, &c. and the Sultan of the Ottoman Empire. London, 1679.

Carlyle, Thomas. "Lecture II. The Hero as Prophet. Mahomet: Islam." 1840. *On Heroes, Hero-Worship, & the Heroic in History.* Eds. Michael K. Goldberg, Joel J. Brattin, and Mark Engel. Berkeley: U of California P, 1993.

Chalmers, A. *The General Biographical Dictionary.* New ed. 32 vols. (London: J. Nichols and Son, 1812–17.

The Character of an Ignoramus Doctor. London, 1681.

Cheynell, Francis. *The Divine Trinunity of the Father, Son, and Holy Spirit.* London, 1650.

———. *The rise, growth, and danger of Socinianisme together with a plaine discovery of a desperate designe of corrupting the Protestant religion.* London, 1643.

Chubb, Thomas. *The Posthumous Works of Mr. Thomas Chubb.* 2 vols. London: R. Baldwin, 1748.

Clarke, Samuel. "A Discourse concerning the unchangeable obligations of Natural Religion and the Truth and Certainty of the Christian Revelation." *The Works of Samuel Clarke.* 4 vols. London, 1738.

A Code of Gentoo Laws. Trans. Nathaniel Brassey Halhed. London, 1776.

Cole, Juan. *Napoleon's Egypt: Invading the Middle East.* New York: Palgrave Macmillan, 2007.

Coleridge, Samuel Taylor. *Anima Poetae.* Ed. Ernest Hartley Coleridge. London: William Heinemann, 1895.

———. *The Collected Letters of Samuel Taylor Coleridge.* Ed. Earl Leslie Griggs. Vols. 1–2. Oxford: Clarendon Press, 1956.

———. "Introductory Address" in *Conciones ad Populum or Addresses to the People. The Collected Works of Samuel Taylor Coleridge.* Gen. ed. Kathleen Coburn. Vol. 1, *Lectures 1795 On Politics and Religion,* eds. Lewis Patton and Peter Mann. Princeton, NJ: Princeton UP, 1971.

———. "Kubla Khan; or, A Vision in a Dream." *The Collected Works of Samuel Taylor Coleridge.* Gen. ed. Kathleen Coburn. Vol. 16, bk. 1, *Poetical Works,* ed. J. C. C. May. Princeton, NJ: Princeton UP, 2001.

———. "Lay Sermons." *The Collected Works of Samuel Taylor Coleridge.* Gen. ed. Kathleen Coburn. Vol. 6, ed. Reginald James White. Princeton, NJ: Princeton UP, 1972.

———. "Lectures on Revealed Religion, Its Corruptions, and Its Political Views." *The Collected Works of Samuel Taylor Coleridge.* Gen. ed. Kathleen Coburn. Vol. 10, *Lectures 1795 on Politics and Religion,* eds. Lewis Patton and Peter Mann. Princeton, NJ: Princeton UP, 1971.

———. "Mahomet." *The Collected Works of Samuel Taylor Coleridge.* Gen. ed. Kathleen Coburn. Vol. 16, bk. 1, *Poetical Works,* ed. J. C. C. May. Princeton, NJ: Princeton UP, 2001.

———. *The Notebooks of Samuel Taylor Coleridge.* Ed. Kathleen Coburn. Vol. 1. London: Routledge & Kegan Paul, 1957.

———. "On the Present War" in *Conciones Ad Populum or Addresses to the People. The Collected Works of Samuel Taylor Coleridge.* Vol. 1, *Lectures 1795 On Politics and Religion.* Eds. Lewis Patton and Peter Mann. Princeton, NJ: Princeton UP, 1971.

———. "The Power of Turkey" in *The Courier,* Aug. 30, 1811. *The Collected Works of Samuel Taylor Coleridge:* Vol. 3, *Essays on His Times,* eds. Kathleen Coburn and David V. Erdman. Princeton, NJ: Princeton UP, 1978.

———. "Religious Musings." *The Collected Works of Samuel Taylor Coleridge.* Gen. ed. Kathleen Coburn. Vol. 16, bk. 1, *Poetical Works,* ed. J. C. C. May. Princeton, NJ: Princeton UP, 2001.

Collins, Anthony. *A Discourse on the Grounds and Reasons of the Christian Religion.* London, 1724.

Copies of Original Letters from the Army of General Bonaparte in Egypt, intercepted by the Fleet under the command of Admiral Nelson. 2nd ed. London, 1798.

A Dialogue between Dr. Sherlock, the King of France, the Great Turk, and Dr. Oates. London, 1691.

Dalrymple, Theodore. "Unenlightened—As Extremist Muslims React to the Danish Cartoons, the Enlightenment Doesn't Look So Bad, Huh?" *National Review.* Feb. 27, 2006.

"Danish Cartoons Arrive (Almost) at N.Y.U." *New York Observer.* Apr. 10, 2006: 2.

"Danish Muhammed Cartoon reprinted." BBC News. Feb. 13, 2008.

Davies, John. Dedication. *The Egyptian History, treating of the Pyramids, the Inundation of the Nile, and other Prodigies of Egypt.* By Murtada ibn al-Khafif. London, 1672.

Davy, Du Perron Jacques. *Luthers Alcoran being a Treatise First Written in French by the learned Cardinall Person, of Famous Memory, against the Hugenots of France.* London, 1642.

Davy, John. *Fragmentary Remains, literary and scientific, of Sir Humphry Davy.* London: J. Churchill, 1858.

Davy, William and Joseph White. "Preface." *Institutes Political and Military . . . by the Great Timour.* Trans. William Davy and Joseph White. Oxford: Clarendon Press, 1783.

Dennis, John. "An Essay on the Opera's After the Italian Manner, which are about to be Establish'd on the English Stage: with some Reflections on the Damage which they may bring to the Publick," *The Critical Works of John Dennis.* 2 vols. Ed. Edward Niles Hooker. Baltimore: The Johns Hopkins UP, 1939.

De Quincey, Thomas. "Notes on Walter Savage Landor (part II)." *The Works of Thomas De Quincey.* Ed. Robert Morrison. 21 vols. London: Pickering & Chatto, 2000.

"A Discourse on the Principles of some Modern Infidels, occasioned by several late Books and Pamphlets." *London Journal* 700. Nov. 25, 1732.

Dr. Oates Answer to Count Teckleys Letter Intercepted at Dover. London, 1683.

Dr. Oates Answer to Count Teckly's Letter giving him a true account of the present horrible plot. London, 1683.

Dr. Oates last Farewell to England he went on ship-board Sunday last, with forescore bums to attend his sir-reverence to stom-bula, where he's a going to be mufty to the Grand Turk. London, 1680.

Dr. Oates last legacy's and his farewell sermon to being sent far to be the high priest to the Grand Turk. London, 1683.

Drummond, William. *Oedipus Judaicus.* London, 1811.

Dryden, John. *A true coppy of the Epilogue to Constantine the Great that which was first published being false and surreptitious.* London, 1684.

Du Bec, Jean. *The History of the Life of Tamerlane the Great.* London: W. Owen, 1753.

Dujardin, Richard C. "Religion, The Year in Review—Cultures in collision—2006 finds faiths at odds at home and abroad." *The Providence* (RI) *Journal.* Dec. 30, 2006.

Edwards, John. *The Socinian Creed, or a brief account of the professed tenents and doctrines of the foreign and english socinians.* London, 1697.

Elwall, Edward. *A Declaration against all the kings and temporal powers under heaven.* London, 1741.

———. *Idolatry discovered and detested.* London, 1744.

———. *The Triumph of Truth: being an account of the trial of Mr. E. Elwall, for heresy and blasphemy. An Appeal to the Serious and Candid Professors of Christianity.* Leeds, 1771.

Emlyn, Thomas. *The Works of Mr. Thomas Emlyn.* Vol. 2. London, 1746.

"An Epistle Dedicatory, to His Illustrious Excellency *Ameth Ben Ameth* Embassador of the Mighty Emperor of *Fez* and *Morrocco,* to *Charles* the 2d, King of *Great Britain.*" *The Socinian Controversy Discuss'd.* Charles Leslie. London, 1708.

Flemming, Rose, ed. "Muhammeds Ansigt." *Jyllands-Posten.* Sept. 3, 2005. *Four Treatises concerning the doctrine, discipline, and worship of the Mahometans.* London: Darby, 1712.

Floyer, Sir John Floyer. *The Sibylline Oracles, Translated from the Best Greek Copies, and Compared with the Sacred Prophecies, Especially with Daniel and the Revelations.* London, 1713.

Freke, William. *Vindication of the Unitarians, against the late reverend author on the Trinity in a letter.* London, 1690.

Fuller, Andrew. *The Calvinistic and Socinian Systems Examined and Compared.* Market-Harborough, UK: Button, Thomas, Matthews, and Gardiner, 1793.

Gibbon, Edward. *The History of the Decline and Fall of the Roman Empire.* 12 vols. London, 1788.

Glendhill, Ruth, and Philip Webster, "Archbishop of Canterbury Argues for Islamic Law in Britain." *The Times.* Feb. 8, 2008, www.timesonline.co.uk/tol/comment/faith/article3328024.ece, accessed Sept. 2, 2010.

Gourgaud, Baron. *Talks of Napoleon at St. Helena.* 1817. Trans. Elizabeth Wormeley Latiner. Chicago: A. C. McClurg and Co., 1904.

Grabe, Joannes Ernestus. *An Essay upon Two Arabick manuscripts of the Bodlejan Library.* London, 1711.

Great Britain House of Commons, *The minutes of what was offered by Warren Hastings . . . at the bar of the House of Commons.* London, 1786.

Great news from Count Teckely, or, An Account of Some Passages 'twixt a True Protestant English Volunteer, and a Teckelytish MAHOMETAN *in the Turkish Camp sent over by the Counts secretary to a brother in London.* London, 1684.

Griffiths, Ben, and Tim McEvoy. "The Right to Offend Belongs to All." *The Daily Illini.* Feb. 6, 2006.

Halsband, Robert, ed. *The Complete Letters of Lady Mary Wortley Montagu.* 3 vols. Oxford: Clarendon, 1965.

Hastings, Warren. *The Defence of Warren Hastings, Esq (late Governor General of Bengal,) at the bar of the House of Commons.* London, 1786.

———. *Memoirs relative to the state of India. A new edition, with additions.* London, 1786.

Higgins, Andrew. "Muslims ask French to cancel 1741 play by Voltaire." *Wall Street Journal.* Mar. 6, 2006.

"Historical and Critical Reflections on Mahometanism and Socinianism." *Four Treatises concerning the doctrine, discipline, and worship of the Mahometans.* London: J. Darby, 1712.

Hobbes, Thomas. *Leviathan.* Ed. C. B. Macpherson. New York: Penguin Books, 1968.

Horsley, Samuel. *Letters from the Archdeacon of Saint Albans, in reply to Dr. Priestley.* London, 1784.

———. *Tracts in Controversy with Dr. Priestley.* Glocester, 1789.

Howe, Thomas. *Critical Observations on books, ancient and modern.* Vol. 4. London: W. Richardson, 1776–.

The Intreigues of the French King at Constantinople to embroil Christendom discovered in several dispatches past betwixt him and the late Grand Seignior, Grand Vizier and Count Teckily: all of them found among that Count's papers seiz'd in December last: with some reflections upon them. London, 1689.

Jeffrey, Francis. Rev. of *Thalaba the Destroyer,* by Robert Southey. *Edinburgh Review, or Critical Journal* 1 (1802): 63–83.

Keith, George. *Oriental Philosophy, showing the Wisdom of Some Renowned Men of the East.* London, 1674.

Knolles, Richard. "The History of the Turkish Empire Continued." *The Turkish history from the original of that nation . . . whereunto is added, the present state of the Ottoman Empire by Sir Paul Pycaut.* London, 1687.

Landor, Walter Savage. "The Birth of Poesy." *The Complete Works of Walter Savage Landor.* Ed. Stephen Wheeler. 16 vols. London: Chapman and Hall, 1927.

———. "Extract from the French Preface." *The Complete Works of Walter Savage Landor.* Ed. Stephen Wheeler. 16 vols. London: Chapman and Hall, 1927.

———. "Gebir." *The Complete Works of Walter Savage Landor.* Ed. Stephen Wheeler. 16 vols. London: Chapman and Hall, 1927.

———. "To the Fellows of Trinity College." *The Complete Works of Walter Savage Landor.* Ed. Stephen Wheeler. 16 vols. London: Chapman and Hall, 1927.

Le Clerc, Jean. *Memoirs of Emeric Count Teckely. In four books.* London, 1693.

Lee, Nathaniel. *Constantine the Great, a Tragedy acted at the Theatre-Royal, by their majesties servants.* London, 1684.

Leibniz, Gottfried Wilhelm. "A Letter from Mr. Leibnitz to the Author of the Reflections upon the Origin of Mahometanism." *Four Treatises concerning the doctrine, discipline, and worship of the Mahometans.* London, 1712.

Leland, John. *A view of the principal deistical writers that have appeared in England in the last and present century.* London, 1754.

Lempriere, John. *Lempriere's Classical Dictionary of Proper Names in Ancient Authors.* Ed. Fredrick Adam Wright. London: Routledge & Kegan Paul, 1958.

Leslie, Charles. *Deism refuted: or the truth of Christianity demonstrated.* London, 1755.

———. *Socinian Controversy Discussed.* London, 1708.

———. *The Truths of Christianity Demonstrated in a dialogue betwixt a Christian and a Deist.* 1711. London, 1799.

A Letter from Count Teckely to the Salamanca doctor: giving an account of the siege of Vienna, and the state of the Ottoman Empire. London, 1683.

Liberty of Conscience Confuted by reasons of Argument and Policie. Delivered in a Discourse betwixt a Turke and a Christian. Occasioned by a Letter written to a Peere of this Realme. London, 1648.

Life and Actions of Mahomet in Four Treatises concerning Mahometanism. London, 1712.

The Life of Mahomet; or the history of that imposture, which has begun, carried on, and finally established him in Arabia. London, 1799.

Locke, John. *A Letter concerning Toleration.* 1668. New York: Bobs Merrill, 1955.

MacCaulay, Catherine. *Letters on Education. With Observations on religious and metaphysical subjects.* London, 1790.

Macgowan, John. *Socinianism Brought to the Test.* London, 1773.

Mackey, Sampson Arnold. *The Mythological Astronomy of the Ancients Demonstrated by Restoring to their Fables and Symbols their Original Meaning.* 1822–23. Minneapolis: Wizards Bookshelf, 1973.

———. *A Reply, intended to be made to the various disputants, on an Essay on Chronology, which was read at the Philosophical Society of Norwich.* Norwich: R. Walker, 1825.

Maizeaux, Des. "Some Memoirs of the life and writings of Mr. John Toland." *A Collection of Several Pieces of Mr. Toland.* 2 vols. London: J. Peele, 1726.

Mangey, Thomas. *Remarks upon Nazarenus.* London, 1718.

Manley, Delariviere. "Almyna: or, the Arabian Vow." *The Selected Works of Delarivier Manley.* 5 vols. London: Pickering & Chatto, 2005.

Manley, Roger. "The History of the Turkish Empire Continued." *Turkish History*, 6th ed. Richard Knolles. London, 1687.

Marana, Giovanni Paolo. *Letters Writ by a Turkish Spy.* 8 vols. London, 1702–3.

McLachlan, John. *Socinianism in Seventeenth-Century England.* Oxford: Oxford UP, 1951.

Montagu, Lady Mary Wortley. *The Letters and Works of Lady Mary Wortley Montagu.* Ed. Lord Wharncliffe. 5 vols. London, 1837.

———. *Life of Lady Mary Wortley Montagu.* Ed. Robert Halsband. Oxford: Clarendon Press, 1956.

———. *The Turkish Embassy Letters.* Ed. Malcolm Jack. London: Virago Press, 1994.

Montesquieu, Charles-Louis de Secondat. *The Spirit of the Laws.* Trans. and eds., Anne M. Cohler, Basia Carolyn Miller, and Harold Samuel Stone. Cambridge: Cambridge UP, 1989.

The Morality of the East; extracted from the Koran of Mohammed. London, 1776.

Morgan, Thomas. *The Moral Philosopher in a dialogue between Philalethes a Christian deist, and Theophanes a Christian Jew.* London, 1737.

Mosheim, Johann Lorenz. *An Ecclesiastical History, Ancient and Modern.* 2 vols. London, 1765.

Muwakkil, Salim. "Islam vs. the West: Clashing Sensibilities." *The Third Coast* (Mar. 6, 2006): 17.

Norris, John. *An Account of Reason and Faith: in Relation to the Mysteries of Christianity.* London, 1697.

———. *A Murnival of Knaves, or Whiggism plainly display'd, and (if not grown shameless) burlesqu't out of countenance.* London, 1683.

Northleigh, John. *A gentle reflection on the modest account, and a vindication of the loyal abhorrers from calumnies of a factious pen by the author of the Parallel.* London, 1682.

Nye, Stephen. *A Brief History of the Unitarians, called also Socinians in Four Letters, written to a friend.* London, 1687.

———. *A Letter of Resolution concerning the doctrines of the Trinity and the Incarnation.* London, 1691?

Oates new shams discovered: and how they carried it on from time to time sent in a letter to his Grace James Duke of Monmouth from Doctor Titus Oates. London, 1688?

———. *True and Exact Narrative of the Horrid Plot and Conspiracy of the Popish Party against the Life of His Sacred Majesty, the Government and the Protestant Religion, etc. published by the Order of the Right Honorable the Lords Spiritual and Temporal in Parliament assembled.* London, 1679.

Ockley, Simon. "Preface." *The history of the Saracens.* 2nd ed. London, 1718.

Paine, Thomas. *The Age of Reason.* Ed. Philip Sheldon Foner. Secaucus: Carol Publishing Group, 1998.

———. "Origin of Freemasonry." *The Life and Works of Thomas Paine.* Ed. William M. Van der Weyde. 10 vols. New Rochelle: Thomas Paine National Historical Association, 1925.

———. *Rights of Man.* Mineola, NY: Dover Publications, 1999.

Paley, William. *The Principles of moral and political philosophy.* 3rd ed. London, 1786.

"Panel Discussion on Free Speech and the Danish Cartoons to Be Held at the University of Chicago; Cartoons Will Be on Display." *US Newswire.* Apr. 17, 2006.

Parkhurt, John. *The divinity and pre-existence of our Lord and Saviour Jesus Christ.* London, 1787.

Pirie, Alexander. *An Attempt to Expose the weakness, fallacy, and absurdity, of the Unitarian or Socinian arguments.* Perth, 1792.

Prideaux, Humphrey. *The True Nature of Imposture Fully Displayed in the Life of Mahomet.* London, 1697.

Priestley, Joseph. *Defences of the History of the Corruptions of Christianity.* London, 1786.

———. *Defences of Unitarianism for the year 1787.* Birmingham, 1788.

———. *Discourses on the Evidence of Revealed Religions.* London, 1794.

————. *Discourses on Various Subjects*. Birmingham, 1787.

————. *Discourses relating to the Evidence of Revealed Religion*. London, 1796.

————. *Disquistions relating to Matter and Spirit*. 2nd ed. 2 vols. Birmingham, 1782.

————. *An history of the corruptions of Christianity*. 2 vols. Birmingham, 1782.

————. *Letters to Dr. Horsley*. Birmingham, 1783–6.

————. *Letters to the Rev. Edward Burn*. Birmingham, 1790.

————. *The Theological and Miscellaneous Works of Joseph Priestley*. 25 vols. London: G. Smallfield, 1817–32.

The Prospect before Us. Being a Series of Papers upon the Great Question which now Agitates the Public Mind. London, 1788.

Rahman, As'ad Abul. "Respect Each Other to Avoid a Clash of Civilizations." *Global News Wire*. Mar. 11, 2006.

The rebels association in Hungary for reformation of religion and advancement of the Empire. London, 1682.

Reflections on Mohammedanism, and the Conduct of Mohammed. Occasioned by a late learned translation and exposition of the Koran or alkoran. London, 1735.

Reid, William Hamilton. *The Rise and Dissolution of the Infidel Societies in the Metropolis*. 1800. Plymouth: Woburn Press, 1971.

Review of Burke's Speech during the Hastings Proceedings. *Gazetteer*. Feb. 15–16, 18–19 1788.

————. *World*. Feb. 18–19, 1788.

Review of *Helga; A Poem. In Seven Cantos*, by William Herbert. *The Edinburgh Review, or the Critical Journal* 25 (1815): 146–68.

Review of "Mackey's "Theory of the Earth." *Notes and Queries* 8.1 (1853): 565–66.

————. *Notes and Queries* 9.1 (1854): 179.

Robinson, John. *Proofs of a conspiracy against all Religions and Governments of Europe*. London, 1798.

Robertson, William. *An Historical Disquisition concerning the Knowledge which the ancients had of India*. London, 1791.

Robinson, Mary. *Thoughts on the Condition of Women, and on the Injustice of Mental Subordination*. 2nd ed. London, 1799.

Rose, H. J. *A New General Biographical Dictionary*. 1853.

Rowe, Nicholas. "Epistle Dedicatory." *Tamberlane. A Tragedy*. 2nd ed. London: Jacob Tonson, 1703.

Sale, George, ed. and trans., *The Koran: or, Alcoran of Mohammed*. 1734. London: Frederick Warne and Co., 1910.

————. "The Preliminary Discourse." *The Koran: or, Alcoran of Mohammed*. 1734. London: Frederick Warne and Co., 1910.

The Salamanca Doctors comment upon the Proclamation. London, 1683.

Sayer, James. *A Reverie of Prince Demetrius Cantemir, Ospidar of Moldavia*. London, 1788.

Scott, Major John. *A Letter to the Right Honourable Charles James Fox, on the extraneous matter contained in Mr. Burke's Speeches*. London, 1789.

Shairani, Hafiz, Mahmud Khan. "Preface" and "Introduction." *The Rise and Progress of Mahometanism*. 1911. Lahore: Orientalia, 1975.

Shelley, Mary. *Frankenstein*. Ed. J. Paul Hunter. New York: W. W. Norton, 1996.

———. "The Last Man." *The Novels and Selected Works of Mary Shelley*. 8 vols. Eds. Jane Blumberg and Nora Crook. London: William Pickering, 1996.

———. *Mary Shelley's Journal*. Ed. Frederick L. Jones. Norman: U of Oklahoma P, 1947.

———. "Preface." *Essays, Letters from Abroad, Translations and Fragments*. By Percy Bysshe Shelley. 2 vols. London: Edward Moxon, 1840.

Shelley, Percy. "The Assassins: A Fragment of a Romance." *The Prose Works of Percy Bysshe Shelley*, vol. 1. Ed. E. B. Murray. Oxford: Clarendon Press, 1993.

———. "Hellas." *Shelley's Poetry and Prose*. Eds. Donald H. Reiman and Sharon B. Powers. New York: W. W. Norton, 1977.

———. "Laon and Cythna; or the Revolution of the Golden City: A Vision of the Nineteenth Century." *The Poems of Shelley*. Eds. Kelvin Everest and Geoffrey Matthews. 2 vols. Essex: Pearson Education Limited, 2000.

———. *The Letters of Percy Bysshe Shelley*. Ed. Roger Ingpen. 2 vols. London: Sir Isaac Pitman & Sons, 1909.

———. "On Christianity." *The Prose Works of Percy Bysshe Shelley*. vol. 1. Ed. E. B. Murray. Oxford: Clarendon Press.

———. "Ozymandias." *The Poems of Shelley*. Eds. Kelvin Everest and Geoffrey Matthews. 2 vols. Essex: Pearson Education Limited, 2000.

———. "A Philosophical View of Reform." *Shelley's Revolutionary Year*. London: Redwords, 1990.

Sheridan, Richard Brinsley. *The Speeches of the Late Right Honourable Richard Brinsley Sheridan*. 2 vols. London, 1816.

Sherlock, William. *A Vindication of the doctrine of the Holy and ever blessed Trinity and the Incarnation of the Son of God*. London, 1691.

Shirley, John. *The History of the state of the present war in Hungary, Austria, Croatia, Moravia, and Silesia*. London, 1683.

Slackman, Michael. "Bin Laden reaffirms role on world stage." *International Herald Tribune* (Apr. 25, 2006): 4.

———. "Bin Laden Says West Is Waging War Against Islam, and Urges Supporters to Go to Sudan." *New York Times* (Apr. 24, 2006): A1.

Smalbroke, Richard. *The New Arian reprov'd: or, a Vindication of some Reflections on the conduct of Mr. Whiston, in his revival of the Arian heresy*. London: Timothy Childe, 1711.

Smith, Joseph. *The Unreasonableness of deism, or the certainty of a divine revelation* London, 1720.

Southey, Robert. *The Commonplace Book*. Ed. John Wood Warter. 4 vols. London: Longman, Brown, Green, and Longmans, 1850.

———. *The Correspondence of Robert Southey with Caroline Bowles*. Ed. E. Dowden. Dublin: Hodges and Friggs; and London: Longmans and Green, 1881.

―――. "The Curse of Kehama." *Robert Southey: Poetical Works 1793–1810*. Ed. Lynda Patt. 5 vols. London: Pickering and Chatto, 2004.

―――. "Joan of Arc." *Robert Southey: Poetical Works 1793–1810*. Ed. Lynda Patt. 5 vols. London: Pickering and Chatto, 2004.

―――. *The Letters of Robert Southey to John May, 1797 to 1838*. Ed. Charles Ramos. Austen: Jenkins Publishing Co., 1976.

―――. *The Life and Correspondence of the Late Robert Southey*. 6 vols. Ed. Charles C. Southey. London: Longman, Brown, Green & Longmans, 1850.

―――. "Mohammed. Book 2." *Robert Southey: Poetical Works 1793–1810*. Ed. Lynda Pratt. 5 vols. London: Pickering and Chatto, 2004.

―――. Review of *Gebir*, by Walter Savage Landor. *Critical Review* 27 (1799): 29–39.

―――. *Selections from the Letters of Robert Southey*. 4 vols. Ed. John Wood Warter. London: Longman, Brown, Green, and Longmans, 1856.

―――. "Speech on Bengal Judicature Bill" (1781), 5:140–41.

―――. "Speech on Moving Resolutions for Conciliation with America" (1775), 2:126.

―――. "Thalaba the Destroyer." *Robert Southey: Poetical Works 1793–1810*. Eds. Lynda Patt and Tim Fulford. 5 vols. London: Pickering and Chatto, 2004.

Southey, Robert and Herbert Hill, *Oliver Newman: a New-England tale (unfinished): with other Poetical Remains*. London: Longman, Brown, Green, & Longmans, 1845.

Stillingfleet, Edward. "Preface." *A Discourse in Vindication of the doctrine of the Trinity*. London, 1697.

Stubbe, Henry. *The Rise and Progress of Mahometanism*. 1911. Lahore: Orientalia, 1975.

The Sum of Nine Articles lately ratified and mutually counterchanged, between the Ottoman Emperour and Count Emeric Techli, leader of the Hungarian Malecontents. London, 1683.

Taylor, William. *A Memoir of the Life and Writings of the Late William Taylor*. 2 vols. London: John Murray, 1843.

A Testimony and Warning against Socinian and Unitarian errors. Glasgow, 1793.

Tindal, Matthew. *Christianity as Old as the Creation*. London, 1730.

Toland, John. *Christianity not Mysterious*. London, 1696.

―――. *A collection of several pieces of Mr. John Toland*. 2 vols. London, 1726.

―――. "English Extracts of *Nazarenus*." 1698. *Nazarenus: or, Jewish, Gentile, and Mahometan Christianity*. Ed. Justin Champion. Oxford: Voltaire Foundation, 1999.

―――. *A letter from an Arabian physician to a famous professor in the University of Hall in Saxony, concerning Mahomet's taking up arms, his marrying of many wives, his keeping of concubines, and his paradise*. London? 1706?

―――. *Nazarenus: or, Jewish, Gentile, and Mahometan Christianity*. 1718. Ed. Justin Champion. Oxford: Voltaire Foundation, 1999.

Toulmin, Joshua. *A Free and Serious Address to the Christian Laity*. London, 1781.

Tracts Printed and Published by the Unitarian Society for promoting Christian Knowledge and the Practice of Virtue. 13 vols. London, 1791–1802.

The Trial of Warren Hastings, Esq. 2 vols. London, 1794.

"200," *South Park.* Comedy Central. Apr. 14, 2010.

"201" *South Park.* Comedy Central. Apr. 21, 2010.

An Universal History, from the earliest account of time to the present. 20 vols. Dublin: Edward Bate, 1746.

Volney, Constantin Francois. *The Ruins, or Meditations on the Revolutions of Empire.* 1792. New York: Peter Eckler, 1890.

———. *Travels through Syria and Egypt.* Vol. 2. London, 1787. 2 vols.

Voltaire, Francois-Marie Arouet. "Essai sur les moeurs," chap. 43, *Oeuvres Complétes de Voltaire.* Ed. Louis Moland. 52 vols. Paris: Garnier Fréres, 1878.

———. "Of the Alcoran; and of Mahomet." *The Works of M de Voltaire. Translated from the French with notes, historical and critical.* Trans. Dr. Smollet. 25 vols. London, 1762.

Vossius, Issac. *Isaaci Vossii De Sibyllinis aliisque quae Christi natalem praecessere oraculis accedit ejusdem responsio ad objectiones nuperae criticae sacrae.* Oxoniae: E Theatro Sheldoniano, 1679.

Wajid, Sara. "Secular, Liberal, and Doggedly Fundamentalist." *The Times Higher Education Supplement* (Mar. 17, 2006): 18.

Warburton, William. *The Divine Legation of Moses demonstrated, on the principles of a religious deist.* 2 vols. London: Mr. Fletcher Gyles, 1742–58.

Warren, Albertus. *An Apology for the Discourse of Human reason written by Martin Clifford.* London, 1680.

Whiston, William. *A Vindication of the Sibylline Oracles.* London, 1715.

Williams, Rowan. "Archbishop's Lecture-Civil and Religious Law in England: A Religious Perspective." *The Archbishop of Canterbury.* N.p. Feb. 7, 2008, www.archbishopofcanterbury.org/1575, accessed Sept. 2, 2010.

Wilmot, John. *The Letters of John Wilmot, Earl of Rochester.* Ed. J. Treglown. Oxford: Oxford UP, 1980.

Wollstonecraft, Mary. *A Critical Edition of Mary Wollstonecraft's 'A Vindication of the Rights of Woman: With Strictures on Political and Moral Subjects.'* Ed. Ulrich H. Hardt. Troy, NY: Whitston Publishing, 1982.

———. *Historical and Moral View of the Origin and Progress of the French Revolution.* London, 1794.

Wood, Anthony. *Athenae Oxoniensis.* 4 vols. London, 1813–20.

Secondary Sources

Aaron, Jane. "The Return of the Repressed: Reading Mary Shelley's *The Last Man.*" *Feminist Criticism: Theory and Practice.* Ed. Susan Sellers. New York: Harvester Wheatsheaf, 1991.

Abrams, M. H. *Natural Supernaturalism: Tradition and Revolution in Romantic Literature.* New York: W. W. Norton, 1971.

Adas, Michael. *Prophets of Rebellion: Millenarian Protest Movements against the European Colonial Order.* Cambridge: Cambridge UP, 1979.

Ahmad, Munir. "Oriental Influences in Romantic Poetry with Special Reference to Coleridge and Southey." Ph.D. diss., U of Birmingham, 1959.

Ahmed, Leila. *Women and Gender in Islam: Historical Roots of a Modern Debate*. New Haven: Yale UP, 1992.

Alam, Muzaffar. *The Languages of Political Islam: India 1200–1800*. Chicago: U of Chicago P, 2004.

Alavi, Seema. "Introduction." *The Eighteenth Century in India*. Ed. Seema Alavi. Oxford: Oxford UP, 2002.

Al-Da'mi, Muhammed A. *Arabian Mirrors and Western Soothsayers: Nineteenth-Century Literary Approaches to Arab-Islamic History*. New York: Peter Lang, 2002.

Allen, Don Cameron. *The Legend of Noah: Renaissance Rationalism in Art, Science, and Letters*. Urbana: U of Illinois P, 1949.

Andrea, Bernadette. *Women and Islam in Early Modern English Literature*. Cambridge: Cambridge UP, 2007.

———. "Women and Their Rights: Gülen's Gloss on Lady Montagu's "Embassy" to the Ottoman Empire." *Muslim Citizens of the Globalized World*. Eds. Robert A. Hunt and Yüksel A. Aslandoğan. Somerset, NJ: The Light, 2007.

Anidjar, Gil. *The Jew, The Arab: A History of the Enemy*. Stanford: Stanford UP, 2003.

Ansari, Humayun. *"The Infidel Within": Muslims in Britain since 1800*. London: Hurst & Co., 2004.

———. "Making Transnational Connections: Muslim Networks in early Twentieth Century Britain." *Islam in Inter-War Europe*. Eds. Nathalie Clayer and Eric Germain. New York: Columbia UP, 2008.

Apetrei, Sarah. "Call No Man Master Upon Earth": Mary Astell's Tory Feminism and an Unknown Correspondence." *Eighteenth-Century Studies* 41.4 (2008): 507–23.

Aravamudan, Srinivas. *Guru English: South Asian Religion in a Cosmopolitan Language*. Princeton, NJ: Princeton UP, 2006.

———. "In the Wake of the Novel: The Oriental Tale as National Allegory." *Novel: A Forum on Fiction* 33.1 (1999): 5–31.

———. "Lady Mary Wortley Montagu in the *Hammam*: Masquerade, Womanliness, and Levantinization." *ELH* 62.1 (1995): 69–104.

———. *Tropicopolitans: Colonialism and Agency, 1688–1804*. Durham: Duke UP, 1999.

Archinstein, Sharon. "Mary Astell, Religion, and Feminism: Texts in Motion." *Mary Astell: Reason, Gender, Faith*. Eds. William Kolbrener and Michal Michelson. Burlington, VT: Ashgate, 2007.

Armitage, David and Sanjay Subrahmanyam, eds. *The Age of Revolutions in Global Context, c. 1760–1840*. New York: Palgrave Macmillan, 2010.

Asad, Talal. *Formations of the Secular: Christianity, Islam, and Modernity*. Stanford: Stanford UP, 2003.

———. *Genealogies of Religion: Discipline and Reasons of Power in Christianity and Islam*. Baltimore: The Johns Hopkins UP, 1993.

Ayalan, Ami. *The Press in the Arab Middle East: A History*. New York: Oxford UP, 1995.

Ayling, Stanley. *Edmund Burke: His Life and Opinions*. New York: St. Martin's Press, 1998.

Backscheider, Paula R. "Barry, Elizabeth (1656/8–1773)." *Oxford Dictionary of National Biography*. 2004.

Bailyn, Bernard. *Ideological Origins of the American Revolution*. Cambridge, MA: Belknap Press of Harvard UP, 1967.

Bainbridge, Simon. *Napoleon and English Romanticism*. Cambridge: Cambridge UP, 1995.

Ball, Bryan W. *A Great Expectation: Eschatological Thought in English Protestantism to 1660*. Leiden: Brill, 1975.

Ballaster, Ros. *Fabulous Orients: Fictions of the East in England, 1662–1785*. Oxford: Oxford UP, 2005.

Bannet, Eve Tavor. "The "Abyss of the Present" and Women's Time in Mary Shelley's *The Last Man*." *The Eighteenth-Century Novel* 2 (2002): 353–81.

———. *The Domestic Revolution: Enlightenment Feminisms and the Novel*. Baltimore: The Johns Hopkins UP, 2000.

Barlas, Asma. *"Believing Women" in Islam: Unreading Patriarchal Interpretations of the Qur'an*. Austin: U of Texas P, 2002.

Barnett, Richard B. "Embattled Begums: Women as Power Brokers in Early Modern India." *Women in the Medieval Islamic World: Power, Patronage, and Piety*. Ed. Gavin R. G. Hambly. New York: St. Martin's Press, 1998.

Barnstone, Willis and Marvin Meyer, eds. *The Gnostic Bible*. Boston: Shambhala, 2003.

Barrel, John. *The Infection of Thomas De Quincey: A Psychopathology of Imperialism*. New Haven: Yale UP, 1991.

Bar-Yosef, Eitan. *The Holy Land in English Culture 1799–1917*. Oxford: Clarendon Press, 2005.

Bayly, Christopher A. *The Birth of the Modern World*, 1780–1914. Malden, MA: Blackwell, 2004.

———. *Empire and Information: Intelligence Gathering and Social Communication in India, 1780–1870*. Cambridge: Cambridge UP, 1996.

———. "The First Age of Global Imperialism, 1760–1830." *Journal of Imperial and Commonwealth History* 26.2 (1998): 28–47.

———. *Imperial Meridian: The British Empire and the World 1780–1830*. London: Longman, 1989.

———. "Van Leur and the Indian Eighteenth Century." *On the Eighteenth Century as a Category of Asian History*. Eds. Leonard Blusse and F. S. Gaastra. Brookfield: Ashgate, 1998.

Beach, Adam R. "Lady Mary Wortley Montagu and Slavery in the Ottoman (and the British) Empire." *Philological Quarterly* 85.3 (2006): 293–314.

Bennison, Amira K. "Muslim Universalism and Western Globalization." *Globalization in World History*. Ed. A. G. Hopkins. London: Pimlico, 2002.

Bentley, G. E., Jr. *Blake Books Supplement*. Oxford: Clarendon Press, 1995.

Berman, David. "Deism, Immortality, and the Art of Theological Lying." *Deism,*

Masonry, and the Enlightenment. Ed. J. A. Leo Lemay. Newark: U of Delaware P, 1987.

Bernal, Martin. *Black Athena: The Afroasiatic Roots of Classical Civilization.* 2 vols. New Brunswick: Rutgers UP, 1985.

Bernhardt-Kabisch, Ernest. *Robert Southey.* Boston: Twayne Publishers, 1977.

Berti, Silvia, Francoise Charles-Daubert, and Richard H. Popkin, eds. *Heterodoxy, Spinozism, and Free Thought in Early-Eighteenth-Century Europe.* Dordrecht: Kluwer, 1996.

Betts, C. J. *Early Deism in France.* Hague: Martinus Nijhoff, 1984.

Beynon, John C. "Lady Mary Wortley Montagu's Sapphic Vision." *Imperial Desire: Dissident Sexualities and Colonial Literature.* Eds. Philip Holden and Richard R. Ruppel. Minneapolis: U of Minnesota P, 2003.

Birchwood, Matthew. "News from Vienna: Titus Oates and the True Protestant Turks." *Cultural Encounters Between East and West.* Eds. Matthew Birchwood and Mathew Dimmock. Newcastle: Cambridge Scholars Press, 2005.

———. *Staging Islam in England: Drama and Culture, 1640–1685.* Cambridge: D. S. Brewer, 2007.

———. "Vindicating the Prophet." *Prose Studies* 29.1 (2007): 59–72.

Blackstone, Bernard. "Byron and Islam: the Triple Eros." *Journal of European Studies* 4 (1974): 63–81.

Blaut, James Morris. *The Colonizer's Model of the World: Geographical Diffusionism and Eurocentric History.* New York: The Guilford Press, 1993.

Blumenberg, Hans. *The Legitimacy of the Modern Age.* Cambridge, MA: MIT Press, 1983.

Bohls, Elizabeth A. *Woman Travel Writers and the Language of Aesthetics, 1716–1818.* Cambridge: Cambridge UP, 1995.

Bolton, Carol. *Writing the Empire: Robert Southey and Romantic Colonialism.* London: Pickering and Chatto, 2007.

Bose, Sugata. *A Hundred Horizons: The Indian Ocean in the Age of Global Empire.* Cambridge, MA: Harvard UP, 2006.

Bourke, Richard. "Edmund Burke and the Politics of Conquest." *Modern Intellectual History* 4.3 (2007): 403–32.

Bowen, H. V. *The Business of Empire: The East India Company, 1756–1833.* Cambridge: Cambridge UP, 2006.

———. *Revenue and Reform: The Indian Problem in British Politics, 1757–1773.* Cambridge: Cambridge UP, 1991.

Boyarin, Daniel. "Hybridity and Heresy: Apartheid Comparative Religion in Late Antiquity." *Postcolonial Studies and Beyond.* Eds. Ania Loomba, Survir Kaul, Matti Bunzl, Antoinette Burton, and Jed Esty. Durham: Duke UP, 2005.

Boyle, Mary L. *Biographical Notices of the Portraits at Hinchingbrook.* London: Victoria Press, 1876.

Bradley, James E. *Religion, Revolution, and English Radicalism: Nonconformity in Eighteenth-Century Politics and Society.* Cambridge: Cambridge UP, 1990.

Bredvold, Louis. "Deism Before Lord Herbert." *Papers of the Michigan Academy of Science, Arts, and Letters* 4 (1924): 431–42.

Brewer, John. *Party Ideology and Popular Politics at the Accession of George III.* Cambridge: Cambridge UP, 1976.

———. *The Sinews of Power: War, Money and the English State.* Cambridge, MA: Harvard UP, 1990.

Brown, Nathaniel. *Sexuality and Feminism in Shelley.* Cambridge, MA: Harvard UP, 1979.

Brown, Norman O. *The Challenge of Islam: The Prophetic Tradition.* Ed. Jerome Neu. Santa Cruz: New Pacific Press, 2009.

———. "The Prophetic Tradition." *Studies in Romanticism* 21.3 (1982): 367–72.

Burgess, Glen. *The Politics of the Ancient Constitution.* University Park: Pennsylvania State UP, 1992.

Burke, Edmund III. "Islamic History as World History: Marshall Hodgson, 'The Venture of Islam.'" *International Journal of Middle East Studies* 10.2 (1979): 241–64.

Burton, Antoinette M. "Introduction: On the Inadequacy and Indispensability of the Nation." *After the Imperial Turn: Thinking with and through the Nation.* Ed. Antoinette Burton. Durham, NC: Duke UP, 2003.

Burton, Jonathan. *Traffic and Turning: Islam and English Drama, 1579–1624.* Newark: U of Delaware P, 2005.

Butler, Marilyn. "Druids, Bards and Twice-Born Bacchus: Peacock's Engagement with Primitive Mythology." *Keats-Shelley Review* 36 (1985): 57–76.

———. "Myth and Mythmaking in the Shelley Circle." *Journal of English Literary History* 49.1 (1982): 50–72.

———. "Orientalism." *The Romantic Period.* Ed. David B. Pirie. London: Penguin Books, 1994.

———. "Plotting the Revolution: The Political Narratives of Romantic Poetry and Criticism." *Romantic Revolutions: Criticism and Theory.* Eds. Kenneth R. Johnston, Gilbert Chaitin, Karen Hansen, and Herbert Marks. Bloomington: Indiana UP, 1990.

———. "Romantic Manichaeism: Shelley's 'On the Devil and Devils' and Byron's Mythological Dramas." *The Sun Is God: Painting, Literature and Mythology in the Nineteenth Century.* Ed. J. B. Bullen. Oxford: Clarendon Press, 1989.

———. "Shelley and the Empire in the East." *Shelley: Poet and Legislator of the World.* Eds. Betty T. Bennett and Stuart Curran. Baltimore: The Johns Hopkins UP, 1996.

Butterfield, Herbert. *The Whig Interpretation of History.* 1931. New York: The Norton Library, 1965.

Byrne, Peter. *Natural Religion and the Nature of Religion: The Legacy of Deism.* London: Routledge, 1989.

Cairncross, John. *After Polygamy Was Made Sin, the Social History of Christian Polygamy.* London: Routledge & Kegan Paul, 1974.

Cannon, John Aston. *The Fox-North Coalition: Crisis of the Constitution, 1782–4.* Cambridge: Cambridge UP, 1969.

Cantor, Paul A. "The Apocalypse of Empire: Mary Shelley's *The Last Man.*" *Iconoclastic Departures: Mary Shelley After Frankenstein.* Eds. Syndy M. Conger, Frederick S. Frank, and Gregory O'Dea. London: Associated UP, 1997.

Canuel, Mark. *Religion, Toleration, and British Writing, 1790–1830.* Cambridge: Cambridge UP, 2002.

Carnall, Geoffrey. *Robert Southey and His Age: The Development of a Conservative Mind.* Oxford: Clarendon Press, 1960.

Carnell, Rachel. *A Political Biography of Delarivier Manley.* London: Pickering & Chatto, 2008.

Casanova, Jose. *Public Religions in the Modern World.* Chicago: U of Chicago P, 1994.

Cernovodeanu, Paul. *England's Trade Policy in the Levant and Her Exchange of Goods with the Romanian Countries under the latter Stuarts.* Bucharest: Academy of the Socialist Republic of Romania, 1972.

Certeau, Michel de. *The Writing of History.* Trans. Tom Cowley. New York: Columbia UP, 1988.

Chakrabarty, Dipesh. *Provincializing Europe: Postcolonial Thought and Historical Difference.* Princeton, NJ: Princeton UP, 2000.

Champion, Justin. "Legislators, Impostors, and the Politic Origins of Religion: English Theories of 'Imposture' from Stubbe to Toland." *Heterodoxy, Spinozism, and Free Thought in Early Eighteenth-Century Europe.* Eds. Silvia Berti, Francois Charles-Daubert, and Richard H. Popkin. Dordrecht: Kluwer, 1996.

———. *The Pillars of Priestcraft Shaken: The Church of England and Its Enemies, 1660–1730.* Cambridge: Cambridge UP, 1992.

———. *Republican Learning: John Toland and the Crisis of Christian Culture, 1696–1722.* Manchester: Manchester UP, 2003.

———. "Toleration and Citizenship in Enlightenment England: John Toland and the Naturalization of the Jews, 1714–1753." *Toleration in Enlightenment Europe.* Eds. Ole Peter Grell and Roy Porter. Cambridge: Cambridge UP, 2000.

Chandler, David. "Robert Southey and the Prelude's 'Arab Dream.'" *Review of English Studies* 52.214 (2003): 203–19.

Chapin, Chester. "Was William Wollaston (1660–1724) a Deist?" *A Quarterly Journal of Short Articles* 7.2 (1994): 72–76.

Chatterjee, Kumkum. "History as Self-Representation: The Recasting of a Political Tradition in Late Eighteenth-Century Eastern India." *Modern Asian Studies* 32.4 (1998): 913–48.

Chérif, Mustapha. *Islam and the West: A Conversation with Jacques Derrida.* Trans. Teresa Lavendar Fagan. Chicago: U of Chicago P, 2008.

Christianson, Paul. *Reformers and Babylon: English Apocalyptic Visions from the Reformation to the Eve of the Civil War.* Toronto: U of Toronto P, 1978.

Clark, Anna. *Scandal: The Sexual Politics of the British Constitution.* Princeton, NJ: Princeton UP, 2004.

Clark, Jonathan. *The Dynamics of Change: The Crisis of the 1750s and English Party.* Cambridge: Cambridge UP: 1982.

———. *English Society 1660–1832: Religion, ideology and politics during the ancien regime*. Cambridge: Cambridge UP, 1985.

———. "Introduction." *Reflections on the Revolution in France*. Stanford: Stanford UP, 2001.

Clvcas, Stephen. "Samuel Hartlib's Ephemerides, 1635–59, and the Pursuit of Scientific and Philosophical Manuscripts: the Religious Ethos of an Intelligencer." *Seventeenth Century* 6.1 (1991): 33–55.

Coleman, Deirdre. *Romantic Colonization and British Anti-Slavery*. Cambridge: Cambridge UP, 2005.

Cobbett, William, *A Complete Collection of State Trials*. Vol. 13, ed. Thomas Bayly Howell. London: T. C. Hansard, 1812.

Cole, Juan. *Napoleon's Egypt: Invading the Middle East*. New York: Palgrave Macmillan, 2007.

———. "Playing Muslim: Bonaparte's Army of the Orient and Euro-Muslim Creolization." *The Age of Revolutions in Global Context, c. 1760–1840*. Eds. David Armitage and Sanjay Subrahmanyam. New York: Palgrave Macmillan, 2010.

Colley, Linda. *Britons: Forging the Nation 1707–1837*. New Haven: Yale UP, 1992.

———. *Captives: Britain, Empire and the World, 1600–1850*. New York: Pantheon Books, 2002.

———. *In Defiance of Oligarchy: The Tory Party, 1714–60*. Cambridge: Cambridge UP, 1982.

———. "Eighteenth-Century English Radicalism before Wilkes." *Transactions of the Royal Historical Society*. 5th series, 31 (1981): 1–20.

Cooke, Arthur L. and Thomas B. Stroup. "The Political Implications in Lee's Constantine the Great." *Journal of English and Germanic Philology* 49 (1950): 506–15.

Corbin, Henry. *Cyclical Time and Ismaili Gnosis*. London: Kegan Paul International, Islamic Publications, 1983.

———. "Divine Epiphany and Spiritual Birth in Ismailian Gnosis." *Man and Transformation: Papers from the Eranos Yearbooks*. Vol. 5, Trans. Ralph Maneheim. Ed. Joseph Campbell. Princeton, NJ: Princeton UP, 1964.

Corbin, Henry and Leonard Fox. *Swedenborg and Esoteric Islam*. West Chester, PA: Swedenborg Foundation, 1995.

Cottle, Joseph. *Reminiscences of Samuel Taylor Coleridge and Robert Southey*. 2nd ed. London: Houlston and Stoneman, 1848.

Courtney, Cecil P. *Montesquieu and Burke*. Oxford: Basil Blackwell, 1963.

Cragg, Gerald R. *Reason and Authority in the Eighteenth Century*. London: Cambridge UP, 1964.

Crawford, Patricia. *Women and Religion in England, 1500–1720*. London: Routledge, 1993.

Crowe, Ian, ed. *An Imaginative Whig: Reassessing the Life and Thought of Edmund Burke*. Columbia: U of Missouri P, 2005.

Cruickshanks, Eveline. *Political Untouchables: the Tories and the '45*. London: Duckworth, 1979.

Cryle, Peter and Lisa O' Connell. *Libertine Enlightenment: Sex, Liberty and License in the Eighteenth Century*. New York: Palgrave Macmillan, 2004.

Cunningham, Allan. *Anglo-Ottoman Encounters in the Age of Revolution: Collected Essays*. Ed. Edward Ingram. 2 vols. Portland, OR: Frank Cass, 1993.

Curran, Stuart. *Shelley's Annus Mirabilis: The Maturing of an Epic Vision*. San Marino, CA: Huntington Library, 1975.

Daftary, Farhad. *A Short History of the Ismailis: Traditions of a Muslim Community*. Princeton, NJ: Markus Wiener, 1998.

Dalrymple, William. *White Mughals: Love and Betrayal in Eighteenth-Century India*. New York: Viking, 2002.

Daniel, Norman. *Islam, Europe, and Empire*. Edinburgh: Edinburgh UP, 1966.

Daniel, Stephen H. *John Toland: His Methods, Manners and Mind*. Kingston: McGill-Queen's UP, 1984.

Davenport, Richard Alfred. "A Sketch of the Life of George Sale." *The Koran: or, Alcoran of Mohammed*. 1734. London: Frederick Warne and Co., 1910.

Derrida, Jacques. "Faith and Knowledge: The Two Sources of 'Religion' at the Limits of Reason Alone." *Religion*. Eds. Jacques Derrida and Gianni Vattimo. Stanford: Stanford UP, 1996.

Derry, John W. *The Regency Crisis and the Whigs, 1788–9*. Cambridge: Cambridge UP, 1963.

Digby, Simon. Review of *Politics and Society during the Early Medieval Period. Collected Works*. Vol. 1. Mohammad Habibi and K. A. Nizami. *Bulletin of the School of Oriental and African Studies, University of London* 39.2 (1976).

Dimmock, Matthew. "'Machomet dyd before as Luther doth nowe': Islam, the Ottomans and the English Reformations." *Reformation* 9 (2004): 99–130.

———. *New Turkes: Islam and the Ottomans in Early Modern England*. Burlington, VT: Ashgate, 2005.

Diouf, Sylviane. *Servants of Allah: African Muslims Enslaved in the Americas*. New York: New York UP, 1998.

Dirks, Nicholas B. *The Scandal of Empire: India and the Creation of Imperial Britain*. Cambridge, MA.: Harvard UP, 2006.

Dobbs, Betty Jo Teeter. *The Foundations of Newton's Alchemy, or the Hunting of the Greene Lyon*. Cambridge: Cambridge UP, 1975.

Drew, John. "'Kubla Khan' and Orientalism." *Coleridge's Visionary Language: Essays in Honor of J. B. Beer*. Eds. Tim Fulford and Morton D. Paley. Cambridge: D. S. Brewer, 1993.

Droge, Arthur J. *Homer or Moses? Early Christian Interpretations of the History of Culture*. Tubingen: J. C. B. Mohr, 1989.

Edward, William Winks. *Lives of Illustrious Shoemakers*. London: Sampson, Low, Marston, Searle and Rivington, 1883.

Ellenzweig, Sarah. *The Fringes of Belief: English Literature, Ancient Heresy, and the Politics of Freethinking, 1660–1760*. Stanford: Stanford UP, 2008.

———. "The Love of God and the Radical Enlightenment: Mary Astell's Brush with Spinoza." *Journal of the History of Ideas* 64.3 (2003): 379–97.

Ellis, Markman. *The Coffee House: A Cultural History.* London: Weidenfeld & Nicolson, 2004.

Elmarsafy, Ziad. *The Enlightenment Qur'an: The Politics of Translation and the Construction of Islam.* Oxford: Oneworld, 2009.

Elofson, W. M. *The Rockingham Connection and the Second Founding of the Whig Party, 1768–1773.* Montreal: McGill-Queens UP, 1996.

Elwin, Malcolm. *Landor: A Replevin.* London: Macdonald, 1958.

Epstein, James. *In Practice: Studies in the Language and Culture of Popular Politics in Modern Britain.* Stanford: Stanford UP, 2003.

———. *Radical Expression: Political Language, Ritual, and Symbol in England, 1790–1850.* New York: Oxford UP, 1994.

Erickson, Amy Louise. *Women and Property in Early Modern England.* London: Routledge, 1993.

Erving, George S. "Coleridge, Priestley, and the Culture of Unitarian Dissent." Ph.D. diss. U of Washington, 2005.

Esposito, John L. *Islam: The Straight Path.* New York: Oxford UP, 1991.

Evans, Robert Rees. *Pantheisticon: The Career of John Toland.* New York: Peter Lang, 1991.

Faroqhi, Suraiya. *Subjects of the Sultan: Culture and Daily Life in the Ottoman Empire.* London: I. B. Tauris, 2000.

Fay, Mary Ann. "Women and *Waqf*: Property, Power, and the Domain of Gender in Eighteenth-Century Egypt." *Women in the Ottoman Empire: Middle Eastern Women in the Early Modern Era.* Ed. Madeline C. Zilfi. Leiden: Brill, 1997.

Ferguson, Moira. *First Feminists: British Women Writers 1578–1799.* Bloomington: Indiana UP, 1985.

Fisch, Audrey A., Anne K. Mellor, and Esther H. Schor, eds. *The Other Mary Shelley: Beyond Frankenstein.* New York: Oxford UP, 1993.

Fisher, Michael. *Counterflows to Colonialism: Indian Travellers and Settlers in Britain 1600–1857.* Delhi: Permanent Black, 2004.

Fleissner, Robert F. *Sources, Meaning, and Influences of Coleridge's Kubla Khan: Xanadu Re-Routed.* Lewiston, UK: The Edwin Mellen Press, 2000.

Force, James E. "Introduction," *An account of the Growth of Deism in England.* By William Stephens. 1696. Repr. Los Angeles: William Andrews Clark Memorial Library, 1990.

———. "The Newtonians and Deism." *Essays on the Context, Nature, and Influence of Isaac Newton's Theology.* Eds. James E. Force and Richard H. Popkin. Dordrecht: Kluwer, 1990.

———. *William Whiston: Honest Newtonian.* Cambridge: Cambridge UP, 1985.

Forman, Frieda Johles and Caoran Sowton, eds. *Taking Our Time: Feminist Perspectives on Temporality.* Oxford: Pergamon Press, 1989.

Forster, John. *Walter Savage Landor: A Biography.* 2 vols. London: Chapman and Hall, 1869.

Fouke, Daniel C. *Philosophy and Theology in a Burlesque Mode: John Toland and "the Way of Paradox."* New York: Humanity Books, 2007.

Franklin, Michael J. ed., *Romantic Representations of British India.* New York: Routledge, 2006.

Froom, Le Roy Edwin. *The Prophetic Faith of Our Fathers.* 4 vols. Washington, DC: Review and Herald, 1948.

Fulford, Tim. "Introduction." *Robert Southey: Poetical Works 1793–1810.* Eds. Lynda Pratt and Tim Fulford. 5 vols. London: Pickering and Chatto, 2004.

———. "Pagodas and Pregnant throes: Orientalism, Millenarianism and Robert Southey." *Romanticism and Millenarianism.* Ed. Tim Fulford. New York: Palgrave, 2002.

——— and Peter J. Kitsan, eds. *Romanticism and Colonialism.* Cambridge: Cambridge UP, 1998.

Gallagher, Catherine. "Embracing the Absolute: The Politics of the Female Subject in Seventeenth-Century England." *Genders* 1 (1988): 24–39.

———. *Nobody's Story: The Vanishing Acts of Women Writers in the Marketplace, 1670–1820.* Berkeley: U of California P, 1994.

Garcia, Humberto. "In the Name of the 'Incestuous Mother': Islam and Excremental Protestantism in De Quincey's *Infidel* Book." *Journal for Early Modern Cultural Studies* 7.2, (2007), 57–87.

Garrett, Clarke. *Respectable Folly: Millenarians and the French Revolution in France and England.* Baltimore: The Johns Hopkins UP, 1975.

Gay, Peter. *Deism: An Anthology.* Toronto: D. Van Nostrand Co., 1968.

"George Sale." *Oxford Dictionary of National Biography.* 2004–6.

Gerrard, Christine. *The Patriot Opposition to Walpole: Politics, Poetry, and National Myth, 1725–1742.* Oxford: Clarendon Press, 1994.

Gibbons, Luke. *Edmund Burke and Ireland: Aesthetics, Politics, and the Colonial Sublime.* Cambridge: Cambridge UP, 2003.

Gibson, William and Robert G. Ingram. *Religious Identities in Britain, 1660–1832.* Aldershot, UK: Ashgate, 2005.

Gilbert, Sandra and Susan Gubar. *The Madwoman in the Attic.* New Haven: Yale UP, 1979.

Gilmartin, Kevin. *Print Politics: The Press and Radical Opposition in Early Nineteenth-Century England.* Cambridge: Cambridge UP, 1996.

———. "Romanticism and Religious Modernity: From Natural Supernaturalism to Literary Sectarianism." *The Cambridge History of English Romantic Literature.* Ed. James Chandler. Cambridge: Cambridge UP, 2009.

Glasse, Cyril, ed. *The Concise Encyclopedia of Islam.* San Francisco: Harper and Row, 1989.

Goffman, Daniel. *Britons in the Ottoman Empire, 1642–1660.* Seattle: U of Washington P, 1998.

Goldsmith, Steven. *Unbuilding Jerusalem: Apocalypse and Romantic Representation.* Ithaca: Cornell UP, 1993.

Goldstone, Jack. *Revolution and Rebellion in the Early Modern World.* Berkeley: U of California P, 1991.

Gomez, Michael A. *Black Crescent: The Experience and Legacy of African Muslims in the Americas.* Cambridge: Cambridge UP, 2005.

Goodman, Lenn Evan. *God of Abraham.* New York and Oxford: Oxford UP, 1996.

———. *Islamic Humanism.* Oxford: Oxford UP, 2003.

Gordon, Alexander. *Heads of English Unitarian History.* 1895. Trowbridge, UK: Redwood Press, 1970.

Grand, Peter. *Islamic Roots of Capitalism.* Syracuse, NY: Syracuse UP, 1998.

Greaves, Richard L. *Enemies Under His Feet: Radicals and Nonconformists in Britain, 1664–1677.* Stanford: Stanford UP, 1990.

Greene, Jody. *The Trouble with Ownership: Literary Property and Authorial Liability in England, 1660–1730.* Philadelphia: U of Pennsylvania P, 2005.

Grendy, M. O. "Orientalism and Propaganda: The Oriental Tale and Popular Politics in Late Eighteenth-Century Britain." *The Eighteenth-Century Novel* 2 (2002): 215–37.

Griffiths, Ben and Tim McEvoy, "The right to offend belongs to all." *The Daily Illini.* Feb. 6, 2006.

Griggs, Earl Leslie. "Diadesté, a Fragment of an Unpublished play by Samuel Taylor Coleridge." *Modern Philology* 34.4 (1937): 377–85.

Grosrichard, Alain. *The Sultan's Court: European Fantasies of the East.* Trans. Liz Heron. London: Verso, 1998.

Grout, Donald Jay and Hermine Weigel Williams. *A Short History of the Opera.* New York: Columbia UP, 2003.

Grundy, Isobel. *Lady Mary Wortley Montagu: Comet of the Enlightenment.* Oxford: Oxford UP, 1999.

Gunny, Ahmad. *Images of Islam in Eighteenth-Century Writings.* London: Grey Seal, 1996.

Haakonssen, Knud, ed. *Enlightenment and Religion: Rational Dissent in Eighteenth Century Britain.* Cambridge: Cambridge UP, 1996.

Hall, M. B. "Arabic Learning in the Correspondence of the Royal Society 1660–1677." *The "Arabick" Interest of the Natural Philosophers in Seventeenth-Century England.* Ed. G. A. Russell. Leiden: Brill, 1994.

Haller, William W. *The Early Life of Robert Southey 1774–1803.* New York: Columbia UP, 1917.

Halm, Heinz. *Shiism.* Edinburg: Edinburg UP, 1991.

———. *The Shi'ites: A Short History.* Trans. Allison Brown. Princeton: Markus Wiener, 2007.

Hambly, Gavin R. G. "Armed Women retainers in the Zenanas of Indo-Muslim Rulers: the Case of Bibi Fatima." *Women in the Medieval Islamic World: Power, Patronage, and Piety.* Ed. Gavin R. G. Hambly. New York: St. Martin's Press, 1998.

Hanson, Laurence. *The Government and the Press, 1695–1763.* Oxford: Clarendon Press, 1936.

Harper, Tim. "Empire, Diaspora and the Languages of Globalism, 1850–1914." *Globalization in World History.* Ed. A. G. Hopkins. London: Pimlico, 2002.

Harrison, John Fletcher Clews. *The Second Coming: Popular Millenarianism 1780–1850*. New Brunswick, NJ: Rutgers UP, 1979.

Harrison, Peter. *'Religion' and Religions in the English Enlightenment*. Cambridge: Cambridge UP, 1990.

Hartley, Robert. "The Uroboros in Shelley's Poetry." *Journal of English and Germanic Philology* 73 (1974): 524–42.

Hassan, Nawal Muhammad. *Hayy Bin Yaqzan and Robinson Crusoe: A Study of an Early Arabic Impact on English Literature*. Baghdad: Al-Rashid House, 1980.

Haykel, Bernard. *Revival and Reform in Islam: The Legacy of Muhammed al-Shawkânî*. Cambridge: Cambridge UP, 2003.

Hearne, Thomas. *Remarks and Collections*. Vol. 3. Ed. Charles Edward Doble. Oxford: Clarendon Press, 1885–1921.

Heffernan, Teresa. "Feminism against the East/West Divide: Lady Mary's *Turkish Embassy Letters*." *Eighteenth-Century Studies* 33.2 (2000): 201–15.

Herman, Ruth. *The Business of a Woman: The Political Writings of Delarivier Manley*. Newark: U of Delaware P, 2003.

Herrick, James A. "The English Deists' Argument for Freedom of Expression." *Free Speech Yearbook* 34 (1996): 131–40.

———. *The Radical Rhetoric of the English Deist: The Discourse of Skepticism, 1680–1750s*. Columbia: U of South Carolina P, 1997.

Highfill, Philip H., Jr., Kalman A. Burnim, and Edward A. Langhans. *A Biographical Dictionary of Actors, Actresses, Musicians, Dancers, Managers, and Other Stage Personal in London: 1600–1800*. 16 vols. Carbondale: Southern Illinois UP, 1973.

Hill, Bridget. *The First English Feminist: "Reflections upon Marriage" and Other Writings by Mary Astell*. Aldershot, UK: Gower Publishing, 1986.

Hill, Christopher. *The Century of Revolution, 1603–1714*. 1961. London: Sphere Books, 1969.

———. *Change and Continuity in Seventeenth-Century England*. Cambridge, MA: Harvard UP, 1975.

———. *The Collected Essays of Christopher Hill*. 4 vols. Amherst: U of Massachusetts P, 1985.

———. *The English Bible and the Seventeenth-Century Revolution*. London: Allen Lane the Penguin Press, 1993.

———. *The Experience of Defeat: Milton and Some Contemporaries*. London: Faber and Faber, 1984.

———. *Intellectual Origins of the English Revolution*. Oxford: Clarendon, 1965.

———. *The World Turned Upside Down*. New York: The Viking Press, 1972.

Hodgson, Marshall G. S. *The Secret Order of the Assassins*. 1955. Philadelphia: U of Pennsylvania P, 2005.

———. *The Venture of Islam*. 3 vols. Chicago: U of Chicago P, 1974.

Hofkosh, Sonia and Alan Richardson, eds. *Romanticism, Race, and Imperial Culture 1780–1834*. Bloomington: Indiana UP, 1996.

Hogan, Charles B., ed. *The London Stage: 1660–1800*. 5 vols. Carbondale: Southern Illinois UP, 1960–68.

Holcombe, Lee. *Wives and Property: Reform of the Married Women's Property Law in Nineteenth-Century England.* Toronto: U of Toronto P, 1983.

Holt, Peter Malcolm. *A Seventeenth-Century Defender of Islam: Henry Stubbe (1632–76) and his Book.* London: Friends of Dr. William's Library, 1976.

———. *Studies in the History of the Near East.* London: Frank Cass, 1973.

Hopkins A. G., ed. *Globalization in World History.* New York: W. W. Norton, 2002.

Hourani, Albert. *Arabic Thought in the Liberal Age, 1798–1939.* 1962; Cambridge: Cambridge UP, 1983.

Houston, Alan and Steve Pincus. "Introduction: Modernity and Later Seventeenth-Century England." *A Nation Transformed: England after the Restoration* Cambridge: Cambridge UP, 2001.

Hunter, Michael M. "Aikenhead the Atheist: The Context and Consequences of Articulate Irreligion in the Late Seventeenth Century." *Atheism from the Reformation to the Enlightenment.* Oxford: Clarendon Press, 1992.

Huntington, Samuel. "The Clash of Civilizations?" *Foreign Affairs* (Summer 1993).

———. *The Clash of Civilizations and the Remaking of the World Order.* New York: Simon and Schuster, 1996.

Ibbetson, David. "Sir William Jones as Comparative Lawyer." *Sir William Jones 1746–1794: A Commemoration.* Ed. Alexander Murray. Oxford: Oxford UP, 1998.

Israel, Jonathan I. *Enlightenment Contested: Philosophy, Modernity and the Enlightenment of Man, 1670–1752.* Oxford: Oxford UP, 2006.

———. "John Locke and the Intellectual Legacy of the Early Enlightenment." *Eighteenth-Century Thought* 3 (2007): 37–55.

———. *Radical Enlightenment: Philosophy and the Making of Modernity 1650–1750.* Oxford: Oxford UP, 2001.

———. "Spinoza, Locke and the Enlightenment Battle for Toleration." *Toleration in Enlightenment Europe.* Eds. Ole Peter Grell and Roy Porter. Cambridge: Cambridge UP, 2000.

Jacob, James R. *Henry Stubbe, Radical Protestantism and the Early Enlightenment.* Cambridge: Cambridge UP, 1983.

Jacob, Margaret C. *Living the Enlightenment: Freemasonry and Politics in Eighteenth-Century Europe.* New York: Oxford UP, 1991.

———. *The Newtonians and the English Revolution, 1689–1720.* Ithaca: Cornell UP, 1976.

———. *The Radical Enlightenment: Pantheists, Freemasons and Republicans.* London: George Allen & Unwin, 1981.

Jager, Colin. "After the Secular: The Subject of Romanticism." *Public Culture* 18.2 (2006): 301–21.

———. *The Book of God: Secularization and Design in the Romantic Era.* Philadelphia: U of Pennsylvania P, 2007.

Janes, Regina. "Edmund Burke's Flying Leap from India to France." *History of European Ideas* 7 (1986): 509–27.

Jasanoff, Maya. *Edge of Empire: Lives, Cultures, and Conquest in the East, 1750–1850.* New York: Knopf, 2005.

Kabitoglou, E. Douka. "Shelley's (Feminist) Discourse on the Female: *The Revolt of Islam.*" *AAA: Arbeiten Aus Anglistik und Amerikanistik* 15.2 (1990): 139–50.

Kahf, Mohja. *Western Representations of the Muslim Woman.* Austin: U of Texas P, 1999.

Katz, David S. "Vossius and the English Biblical Critics." *Scepticism and Irreligion in the Seventeenth and Eighteenth Centuries.* Eds. Richard H. Popkin and Arjo Vanderjagt. Leiden: Brill, 1993.

Keeble, N. H. *The Restoration: England in the 1660s.* Oxford: Blackwell, 2002.

Kelley, Linda. *Richard Brinsley Sheridan: A Life.* London: Sinclair-Stevenson, 1997.

Kietzman, Mary Jo. "Montagu's *Turkish Embassy Letters* and Cultural Dislocation." *SEL* 38 (1998): 537–51.

Khan, Gulfishan. *Indian Muslim Perceptions of the West during the Eighteenth Century.* Karachi: Oxford UP, 1998.

Khoury, Dina Rizk. "Slippers at the Entrance or Behind Closed Doors: Domestic and Public Spaces for Mosuli Women." *Women in the Ottoman Empire: Middle Eastern Women n the Early Modern Era.* Ed. Madeline C. Zilfi. Leiden: Brill, 1997.

Kidwa, A. R. "The Outline of Coleridge's and Southey's 'Mohammed.'" *Notes and Queries* 238.40 (1993): 38–39.

King, Richard. *Orientalism and Religion: Postcolonial Theory, India and "the Mystic East."* New York: Routledge, 1999.

Knoespel, Kenneth. "Newton in the School of Time: The Chronology of the Ancient Kingdoms Amended and the Crisis of Seventeenth-Century Historiography." *The Eighteenth Century: Theory and Interpretation* 30.3 (1989): 19–41.

Kohn, Margaret and Daniel I. O'Neill. "A Tale of Two Indias: Burke and Mill on Empire and Slavery in the West Indies and America." *Political Theory* 34.2 (2006), 192–228.

Kontler, László. *A History of Hungary.* New York: Palgrave Macmillan, 2002.

———. "The Idea of Toleration and the Image of Islam in Early Enlightenment English Thought." *Sous le signe des lumieres.* Budapest: ELTE, 1987.

Kowaleski-Wallace, Elizabeth. *Consuming Subjects: Women, Shopping, and Business in the Eighteenth Century.* New York: Columbia UP, 1997.

Kozlowski, Gregory C. "Private Lives and Public Piety: Women and the Practice of Islam in Mughal India." *Women in the Medieval Islamic World: Power, Patronage, and Piety.* Ed. Gavin R. G. Hambly. New York: St. Martin's Press, 1998.

Kucich, Greg. "Inventing Revolutionary History: Romanticism and the Politics of Literary Tradition." *The Wordsworth Circle* 25.3 (1994): 138–45.

Kuhn, Albert J. "English Deism and the Development of Romantic Mythological Syncretism." *PMLA* 71 (1956): 1094–1116.

Lahir, Shampa. *Indians in Britain: Anglo-Indian Encounters, Race and Identity, 1880–1939.* London: Frank Cass, 2000.

Langford, Paul, gen. ed. *The Writings and Speeches of Edmund Burke.* 7 vols. Oxford: Oxford UP, 1981.

Leask, Nigel. *British Romantic Writers and the East: Anxieties of Empire* Cambridge: Cambridge UP, 1992.

———. *The Politics of Imagination in Coleridge's Critical Thought.* Houndmills, UK: The Macmillan Press, 1988.

———. "'Travelling the other way': *The Travels of Mirza Abu Taleb Khan* (1810) and Romantic Orientalism." *Romantic Representations of British India.* Ed. Michael J. Franklin. New York: Routledge, 2006.

Lelyveld, David. *Aligarh's First Generation: Muslim Solidarity in British India.* Princeton, NJ: Princeton UP, 1978.

Levine, Joseph M. "Deists and Anglicans: The Ancient Wisdom and the Idea of Progress." *The Margins of Orthodoxy: Heterodox Writing and Cultural Response, 1660–1750.* Ed. Roger D. Lund. Cambridge: Cambridge UP, 1995.

Levtzian, Nehemiah and John O. Voll, eds. *Eighteenth-Century Renewal and Reform in Islam.* Syracuse, NY: Syracuse UP, 1987.

Levy, Leonard W. *Treason against God: A History of the Offense of Blasphemy.* New York: Schocken Books, 1981.

Lew, Joseph W. "The Deceptive Other: Mary Shelley's Critique of Orientalism in 'Frankenstein.'" *Studies in Romanticism* 30 (1991): 255–83.

———. "Lady Mary's Portable Seraglio." *Eighteenth Century Studies* 24 (1991): 432–50.

———. "The Plague of Imperial Desire: Montesquieu, Gibbon, Brougham, and Mary Shelley's *The Last Man.*" *Romanticism and Colonialism: Writing and Empire, 1780–1830.* Eds. Tim Fulford and Peter J. Kitson. Cambridge: Cambridge UP, 1998.

Lewis, Bernard. *The Assassins: A Radical Sect in Islam.* New York: Basic Books, 1968.

———. *From Babel to Dragomans: Interpreting the Middle East.* London: Oxford UP, 2004.

———. *British Contributions to Arabic Studies.* Cambridge: Cambridge UP, 1937.

———. *The Crisis of Islam: Holy War and Unholy Terror.* New York: The Modern Library, 2003.

———. *From Babel to Dragomans: Interpreting the Middle East.* London: Oxford UP, 2004.

———. *What Went Wrong? Western Impact and Middle Eastern Response.* Oxford: Oxford UP, 2002.

Lewis, Bernard and Stanley Burstein, eds. *Land of Enchanters: Egyptian Short Stories from the Earliest Times to the Present Day.* Princeton, NJ: Markus Wiener, 2001.

Lewis, William Roger, gen. ed. *The Oxford History of the British Empire.* 5 vols. Oxford: Oxford UP, 1998-99.

Lieberman, Victor. *Strange Parallels: Southeast Asia in a Global Context c. 800–1830.* Cambridge: Cambridge UP, 2003.

Littleton, Charles G. D., "Ancient Languages and New Science: The Levant in the Intellectual Life of Robert Boyle." *The Republic of Letters and the Levant.* Eds. Alastair Hamilton, Maurits H. Van Den Boogart, and Bart Westerweel. Leiden: Brill, 2005.

Lock, F. P. *Edmund Burke: Volume II, 1784–1797.* Oxford: Clarendon Press, 2006.

Lowenthal, Cynthia. *Lady Mary Wortley Montagu and the Eighteenth-Century Familiar Letter.* Athens: U of Georgia P, 1994.

Lowes, John Livingston. *The Road to Xanadu: A Study in the ways of the Imagination.* 1929. Boston: Houghton Mifflin, 1959.

Lund, Roger D. "Introduction." *The Margins of Orthodoxy: Heterodox Writing and Cultural Response, 1660–1750*. Ed. Roger D. Lund. Cambridge: Cambridge UP, 1995.

———. "Irony as Subversion: Thomas Woolston and the Crime of Wit." *The Margins of Orthodoxy: Heterodox Writing and Cultural Response, 1660–1750*. Ed. Roger D. Lund. Cambridge: Cambridge UP, 1995.

———, ed. *The Margins of Orthodoxy: Heterodox Writing and Cultural Response, 1660–1750*. Cambridge: Cambridge UP, 1995.

Lurbe, Pierre. "John Toland and the Naturalization of the Jews." *Eighteenth-Century Ireland* 14 (1999): 37–48.

Lyles, William H. *Mary Shelley: An Annotated Bibliography*. New York: Garland Publishing, 1975.

Mahmood, Saba. "Secularism, Hermeneutics, and Empire: The Politics of Islamic Reformation." *Public Culture* 18.2 (2006): 323–47.

Mahmoud, Fatma Moussa. "The Arabic Original of Landor's *Gebir*." *Cairo Studies in English* (1960): 69–86.

Majeed, Javed. *Ungoverned Imaginings: James Mill's the History of British India and Orientalism*. Oxford: Clarendon Press, 1992.

Makdisi, Saree. *Romantic Imperialism: Universal Empire and the Culture of Modernity*. Cambridge: Cambridge UP, 1998.

———. *William Blake and the Impossible History of the 1790s*. Chicago: U of Chicago P, 2003.

Makdisi, Saree and Felicity Nussbaum. The Arabian Nights *in Historical Context: Between East and West*. Oxford: Oxford UP, 2008.

Manuel, Frank E. *The Eighteenth Century Confronts the Gods*. New York: Atheneum, 1967.

———. *The Religion of Isaac Newton*. Oxford: Clarendon Press, 1974.

Markley, Robert. *The Far East and the English Imagination 1660–1730*. Cambridge: Cambridge UP, 2006.

———. "Newton, Corruption, and the Tradition of Universal History." *Newton and Religion*. Eds. James E. Force and Richard H. Popkin. Dordrecht: Kluwer, 1999.

Marr, Timothy. *The Cultural Roots of American Islamicism*. Cambridge: Cambridge UP, 2006.

Marshall, Allan. "Oates, Titus (1649–1705)." *Oxford Dictionary of National Biography*. Oxford: Oxford UP, 2004. Online ed., Jan. 2008, www.oxforddnb.com.proxy .library.vanderbilt.edu/view/article/20437, accessed Apr. 6, 2011.

Marshall, John. *John Locke, Toleration and Early English Enlightenment Culture*. New York: Cambridge UP, 2006.

Marshall, Peter J. "Britain and the World in the Eighteenth Century: IV The Turning Outwards of Britain." *Transactions of the Royal Historical Society*, 6th series, 11 (2001): 1–15.

———. *The Great Map* of *Mankind*. Cambridge, MA: Harvard UP, 1982.

———. *The Impeachment of Warren Hastings*. London: Oxford UP, 1965.

————. *The Making and Unmaking of Empire: Britain, India, and America c. 1750–1783*. Oxford: Oxford UP, 2005.

————., ed. *The Oxford History of the British Empire*. Vol. 2 Oxford: Oxford UP, 1998.

Masuzawa, Tomoko. *The Invention of World Religions: Or, How European Universalism Was Preserved in the Language of Pluralism*. Chicago: U of Chicago P, 2005.

Matar, Nabil. *Britain and Barbary, 1589–1689*. Gainesville: UP of Florida, 2005.

————. *Islam in Britain, 1558–1685*. Cambridge: Cambridge UP, 1998.

————. "Islam in Britain, 1689–1750." *Journal of British Studies* 47.2 (2008): 284–300.

————. "John Locke and the 'Turbanned Nations.'" *Journal of Islamic Studies* 2 (1991): 67–77.

————. "Some Notes on George Fox and Islam." *The Journal of the Friends' Historical Society* 55 (1989): 271–76.

McCalman, Iain. "The Infidel as Prophet: William Reid and Blakean Radicalism." *Historicizing Blake*. Eds. Steve Clarke and David Worrall. New York: St. Martin's Press, 1994.

————. "New Jerusalems: Prophecy, Dissent and Radical Culture in England, 1786–1830." *Enlightenment and Religion: Rational Dissent in Eighteenth-Century Britain*. Ed. Knud Kaakonssen. Cambridge: Cambridge UP, 1996.

————. *Radical Underworld: Prophets, Revolutionaries and Pornographers in London, 1795–1840*. Cambridge: Cambridge UP, 1988.

McDermott, Gerald R. *Jonathan Edwards Confronts the Gods*. Oxford: Oxford UP, 2000.

McDowell, Paula. *The Women of Grub Street: Press, Politics, and Gender in the London Literary Marketplace, 1678–1730*. Oxford: Clarendon Press, 1998.

Mcfarland, Thomas. *Coleridge and the Pantheist Tradition*. Oxford: Clarendon Press, 1969.

McKelvy, William R. *The English Cult of Literature: Devoted Readers, 1774–1880*. Charlottesville: U of Virginia P, 2007.

Mee, Jon. *Dangerous Enthusiasm: William Blake and the Culture of Radicalism in the 1790s*. Oxford: Clarendon Press, 1992.

————. *Romanticism, Enthusiasm, and Regulation*. Oxford: Oxford UP, 2003.

Mellor, Anne K. "Blake, the Apocalypse and Romantic Women Writers." *Romanticism and Millenarianism*. Ed. Tim Fulford. New York: Palgrave, 2002.

————. *Mary Shelley: Her Life, Her Fiction, Her Monsters*. New York: Routledge, 1988.

————. *Romanticism and Gender*. New York: Routledge, 1993.

Melman, Billie. *Women's Orients: English Women and the Middle East, 1718–1918*. Houndmills, UK: Macmillan, 1992.

Mernissi, Fatima. *Women's Rebellion and Islamic Memory*. London: Zed, 1996.

Millar, Simon. *Vienna 1683: Christian Europe Repels the Ottomans*. Oxford: Osprey Publishing, 2008.

Mitchell, L. G. *Charles James Fox and the Disintegration of the Whig Party 1782–1794*. Oxford: Oxford UP, 1971.

Molnár, Miklós. *A Concise History of Hungary.* Cambridge: Cambridge UP, 2001.

Morgan, Fidelis. *A Women of No Character: An Autobiography of Mrs. Manley.* London: Faber and Faber, 1986.

Morton, Timothy and Nigel Smith. *Radicalism in British Literary Culture, 1650–1830.* Cambridge: Cambridge UP, 2002.

Mulsow, Martin. "The 'New Socinians': Intertextuality and Cultural Exchange in Late Socinianism." *Socinianism and Arminianism: Antitrinitarians, Calvinists and Cultural Exchange in Seventeenth-Century Europe.* Eds. Martin Mulsow and Jan Rohls. Leiden: Brill, 2005.

Murray, Eugene Bernard. "The Dating and Composition of Shelley's *The Assassins*." *Keats-Shelley Journal* 35 (1985): 14–17.

Norbrook, David. *Writing the English Republic: Poetry, Rhetoric and Politics 1627–1660.* Cambridge: Cambridge UP, 1999.

Nussbaum, Felicity A. ed. *The Global Eighteenth Century.* Baltimore: The Johns Hopkins UP, 2003.

———. *Rival Queens: Actresses, Performances, and the Eighteenth-Century British Theater.* Philadelphia: U of Pennsylvania P, 2010.

———. *Torrid Zones: Maternity, Sexuality, and Empire in Eighteenth-Century English Narratives.* Baltimore: The Johns Hopkins UP, 1995.

Ober, Warren U. "'MOHAMMED': The Outline of a Proposed Poem by Coleridge and Southey." *Notes and Queries* 5 (1958): 448.

———. "Southey, Coleridge, and "Kubla Khan." *Journal of English and Germanic Philology* (1959): 414–22.

O'Brien, Karen. *Narratives of Enlightenment: Cosmopolitan History from Voltaire to Gibbon.* New York: Cambridge UP, 1997.

Oliver, W. H. *Prophets and Millennialists: The Uses of Biblical Prophecy in England from the 1790s to the 1840s.* New Zealand: Auckland UP, 1978.

O'Quinn, Daniel. *Staging Governance: Theatrical Imperialism in London, 1770–1800.* Baltimore: The Johns Hopkins UP, 2005.

Orr, Bridget. *Empire and the English Stage, 1660–1714.* Cambridge: Cambridge UP, 2001.

The Oxford History of the British Empire. Gen. ed. William Roger Lewis. Vol. 2, *The Eighteenth Century*, ed. P. J. Marshall (Oxford: Oxford UP, 1998–99).

Ozcan, Azim. *Pan-Islamism: Indian Muslims, the Ottomans and Britain (1877–1924).* Leiden: Brill, 1997.

Pailin, David A. *Attitudes to Other Religions: Comparative Religion in Seventeenth- and Eighteenth-Century Britain.* Manchester: Manchester UP, 1984.

Paley, Morton D. *Apocalypse and Millennium in English Romantic Poetry.* Oxford: Clarendon Press, 1999.

———. "*The Last Man*: Apocalypse without Millennium." *The Other Mary Shelley: Beyond Frankenstein.* Eds. Audrey A. Fisch, Anne K. Mellor, and Esther H. Schor. New York: Oxford UP, 1993.

Park, Roy, ed. *Sales Catalogues of Libraries of Eminent Persons: Poets and Men of Letters.* 10 vols. London: Scholar Press, 1974.

Parker, Kenneth. "Introduction." *Early Modern Tales of Orient: A Critical Anthology.* London: Routledge, 1999.

Pateman, Carole. *The Sexual Contract.* Stanford: Stanford UP, 1988.

Patton, Lewis and Peter Mann. "Introduction." *The Collected Works of Samuel Taylor Coleridge: Lectures 1795 On Politics and Religion.* 16 vols. Ed. Lewis Patton and Peter Mann. Princeton, NJ: Princeton UP, 1971.

Paulin, David A. *Attitudes to Other Religions.* Manchester: Manchester UP, 1984.

Peirce, Leslie P. *The Imperial Harem: Women and Sovereignty in the Ottoman Empire.* New: Oxford UP, 1993.

Peter, Ole and Roy Porter. "Toleration in the Eighteenth Century." *Toleration in Enlightenment Europe.* Eds. Ole Peter Grell and Roy Porter. Cambridge: Cambridge UP, 2000.

Philip, Mark. "English Republicanism in the 1790s." *Journal of Political Philosophy* 6.1 (1998): 1–28.

Piper, Herbert Walter. *The Active Universe: Pantheism and the Concept of Imagination in English Romantic Poets.* London: The Athlone Press, 1962.

———. "Coleridge and the Unitarian Consensus." *The Coleridge Connection: Essays for Thomas Mcfarland.* Eds. Richard Gravil and Molly Lefebure. New York: St. Martin's Press, 1990.

Pocock, John Greville Agard. *The Ancient Constitution and the Feudal Law . . . A Reissue with a Retrospect.* 1957. New York: Cambridge UP, 1987.

———. *Barbarism and Religion.* 3 vols. *The Enlightenment of Edward Gibbon, 1734–64.* Cambridge: Cambridge UP, 1999.

———. "Burke and the Ancient Constitution—A Problem in the History of Ideas." *Historical Journal* 3.2 (1960): 125–43.

———. "Criticism of the Whig Order in the Age between the Revolutions." *The Origins of Anglo-American Radicalism.* Eds. Margaret Jacob and James C. Jacob. London: Allen and Unwin, 1984.

———. *The Machiavellian Moment: Florentine Political Thought and the Atlantic Republican Tradition.* 1975. Repr. with a New Afterword. Princeton, NJ: Princeton U P, 2003.

———. *Political Works of James Harrington.* Cambridge: Cambridge UP, 1977.

———. "The Varieties of Whiggism." *Virtue, Commerce, and History.* Cambridge: Cambridge UP, 1985.

Pohl, Nicole. *Women, Space and Utopia: 1660–1800.* Aldershot, UK: Ashgate, 2006.

Poovey, Mary. *The Proper Lady and the Woman Writer.* Chicago: U of Chicago P, 1984.

Popkin, Richard H. "The Deist Challenge." *From Persecution to Toleration.* Eds. Ole Peter Grell, Jonathan I. Israel, and Nicholas Tacke. Oxford: Clarendon Press, 1991.

———. "Newton as a Bible Scholar." *Essays on the Context, Nature, and Influence of Isaac Newton's Theology.* Eds. James E. Force and Richard H. Popkin. Dordrecht: Kluwer, 1990.

———. "Polytheism, Deism, and Newton." *Essays on the Context, Nature, and Influence of Isaac Newton's Theology.* Eds. James E. Force and Richard H. Popkin. Dordrecht: Kluwer, 1990.

Porter, Roy. *The Creation of the Modern World: The Untold Story of the British Enlight-enment*. New York: W. W. Norton, 2000.

———. "Mixed Feelings: The Enlightenment and Sexuality in Eighteenth-Century Britain." *Sexuality in Eighteenth-Century Britain*. Ed. Paul-Gabriel Boucé. Totowa: Manchester UP, 1982.

Pratt, Mary Louise. *Imperial Eyes: Travel Writing and Transculturation*. New York: Routledge, 1992.

Quataert, Donald. *The Ottoman Empire, 1700–1922*. Cambridge: Cambridge UP, 2000.

Rabb, Melinda Alliker. *Satire and Secrecy in English Literature from 1650 to 1750*. New York: Palgrave Macmillan, 2007.

Rahman, Fazlur. "Revival and Reform in Islam." *The Cambridge History of Islam*. Eds. Peter M. Holt, Ann K. S. Lambton, and Bernard Lewis. 2 vols. Cambridge: Cambridge UP, 1970.

Rahman, Tariq. "The Urdu-English Controversy in Pakistan." *Modern Asian Studies* 31.1 (1997): 177–207.

Redwood, John. *Reason, Ridicule and Religion*. London: Thames and Hudson, 1976.

Reid, John Phillip. *The Ancient Constitution and the Origins of Anglo-American Liberty*. Dekalb: Northern Illinois UP, 2005.

Reiman, Donald. *Intervals of Inspiration: The Skeptical Tradition and the Psychology of Romanticism*. Greenwood, FL: Penkevill, 1988.

Richardson, Alan. "Epic Ambivalence: Imperial Politics and Romantic Deflections in William's *Peru* and Landor's *Gebir*." *Romanticism, Race, and Imperial Culture, 1780–1834*. Eds. Alan Richardson and Sonia Hofkosh. Bloomington: Indiana UP, 1996.

Rivers, Isabel. *Reason, Grace, and Sentiment: A Study of the Language of Religion and Ethics in England, 1660–1780*. 2 vols. Cambridge: Cambridge UP, 1999–2000.

Robbins, Caroline. *The Eighteenth-Century Commonwealthman*. Cambridge, MA: Harvard UP, 1961.

Roberts, Marie. *British Poets and Secret Societies*. London: Croom Helm, 1986.

Robinson, Maxime. *Europe and the Mystique of Islam*. Trans. Roger Venius. Seattle: U of Washington P, 1987.

Rogers, Katharine M. *Feminism in Eighteenth-Century England*. Urbana: U of Illinois P, 1982.

Roosbroeck, Gustave Leopold Van. *Persian Letters Before Montesquieu*. New York: Publications of the Institute of French Studies, 1932.

Rossi, Paolo. *The Dark Abyss of Time: The History of the Earth and the History of Nations from Hooke to Vico*. Trans. Lydia G. Cochrane. Chicago: U of Chicago P, 1984.

Rubin, Gayle. "The Traffic in Women: Notes on the Political Economy of Sex." *Toward an Anthropology of Women*. New York: Monthly Review Press, 1975.

Russell, G. A., ed. *The "Arabick" Interest of the Natural Philosophers in Seventeenth-Century England*. Leiden: Brill, 1994.

Ryan, Robert. *The Romantic Reformation: Religious Politics in English Literature, 1789–1824*. Cambridge: Cambridge UP, 1997.

Ryley, Robert M. *William Warburton*. Boston: Twayne, 1984.

Sachedina, Abdulaziz Abdulhussein. *Islamic Messianism: The Idea of the Mahdi in-Twelver Shi'ism*. Albany: State U of New York P, 1981.

Said, Edward W. *Orientalism*. New York: Vintage Books, 1978.

Sambrook, A. J. "A Romantic Theme: The Last Man." *Forum for Modern Language Studies* 2 (1966): 25–33.

Schmitt, Charles B. "Perennial Philosophy: From Agostino Steuco to Leibniz." *Journal of the History of Ideas* 27 (1966): 505–32.

Schneider, Elisabeth. *Coleridge, Opium and "Kubla Khan."* 1953. New York: Octagon Books, 1968.

Schofield, Robert. *The Enlightened Joseph Priestly: A Study of His Life and Work from 1773 to 1804*. University Park: Pennsylvania State UP, 2004.

———. "Joseph Priestly, Eighteenth-Century British Neoplatonism, and S. T. Coleridge." *Transformation and Tradition in the Sciences*. Ed. Everett Mendelsohn. Cambridge: Cambridge UP, 1984.

Schreps, Hans Joachim. *Jewish Christianity*. Philadelphia: Fortress Press, 1969.

Schulze, Reinhard. "Das islamische achtzehnte jahrhundert: Versuch einer historiographischen kritik." *Die Welt des Islams* 30 (1990): 140–49.

———. "Was ist die islamische Aufkärung?" *Die Welt des Islams* 36 (1996): 276–325.

Scott, Jonathan. "England's Troubles: Exhuming the Popish Plot." *The Politics of Religion in Restoration England*. Eds. Tim Harris, Paul Seaward, and Mark Goldie. Oxford: Basil Blackwell, 1990.

Seed, John. "The Role of Unitarianism in the Formation of Liberal Culture 1775–1851: A Social History." Ph.D. diss., U of Hull, 1981.

Sen, Amartya. "Passage to China." *New York Review of Books* 51.19 (2004): 61–65.

Sen, Sudipta. *Distant Sovereignty: National Imperialism and the Origins of British India*. New York: Routledge, 2002.

Setton, Kenneth M. "Lutherism and the Turkish Peril." *Balkan Studies*. 3.1 (1962): 133–68.

———. *Venice, Austria, and the Turks in the Seventeenth Century*. Philadelphia: American Philosophical Society, 1991.

Shaffer, Elinor S. *"Kubla Khan" and the Fall of Jerusalem: The Mythological School in Biblical Criticism and Secular Literature 1770–1880*. Cambridge: Cambridge UP, 1975.

Sharafuddin, Mohammed. *Islam and Romantic Orientalism*. London: I. B. Tauris, 1994.

Sharp, Jenny. *Allegories of Empire: The Figure of Women in the Colonial Text*. Minneapolis: U of Minnesota P, 1993.

Shaw, Ezel Kural Shaw. "The Ottoman Aspects of *Pax Ottomanica*." *Tolerance and Movements of Religious Dissent in Eastern Europe*. Ed. Béla K. Király. New York: Columbia UP, 1975.

Shaw, Jane. "Gender and the 'Nature' of Religion: Lady Mary Wortley Montagu's Embassy Letters and Their Place in Enlightenment Philosophy of Religion." *Bulletin of the John Rylands University Library of Manchester* 80.3 (1998): 129–45.

Shelley, Bryan. *Shelley and Scripture: The Interpreting Angel*. Oxford: Clarendon Press, 1994.

Smith, Hilda L. *All Men and Both Sexes: Gender, Politics, and the False Universal in England, 1640–1832.* University Park: Pennsylvania State UP, 2002.

———. "'Cry up Liberty': The Political Context for Mary Astell's Feminism." *Mary Astell: Reason, Gender, Faith.* Eds. William Kolbremer and Michal Michelson. Burlington, VT: Ashgate, 2007.

———. "Introduction: Women, Intellect, and Politics: Their Intersection in seventeenth-century England." *Women Writers and the Early Modern British Political Tradition.* Ed. Hilda L. Smith. Cambridge: Cambridge UP, 1998.

———. *Reason's Disciples: Seventeenth-Century English Feminists.* Urbana : U of Illinois P, 1982.

Sonbul, Amira El Azhary. Introduction. *Women, the Family, and Divorce Laws in Islamic History.* Ed. Amira El Azhary Sonbul. Syracuse, NY: Syracuse UP, 1996.

Spacks, P. M. "Ev'ry Woman Is at Heart a Rake." *Eighteenth Century Studies* 8.1 (1974–5): 27–46.

Spencer, Jane. *The Rise of the Woman Novelist.* Oxford: Basil Blackwell, 1986.

Springborg, Patricia. *Mary Astell: Theorist of Freedom from Domination.* Cambridge: Cambridge UP, 2005.

Spurr, John. *England in the 1670s: "This Masquerading Age."* Malden, MA: Blackwell, 2002.

Stabler, Jane, "Space for Speculation: Coleridge, Barbauld, and the Poetics of Priestley." *Samuel Taylor Coleridge and the Sciences of Life.* Ed. Nicholas Roe. Oxford: Oxford UP, 2001.

Storey, Mark. *Robert Southey: A Life.* Oxford: Oxford UP, 1997.

Stowasser, Barbara Freyer. "Women and Citizenship in the Qur'an." *Women, the Family, and Divorce Laws in Islamic History.* Ed. Amira El Azhary Sonbul. Syracuse, NY: Syracuse UP, 1996.

Stoye, John. *Siege of Vienna: The Last Great Trial Between the Cross and Crescent.* New York: Pegasus Books, 2006.

Stretton, Tim. "Women, Property and Law." *A Companion to Early Modern Women's Writing.* Ed. Anita Pacheco. Oxford: Blackwell, 2002.

Strong, Rowan. *Anglicanism and the British Empire, c. 1700–1850.* Oxford: Oxford UP, 2007.

Stroumsa, Sarah. *Freethinkers of Medieval Islam: Ibn Al-Rawandi, Abu Bakr Al-Razi and Their Impact on Islamic Thought.* Leiden: Brill, 1999.

Subrahmanyam, Sanjay. "Connected Histories: Notes towards a Reconfiguration of Early Modern Eurasia." *Modern Asian Studies* 31.3 (1997): 735–62.

Suleri, Sara. *The Rhetoric of English India.* Chicago: U of Chicago P, 1992.

Sullivan, Robert E. *John Toland and the Deist Controversy.* Cambridge, MA: Harvard UP, 1982.

Taylor, Charles. *Modern Social Imaginaries.* Durham: Duke UP, 2004.

———. *A Secular Age.* Cambridge, MA: Harvard UP, 2007.

Thomas, Donald. *A Long Time Burning: The History of Literary Censorship in England.* London: Routledge & Kegan Paul, 1969.

"Thomas Emlyn." *Oxford Dictionary of National Biography.* 2004–6.

Thomas, Keith. "The Double Standard." *Journal of the History of Ideas* 20 (1959): 195–216.

Thomas, Peter D. G. *George III: King and Politicians, 1760–1770*. Manchester: Manchester UP, 2002.

Thomson, Ann. *Barbary and Enlightenment: European Attitudes Towards the Maghreb in the 18th Century*. Leiden: Brill, 1987.

Todd, Janet. *The Sign of Angellica: Women, Writing and Fiction, 1660–1800*. New York: Columbia UP, 1989.

Tolan, John. "Looking East Before 1453: The Saracen in the Medieval European Imagination." *Cultural Encounters Between East and West*. Eds. Matthew Birchwood and Mathew Dimmock. Newcastle: Cambridge Scholars Press, 2005.

Toomer, G. J. *Eastern Wisdome and Learning: The Study of Arabic in Seventeenth-Century England*. Oxford: Clarendon Press, 1996.

Travers, Robert. *Ideology and Empire in Eighteenth-Century India: The British in Bengal*. Cambridge: Cambridge UP, 2007.

Tumbleson, Raymond D. *Catholicism in the English Protestant Imagination*. Cambridge: Cambridge UP, 1998.

Turhan, Filiz. *The Other Empire: British Romantic Writings about the Ottoman Empire*. New York: Routledge, 2003.

Turnbull, G. H. *Hartlib, Dury and Comenius: Gleamings from Hartlib's papers*. London: UP of Liverpool, 1947.

———. "Johann Valentin Andreae's Societas Christiana." *Zeitschrift Fur Deutsche Philologie* 74 (1955): 161–66.

———. "John Hall's Letters to Samuel Hartlib." *The Review of English Studies* 4.15 (1953): 222–24.

Turner, James G. *Libertines and Radicals in Early Modern London: Sexuality, Politics, and Literary Culture*. Cambridge: Cambridge UP, 2002.

———. "The Properties of Libertinism." *'Tis Nature's Fault: Unauthorized Sexuality during the Enlightenment*. Ed. Robert Purks Maccubbin. Cambridge: Cambridge UP, 1985.

Underwood, David. *A Freeborn People: Politics and the Nation in Seventeenth-Century England*. Oxford: Clarendon Press, 1996.

"Unitarian." *Oxford English Dictionary*. 2nd ed. 1989.

Veer, Peter Van Der. *Imperial Encounters: Religion and Modernity in India and Britain*. Princeton, NJ: Princeton UP, 2001.

Venturi, Franco. "Oriental Depotism." *Journal of the History of Ideas* 24 (1963): 133–42.

Vitkus, Daniel. *Turning Turk: English Theater and the Multicultural Mediterranean, 1570–1630*. New York: Palgrave Macmillan, 2003.

Voegelin, Eric. "Machiavelli's Prince: Background and Formation." *Review of Politics* 12 (1951): 142–68.

Voll, John Obert. "Foundations for Renewal and Reform: Islamic Movements in the Eighteenth and Nineteenth Centuries." *The Oxford History of Islam*. Ed. John Esposito. New York: Oxford UP, 1999.

———. "Renewal and Reform in Islamic History: *Tajdid* and *Islah*." *Voices of Resurgent Islam.* Ed. John L. Esposito. New York: Oxford UP, 1983.

Waldman, Peter. "A Historian's Take on Islam Steers US in Terrorism Fight." *Wall Street Journal*, Feb. 4, 2004.

Walker, Daniel P. *The Ancient Theology: Studies in Christian Platonism from the Fifteenth to the Eighteenth Century.* Ithaca: Cornell UP, 1972.

Walsh, Clement. "A Note on the Meaning of 'Deism.'" *Anglican Theological Review* 38 (1956): 160–65.

Walther, Weibke. *Women in Islam.* Princeton, NJ: Markus Wiener, 1981.

Wasti, Syed Tanvir. "Halil Halid: Anti-imperialist Muslim Intellectual." *Middle Eastern Studies* 29.3 (1993): 559–79.

Watt, Katherine. "Thomas Walker Arnold and the Re-Evaluation of Islam, 1864–1930." *Modern Asian Studies* 36.1 (2002): 1–98.

Webb, R. K. "Religion." *An Oxford Companion to the Romantic Age.* Ed. Iain McCalman. Oxford: Oxford UP, 1999.

Webster, Charles. *The Great Instauration: Science, Medicine and Reform, 1626–1660.* New York: Holmes and Meier, 1975.

Weitzman, Arthur J., ed. *Letters Writ by a Turkish Spy, by Giovanni P. Marcana.* London: Routledge, 1970.

———. "The Oriental Tale in the Eighteenth Century: A Reconsideration." *Studies in Voltaire and the Eighteenth Century* 58 (1967): 1839–55.

Wells, Lynn. "The Triumph of Death: Reading the Narrative in Mary Shelley's *The Last Man*." *Iconoclastic Departures: Mary Shelley After Frankenstein.* Eds. Syndy M. Conger, Frederick S. Frank, and Gregory O'Dea. London: Associated UP, 1997.

Westfall, Richard S. "Isaac Newton's *Theolofiae Gentilis Origines Philosophicae*." *The Secular Mind: Essays Presented to Franklin L. Baumer.* Ed. Warren Wagar. New York: Holmes and Meier Publishers, 1982.

———. *Never at Rest.* Cambridge: Cambridge UP, 1980.

Whalley, George. *The Bristol Library Borrowings of Southey and Coleridge, 1793–8.* London: The Bibliographical Society, 1949.

Wheeler, Richard S. "Pakistan in 1975: The Hydra of Opposition." *Asian Survey* 16.2 (1976): 111–18.

Whelan, Frederick G. *Edmund Burke and India.* Pittsburgh: U of Pittsburgh P, 1996.

———. "Burke, India, and Orientalism." *An Imaginative Whig: Reassessing the Life and Thought of Edmund Burke.* Ed. Ian Crowe. Columbia: U of Missouri P, 2005.

———. "Oriental Despotism: Anquetil-Duperron's Responses to Montesquieu." *History of Political Thought* 22 (2001): 619–47.

White, Daniel E. *Early Romanticism and Religious Dissent.* Cambridge: Cambridge UP, 2006.

———. "'Mysterious Sanctity': Sectarianism and Syncretism from Volney to Hemans." *European Romantic Review* 15.2 (2004): 269–76.

Wickens, G. M. "*Lalla Rookh* and the Romantic Tradition of Islamic Literature in English." *Year Book of Comparative and General Literature* 20 (1971): 61–66.

Wilbur, Earl Morse. *A History of Unitarianism.* 2 vols. Cambridge, MA: Harvard UP, 1952.

Wilson, Adrian. *The Making of Man-Midwifery: Childbirth in England 1660–1700.* London: UCL Press, 1995.

Wilson, Kathleen. "The Female Rake: Gender, Libertinism and Enlightenment." *Libertine Enlightenment: Sex, Liberty and License in the Eighteenth Century.* Eds. Peter Cryle and Lisa O' Connell. New York: Palgrave Macmillian, 2004.

———. *The Island Race: Englishness, Empire and Gender in the Eighteenth Century.* London: Routledge, 2003.

———, ed. *A New Imperial History: Culture, Identity, and Modernity in Britain and the Empire, 1660–1840.* Cambridge: Cambridge UP, 2004.

Winnett, Arthur R. "Were the Deist 'Deists'?" *Church Quarterly Review* 161 (1960): 70–77.

Wolpert, Stanley. *A New History of India,* 8th ed. New York: Oxford UP, 2009.

Wood, Alfred Cecil. *A History of the Levant Company.* New York: Barnes & Noble, 1964.

Worrall, David. *Radical Culture: Discourse, Resistance and Surveillance, 1790–1820.* Detroit: Wayne State UP, 1992.

Wright, Eamon. *British Women Writers and Race, 1788–1818.* New York: Palgrave Macmillan, 2005.

Wunder, Jennifer N. *Keats, Hermeticism, and the Secret Societies.* Aldershot, UK: Ashgate, 2008.

Wykes, David L. "Elwall, Edward (*bap.* 1676, d. 1744)." *Oxford Dictionary of National Biography.* Oxford University Press, 2004, www.oxforddnb.com.proxy.library.vanderbilt.edu/view/article/8775, accessed Apr. 12, 2011.

Wylie, Ian. *Young Coleridge and the Philosophers of Nature.* Oxford: Clarendon Press, 1989.

Yates, Francis. *Giordano Bruno and the Hermetic Tradition.* 1964. Repr. Chicago: U of Chicago P, 1979.

———. *The Rosicrucian Enlightenment.* London: Routledge, 1972.

Young, Brian W. *Religion and Enlightenment in Eighteenth-Century England: Theological Debate from Locke to Burke.* Oxford: Oxford UP, 1998.

Zaller, Robert. "The Continuity of British Radicalism in the Seventeenth and Eighteenth Centuries." *Eighteenth-Century Life* 6. 2–3 (1981): 17–38.

Zonana, Joyce. "The Sultan and the Slave: Feminist Orientalism and the Structure of *Jane Eyre.*" *Signs: the Journal of Women in Culture and Society* 18.3 (1993): 592–617.

———. "'They will prove the truth of my tale': Safie's Letters as the Feminist Core of Mary Shelley's Frankenstein." *Journal of Narrative Technique* 21.2 (1991): 170–84.

0000121755177